Post-Nationalist American Studies

EDITED BY

John Carlos Rowe

UNIVERSITY OF CALIFORNIA PRESS

Berkeley   Los Angeles   London

University of California Press
Berkeley and Los Angeles, California

University of California Press, Ltd.
London, England

© 2000 by
The Regents of the University of California

Library of Congress Cataloging-in-Publication Data

Post-nationalist American studies / edited by John Carlos Rowe.
     p.   cm.
    Includes bibliographical references and index.
    ISBN 0-520-22438-8 (cloth : alk.) — ISBN 0-520-22439-6 (pbk. : alk)
    1. United States—Civilization—Study and teaching.   2. United
States—Civilization—1970—Study and teaching.   3. Nationalism—
United States—Study and teaching.   4. United States—Ethnic relations—Study and teaching.   5. United States—Race relations—Study
and teaching.   6. Pluralism (Social sciences)—United States—Study
and teaching.   I. Rowe, John Carlos.
E175.8 .P7   2000
973—dc21   99-056775

Manufactured in the United States of America

09 08 07 06 05 04 03 02 01 00

10 9 8 7 6 5 4 3 2 1

The paper used in this publication is both acid-free and to-
tally chlorine-free (TCF). It meets the minimum requirements of ANSI/NISO Z39.48–1992 (R 1997) (*Permanence of
Paper*).

For our students

CONTENTS

Preface   ix

Introduction   1

Post-Nationalism, Globalism, and the New American Studies
JOHN CARLOS ROWE   23
Syllabus: Comparative American Studies: An Introduction   38

Creating the Multicultural Nation: Adventures in Post-Nationalist
American Studies in the 1990s
GEORGE J. SÁNCHEZ   40
Syllabus: Introduction to American Studies and Ethnicity   59

Rethinking (and Reteaching) the Civil Religion in Post-Nationalist
American Studies
JAY MECHLING   63
Syllabus: (Re)Teaching the Civil Religion: Religion in American Lives   81

Foreign Affairs: Women, War, and the Pacific
KATHERINE KINNEY   84
Syllabus: Pacific America: War, Memory, and Imagination   107

Making Comparisons: First Contact, Ethnocentrism, and
Cross-Cultural Communication
STEVEN MAILLOUX   110
Syllabus: Making Comparisons   126

Race, Nation, and Equality: Olaudah Equiano's *Interesting Narrative* and a Genealogy of U.S. Mercantilism

DAVID KAZANJIAN 129

Syllabus: Enclosing the "Open Sea": Race, Nation, Gender, and Equality in the Northern Atlantic 164

Joaquín Murrieta and the American 1848

SHELLEY STREEBY 166

Syllabus: 1848: Empire, Amnesia, and American Studies 197

My Border Stories: Life Narratives, Interdisciplinarity, and Post-Nationalism in Ethnic Studies

BARBARA BRINSON CURIEL 200

Syllabus: Race and Gender in American Autobiography 219

How Tiger Woods Lost His Stripes: Post-Nationalist American Studies as a History of Race, Migration, and the Commodification of Culture

HENRY YU 223

Syllabus: Buying and Selling the Exotic: Transnational Culture and Global History 247

List of Contributors 249

Index 253

PREFACE

In the fall of 1996, nine scholars participated in the residential research group, "Post-Nationalist American Studies," at the University of California's Humanities Research Institute (UCHRI) on the Irvine campus: Barbara Brinson Curiel, at that time lecturer in Liberal Studies and Women's Studies at California State University, San Marcos, currently assistant professor of English at Humboldt State University, who had recently earned her Ph.D. in Literature from the University of California, Santa Cruz (UCSC); David Kazanjian, now an assistant professor of English at Queens College, the City University of New York, at that time a Ph.d. candidate in Rhetoric at the University of California, Berkeley; Katherine Kinney, associate professor of English at the University of California, Riverside; Steven Mailloux, professor of English at the University of California, Irvine; Jay Mechling, professor of American Studies at the University of California, Davis; John Carlos Rowe, professor of English at the University of California, Irvine; George Sánchez, now professor of Chicano Studies at the University of Southern California, and at that time Chair and professor of American Cultures at the University of Michigan; Shelley Streeby, assistant professor of Literature at the University of California, San Diego; and Henry Yu, assistant professor of History and Asian American Studies at the University of California, Los Angeles. John Rowe developed the idea for this research group from the discussion at a one-day disciplinary forum, "American Studies in the University of California," which he had convened at the Humanities Research Institute in October 1994.

In that disciplinary forum, University of California faculty discussed scholarly, curricular, and institutional changes in American Studies nationally, internationally, and within the University of California (UC) system. Such one-day forums often lead to formal applications to the Humanities

Research Institute for residential research projects, and in our discussion of such a project we stressed the need to connect in specific ways the research and teaching components of the new American Studies. Thus when John Rowe did apply in 1995 to convene a UCHRI research group in 1996–97, he divided the work into two parts: a residential research group in the fall of 1996 and a series of visits to UC campuses by members of the research group, in order to connect scholarly questions with local curricular and pedagogical issues in the field. Between January and May 1997, we held seven forums for such discussions on the following campuses: Davis, Riverside, Los Angeles, Santa Cruz, Berkeley, Irvine, and San Diego. What members of the research group learned at these forums informs the chapters that follow, including the sample syllabi we have designed to accompany them. As we expected, there is no general lesson to be drawn from the very different institutional situations in which research and teaching in American Studies, Ethnic Studies, and Women's Studies are diversely pursued in this public university, unless the very diversity of approaches teaches us that our scholarly models and theories should take better account of such local knowledges and institutional situations.

During the fall of 1996, when we were in residence at the UCHRI on the Irvine campus, we divided our time among three projects: each scholar's research project, which was the basis for each applicant's acceptance into the research group; organization of our visits to the UC campuses during the winter and spring quarters; and work on the introduction and on each scholar's essay for the present volume. We met together once a week to work on one or more of these projects, and we agreed to share the responsibility for organizing each weekly seminar by delegating each week to two or more members of the group with interest in a particular topic or project. With a modest budget to invite visitors to these weekly seminars, we conducted a variety of private "working sessions" and several public forums, many of which are mentioned in the following pages. The general format for both the private and public seminars was the discussion of new work by members of the research group and/or invited scholars. Whenever possible, the work to be discussed was distributed and read in advance, so that the majority of our time could be devoted to careful discussion.

The general topics and names of the scholars in each of these seminars help clarify not only our working relations but some of the discussion below. We organized three public events during the fall of 1996. Steven Mailloux and John Rowe organized a discussion entitled "Curricular Changes in English, Ethnic, Women's, and American Studies," which began with remarks from a panel composed of faculty involved in Irvine's new interdisciplinary programs (Robyn Wiegman, Steven Mailloux, John Rowe, and Thelma Foote) and two members of the research group associated with established American Studies programs (George Sánchez, then chair of American Cultures at the University of Michigan, and Jay Mechling, American Studies at UC, Davis). Shelley Streeby and Barbara Brinson Curiel organized a public forum entitled "Chicano Studies, American Studies, and the Politics of Memory," which included presentations by Rosaura Sánchez and Beatrice Píta (both from the Department of Literature at UC, San Diego), and by José David Saldívar (Ethnic Studies, UC, Berkeley). David Kazanjian organized the third public forum, "Studying U.S. Racial Formations in a Global Frame," which included contributions from Vilashini Cooppan (Literature, UCSC), David Eng (English and Comparative Literature, Columbia), Colleen Lye (English, UC, Berkeley), and María Josefina Saldaña-Portillo (then in English at UC, Santa Barbara, now at Brown). We were fortunate to be able to arrange visits by several other scholars to our private, working seminars, including Jonathan Holloway and George Lipsitz (both from Ethnic Studies, UC, San Diego), Cheryl Walker (Scripps College), Melani Budianta (English and American Studies, University of Indonesia, Jakarta), Emory Elliott (English and Center for Ideas and Society, UC, Riverside), Nadilza Moreira (Brazil), and Ewa Luczak (Poland).

Recognizing that the institutional aspects of our research subject have local, national, and international components, we decided to sponsor forums at the American Studies Association convention in Kansas City (October 31–November 3, 1996) and the California American Studies Association conference in Berkeley (May 2–4, 1997). At both of these professional meetings, we were able to discuss our ideas about "post-nationalist American Studies" with scholars representing a wide variety of institutions of higher education, regions, and nationalities.

Our interests in connecting institutional, curricular, and scholarly issues are treated in all of the chapters that follow, but we wanted to be more explicit than most scholarly studies about how such interconnections influence our pedagogies. We decided early in our discussions of this project to include a syllabus for a course, real or imagined, with each essay included in the book. These syllabi are not included as models to be followed by our readers. We know that the best teaching emerges from scholarly interests and institutional concerns specific to the instructor and his/her students. Instead, we understand these syllabi as providing exemplifications of the ideas, theories, and interpretations that structure our scholarly essays. "How would you develop a course out of these ideas?" was the question we asked ourselves, and we think it is a question that should always be asked by teacher-scholars, no matter how esoteric the topic. Each syllabus follows the appropriate essay in the book. Each syllabus has a somewhat different form, suggesting the different styles of our contributors and the different institutions where we teach. Taken together, these syllabi do not offer a curriculum for a new "post-nationalist American Studies," but they do suggest how the new topics, interests, and questions discussed in these essays can and should become parts of our everyday teaching practices.

Early in our discussions of this project, we decided that our introduction should be written cooperatively and that the entire volume should be edited by all nine scholars. We are by no means the first scholars to write in this cooperative manner; we are following the lead of others, especially in Women's and Ethnic Studies. In the final seminar of the fall quarter, we divided up the main topics of our introduction and asked two or more scholars in our group to write a few pages on each topic. We distributed drafts by electronic mail, and George Sánchez created an approximate order for those drafts, redistributing this second draft by electronic mail. When we met in April 1997 to revise our introduction and arrange the contents of this book, we spent two days working as a group and revising paragraph by paragraph. The final editing and compilation of the volume took considerably longer and could not be done practically as a cooperative effort. John Rowe agreed to serve as volume editor, gathering and compiling revisions, and finally editing and assembling the final manuscript for submission to the University of California Press.

What follows, then, is the result of such intellectual cooperation, including not only the mutual work of nine scholars but also the contributions of our colleagues in the UC system, our visitors from other universities around the world, and scholars attending our forums at the national and California American Studies Association meetings in 1996–97. Large and diverse as the group of scholars involved in this project is, it by no means represents adequately the different cultures, disciplines, and media that should constitute a new, post-nationalist American Studies. The essays and syllabi in this book are also not intended to provide a comprehensive map of the new American Studies. Although we address issues relevant to Native American Studies, none of our contributions engages the main theoretical, historical, and curricular issues of this field. Despite our call in several places for a new comparatism that would be attentive to the social and cultural diversity of the Western Hemisphere, none of the following essays deals centrally with Caribbean, Latin American, or Canadian Studies. Our purpose is not to offer a set of essays that will "cover" the many fields and disciplines of American Studies—such a task is beyond the scope of any single volume—but to suggest instead how the different specializations represented by the members of our research group might be reimagined in terms of the contemporary challenges facing the new American Studies.

We have mentioned above each of the scholars who visited our research group during our residency at UCHRI. We want to take this opportunity to thank them for challenging and inspiring us. We are also grateful to the American Studies Association and California American Studies Association for allowing us to schedule forums at their annual conventions. We are grateful to administrators and staff at the following UC campuses for help-ing us organize our public forums: Riverside, Davis, Santa Cruz, Irvine, Los Angeles, Berkeley, and San Diego.

Patricia O'Brien, director of UCHRI during our residency, and Debra Massey, assistant director, made certain that we could accomplish practi-cally the diverse events and tasks we considered crucial for our collabora-tive research. Our plans to hold forums at the American Studies Associa-tion and California American Studies Association conventions, as well as on the different campuses of the UC system, were not usual for residential re-search groups and thus required special expenses and logistical arrange-ments. Our determination to write collaboratively the introduction to this book required us to meet again in the spring of 1997 to revise a working draft. That, too, cost time and money and required special arrangements that the staff of the UCHRI promptly and efficiently provided.

Introduction

Barbara Brinson Curiel, David Kazanjian, Katherine Kinney,
Steven Mailloux, Jay Mechling, John Carlos Rowe, George Sánchez,
Shelley Streeby, and Henry Yu

Our group was initially organized under the title "Post-Nationalist American Studies." In the call for applications, the description beneath the title,
however, emphasized the intersections between changing models of American Studies and " 'post-national' models for community and social organization." During our weekly conversations, we frequently talked about the
differences between the terms *post-nationalist* and *post-national* as well as the
implications of the prefix *post-* more generally. Some of us were wary of the
implications of the *post-* in the phrase "post-national American Studies."
While *post-national* has gained a certain currency in discussions of globalization and in revisionary "New Americanists" projects, many of us worried
about the term's developmental trajectory and the sense of belatedness it
evoked, as though the time of the nation-state had passed.[1] Although we
agree that the flexible regimes of accumulation underpinning what David
Harvey has described as the condition of postmodernity are dramatically
changing the meaning and significance of nationalisms and the nation-
state, none of us believes that the nation-form has been or will any time in
the near future be superseded.

California's passage of Proposition 187, which sought to withdraw benefits from undocumented workers, and the University of California Regents'
decision to rescind affirmative action in admissions and hiring made it particularly unsettling to meet under the rubric of "post-national American
Studies," because both national borders and citizenship privileges were once
again being marked off in restrictive ways. Even as debates about the movements of capital and people across national boundaries intensify, nationalist
nativisms are repeatedly mobilized to oppose immigration; transnational
corporations continue to rely on nation-states for labor control; state intervention in "unstable financial markets" has become, according to Harvey,

more rather than less pervasive; and the "National Symbolic," as Lauren Berlant puts it, with its "traditional icons, its metaphors, its heroes, its rituals, and its narratives" in many ways continues to "provide an alphabet for a collective consciousness or national subjectivity."[2] Indeed, in the current context, invocations of the post-national by U.S. intellectuals can function as disturbing disavowals of the global reach of U.S. media and military might. Our use of the word *national* thus refers to a complex and irreducible array of discourses, institutions, policies, and practices which, even if they are in flux or in competition with other structures and allegiances, cannot be easily wished away by the application of the *post-* prefix.

The term *post-nationalist,* of course, is open to many of the same objections. If we have not superseded the nation-state, neither have we superseded nationalism. On the one hand, the insistence that the fall of the Soviet Union means that the United States "won" the Cold War has re-engendered narratives of American global superiority. In some instances, especially in other parts of the Americas in the age of NAFTA, a "nationalistic emphasis on meaningful autonomy and independence" could provide a source of "resistance to the increasingly total consolidation of the system of international capitalism."[3] Within the United States, moreover, it is important to distinguish between nationalisms which are aligned with the nation-state and those which challenge "official" nationalism. As George Lipsitz reminded us when he joined our seminar one week, despite their limitations, black and Chicano nationalisms, for instance, are not identical with or reducible to U.S. nationalism.[4] In other words, we need to critique the limits and exclusions of nationalism without forgetting the differences between nationalisms or throwing all nationalisms into the trash-can of history.

Despite the paradoxes and dangers of a post-nationalist approach to American Studies, however, that adjective does begin to describe the desire of those in our group to contribute to a version of American Studies that is less insular and parochial, and more internationalist and comparative. In this sense, our efforts to formulate a post-nationalist American Studies respond to and seek to revise the cultural nationalism and celebratory American exceptionalism that often informed the work of American Studies scholars in the Cold War era. If our post-nationalism wrestles with an earlier version of American Studies, it is also inevitably informed by our respective locations and workplaces. This residential research group was convened on a university campus in Southern California, where disputes about immigration, assimilation, and citizenship are debated daily in the local media. The New Year in this part of the country means festivities and celebrations, as well as an inevitable "border crack-down" to monitor more stringently the human traffic across the United States–Mexico border. The fall 1996 elections included a local congressional race in which Robert

Dornan, the loser, alleged that the victor, Loretta Sanchez, won because noncitizens had voted in large numbers.[5] The ideal of a closed American nation and a fixed national culture will only recognize outsiders by excluding or assimilating them. Yet the post-nationalist recognizes that even in moments like the present one—in which the American nation-state seems to be extremely hostile to the incursions of cultural and political outsiders—there is plenty of evidence of resistance to U.S. hegemony, and in particular to narrow definitions of national character.

As a critical perspective, post-nationalist American Studies values the work, both recent and historical, of scholars whose concept of the nation and of citizenship has questioned dominant American myths rather than canonized them. Of course, we refer principally to scholarship in Ethnic and Women's Studies, at one time marginalized in the academy, but now key to a dynamic understanding of American culture and institutions, and the foundation of that critical practice which we call the post-nationalist. The post-nationalist is not a new critical practice; it builds upon previous work, within and outside of American Studies, that is critical of U.S. hegemony and the constructedness of both national myths and national borders.[6]

Despite a long history of dissent, nationalist paradigms and assumptions have held sway in the popular imagination as well as in scholarly discourse. "American exceptionalism" is the crucial term of order for such nationalist thinking. The origins of the doctrine of American exceptionalism are traditionally traced to two key documents in the history of the early republic: Washington's "Farewell Address" (1796) and the Monroe Doctrine (1823). George Washington warned the young republic against entanglement in the affairs of Europe, while the Monroe Doctrine warned the nations of Europe to forego claims to their former colonies in North and South America and to end "interference" in the affairs of the Western Hemisphere. This turn away from Europe marks the primary meaning of American exceptionalism—the conviction that the United States marked a break from the history of Europe, specifically the history of feudalism, class stratification, imperialism, and war. Puritan tropes such as the "City on the Hill" and the "Errand into the Wilderness" were later reclaimed to figure American exceptionalism. John Winthrop's words delivered aboard a ship bound for New England in 1630, "We shall be as a city upon a hill, the eyes of all people upon us," came to define the persuasive image of the United States as literally above other nations, separate and inviolate, righteous and exemplary.[7]

Traditionally, this imagined break with Europe was seen as inextricably tied to the "Westward movement" of American history. The foreignness of Europe rhetorically domesticated claims to the conquered territories of the West. In Frederick Jackson Turner's classic 1894 formulation, "The Significance of the Frontier in American History," the advance of the frontier meant "the steady movement away from Europe, a steady growth of independence on American lines."[8] As Michael Rogin has argued, "the linkage of expansion to freedom instead of the acquisition of colonies" has shaped American nationalism "from the beginning."[9] If American society was moving away from Europe, it could not be "colonizing" the North American continent as European powers had done; the United States was instead claiming land which was understood to be its "manifest destiny." The frontier thesis shared the basic assumptions Amy Kaplan finds in Perry Miller's *Errand into the Wilderness:* "That America—once cut off from Europe—can be understood as a domestic question, left alone, unique, divorced from international conflicts—whether the slave trade or the Mexican War—in which that national identity takes shape."[10]

The Turner thesis has been thoroughly superseded as a historical paradigm by new western historians such as Patricia Limerick and Richard White.[11] But its power has always been symbolic. The assumption that American history moves from east to west remains deeply ingrained in cultural imagination. In such national narratives Chicanos and Asian Americans remain perpetual latecomers, cast in the role of "recent" immigrants and foreign nationals, as if the War with Mexico did not predate the Civil War or the transcontinental railway had not been built from west to east as well from east to west. Race has long been the fault line in the logic equating American nationalism with the expansion of freedom. Turner overtly offers his "frontier thesis" as an alternative to the argument that slavery was the "peculiar" feature of American culture and history.[12] Perry Miller, as Kaplan so adroitly foregrounds, came to his discovery of American uniqueness along "the banks of the Congo," and had to actively suppress the past and present significance of Africa in his formulation of "the origins of America . . . from a dyadic relationship between Europe and an empty continent. . . ."[13] Scholars and intellectuals such as W. E. B. Du Bois and José Martí challenged such exclusionary racial and nationalist models long before the institutionalization of Ethnic Studies in the 1960s and 1970s.[14]

The question of a "Post-Nationalist American Studies" also reminds us of the ways the birth and early development of American Studies were entangled with nationalist ideologies. Gene Wise's famous essay, "Paradigm Dramas," and several addresses by presidents of the American Studies Association tell this history, which is worth a brief sketch here.[15] The field originated in the 1930s amid the social and economic upheavals of the Great Depression. It is rooted in anxieties about the special claims and desires of Americanists to legitimate the study of the United States in the university, especially in some of the elite universities where American Studies began. By the 1940s, when the first American Civilization Ph.D.s emerged from Harvard and then Yale and the University of Pennsylvania, American Studies was fully implicated in the wartime and postwar celebration of

American exceptionalism. A classic in American Studies scholarship of this time, John Kouwenhoven's *The Arts in Modern American Civilization* (1948), bursts with pride over America's unique styles and contributions, and the "consensus" scholarship of the 1950s continued the argument that American culture was exceptional both in its character and in its mission of spreading democratic liberalism around the world.[16] Daniel Boorstin's *The Genius of American Politics* (1953) made the boldest claims for the "givenness" of American democratic experience, but Boorstin's claims and mood pervade much of the American Studies scholarship of the 1950s and early 1960s, including David Potter's *People of Plenty* (1954) and such classic myth-and-symbol studies as Henry Nash Smith's *Virgin Land,* R. W. B. Lewis's *American Adam,* and Leo Marx's *The Machine in the Garden.*[17]

Of course, careful readers of some of this work will notice ambivalence in the claims, such as Potter's doubts that American democratic traditions could be exported or Leo Marx's worries about the givenness of American democratic traditions. But in general the scholars of American Studies from the end of the Second World War to the mid-1960s justified American exceptionalism, rarely challenged the assumption that the nation-state was the proper unit of analysis for understanding American experience, and endorsed an American ideal of internationalism. In the latter case, scholars of American Studies often developed notions of the United States as the economic, social, and political utopia toward which other nations ought to aspire, contributing thereby to a familiar Cold War ideology in which both the United States and the Soviet Union claimed international "destinies" for their respective worldviews.

Just when the consensus paradigm in American Studies came apart is hard to say; these things happen slowly. In retrospect we do see how the increasingly visible Civil Rights movement, then the Black Power movement, the women's movement, the gay rights movement, and labor movements, such as that of California's migrant farmworkers, meant that American Studies practitioners could no longer sustain the fiction that Americans "shared" a national character based on common experiences. The Vietnam war forced many scholarly communities, including the American Studies Association (ASA), to debate the proper role of intellectuals in the Cold War. As in many other scholarly societies, a "radical caucus" emerged in the ASA at the end of the 1960s and began pushing American Studies practitioners toward C. Wright Mills's stance that the proper goal of the sociological imagination was "connecting private troubles with public issues."[18]

Meanwhile, just as the radical caucus and others were assaulting the collaboration of American Studies with nationalist ideologies, new sorts of particularist nationalism emerged with the Black Power movement, a nationalist Chicano/a movement (La Raza), and a general move into identity the 1970s and 1980s. These social movements and their criticism of American nationalism showed up in the university as programs and departments of Ethnic Studies and Women's Studies. Those "left behind" in traditional American Studies programs struggled to avoid being perceived as "white heterosexual male studies" in the new constellation of programs and scholarly specialties. By the mid-1980s the ASA—as evidenced by the articles published in *American Quarterly*, its convention programs, and the diversity of its national council and officers—embraced a multicultural view of the American Studies project. But the question remained how the new American Studies would find a distinctive, interdisciplinary, scholarly and teaching role for the specialty without slipping again into a rhetoric that privileged national identity. How could the new American Studies take "nation," "nationality," and "nationalism" as phenomena that are simultaneously fictional and real?

Another crucial question for the new American Studies is how it will draw on previous traditions of scholarship. If the aims of American Studies have changed, then how are its practitioners to assess and use scholarship, much of it based on time-consuming empirical research, produced according to the nationalist paradigm? For example, there has been much work in a postmodern vein about diaspora, migration, and modern consciousness which nonetheless echoes (unknowingly, much of the time) the themes of the older immigration history (itself part of American exceptionalism) by scholars such as Oscar Handlin. The old version painted America as the melting pot of the world, reading sources such as Crèvecoeur, Tocqueville, and social scientific work on immigration, in order to portray American national consciousness as a unique process of transformation.

Current American scholarship has actively criticized that version of American exceptionalism, but much of the recent theoretical emphasis on global migration and movement has paradoxically left some of us wondering why it is that some Americans still feel unique, others look for more specific forms of identification within the nation-state, and others reject the very idea of national affiliation. Placing American national consciousness within the historical context of the rise of modern nationalism, ethnic consciousness, and cultural identity in general would be one way for American Studies to be self-reflective about the "American" part of the endeavor.[19]

If it does not exactly describe, prescribe, or proscribe, our use of "postnationalism," like any act of nomination, certainly produces and performs; that is, it not only unsettles, but also acts in the world of critical practice. Most immediately, "post-nationalism" acts by addressing the question not only of how areas and objects of study within American Studies might change, but also of how methodologies might change. In fact, we want to suggest that efforts at "post-nationalist" American Studies ought to incorporate a thorough recognition of the dynamic imbrication of the methodological and the conceptual. Recent shifts in objects and areas of study within American Studies are calling forth new methods of study and paradigms of research, while engagements by American Studies scholars with multiple disciplines and methodologies are redefining those very objects and areas.

Our group's discussions about the methodological and conceptual shifts that a "post-nationalist" practice might bring to American Studies focused on the possibilities and limits of three current movements in this direction within American Studies: the embrace of "cosmopolitanism" or "critical internationalism;" the engagement with Postcolonial Studies; and the appropriation of Gramscian and/or the Subaltern Studies Collective's theories of subalternity.

In one sense, then, we join the current chorus of calls to move U.S.-based American Studies, Women's Studies, and Ethnic Studies away from uncritical nationalist perspectives and toward what has been variously called critical internationalism, transnationalism, or globality. In particular, we are concerned with how one negotiates among local, national, and global perspectives, while remaining vigilantly self-critical about the epistemologically and historically deep ties that American Studies has had to U.S. imperialism.

An essay by Jane Desmond and Virginia Domínguez in *American Quarterly* exemplifies a particularly pervasive version of the call for "cosmopolitanism" or "critical internationalism" within American Studies. Echoing Linda Kerber and Benjamin Lee, Desmond and Domínguez call for " 'an authentically cosmopolitan intellectual culture,' " a "true internationalization" of American Studies.[20] Concretely, Desmond and Domínguez advocate more interaction between U.S. scholars and international scholars, by which they mean that U.S. scholars should read more work by non-U.S. scholars on the United States; more international meetings and exchange programs should be held; new transnational technologies should be adopted more rapidly and democratically; and more funding for all of the above should be provided by departments, universities, and professional institutions (486–7). These steps could certainly open up opportunities for organized as well as chance encounters with non-U.S. scholars that could affect the transformation of U.S.-based American Studies scholarship. In fact, we would emphasize how the very possibility of such opportunities is currently being threatened by cuts in U.S. government funding of the humanities.

Yet Desmond and Domínguez stop short of a sustained discussion of what "new paradigms of research" a critical internationalism would involve. Rather, they seem to suggest that a certain international, intellectual equal exchange will necessarily erode the nationalist tendencies of American Studies and "generate" new, cosmopolitan paradigms of research (484–8).

But what, exactly, does the "cosmopolitan" mean when it is transformed from a practice of international intellectual exchange into a paradigm of American Studies research? Are we sure that such a "cosmopolitan" practice will overthrow, rather than export and reinforce, the imperialist and nationalist traditions of American Studies?

Desmond and Domínguez's understanding of "cosmopolitanism" seems to stem from their agreement with popular celebrations of the death of the nation-state at the hands of the supposedly increasing globalization of capitalism. They take this increasing globalization of capitalism as a historical rationale for a shift toward "critical internationalism" within American Studies. However, the research of, for example, Karl Polanyi, Annales school founder Marc Bloch, Fernand Braudel, Ernesto Laclau, world-system theorists (such as Immanuel Wallerstein, Giovanni Arrighi, and Janet Abu-Lughod), and contemporary geographers (such as Peter J. Hugill), has shown that capitalist and even precapitalist economic and cultural systems have long been "global."[21] If "globalization" is not, in fact, increasing in any simple, quantifiable, or progressive sense today, then we ought to ask from whence the optimism of American Studies critics, such as Desmond and Domínguez, derives? If the global is not progressively obliterating the national or the local today, but rather global, national, and local forces are articulating with each other in complex modalities, then the elucidation of these articulations rather than a celebration of them is the urgent task before us. A rush to celebrate what Desmond and Domínguez call the "cosmopolitan" runs the risk of entrenching current raced, gendered, and classed values of transnational capitalism at least as much as it challenges current U.S. hegemony within transnational capitalism. For us, then, "post-nationalist" names a negotiation among local, national, and global frames of analysis that seeks its justification neither in objective and progressive historical processes of globalization nor in implicit celebrations of the obliteration of the local and the national. What the result of this negotiation might look like, and how it might authorize itself, are crucial questions to consider. The questions themselves, rather than quick answers to them, would seem to be more fruitful occasions for a new American Studies.[22]

Other recent efforts at specifying "paradigms for research" for a "critically international" American Studies have engaged with Postcolonial Studies, while related efforts have mobilized the concept of subalternity to name and examine the marginalization of people of color in the United States. By making visible the white settler colonial history of the United States, such efforts can help overcome such founding American Studies myths— or, to borrow Houston A. Baker, Jr.'s use of Foucault, "governing statements"—as "the individual in the wilderness," "migratory errand," "self-reliance," and North America as *tabula rasa.*"[23] In addition, these efforts can push Postcolonial Studies itself to consider the relationship of North American colonialism in general, and U.S. racial formations in particular, to Marxian narratives of, primarily, European colonialism and imperialism.

Yet, as Jenny Sharpe has argued, a number of problems attend the "re-fashioning" of Postcolonial Studies and theories of "subalternity" as American Studies or even Minority Discourse Studies.[24] What happens, Sharpe asks, to North-South or East-West power relations when the metropolitan North reclaims the margins of global power? What does the fundamentally political and historically specific analogy between the marginalized or minoritized subject in the North and the entire marginalized world of the South (from international bourgeoisie to rural subaltern) make visible and obscure? Sharpe calls on us to keep track of the gains and losses of appropriating critical terminology from Postcolonial Studies to analyze North America in general and the United States in particular.[25]

At the same time, as George Lipsitz suggested in a paper he presented to our group, these recent American Studies efforts to engage with Postcolonial Studies have roots in the Black Power and Chicano nationalist movements' claims to the discourses of marginalization and resistance forged by the great decolonization movements of the twentieth century, claims realized in the "internal colonization" model as well as in powerful, if flawed and fleeting, transnational political alliances. Despite post-Bandung, "post-1968," and post–Civil Rights era disillusionment, the "internal colonization" claims were too sustained and complex to be dismissed simply as naive or out of date. They offer us concrete attempts to negotiate methodologically and conceptually among local, national, international, transnational, and global frames and objects of analysis. While Sharpe's caution gives pause to American Studies work that engages with postcolonial theory in general, and the notion of subalternity in particular, Lipsitz urges us not to simply eschew such engagement, but rather to proceed with a critical and active awareness of the "internal colonization" legacy.[26]

The intersections among formations of race, culture, and mass consumption are also crucial subjects for post-nationalist American Studies. Historians and critics have thoroughly examined U.S. mass consumption and consumer capitalism.[27] Critical work remains to be done on how race and culture have been commodified in these processes. At a macro-level, theorists of post-modernity have examined such phenomena, but new work is needed on social practices at a local level. Some of the most interesting insights regarding the commodification of culture have come from critics of anthropology, and a post-nationalist American Studies might benefit immensely from the transnational perspectives involved in criticizing imperial anthropology.

Racial and ethnic issues in the United States are often treated as problems specific to the multicultural United States, rather than as specific instances of divisions, hierarchies, and conflicts that can be found in virtually every society. There is a need for a greater awareness of the commodification of racial difference and exotic cultures which lies at the heart of multinational capitalism. For example, an American Express television commercial of several years ago featured the founder of The Body Shop expressing her company's corporate policy regarding indigenous peoples around the world—they would pay "natives" for the products they produced, commodifying their authentically exotic origins, but in her words: "We don't touch the culture." Her fantasy of benevolence and the nostalgic desire to "preserve" "primitive culture" have a long history dating back to the gunboat anthropology of Western imperialism. The "spread of the American Dream" requires a careful examination of the historical intersections between multinational capitalism, state power, and representations of race and culture.[28] Recent studies, such as *Coca-Colonization and the Cold War,* though suggestive, only begin to examine the ways in which the U.S. government and multinational corporations have imported and exported what they defined as cultural products.[29]

Over the past fifteen years, one of the major developments in American Studies across the nation has been the adoption of multiculturalism as a central, if not the central, organizing principle in how to study culture in the United States. As many faculty abandoned perspectives which focused on American exceptionalism, most American Studies programs emerged at the forefront of their campuses in integrating new writings on and by people of color into required courses for undergraduate majors and graduates, as well as into general education courses on U.S. society for the entire campus. In the early 1970s, prominent American Studies programs, along with Ethnic Studies programs, led efforts at hiring faculty of color. On campuses which did not establish Ethnic Studies departments or stand-alone programs focusing on specific racial populations, American Studies by the 1980s often played an umbrella function in providing courses which dealt primarily with issues of race and ethnicity in the United States.

During this same period, prominent programs and departments in Ethnic Studies have increasingly grown from individualized programs centered on a specific ethnic group—for example, African American Studies or Chicano/a Studies—to diverse settings whose intellectual role has become the theoretical study of race and ethnicity across various groups. Newly developed Ethnic Studies departments, like the one recently instituted at the University of California, San Diego, are not compartmentalized into separate ethnicities; instead, they take as their direction issues of race and ethnicity nationally and globally. Stand-alone programs in African American Studies, for example, have increasingly taken on a diasporic perspective which examines race not only in a U.S. context, but often in relatiqn to discussions in Africa, Latin America, and the Caribbean, not to mention other sites in the Black Atlantic, like Great Britain.

These intellectual developments have increasingly led to significant borrowings across the lines of American and Ethnic Studies. The disciplinary crossroads of American Studies should provide a fertile ground for the growth of various cultural studies, Ethnic Studies, Women's Studies, and other enterprises which thrive on criticizing the dominant within American society. The perspectives of dominated and excluded classes or groups within America have long helped us to challenge the ideological and nationalist presumptions of American scholarship. To the extent that American Studies has sought or welcomed such critical points of view, and considering the critical tenor of much of what American Studies has produced in the last twenty years, it has probably been quite a while since many American Studies scholars have been involved in unreflective nationalist enterprises.

Unfortunately, these intellectual developments have occurred at a time in which American universities have been under attack on both political and financial grounds, and interdisciplinary perspectives have often been the main casualties of these attacks. Several Ethnic Studies programs have been significantly downsized or eliminated during the late 1980s and 1990s, and a few once-prestigious American Studies programs, like the American Civilization program at the University of Pennsylvania, have been entirely eliminated.[30] One would expect this period to have produced a new coalition politics among American and Ethnic Studies faculty, given increasingly similar intellectual perspectives and often common assaults on their intellectual integrity. On some campuses, this did occur as faculty and students decided to stand together and reshape existing programs to take into account the new, expansive intellectual and theoretical perspectives which took on questions of race and ethnicity in a wide-lensed fashion.[31]

On the other hand, at institutions as different as Columbia University and the University of Washington, student demands and protests for Ethnic Studies, often prompted by changing student demographics, were met with administrative proposals for American Studies. As George Sánchez argues in his essay, many college administrators, for both financial and ideological reasons, have tried to assimilate Ethnic Studies into American Studies. On some campuses, like the University of California, Berkeley, and the University of Colorado, a large proportion of Ethnic Studies faculty fought against this incorporation to preserve long-standing Ethnic Studies departments and programs. It seemed to some as if American Studies now loomed as a new imperializing force, driven by fiscal crises and ideological imperatives to "control difference" under a rubric of newfound Americanism. As John Carlos Rowe points out in his essay, congressional reductions in funding for the U.S. Information Agency also come at a particularly in-opportune historical moment, when many international scholars need more than ever to understand the United States in terms of its multicultural realities and global ambitions, including the legacy of cultural imperialism to which the U.S. Information Agency has contributed.

A post-nationalist American Studies must find a way to incorporate the various intellectual traditions in a multicultural United States and the specific histories at different colleges and universities without assuming a position of ideological control over the study of race and ethnicity. Moreover, few faculty of color want to face the age-old question, "Are you American?" by having to decide to contribute either to an overarching American Studies program or a marginalized Ethnic Studies program. And certainly a multicultural curriculum can not be sustained without advances in the hiring and promotion of faculty of color who specialize in the study of specific racial/ethnic groups in the United States.

The increasing value of knowledge about racial and ethnic minorities has come to intersect with the need for more intellectuals of color within "white" academia; as a result, issues involving the commodification of ethnic knowledge and of racialized bodies have become intertwined. At times when most of academia ignored the existence of race in American history, intellectuals of color often chose to study racial and ethnic groups left out of American narratives. For such intellectuals, the value of their expert knowledge paralleled the need for their bodies to represent minority populations in academia. Not all academics of color studied race and ethnicity, though, and the conflating within academia of raced knowledge and raced bodies often led to awkward evaluations of intellectual worth. Belittled by standards applied only to them, intellectuals of color have had to fight against a ghettoization of their knowledge if they studied ethnicity, while those who did not study ethnicity encountered assumptions about their ethnic expertise because of the conflation between expert knowledge and racialized bodies.

Even with the success of equal-opportunity hiring practices and a commitment to affirmative action, universities remain alienating places for minorities, and much of the difficulty lies not in the continuing existence of racial hostility, but in the very ways by which race and ethnicity have been valued within academia. Despite claims to intellectual purity beyond the reach of the marketplace, higher education is embedded within the practices of American capitalist culture and society.

We need to examine the ways in which ethnicity and race have themselves become commodified by intellectuals in America. Beyond the often bizarre ways in which exotic knowledge and intellectuals of color have been commodified within academia, American intellectuals have had a problematic relationship with the workings of the capitalist market, founding their critiques upon the assumption that they have been somehow removed from its operations. Academics who have long disdained the workings of the market paradoxically find themselves implicated in the commodification of ethnicity and difference in America. Intellectuals who have evaluated and treasured the exotic and the strange, the ethnic and the different, yet at the same time railed against the workings of mass consumption and mass production, find it strange to see corporate America outracing them in the effort to place a value on ethnicity. Consumer products such as leisure, sports, and fashion, seen from the perspective of the Frankfurt school and neo-Marxist theories of fetishism and alienation, are often objects of disdain among academic scholars, and their treatments of such subjects reflect such distaste. When such intellectuals themselves value racial and cultural difference, however, their own commodification of exoticism passes unnoticed within the larger context of racial and cultural commodification produced by global capitalism.

The quandary of placing a value on racial difference without succumbing to a bourgeois fascination with "authentic" and "exotic" cultures is related to the problem of public intellectual life. Whether intellectuals trivialize or exaggerate the importance of consumption in the production of social values, they must justify their work in relation to market forces. There is a need for public intellectuals who can engage with a listening and reading audience who see themselves not as the victims of a capitalist market, but as active and empowered consumers. An American Studies which sees as its main task the unmasking of bourgeois foibles is in danger of missing its own bourgeois, cosmopolitan values, but much more dangerous is the threat of public irrelevance. Put another way, how will the new American Studies define the responsibilities of the public intellectual in this postmodern situation?

The commitment of several members of the research group to holism represents an important group of scholars in the discipline of American Studies. The ideas of systems, holism, and pattern have a long and particular history in disciplines associated with cultural studies, and some might say that the ideas belong to a "consensus" view of history and society discarded with the sixties' awareness of conflict and diversity as characteristic of American experience. On the other hand, the pursuit of a holistic understanding of culture does not inevitably depend on a model of culture as a mechanism for "the replication of uniformity," as one anthropologist puts it.[32] Keeping the systems model or metaphor, we can see systems as complex constructions of diverse elements and still ask how the parts of the system might be connected. Old American Studies questions of style—such as inquiries into the ways modernism might be expressed in fiction, painting, architecture, music, and dance, to say nothing of religious and social thought—have not lost their salience, even if we now must sort out the connections between hip-hop styles and postmodernity in fiction. What is perhaps most important is that scholars debate openly the assumptions behind theories of American culture as holistic or differential.

Another traditional goal still important for American Studies is interdisciplinary thinking about American experience. American Studies can count as a success whatever it has contributed to the increased interdisciplinarity of the disciplines, especially history and literary criticism. But we note that with the success of "interdisciplinarity" has come a certain sloppiness in what gets called "interdisciplinary." Theories and methods in history and literary studies have crossed boundaries enough that we are tempted to call all the work in cultural studies interdisciplinary; in a real sense, it is. But before we get too self-congratulatory about this work, we should ask ourselves what disciplines we are avoiding as we do our work. To be "interdisciplinary" would mean to have the tools and frame of mind that prepare the teacher or scholar to draw from many relevant disciplines when thinking about a particular cultural studies question. So where are the theories and methods from some of the disciplines continually neglected in American Studies, such as political science, economics, psychology, rhetoric, and even the cognitive sciences? Our range of interdisciplinary inquiry often turns out to be embarrassingly narrow. The disciplines themselves are extremely internally diverse and in some cases change rapidly. People in American Studies are most likely to know and draw from work in the "cultural studies" corners of some disciplines, such as sociology and anthropology, but other disciplines remain poorly understood by American Studies practitioners. In addition, interdisciplinarity should mean more than reading historical or scientific texts, for instance, exclusively for purposes of *literary* interpretation.

In our view the new American Studies needs to face these tough questions about how we can be more interdisicplinary in our research and teaching. Researchers need aids, such as the "disciplinary access essays" that used to be published in *American Quarterly*.[33] The electronic revolution offers new formats for American Studies scholars to help one another with maps of interesting work in other disciplines, as the work posted to the T-Amstudy listserv and American Crossroads electronic discussion have demonstrated over the past few years.[34] Teachers and students need to develop an intellectual culture that keeps track of what is going on in all the relevant disciplines, including the hard (versus soft) corners of the social sciences. The American Studies program at New York University and the Modern Thought and Literature Program at Stanford require their students to become "literate" in quantitative methods of research, at least enough to read that research if not to replicate it. Following their leads, scholars in American Studies need to work toward the goal of minimal literacy in all the cultural studies disciplines.

No single curricular model and no general institutional definition can address the different problems facing American Studies as a discipline today. Nevertheless, it is important for scholars to begin to address these questions in terms of the consequences of their intellectual and scholarly arguments. One of the common assumptions of the essays in this volume is that every scholarly argument has curricular and institutional relevance that should be made more explicit in our scholarly exchanges. The usual "Academic Darwinism" by which competing programs are imagined to survive or vanish as a consequence of competition for students, funds, and reputation should not determine the mutual futures of Ethnic, Women's, and American Studies. There must be a variety of curricular designs that will encourage the development of what is unique in each of these fields and yet find ways of identifying and thus sharing the several points where these fields intersect and complement each other.

Such intersections are profoundly historical, including as they do the critical moments of historical contact among different cultures—the history of slavery and its abolition, colonization and decolonization, diasporas of many sorts, and war, for example. They are also fundamentally theoretical, insofar as our most influential critical theories have attempted to generalize about otherwise disparate, uncanny, or incommensurate categories, the majority of which involve basic cultural and social differences. Every scholarly investigation of the concrete historical realities of African-American or Asian-American experience, for example, enacts a theory of how and why such histories and experiences have been variously excluded from the dominant model of "American Experience," often by way of specific practices such as slavery, segregation, and the Chinese Exclusion Laws. Theorizing such exclusions is one of our collective obligations as intellectuals committed to the various fields that claim commonly to represent knowledges that are otherwise unrepresentable in the liberal educational project.

All of this suggests the possibility that American Studies, either under this name or a different title, might begin to reimagine its curricular design in terms of such historical and theoretical intersections with the complementary disciplines of Ethnic Studies, Women's Studies, and the several area studies belonging to the horizon of the Western Hemisphere. Such curricular models—there would, of course, be many—would no longer be committed to any sort of "coverage" of the many different historical, geographical, and theoretical areas that the new American Studies claims to encompass.

Once the coverage model has been abandoned, of course, then we have the more challenging task of justifying the education we offer our students at both undergraduate and graduate levels. If only "intersections" were studied in American Studies, then would we in fact be offering students sufficient content to constitute competency in an intellectual field? "Intersectionality" should not be confused with interdisciplinarity, which too often has meant the incorporation of many different disciplines into a single research project or instructional situation. Of course, a certain degree of interdisciplinarity is crucial to the new work being done in the various fields represented in the new American Studies. But we must recognize that the claim for interdisciplinary inclusion within the traditional curriculum of discrete courses and individual instructors can lead to unachievable goals of "comprehensiveness" or troublesome choices of "representative" examples.

When we pose the related questions, "For whom and to what ends are we teaching (and writing)?" we should consider them to encompass the related question of how education and public policy are related. Earlier versions of American Studies, such as the myth and symbol school, have been criticized for contributing to the cultural imperialism integral to U. S. foreign policy in the post–World War II era. Leading figures of that approach, such as Leo Marx, have vigorously denied such connections, defending their commitments to criticize government policies and their identification with the great tradition of American dissent.[35] Yet, how our scholarly and instructional works are used outside the university does not always agree with our best intentions in writing and teaching; every message can be detoured from its proper destination. The lessons of the recent "culture wars" certainly teach educators that we have an obligation to represent ourselves in the public sphere and thus take an active part in shaping those public policies that intersect with our areas of specialization. If we claim truly to be specialists in American cultures, then there should be many such intersections of our work with public policy. Rather than accept the caricature of contemporary scholars as ivory-tower intellectuals, we ought to show how the university is itself one of the important institutions in the formation of public opinions, behaviors, values, and thus policies.

We do not pretend to answer all of these questions in the essays that follow. Each of us was also working toward his or her book-length contribution to the "new American Studies" as we wrote our respective parts of this volume, and those nine books might be considered fuller developments of our different interpretations of post-nationalist American Studies. These conventional qualifications aside, we do think that the essays in this volume provide a good index to the more inclusive, culturally diverse, and comparative American Studies today urged in many scholarly quarters. Because we also think that these scholarly questions must be connected directly with curricular and pedagogical concerns, we have included sample syllabi for courses, real or imagined, that we consider appropriate to the topics discussed in our essays. Like our essays, these syllabi are not prescriptions for how to "do" American Studies; they are instead, like that aggravating title, "post-nationalist American Studies," intended to provoke discussion, research, and teaching.

NOTES

1. Arjun Appadurai, *Modernity at Large: Cultural Dimensions of Globalization* (Minneapolis: University of Minnesota Press, 1996); Donald Pease, "National Identities, Postmodern Artifacts, and Postnational Narratives," in *National Identities and Post-Nationalist Narratives,* Donald Pease, ed. (Durham, N.C.: Duke University Press, 1994), 1–13.

2. See David Harvey, *The Condition of Postmodernity: An Enquiry into the Origins of Cultural Change* (Oxford: Basil Blackwell, 1990), 168; Lauren Berlant, *The Anatomy of National Fantasy: Hawthorne, Utopia, and Everyday Life* (Chicago: University of Chicago Press, 1994), 20.

3. Alok Yadav, "Nationalism and Contemporaneity: Political Economy of a Discourse," *Cultural Critique* 26 (Winter 1993–94): 213, concludes that this "implies not simple endorsement of nationalist projects, but rather contestation for the meaning and direction of nationalist discourses and their appropriation for progressive projects." It is not always easy to cleanly separate "progressive" aspects of nationalist projects; anticapitalist nationalisms often thrive on xenophobic sentiments. While U.S. labor unions oppose transnational capitalism, for instance, the nationalist frame of their vision of worker solidarity has in most cases made it difficult to forge cross-border ties to other workers. As Masao Miyoshi suggests in "A Borderless World? From Colonialism to Transnationalism and the Decline of the Nation-State," in *Global/Local: Cultural Production and the Transnational Imaginary* (Durham, N.C.: Duke University Press, 1996), "How to situate oneself in this . . . configuration of transnational power and culture without being trapped by a dead end nativism seems to be the most important question that faces every critic and theorist the world over at this moment" (91).

4. See Michael Omi and Howard Winant, *Racial Formation in the United States: From the 1960s to the 1990s,* 2d ed. (New York: Routledge, 1994), 35–50. Despite their trenchant critique of race-as-nation paradigms, they agree that the "great insight of nation-based approaches has always been their ability to connect U.S. conditions with global patterns based in the legacy of colonialism" (50).

5. Since then, a Congressional investigation has rejected Dornan's claims, and Loretta Sanchez was reelected to Congress in the November 1998 election.

6. By stressing the many different cultures of the Americas, José Martí and C. L. R. James have influenced the comparatist dimension of post-nationalist American Studies. By focusing on the cultural and geographical contact zones of Mexican, Mexican-American, and Euroamerican cultures, Americo Paredes anticipated the new interest in "border studies."

7. John Winthrop, "A Model Of Christian Charity," in *The Norton Anthology of American Literature,* 4th ed., vol. 1, Nina Baym et al., eds. (New York: Norton, 1994), 180. See Perry Miller, *Errand into the Wilderness* (Cambridge: Harvard University Press, 1956) for the most influential appropriation of Puritan metaphors as Americanist tropes.

8. Frederick Jackson Turner, *Frontier and Section* (New York: Prentice-Hall, 1961), 37–62.

9. Michael Rogin, " 'Make My Day!' Spectacle as Amnesia in Imperial Politics [and] the Sequel," in *The Cultures of United States Imperialism,* Amy Kaplan and Donald Pease, eds. (Durham, N.C.: Duke University Press, 1993), 510. See also Michael Rogin, *Fathers and Children: Andrew Jackson and the Subjugation of the American Indian* (1975), and *Ronald Reagan, the Movie and Other Episodes in Political Demonology* (1987); Richard Drinnon, *Facing West: The Metaphysics of Indian-Hating and Empire-Building* (1980); Richard Slotkin, *Regeneration through Violence: The Mythology of the American Frontier, 1600–1860* (1973), *The Fatal Environment: The Myth of the Frontier in the Age of Industrialization, 1800–1890* (1985), and *Gunfighter Nation: The Myth of the Frontier in Twentieth-Century America* (1992).

10. Amy Kaplan, "Left Alone with America: The Absence of Empire in the Study of American Culture," in *Cultures of United States Imperialism,* 7.

11. See Patricia Limerick, *The Legacy of Conquest: The Unbroken Past of the American West* (1987); and Richard White, *"It's Your Misfortune and None of My Own": A New History of the American West* (1991).

12. Turner, *Frontier and Section,* 53.

13. Kaplan, "Left Alone with America," 6.

14. Internationalist critiques of United States nationalism run throughout both men's careers. See especially W. E. B. Du Bois, *The Suppression of the African Slave Trade* (1896), and *Dusk of Dawn* (1940); and José Martí, *Our America: Writings on Latin America and the Struggle for Cuban Independence,* trans. Elinor Randall, Juan de Onis, and Roslyn Held Foner (New York: Monthly Review Press, 1977).

15. Gene Wise," 'Paradigm Dramas' in American Studies: A Cultural and Institutional History of the Movement," *American Quarterly* 31 (1979): 293–337.

16. John Kouwenhoven, *The Arts in Modern Civilization* (New York: W. W. Norton, 1948).

17. Daniel J. Boorstin, *The Genius of American Politics* (Chicago: University of Chicago Press, 1953); David Potter, *People of Plenty: Economic Abundance and the American Character* (Chicago: University of Chicago Press, 1954); Henry Nash Smith, *Virgin Land: The American West as Symbol and Myth* (Cambridge: Harvard University Press, 1950); R. W. B. Lewis, *American Adam: Innocence, Tragedy, and Tradition in the Nineteenth Century* (Chicago: University of Chicago Press, 1955); Leo Marx, *The Machine in the Garden: Technology and the Pastoral Ideal in America* (New York: Oxford University Press, 1964).

18. C. Wright Mills, *The Sociological Imagination* (New York: Oxford University Press, 1959). The Radical Caucus named its journal *Connections* and subsequently named itself The Connections Collective.

19. "Identity" as an analytical device seems all the rage right now, offering a neat way of understanding the bridge between present-day identity politics, ethnic/nationalist consciousness, and political battles over narratives of the historical past. We need to examine a little more what we mean by identity, and the history of how we came to think about identity as an analytical concept. The problems we have with anthropological conceptions of culture (that culture as an analytical tool is too holistic, static, ahistorical, and structural) have been pointed out by critics of anthropology such as James Clifford, *The Predicament of Culture: Twentieth-Century*

Ethnography, Literature, and Art (Cambridge: Harvard University Press, 1988). In trying to replace the culture concept with something more dynamic, situational, historical, and contingent, historians have suddenly become popular intellectuals, eclipsing anthropologists and sociologists. Identity, as a mode of understanding which is dynamic and involves historical narratives of self and group consciousness, appears to offer a solution to the problems of overly synchronic structural analyses. The intellectual history of the "identity concept" still needs to be examined in order to place its rise within the historical context of modernity.

20. Jane C. Desmond and Virginia R. Domínguez, "Resituating American Studies in a Critical Internationalism," *American Quarterly* 48 (1996): 483–97. Further references given parenthetically in the text.

21. Janet L. Abu-Lughod, *Before European Hegemony: The World System, A.D. 1250–1350* (New York : Oxford University Press, 1989); Giovanni Arrighi, *The Long Twentieth Century* (New York: Verso, 1994); Marc Bloch, *Feudal Society,* trans. L. A. Manyon (Chicago : University of Chicago Press, 1974); Fernand Braudel, *Civilization and Capitalism, Fifteenth–Eighteenth Century,* vol. 1, *The Structures of Everyday Life* (Berkeley: University of California Press, 1981 [1979]), vol. 2, *The Wheels of Commerce* (Berkeley: University of California Press, 1982 [1979]), and vol. 3, *The Perspective of the World* (Berkeley: University of California Press, 1992); André Gunder Frank, *World Accumulation, 1492–1789* (New York: Monthly Review Press, 1978); Peter J. Hugill, *World Trade Since 1431: Geography, Technology, and Capitalism* (Baltimore: Johns Hopkins University Press, 1993); Ernesto Laclau, "Feudalism and Capitalism in Latin America," in *Politics and Ideology in Marxist Theory: Capitalism, Fascism, Populism* (London: New Left Books, 1977); Jorge Larrain, *Theories of Development Capitalism, Colonialism, and Dependency* (Cambridge: Polity Press, 1989); Karl Polanyi, *The Great Transformation* (Boston: Beacon Press, 1957 [1944]); Immanuel Wallerstein, "The Rise and Future Demise of the World Capitalism System: Concepts for Comparative Analysis," in *The Capitalist World-Economy* (Cambridge: Cambridge University Press, 1979), *The Modern World-System,* vol. 2, *Mercantilism and the Consolidation of the European World-Economy, 1600–1750* (New York: Academic Press, 1980), and vol. 3, *The Second Era of Great Expansion of the Capitalist World-Economy, 1730s–1840s* (New York: Academic Press, 1989).

22. In his visit to our group as part of a forum entitled "Studying U.S. Racial Formations in a Global Frame," David L. Eng discussed Mark Chiang's "Coming Out into the Global System: Postmodern Patriarchies and Transnational Sexualities in *The Wedding Banquet,*" one of the essays included in an anthology Eng has coedited with Alice Y. Hom, entitled *Q & A: Queer in Asian America* (Philadelphia: Temple University Press, 1998). Chiang's interpretation of Ang Lee's film offers a crucial caution to notions of "cosmopolitanism" that are based on a celebration of, or optimism about, the current period of globalization. By showing how the film offers an "antihomophobic or homophilic resolution," which simultaneously secures the subordinated place of Asian women and an Asian underclass in the capitalist world-system, Chiang's essay takes the "cosmopolitan" itself as its object of critique and carefully negotiates among local, national, and global perspectives (384).

23. Houston A. Baker, Jr., *Blues, Ideology, and Afro-American Literature: A Vernacular Theory* (Chicago: University of Chicago Press, 1984), 18–19.

24. Jenny Sharpe, "Is the United States Postcolonial? Transnationalism, Immigration, and Race," *Diaspora* 4: 2 (Fall 1995).

25. When "subalternity" is used generally to mean marginalized or oppressed subjects of First World states, it runs the risk of erasing the international division of labor and thus silencing the very subjects to whom "subalternity" had so carefully and tenuously referred.

26. Excellent examples of this kind of careful yet active interpretation of U.S. racial formations were presented to our group by four scholars who shared their work with us at the forum entitled "Studying Racial Formations in a Global Frame": Vilashini Cooppan, who presented unpublished research on the intercultural traffic between black political activists and theorists in the United States and in South Africa; David L. Eng, who presented work from his coedited anthology mentioned above; Colleen Lye, who presented unpublished research on the representation of the Asian American "anomalous minority" as a racial ideology at the crossroads of domestic and geopolitical discourses of imperialism; and María Josefina Saldaña-Portillo, who presented research on the relationships between *mestizaje, indigenismo,* and citizenship in Mexico and in Chicano nationalist discourse, forthcoming as "Who's the Indian in Aztlán? Re-writing *Mestizaje, Indigenismo,* and Citizenship from the Lacandon," in *Ungovernability and Citizenship,* John Beverly, Milagros Lopez, and Ileana Rodriguez, eds. (Durham, N.C.: Duke University Press).

27. For theories of modernization, see Larrain, *Theories of Development;* and Harvey, *Condition of Postmodernity.* For theories of modern and postmodern mass consumption, see Stuart Ewen, *All Consuming Images: The Politics of Style in Contemporary Culture* (New York: Basic Books, 1988); Arjun Appadurai, ed., *The Social Life of Things: Commodities in Cultural Perspective* (New York: Cambridge University Press, 1986); Jean-Christophe Agnew, *Worlds Apart: The Market and the Theater in Anglo-American Thought, 1550–1750* (New York: Cambridge University Press, 1986); Richard Wightman Fox and T. Jackson Lears, eds., *The Culture of Consumption, 1880–1980* (New York: Pantheon, 1983). For historical analyses of the globalization of mass consumption, see John Brewer and Roy Porter, eds., *Consumption and the World of Goods* (New York: Routledge, 1993); and Eric Hobsbawm and Terence Ranger, eds., *The Invention of Tradition* (New York: Cambridge University Press, 1992).

28. The imperialist trope of saving "authentic cultures" from obliteration by the modern forces of imperialism and capitalism can be seen at the heart of the missionary and anthropological efforts which accompanied imperialism, and Americans are still left with the remains of such a narrative structure for purveying "other" cultures. For a wonderful example, see the Polynesian Cultural Centre on Oahu, operated by Mormon missionaries at the nearby campus of Brigham Young University. Displaying a static and ahistorical representation of a lost Polynesian past, the Mormon center employs converts from all over the Polynesian islands, making money from displaying them as "primitives" while converting them to Mormonism and modernity.

29. Reinhold Wagnleitner, *Coca-Colonization and the Cold War: The Cultural Mission of the United States in Austria after the Second World War,* trans. Diana F. Wolf (Chapel Hill: University of North Carolina Press, 1994).

30. American Civilization at the University of Pennsylvania was discontinued in 1997–98, and its faculty positions assigned to other departments, such as Anthropology and History. Graduate students in the program with dissertations in progress at that time are completing them. Comparative Cultures at the University of California, Irvine, which was primarily an American Studies program housed in

the School of Social Sciences, was discontinued in a similar manner in the mid-1990s.

31. New interdisciplinary programs in Ethnic and Women's Studies at the University of California, Irvine, gained institutional identity in the mid-1990s. A curriculum in "Comparative Americas" was designed at the University of California, Santa Cruz, around 1995 and is being tried out as the possible foundation for a Ph.D. or graduate emphasis in the field. Variations on the "Comparative Americas" have appeared at several different universities, including New York University and Northwestern University.

32. Anthony F. C. Wallace, *Culture and Personality*, 2d ed. (New York: Random House, 1970).

33. For a taste of these interdisciplinary "access essays," see Albert E. Stone, "Psychoanalysis and American Literary Culture," *American Quarterly* 28 (1976): 309–23; Marsha Peters and Bernard Mergen, " 'Doing the Rest': The Uses of Photographs in American Studies," *American Quarterly* 29 (1977): 280–303; L. Ling-chi Wang, "Asian American Studies," *American Quarterly* 33 (1981): 339–54; John L. Caughey, "The Ethnography of Everyday Life: Theories and Methods for American Culture Studies," *American Quarterly* 34 (1982): 222–43; Dell Upton, "The Power of Things: Recent Studies in American Vernacular Architecture," *American Quarterly* 35 (1983): 262–79; and Michael Denning, " 'The Special American Conditions': Marxism and American Studies," *American Quarterly* 38 (1986): 356–80.

34. See John Carlos Rowe's essay in this volume for a discussion of these electronic resources, sponsored jointly by Georgetown University and the American Studies Association.

35. Leo Marx, "Pastoralism in America," in *Ideology and Classic American Literature,* Sacvan Bercovitch and Myra Jehlen, eds. (New York: Cambridge University Press, 1986), 62–6, quite ingeniously but erroneously interprets the New Left as an elaboration of the main thrust of American dissent developed by Marx in his classic study, *The Machine in the Garden.* To do so, Marx must ignore the association of his own Jeffersonian utopianism with what by the sixties had become reactionary political and cultural positions, and he must force "pastoralism" as a utopian goal of the Civil Rights and antiwar movements by exaggerating the influence of such works as Charles Reich's *The Greening of America: How the Youth Revolution Is Trying to Make America Livable* (New York: Random House, 1970). Recognizing the importance of television news and other electronic media in shaping social reality and thus public policies, both the Civil Rights and antiwar movements incorporated technology into their political theories and praxes in ways that marked a sharp departure from what Marx had interpreted as the American "pastoral ideal" in *The Machine in the Garden.*

Post-Nationalism, Globalism, and the New American Studies

John Carlos Rowe

Curricula and scholarship in American Studies have changed significantly over the past decade, reflecting the important influences of Women's Studies, Ethnic Studies, and postmodern and postcolonial theories. Earlier approaches, such as the Puritan Origins and Myth-and-Symbol schools, attempted to elaborate those features of American identity and social organization that are unique national characteristics. Often implicit in this nationalist approach to the study of U.S. culture was the assumption that the United States constitutes a model for democratic nationality that might be imitated or otherwise adapted by other nations in varying stages of their "development."

The criticism of such "American Exceptionalism" has focused on both its contributions to U.S. cultural imperialism and its exclusions of the many different cultures historically crucial to U.S. social, political, and economic development. In response to concepts of American identity shaped by Western patriarchy and Eurocentric models for social organization, more recent critical approaches have focused on the many cultures that have been marginalized by traditional American Studies or subordinated to an overarching nationalist mythology. In articulating the many different cultures and social identities in the United States, scholars have often focused on the cultural, political, and economic boundaries dividing these cultures both from the dominant social order and from each other.

Such "border studies" of the intersections and interactions of the different cultures of the United States must also include a reconsideration of national cultural boundaries. If a single nationalist mythology of the United States no longer prevails, then our understanding of just what constitutes the cultural border of the United States is no longer clear. Immigration has always shaped the United States in ways that demonstrate the shifting nature of such cultural boundaries. More traditional American Studies relied on the model of a single dominant culture assimilating immigrant cultures in a gradual, evolutionary manner. More recent approaches have stressed the cultural hybridities that have occurred historically among the many different cultures constituting the United States. Attention to these hybridities requires scholars to look at the multiple cultural influences involved in important social formations; such cultural complexity is often invisible when historical changes are viewed primarily in terms of the assimilation of "minor" cultures to a "dominant" social system.

The borders both of division and contact are also linguistic, and we should not equate and thereby confuse linguistic, cultural, ethnic, and national categories, even though there are many ways in which they may overlap and complement each other. In his recent essay, "For a Multilingual Turn in American Studies," and his long-term project to republish non-English-language works of U.S. literature, Werner Sollors has argued persuasively for the study of U.S. culture as a polylingual as well as multicultural discipline.[1] Despite the long history of an ideology of a monolingual United States, revived quite hysterically in recent years by E. D. Hirsch, Jr., and Arthur Schlesinger, Jr., among others, the United States continues to be a multilingual society with large segments of its population working and living successfully in multilingual contexts.[2] Statistical studies do not support the fear prevalent among conservatives and many liberals that recent immigrants fail to learn English or that polylingual communities, such as major metropolitan areas, are linguistically, culturally, and nationally fragmented. Recent studies have shown that immigrant populations in the United States in the last half of the twentieth century have learned English, even as they have often preserved their native languages, more rapidly and universally than immigrants at any other time in U.S. history.[3] Far more likely to divide recent immigrants from U.S. "national culture," as it is sometimes called, are social disparities in educational and economic opportunities. Class hierarchies, in other words, are far more divisive of peoples in the United States in the late twentieth century than language or culture. Of course, class as a category is often bound up in social practice with historically established hierarchies of race, ethnicity, gender, sexuality, and religion. As Sollors and many of the respondents to his essay in the *Interroads* postings argued, the new American Studies must address the multilingual reality of the United States in the curricular and scholarly reforms now underway in the field.[4]

By the same token, the dominance of the United States according to the nationalist paradigm has often led to the neglect of other nations in the Western Hemisphere, each of which has its own complex multicultural and multilingual history, as well as its own interactions with the other nationalities of the region. The new American Studies tries to work genuinely as a comparatist discipline that will respect the many different social systems and cultural affiliations of the Americas. Rather than treating such cultural differences as discrete entities, however, this new comparative approach stresses the ways different cultures are transformed by their contact and interaction with each other. If we are to preserve the name "American Studies," then we must take into account at the very least the different nationalities, cultures, and languages of the Western Hemisphere, including Canada. If we find this field too large and challenging, then we should consider area studies models that would redefine the American Studies taught at most U.S. colleges and universities today as "U.S. Studies" or "North American Studies." Such comparatist work thus focuses with special interest on just the points of historical, geographical, and linguistic "contact" where two or more communities must negotiate their respective identities. This new interest in border studies should include investigations of how the many different Americas and Canada have historically influenced and interpreted each other. With very different histories of responding to ethnic and racial minorities, as well as of constructing gendered and sexual hierarchies, these different Americas also help foreground the multilingual and multicultural realities of social life and economic opportunity in any of the Americas.

Such fundamental reconsiderations of what constitutes "American Studies" as a field (or *fields*) of study should be accompanied by theoretical investigations of our methodologies for conducting research and interpreting data. The history of the impact of various critical theories and methodologies on American Studies is complex and often contradictory; it is a subject especially in need of scholarly attention at this crucial moment in the reconceptualization of the field. As an interdisciplinary field, American Studies declared its theoretical purposes from its earliest years in the 1930s, and yet American Studies has often been particularly intransigent with respect to new theoretical models, ranging from modernist theories, like phenomenology, the Frankfurt School, structuralism, post-structuralism and deconstruction, to more contemporary approaches, like critical race theory, feminism, queer theory, and postcolonial theory.

A certain anti-theoretical bias lingers in American Studies, sometimes disguised by appeals to "native" methodologies or vaguely defined traditions of "American pragmatism."[5] At other times, an antitheoretical air surrounds those who insist that American Studies has anticipated (and often does better) the knowledge-production claimed by new methods. Such has often been the case with defenders of the Myth-and-Symbol school and specialists in popular culture, especially in their responses to ideological criticism, New Historicism, and cultural studies. Without even attempting to adjudicate these conflicting claims to priority for the centrality of "culture" as the key element constituting the object of study from the founders of American Studies to recent theorists and practitioners of "cultural studies,"

I would simply point out that the very claim for priority by some scholars in American Studies ought to give new critical theories and cultural studies particular appeal as part of a tradition of social criticism, instead of being viewed as competitors for scholarly attention and institutional space.[6]

Indeed, many of the most compelling "post-nationalist" challenges to the study of the Americas as primarily (if not exclusively) coherent "nation-states" are the consequences of the impact of cultural studies on American Studies and related area, Ethnic, Women's, and Gender Studies. Developing in part out of earlier "critical studies of colonial discourse" and "colonial studies," as well as the *Ideologie-kritik* of the Frankfurt School, the materialist criticism and attention to popular and mass media of the Birmingham School, and important traditions of Latin American, African, South Asian, and East Asian anticolonialist writings and political activism, cultural studies often investigate the relationship between the rise of the Western nation-state and the development of European imperial systems of economic, political, linguistic, and cultural domination.[7] Thus the relevance of a post-nationalist perspective for the new American Studies is evident in the new work being done on U.S. national ideology and its concomitant imperialist ambitions in North America, Latin America, and outside the Western Hemisphere. The contemporary scholarly efforts to link the earlier "internal colonization" thesis of crucial American Studies' scholars—like Robert Berkhofer, Richard Drinnon, Reginald Horsman, Annette Kolodny, Richard Slotkin, Ronald Takaki, and Jane Tompkins—with the argument that the United States has traditionally defined itself as a "global power" have obvious connections with the intellectual and political purposes of cultural studies' general interest in the origins, legitimation, and perpetuation of Euroamerican imperial and neo-imperial forms of global domination.[8]

In its claims to encompass the many cultures and political organizations in the Western Hemisphere, the new American Studies threatens its own kind of cultural imperialism, a tendency often overlooked even by the most ideologically attentive scholars. We are now familiar with the ways American Studies of the post–World War II era "often was enlisted in the service of quasi-official governmental policies and institutions" and how its "success" as a field of study could sometimes be tied to the exportation of "American" cultural ideals based on extraordinarily limited models of American identity and experience.[9] There are commonly overlooked practical factors driving the popularity of American Studies outside the United States, such as "the growing number of American-educated Ph.D.s teaching in other countries, the lure of relatively high-paying research grants and temporary teaching positions in the United States, and the prestige of publishing in the United States."[10] In short, the border dividing "native" and "foreign" versions of American Studies is increasingly difficult to draw. We distinguish the new American Studies from older versions not only for being more inclusive and diverse but also for its vigilance with respect of its possible uses in the cultural imperialist agendas central to U.S. foreign policies from the Marshall Plan in postwar Europe to the multinational "alliance" we assembled to fight (and legitimate) the Gulf War. Yet just what separates cultural understanding from cultural imperialism is increasingly difficult to articulate in an age of technologically accelerated human and cultural mobility.

Often what U.S. specialists in American Studies overlook is our tendency to universalize our own interests and to appeal, however unconsciously, to our own "nativist expertise" as implicated in a larger agenda of cultural imperialism that both includes and exceeds specific articulations of foreign policies. In another discussion on the *Interroads* listserv, Jim Zwick expressed his surprise at the equivocal response from non-U.S. scholars to his idea for a centennial conference on the Spanish-American and Philippine-American wars. Unaware that some non-U.S. scholars considered such a project as yet another effort by U.S. specialists to control the intellectual reception of these colonial wars, to disregard once again work already done by scholars in the Philippines, Spain, Cuba, and Latin America, and to publicize the latest U.S. theoretical approach (cultural studies, critical study of colonial discourse, etc.) as the most appropriate for specialists in other political and intellectual communities, Zwick found himself criticized for an intellectual "provincialism" he thought he was working to overcome.[11] Many scholars, like Paul Lauter, Emory Elliott, and Alice Kessler-Harris, have worked recently to increase the participation of non-U.S. American Studies specialists in the American Studies Association and in the exchange of scholarly work at conferences (and now by way of the Internet) for the benefit of both U.S. and non-U.S. scholars and to promote recognition of the very different purposes, interests, and institutional configurations that American Studies may have around the globe.[12]

New institutes and forums for international scholars in American Studies are doing important work at many different U.S. colleges and universities; such work is more important than ever now that the United States Information Agency is being significantly downsized and valuable programs it sponsored lost to fiscal "exigencies."[13] As we contribute to this important work, however, we should remember the dialectical and dialogical purposes of such intellectual exchanges. An older "international" American Studies in the 1950s and 1960s often drew upon the cosmopolitanism of Euroamerican modernism, together with its implicit cultural mission to "enlighten" the foreign cultures from which it drew many of its most avant-garde materials and ideas. The new American Studies requires a new internationalism that will take seriously the different social, political, and educational purposes American Studies serves in its different situations around

the globe. In short, U.S. and other scholars in the Western Hemisphere
have as much to learn from our international colleagues as they from us.[14]

A common purpose linking these different versions of American Studies
should be the critical study of the circulation of "America" as a commodity
of the new cultural imperialism and the ways in which local knowledges
and arts have responded to such cultural importations—the study of what
some have termed "coca-colonization."[15] What some cultural critics have
termed the capacity of local cultures to "write back" against cultural and
even political and economic domination should be considered part of
American Studies, even as we recognize the practical impossibility of expanding our scope to include all aspects of global experience simply because of the global pretensions of First World nations like the United
States. Nevertheless, the study of U.S. imperialist policies toward Native
Americans should not be conducted without consideration of how native
peoples responded to the specific historical circumstances investigated, just
as the Philippine-American War should not be studied exclusively from the
perspective of the United States or the response to the Vietnam War studied solely through U.S. texts. The Native American, Philippine, and Vietnamese perspectives must be represented in such studies (whether published research or classroom instruction), once again in keeping with the
comparatist aims of the new American Studies.

These are only some of the ways in which the new American Studies
should begin to reconstitute its fields of study, especially as the United
States (along with other First World nations) claims an ever-greater responsibility for global economics, politics, language, and identity. I have
written elsewhere about how we might adapt Mary-Louise Pratt's theoretical model of the "contact zone" to articulate a Comparative American Studies that would include as one of its areas of specialization "comparative U.S.
cultures."[16] Like the geopolitical, linguistic, cultural, ethnic, and economic
"borders" I discussed above as crucial to the reformulation of American
Studies, the "contact zone" is a semiotic site where exchanges may occur
from both (or more) sides, even when the configurations of power are in-
equitable (as they usually are).

Intellectuals who work closely with peoples and issues relevant to the actual borders where immigration is controlled, economic destinies decided,
and individual lives immediately and irrevocably affected often warn us not
to generalize too casually or abstractly with regard to these "border regions."[17] We should heed their warnings and learn from their experiences,
but we should also recognize that, however "real" the border between the
United States and Mexico or the border separating Southeast Asian or
Haitian boat people from safety in the United States, there are also discursively constructed borders made all too often to have terrible physical con-

sequences for those forbidden to cross them. In other words, we can begin to reconfigure such borders by establishing intellectual and cultural "contact zones," where a certain dialectics or dialogics of cultural exchange is understood to be a crucial aspect of how the field of American Studies is constituted and how the related territories of "the Americas" and "the United States" ought to be understood. In this respect, teaching and scholarship become direct, albeit never exclusive, means of effecting necessary social changes.

How is it possible for us to accomplish work so vast in scope and involving so many different specializations? One of the commonest reactions to the progressive aims of the new American Studies is to reassert the study of a "common" and "national" culture for reasons both ideal and practical. We must have a common culture, Hirsch and others tell us, to avoid the intellectual anarchy into which we are already drifting. We must, as Sean Wilentz and others warn us, have a unified American Studies discipline, department, program, and professional organization—which usually means one devoted to some version of nationalist study or "American Exceptionalism"—because we haven't the resources, the time, or the expertise to do more, as new programs in Ethnic, Women's, Gender and Sexuality, and Cultural Studies proliferate on college campuses around the world.[18] What, then, are the practical implications of the preceding description of what seems intellectually crucial for the new American Studies to pursue if it is to avoid the mistakes of the past and draw upon the best of its traditions?

Part of the problem facing those committed to this new vision of American Studies is related to the increasingly antiquated model of the university, its disciplinary division of knowledges, and its model of instruction as the transmission of knowledge as information from an authority to receptive students. The conflict of the modern, enlightenment model for the university and its liberal educational ideals with new conceptions of education, the character of knowledge, and the circulation of such knowledge is by no means unique to American Studies.[19] We may simply face it more directly and immediately because we are in the course of reconstituting our field, forced by the exigencies of rapidly changing ideas of the Americas, and because we have a heritage of challenging established academic procedures. But to achieve any part of what I have described in the preceding paragraphs, we will have to bring about fundamental changes in the way most modern universities *educate*.

However sweeping such changes may seem when described in this general manner, they may be realized in many small steps. First, we should not rush to defend American Studies as a program or department, especially against emerging programs in Ethnic, Women's, and Gender and Sexual

Studies that often devote much of their curricula to topics relevant to the study of the United States, the Americas, and the "borders" or "contact zones" I have described above. As part of the work of our research group at the University of California's Humanities Research Institute (UCHRI) in the fall and winter quarters of 1996–97, we met with faculty in American Studies and related programs on the different campuses of the University of California system. On every campus, important curricular changes were underway in the several fields relevant to American Studies, most of those changes reflecting various intellectual and educational responses to the issues discussed above. Each campus had very different ideas about the future of American Studies as a formal program on that campus, and it was instructive to discover how important local institutional and political factors were in shaping these attitudes. Whereas established American Studies programs at the Davis and Santa Cruz campuses are working to help focus and organize curricular changes in their own and collateral disciplines, there were no plans to revive Riverside's program, which was discontinued in the late 1970s, or Irvine's Comparative Cultures program, which was discontinued in 1993, or to expand a small, primarily instructional, undergraduate American Studies program at UCLA to include a graduate (and thus more research-intensive) component.

Open forums that we held at the 1996 American Studies Association Convention in Kansas City and the 1997 California American Studies Association Convention in Berkeley confirmed our sense that there can be no general model for the institutional future of American Studies in U.S. universities, even when interested faculty agree generally with the aims of the new American Studies I have outlined in this essay. Different local issues, both specific to the university and its surrounding community, affect institutional arrangements in ways that can only be generalized in terms of a new intellectual regionalism that must be taken into account as we discuss the multiple futures of American Studies and the established and emerging disciplines with which American Studies must collaborate in the coming decades. This intellectual regionalism is often inflected by the new regionalisms established by the different demographies, ethnicities, and global economic and cultural affiliations characterizing such important border or contact zones as Southern California's relation to Asia, Mexico, Central America, and the Caribbean; greater Houston's relation to Mexico and the Caribbean; Atlanta and the Southeast's relation to the Black Atlantic; and Miami's relation to Cuba, Haiti, and Latin America.[20] Universities ought to mediate between local and international knowledges, and the new regionalisms, not to be confused with older, more discrete regional identities, even those shaped in the major period of European immigration, ought to be taken into account by academics reconstituting American Studies and related fields on their different campuses.

Our consideration of the academic implications of these new regionalisms should also inform the "internationalizing" of American Studies I discussed above—an internationalizing that should avoid the one-sided, often neo-imperialist cosmopolitanism of an earlier American Studies and might complement established international relations (cultural, economic, political) already shaping the college or university's local community.[21] Because new sources of academic funding, especially in support of the sciences, are following the channels of this new regionalism, there will be growing pressure from academic administrators for us to follow such leads. Properly vigilant and often resistant as American Studies scholars have been to the ideological consequences of certain academic funds—a vigilance as important in today's private funding situation as when the Department of Defense was our secret source—we should make serious efforts to direct some of this funding to cultural understanding and criticism, as well as to the expansion of foreign language instruction. Regard for these new regionalisms should, of course, avoid provincialisms of their own; University of California, Irvine, students need to know about the Black Atlantic as well as the Pacific Rim, Mexico, and Latin America. In short, our consideration of these local conditions should be contextualized in a larger understanding of the United States in the comparative contexts of Western Hemispheric and finally global study I have described earlier.

Despite the booming U.S. economy, colleges and universities continue to operate in a state of fiscal crisis as a means of justifying the downsizing that includes drastic transformations of the research mission, especially in the humanities, and the "consolidation" of academic programs. Smaller, newer, underfunded programs are, of course, at the greatest risk, even though the overall savings they offer most universities have little impact on the total budget picture of the institution. In this academic climate, established American Studies programs should work cooperatively with traditionally allied programs in Ethnic, Women's, Gender and Sexual, and Cultural Studies, and in Critical Theory by spelling out protocols for sharing courses, existing faculty, and the definition and recruitment of new faculty positions. Successful American Studies programs should be aware of inclinations by administrators to use them to "consolidate" different programs that those administrators often view as "fragmented," "incoherent," or "needlessly proliferating," especially when those programs are leading the changes in our understanding of the limitations of traditional knowledge-production and its established disciplines.

Much as those of us at colleges and universities without formal American Studies programs might wish to have the opportunity to realize some of the ambitions of the new American Studies in established curricula and degree requirements, we ought to work toward those ends in cooperation, rather than competition, with colleagues in the fields of African-American, Asian-American, Latino and Chicano/a, Native American, Women's, and Gender and Sexual Studies, as well as those in Critical Theory and Cultural Studies.[22] Local, national, and international interests should be worked out in cooperation among such complementary fields. What eventually emerges from such collaborative work may well be different from any of the American Studies, Women's Studies, and Ethnic Studies programs we have known before, and this flexibility with respect to the emerging knowledges and institutional means of producing and sharing such knowledges should help us avoid the failed intellectual orthodoxies of the past and perhaps bring about unexpected changes in traditional departments, where many of us working for such ends hold our primary appointments. Just such an openness to emerging fields, whose methods and objects of study are still debated and contested, characterizes the attitudes of many scholars who are in no hurry to revive or inaugurate formal American Studies under-graduate or graduate programs at colleges and universities presently lacking them. The absence of formal programs, in other words, need not indicate a lack of vitality on the part of the new American Studies, especially when it anticipates its future strength as a consequence of educational coalitions with Ethnic, Women's, Gender and Sexual, and Cultural Studies, and Critical Theory.

Cooperative work of this sort is based on our intellectual experience with the many different fields now involved in American Studies and the challenging theoretical questions the coordination of these fields involves. No scholar can claim to command any part of American Studies; the field is not just multidisciplinary, it is also a cooperative intellectual venture. No matter how innovatively we design curricula, cross-list courses, and bring in visitors to our own classes, we can never approximate this collaborative and collective intellectual enterprise until we transform the classroom from the traditional "scene of instruction" (often a theater of cruel disciplining or trivial imitation) into a joint venture involving many scholars, including our students as active researchers. Team-teaching, coordinated classes, and other traditional responses to the active/passive and master/servant models of teacher/student can today be considered crude versions of the sorts of alternative learning situations offered by the Internet, distance-learning, and other electronic means of instruction. Electronic MUDs (multiuser dimensions) and MOOs (multiobject orientations), virtual conferences, and hypertext databases should be used as more than merely *tools* in traditional classroom education and conventional research; they should be imagined as means of achieving changing ideas of what constitutes education and knowledge in the humanities and social sciences. In these ways, we might also balance our national and international aims with different local interests.

The American Studies Association's support of Randy Bass's and Jeff Finlay's *American Crossroads Project* and *Teaching American Studies* at Georgetown University has led the way of many other academic professional organizations in experimenting with education that transcends specific university sites.[23] There are, of course, ideological consequences to the use of the Internet in education that must be recognized; as primarily an English-language medium and a technology often shaped by U.S. information-industry protocols, the Internet is in its own right another topic in the study of U.S. cultural imperialism. Yet as a medium that we can use to put faculty and students from around the world in regular and immediate contact with each other, increasingly in a variety of languages, the Internet can be used to criticize, resist, and perhaps transform such cultural imperialism. Many "virtual research centers" already link international faculty and students for a fraction of the cost of actual conferences. Our work as scholars must also be complemented by academic publishers, who must now take the initiative in defining the directions for the future of the electronic dissemination of scholarly work and assuring that appropriate standards for the quality of publication are met even as such publishers guarantee the variety of different approaches and subjects.[24]

Michael Clough, senior fellow at the Council on Foreign Relations and a research associate at the Institute of International Studies at the University of California, Berkeley, and cochair of the New American Global Dialogue, wrote recently in an op-ed piece in the *Los Angeles Times*, "For better and worse, it is less and less possible for nationally minded elites, sitting in Washington and New York, to construct policies that simultaneously protect and promote the interests of Los Angeles, San Francisco and other emerging regional metropoles. Instead, a new, much more decentralized model of governance, one capable of accommodating the growing diversity of the American politico-cultural economy, must be developed."[25] A specialist in international relations, Clough is not thinking about postnationalist American Studies, but the new American Studies has been developing in its own way a more "decentralized model," one that is attentive to the different intellectual "regions," or "contact zones," that represent more adequately the domestic and foreign determinants of the United States and the Americas than previous "American Studies." Nationalisms and neonationalisms of all sorts are, of course, very much alive, not only in the politically, culturally, and linguistically diverse United States, but around the globe. The persistence and even revival of nationalism need not prevent us from trying to think of social organizations in contexts other than "national consensus" and its stereotypes of "national experience" and "character." *Post-nationalist* thinking about what constitutes the United States and the Americas may well offer us our best chance of learning from, rather than repeating, the past.

NOTES

1. Werner Sollors, "For a Multilingual Turn in American Studies," *American Studies Association Newsletter* (1997); also posted for discussion on Randy Bass's *Interroads,* a discussion list that "encourages discussions of American Studies from an international comparative perspective" (http://home.dc./soft.com/archives/interroads.html). Sollors, Marc Shell, and other scholars are working through the Longfellow Institute at Harvard and with Johns Hopkins University Press to publish the Longfellow Institute Series in American Languages and Literatures, "the first systematic attempt to republish historically, aesthetically, and culturally significant works written in what is now the United States and published in languages other than English." The Longfellow anthology has already been published, and will be followed by bilingual and trilingual translations of individual works in this area.

2. E. D. Hirsch, Jr., *Cultural Literacy: What Every American Needs to Know* (Boston, Mass.: Houghton Mifflin, 1987), pp. 70–93; Arthur Schlesinger, Jr., *The Disuniting of America: Reflections on a Multicultural Society* (New York: W. W. Norton, 1992).

3. In his response to discussion of his essay on the *Interroads* list, Sollors notes, "It is also simply not true that monolingualism reduces illiteracy or technological ineffectiveness. . . . It is a myth that bilingualism lowers language performance in first languages. . . . It seems doubtful to me whether 'English only' education, based on the false myths of a monolingual past and of better language skills of monolingual people, makes for more civic cohesion than would a fuller understanding of the pervasive multilingualism in U.S. history and society" ("From 'English Only' to 'English-Plus' in American Studies," *Interroads,* August 2, 1997).

4. Paul Lauter, in his response to Sollors's essay (*Interroads,* July 26, 1997), makes a particularly important point about the need to study the ideological assumptions behind previous foreign-language requirements for graduate programs in American Studies. Earlier arguments favoring the so-called "tool languages" of French and German, usually to the neglect of Spanish, Portuguese, Chinese, Japanese, Korean, Vietnamese, and the many other languages crucial to the history of nations and immigrant populations in the Western Hemisphere and the virtual repression of the study of Native American languages, except by specialists in these fields, have played their parts not only in reinforcing the monolingual ideology of the United States but also in perpetuating what I would term the heritage of Euro-cultural colonialism in the United States.

5. I do not include here rigorous accounts of "American pragmatism" as a methodology, theory, and philosophy in its own right, rather than a vaguely invoked synonym for "American character." For an excellent account of American pragmatism in this precise sense, see Mark Bauerlein, *The Concept of Pragmatic Mind: Emerson, William James, Charles Sanders Peirce* (Durham, N.C.: Duke University Press, 1997); for a version of how "American pragmatism" can be used as a substitute for "American (national) character," see Richard Poirier, *The Renewal of Literature: Emer-*

sonian Reflections (New York: Random House, 1987), and *Poetry and Pragmatism* (Cambridge, Mass.: Harvard University Press, 1992).

6. Leo Marx, "Rethinking the American Studies Project," in *American Studies in Germany: European Contexts and Intercultural Relations*, ed. Günter Lenz and Klaus J. Milich (New York: St. Martin's Press; Frankfurt: Campus Verlag, 1995), p. 54.

7. Cary Nelson, *Manifesto of a Tenured Radical* (New York: New York University Press, 1997), pp. 64–70, provides a concise and relevant manifesto of cultural studies, outlining what cultural studies at their best ought to achieve. Missing from his manifesto, however, is any consideration of "nationalism" and "imperialism" as central topics for cultural critics.

8. I am thinking here of my own *Literary Culture and U.S. Imperialism: From the Revolution to World War II* (New York: Oxford University Press, 2000), in which I develop this thesis about U.S. nationalism and imperialism from the first decades of the U.S. republic—the Alien and Sedition Acts, for example—up to the 1940s. In this context, see also the work of Amy Kaplan, who is also writing a book on literature's contribution to U.S. imperialism in the early modern period, from the Spanish-American to the First World wars. There are, of course, other scholars working in this area, many of them represented in Amy Kaplan and Donald Pease, eds., *Cultures of United States Imperialism* (Durham, N.C.: Duke University Press, 1993); and Donald Pease, ed., *National Identities and Post-Americanist Narratives* (Durham, N.C.: Duke University Press, 1994).

9. Leo Marx, "Rethinking," p. 54.

10. Richard P. Horwitz, "Preface," in *Exporting America: Essays on American Studies Abroad*, ed. Richard P. Horwitz (New York: Garland, 1993), p. xv. The essays in this collection by U.S. and non-U.S. specialists in American Studies offer interesting complements and case studies for my argument.

11. See Jim Zwick, "Towards Critical Internationalism within U.S.-based American Studies" (February 18, 1997), and my response (February 18, 1997) on the *Interroads* discussion, administered by Jeff Finlay (FINLAYJI@guvax.acc.georgetown.edu). See also the information page for *Interroads* (http://www.georgetown.edu/crossroads/interroads).

12. Emory Elliott initiated this work as former chair of the International Committee of the ASA. Like Paul Lauter, Elliott has visited many international American Studies programs and helped bring many international scholars to the United States for extended visits. Thanks to both Paul and Emory, our research group was visited by American Studies specialists from Brazil, Poland, and Indonesia.

13. Giles Gunn has conducted a valuable program for international scholars in American Studies at the University of California, Santa Barbara (UCSB), since the summer of 1996, with extramural funding from the U.S. Department of State. The Rockefeller Foundation is funding an International Forum for U.S. Studies from 1997 to 1999 at the University of Iowa. Giles Gunn, Chris Newfield, Elliott Butler-Evans (UCSB), Jeff Peck (Georgetown), Mark Poster, Gabriele Schwab, and I (UC, Irvine) have been working with American Studies scholars at the Humboldt University (Berlin) on a transatlantic cooperative research project since 1995.

14. As we learned from the international scholars visiting our research group and from those attending the public forums we sponsored at the ASA and CASA conventions in 1996–1997, American Studies may serve a wide range of different educational and intellectual purposes around the world. Local political, cultural,

and intellectual issues are often interestingly woven into the curricula and peda-
gogy of American Studies in non-U.S. cultures in ways that U.S. scholars unfamiliar
with those cultures (and their languages and histories) do not understand. Such hy-
bridizations of local and international knowledges range from explicit efforts to cir-
cumvent repressive regimes and local censorship to subtler modes of responding to
U.S. cultural imperialism by *transforming* the ineluctable importation of U.S. cultural "goods."

15. For example, see Reinhold Wagnleitner, *Coca-Colonization and the Cold War:
The Cultural Mission of the United States in Austria after the Second World War,* trans. Diana M. Wolf (Chapel Hill: University of North Carolina Press, 1994), which interprets critically the post–World War II competition between the United States and
Soviet Union for the control of Austrian culture.

16. John Carlos Rowe, "A Future for American Studies: The Comparative U.S.
Cultures Model," in *American Studies in Germany: European Contexts and Intercultural
Relations*, pp. 262–78.

17. During her participation in the Minority Discourse Project at UCHRI in
1993–1994, Norma Alarcón took colleagues on a tour of the United States–Mexico
border, both to familiarize them with an important site of political and social conflict and to remind them that all "border studies" must be mindful of the actual border zones and their consequences for individual lives. I agree that Alarcón's purpose is an important one for us to keep in mind, but I also think that the United
States–Mexico border was discursively constructed long before physical barriers
were erected (by the Treaty of Guadalupe-Hidalgo, for example) and discursively as
well as physically policed.

18. Sean Wilentz, "Integrating Ethnicity into American Studies," *Chronicle of
Higher Education* (November 29, 1996), p. A56. Lawrence Buell, "Are We Post-
American Studies?" in *Field Work: Sites in Literary and Cultural Studies*, eds. Marjorie
Garber, Paul B. Franklin, and Rebecca Walkowitz (New York: Routledge, 1996), p.
89, argues that "nation and culture aren't coextensive, but neither are they dis-
junct." Acknowledging that the "familiar debates about national identity vs. cultural
particularism" have been replaced by "the issue of whether a model of cultural
identity at any level can hold its ground against a model of cultural hybridization or
syncretism" (89), Buell concludes with a markedly colonialist metaphor for the
apocalypse facing American Studies scholars who abandon the nationalist and exceptionalist models of the previous generation's work: "The more decentered so-
called American literary studies becomes, the more suspect the category of nation
as a putative cultural unit, and the more likely United States literature specialists
may be to oscillate between clinging to discredited assumptions about national dis-
tinctiveness vs. throwing ourselves wholly, *amor fati*-like, on the pyre of postnationalism (in a kind of subdisciplinary suttee)" (91). It is quite a rhetorical stretch to
link post-nationalist discussions with the outlawed practice of Hindu suttee, but
Buell's choice of metaphors reveals his intention of suggesting thereby the "primitivism" of other cultures—a "primitivism" American Studies must avoid. Buell's Ori-
entalism in this instance is interestingly, albeit predictably, complemented by appeals to scientific rationality and the rhetoric of Christian belief: "[I]f we're *truly
rigorous* in trying to get to whatever *empirical bedrock underlies* those assumptions
while at the same time remaiing attentive to the distinction between culture and na-

tion (and with this the promise of border, diaspora, and global culture studies), then we will be *faithful* to our *posts* as post-American Americanists, whatever the outcome of the culture wars" (emphasis mine, 91). How extraordinary that such "rigor" and "empiricism" and "bedrock" investigation should conclude in a merely rhetorical flourish, redolent of religion (now of the Euroamerican Christian varieties, to be sure): "faithful to our posts as post-American Americanists"!

19. For a more general treatment of the problem of the enlightenment university and the new modes of knowledge, see David Lloyd, "Foundations of Diversity: Thinking the University in a Time of Multiculturalism," in *"Culture" and the Problem of the Disciplines,* ed. John Carlos Rowe (New York: Columbia University Press, 1998), pp. 15–43.

20. For a good discussion of the new regionalism that has emerged as a consequence of the new global economy, see Michael Clough, "Birth of Nations," *Los Angeles Times* (July 27, 1997), pp. M1, M6.

21. Paul Gilroy's model of the "Black Atlantic," *The Black Atlantic: Modernity and Double Consciousness* (London: Verso, 1993), is being used as one model in an international exchange program planned by Southern universities—Miami, Florida, LSU, and Houston, among others—to enable their students to study at European, Caribbean, African, and Latin American universities that will share in this curriculum. Rethinking the educational aims of "education abroad" programs in terms of the global significance of American Studies should thus be one of our tasks.

22. Jesse Vasquez, President of the National Association for Ethnic Studies and Professor of Education and Puerto Rican Studies at Queens College, responded in an understandably angry way to Wilentz's article, "Integrating Ethnicity into American Studies," in his letter to the *Chronicle* (January 31, 1997), concluding an otherwise sensible critique of Wilentz's arguments by challenging: "It may be that it is ethnic studies that now should consider taking over American studies, and not the other way around" ("Opinion," p. B3).

23. Randy Bass and Jeff Finlay, *Engines of Inquiry: A Practical Guide for Using Technology to Teach American Culture* (Washington, D.C.: Georgetown University Press, 1997).

24. The Columbia Online Project, which makes available portions of recent scholarly books published by Columbia and Oxford University Presses, and *Literature Online* from Chadwyck-Healey, an electronic publisher, are steps in this direction, but academic presses have been slow to adapt to the electronic means of scholarly dissemination currently available.

25. Clough, "Birth of Nations," p. M1.

Syllabus COMPARATIVE AMERICAN STUDIES: AN INTRODUCTION
An Undergraduate Seminar for Juniors and Seniors

Instructor: John Carlos Rowe

READINGS (IN COURSE SEQUENCE)

A Course Reader containing the following essays:

Leo Marx, "Pastoralism in America," and Richard Slotkin, "Myth and the Production of History," in Sacvan Bercovitch and Myra Jehlen, eds., *Ideology and Classic American Literature* (New York: Cambridge University Press, 1986), pp. 36–90.

Sacvan Bercovitch, "The Problem of Ideology in a Time of Dissensus," in *The Rites of Assent: Transformations in the Symbolic Construction of America* (New York: Routledge, 1993), pp. 353–76.

Mary Louise Pratt, "Arts of the Contact Zone," *Profession* 91: 33–41.

John Carlos Rowe, "A Future for American Studies: The Comparative U.S. Cultures Model," in Günter Lenz and Klaus Milich, eds., *American Studies in Germany: European Contexts and Intercultural Relations* (New York: St. Martin's Press, 1995), pp. 262–78.

A Textbook of American Literary Works

Paul Lauter et al., eds. *The Heath Anthology of American Literature,* rev. ed., 2 vols.; and the *Heath Anthology Instructor's Manuals* (Lexington, KY: D. C. Heath, 1997).

Comparative Approaches and the New American Studies

José Martí, *Our America: Writings on Latin America and the Struggle for Cuban Independence,* trans. Elinor Randall, Juan de Onís, and Roslyn Held Foner (New York: Monthly Review Press, 1977).

C. L. R. James, *American Civilization,* ed. Anna Grimshaw and Keith Hart (Cambridge, MA: Blackwell, 1993).

Gloria Anzaldúa, *Borderlands/La Frontera: The New Mestiza* (San Francisco, CA: Spinsters/aunt lute, 1987).

Henry Louis Gates, Jr., *The Signifying Monkey: A Theory of Afro-American Literary Criticism* (New York: Oxford University Press, 1988).

Lucy Maddox, *Removals: Nineteenth-Century American Literature and the Politics of Indian Affairs* (New York: Oxford University Press, 1991).

Paul Gilroy, *The Black Atlantic* (London: Verso, 1993).

Lisa Lowe, *Immigrant Acts: An Asian American Cultural Politics* (Durham, NC: Duke University Press, 1996).

COURSE DESCRIPTION AND PROGRAM

We will begin by reading several recent revisions of traditional American Studies, including such defenses of the latter as offered by Leo Marx. The essays included in the course reader will be ways of identifying the major issues and problems both in traditional American Studies and for the so-called new and comparative American Studies. In order to test some of the claims we make in the course, we will use the recently revised *Heath Anthology of American Literature* both as a source of useful literary and cultural examples and as an object of study in its own right: an anthology that attempts not only to broaden what is understood as "American literature" but also to change the way the literatures of the United States are taught. For these reasons, we will read selectively in the *Instructor's Manuals* that are meant to assist teachers who are using the two-volume Heath *Anthology*. The use of the Heath *Anthology* will also help foreground the literary emphasis of the course, which should merely indicate the instructor's primary specialization in American Studies and the fact that this course is offered in satisfaction of the Major in English.

In the second half of the course, we will look at some classic approaches to American Studies by scholars outside the United States—Martí and C. L. R. James—as a prelude to considering how the new American Studies invites comparative work on the several Americas in the Western Hemisphere and on the many cultures that inform and shape U.S., Latin American, and Caribbean cultures.

The actual readings in the second half of the course will be selected collaboratively by students and the instructor, and this process of selection will be part of the education involved in the course. Working with our understanding of the important issues for the new American Studies from the essays included in the course reader, we will then discuss which chapters and essays by Martí, James, Anzaldúa, Gates, Maddox, Gilroy, and Lowe will be read for class discussions and used for the various assignments in the course. Obviously, our aim will be to understand the new American Studies in terms of a field (or fields) that includes the influences of African, Asian, European, and Native American cultures and peoples in the various racial/ethnic, gender, sexual, class, and national configurations of identity and community shaping the histories of Americas.

Creating the Multicultural Nation

Adventures in Post-Nationalist
American Studies in the 1990s

George J. Sánchez

Mankind—that word should have more meaning for all of us today. We can't be consumed by our petty differences anymore. We will be united in our common inter-ests. Perhaps it is fate that today is the Fourth of July and you will once again be fighting for our freedom—not from tyranny, oppression, or persecution, but from an-nihilation. We are fighting for our right to live, to exist. And should we win the day, the Fourth of July will no longer be known as an American holiday, but as the day when the world declared in one voice, "We will not go quietly into the night. We will not vanish without a fight." We are going to live on. We are going to survive. Today we celebrate our Independence Day!

Actor Bill Pullman as President Thomas J. Whitmore
in the 1996 movie, *Independence Day*

In the summer of 1996, the movie blockbuster *Independence Day* reflected many of the attractions, contradictions, and ironies of post-nationalism in the United States embodied in both popular culture and academic dis-course.[1] On one level, the previews for that movie enticed us to the theaters by depicting the explosion of virtually every important architectural symbol of nationalism in the United States: the White House and Capitol in Wash-ington, D.C., the Empire State Building in New York (and in the movie a fallen Statue of Liberty in New York Harbor), and even Capitol Records Tower in Los Angeles—that odd mixture of national pride, phallic symbol-ism, and international capitalism embedded in popular culture. Once in the theaters, audiences were treated to the vicarious pleasure of watching the outer space invaders defeated by a polyglot team of U.S. citizens, most conspicuously headed by an African-American fighter pilot (played by ac-tor/rapper Will Smith) and a Jewish electronics/mathematical genius (played by actor Jeff Goldblum), while the rest of the world's fighting forces combine across all historical and socio-political divides to back up the American charge. It was in battle against alien invaders that, through the voice of the actor playing the President of the United States, July

Fourth became everyone's independence day. As audiences cheered, nationalism, it seemed, had given way to a global internationalism in the wake of invasion from extraterrestrial aliens.

In truth, however, this film reflected a new-fashioned nationalism, one now ripe in its confidence of a multicultural future for the United States and America's lone role as a military and cultural superpower that could export its diverse, yet unified, values across all national boundaries.² Multiculturalism seemed to have emerged as a quintessential American value, marking the United States as a unique society among nations, while giving it alone the status to lead all nations to a new future devoid of interethnic strife. This cinematic fantasy—ahistoric as it may be—is also a central vision of some leading Americanists in this country and, just as importantly, the rationale behind several new versions of American Studies on various campuses.

This essay intends to critically examine the relationship between the fields of Ethnic Studies, as it has developed in the United States since the 1960s, and a newly revamped American Studies, which hopes to cast aside older notions of American exceptionalism and contribute to a newfound examination of multicultural U.S. society. In an attempt to fully investigate the multiple meanings behind the movement toward a "post-national" American Studies, I will explore one particular ideological focus of much recent work in American Studies that purports to be "post-ethnic" in analysis and motivation.³ I argue that current discussions regarding the place of the two fields of American Studies and Ethnic Studies in academia and on specific U.S. campuses reflect the deep ambivalence toward difference and unity in discussions of nationalism among liberal/left thinkers in the United States struggling with how to conceptualize a new, progressive multicultural agenda for the nation.

In a recent review of the institutional changes toward diversity in the national American Studies Association, 1997 President Mary Helen Washington reported,

> None of these changes happened of its own accord, but at each critical moment in the history of the ASA, an individual has pushed for change, and the organization, with support from the presidents and executive boards, has responded. The pushing, protesting, and organizing of African American, Chicano/a, and Asian American scholars from 1985 to 1997 has resulted in a sea change in the involvement of scholars of color in ASA. . . . If ASA finds itself now on the threshold of change, it is because of the efforts of individuals with extraordinary singularity of purpose.⁴

Significant institutional collaboration on individual campuses, however, has been much more difficult than the changes in the American Studies Association described by Washington. She herself reminds us that a great deal of common interdisciplinary ferment in the 1970s and beyond "should have made, but did not make, African American studies and American studies natural collaborators, fraternal, if not identical, twins."[5]

The failure of cooperation between Ethnic Studies and American Studies faculty and programs was especially the case at smaller college campuses that did not have the resources to engage in widespread faculty hiring that would diversify the traditional curriculum while also building much-needed Ethnic Studies programs demanded by students. At colleges such as Pomona, Oberlin, and Williams, new faculty of color were hired to offer new courses in minority history, literature, and culture, but also had to be able to teach larger surveys in their respective disciplines. These obligations, coupled with the larger demands placed on them for advising and mentoring minority and other students, meant that few of these new hires had the time or energy to contribute to interdisciplinary programs such as American Studies, which continued to rely on volunteer activity. Moreover, many of these faculty banded together to create new Ethnic Studies programs which better met the increased demand for coherency and regularity in course offerings made by students and administrators alike. While American Studies faculties often worked hard at these institutions to implement multiculturalism, they were usually stymied in their attempts to actually involve minority faculty in the inner workings of the interdisciplinary enterprise of American Studies.

Such institutional developments can best be explored by looking at local histories of this intersection between Ethnic Studies and American Studies at specific colleges and universities, rather than less concrete, but more recognized, trends at the national level.[6] Over the past few years, the ground has continued to shift at several U.S. campuses struggling with the academic and institutional boundaries between American Studies and Ethnic Studies. At the University of Michigan, the Program in American Culture uncomfortably fits three Ethnic Studies programs inside a larger American Studies program, combining efforts toward a multicultural vision of U.S. society while uncomfortably competing for resources and often distinctly separate academic agendas under one national umbrella. At the University of Minnesota, an interdisciplinary program operates a tension-ridden alliance with three underfunded Ethnic Studies departments, while the larger administration is paralyzed to move forward for fear of bringing offense to one or more of the parties or having to respond with monies in this belt-tightening era. These umbrella-style programs, although at the forefront of local multiculturalism in American Studies nationwide, exist often in tension with campus efforts at promoting Ethnic Studies.

At these and other institutions, American Studies programs have tried to promote the hiring of faculty who concentrate on racial minorities in order to lead campus efforts at diversification, as well as diversifying their own curricular offerings. Yet even the best attempts to create a "home" for Ethnic Studies within American Studies inevitably bring both successes and frustrations for programs. At the University of California at Santa Cruz, tenured white faculty combine with untenured minority faculty in trying to reshape an American Studies program and promote a new Ph.D. in the field, yet their efforts are often stymied by departing ethnic faculty, a growing anti-U.S. nationalist sentiment among other faculty, and the very power differentials in appointment and prestige that they hope to examine in American society. All these "ground-up" efforts at reform and diversity should be commended, but none has been an unqualified success at removing pressures and frustrations over the state of Ethnic Studies on its campus.

Indeed, attempts to jumpstart relatively new American Studies programs at institutions with longer histories of established Ethnic Studies departments and/or programs have often led directly to tension. At the University of Colorado, a fledging American Studies program tries to assert itself with a decidedly pan-American vision stretching across both northern and southern boundaries of the United States, but is looked at suspiciously by an embattled Ethnic Studies faculty and moves forward with little contact with an established Latin American Studies program. Similar situations have erupted at both the University of California at Berkeley and the University of Washington, even though Ethnic Studies faculty at both institutions are heavily involved in the national American Studies movement. On the local campus level, particularly at institutions in the American West, it often appears (and sometimes is) as if cautious administrators are attempting to "pacify" Ethnic Studies by placing the study of race and ethnicity solely within the confines of a more nationalist, if still interdisciplinary, project.

These fears of containment have, in fact, been actualized when one looks at the state of student politics for academic diversity in the 1990s. At Columbia University, undergraduate students protesting for an Ethnic Studies department were, instead, offered an umbrella American Studies program with appointments in traditional departments as this administration talked of combating intellectual separatism among ethnic faculty when established departments were noticeably lacking in racially specific courses or scholars of color. As administrators at East Coast institutions struggled with calls for ethnic programs that went beyond traditional Black Studies efforts, they increasingly sought to minimize what they perceived as "duplication" of departments born of newly recognized American racial diversity that extends beyond a black-white paradigm.

The latest American Studies program to declare itself as guiding the way to the future in the study of race and ethnicity is that of Princeton University, headed by historian Sean Wilentz. After students occupied the main administration building in 1993 demanding an increase of Latino Studies and Asian American Studies faculty, the university responded by placing these demands within the context of a newly diversified American Studies project. A university committee assigned to respond to these student demands advised the administration that "the intellectual leadership for bolstering its teaching and scholarship in Latino-American and Asian-American studies" should come from the American Studies program, which it deemed "particularly well-suited to encompass studies of the comparative experience of the peoples of America, broadly defined."[7]

Wilentz, while carefully avoiding mention of the almost total lack of faculty in either of these teaching areas at Princeton and of the student protests which led to this report, did take the time to assail the field of Ethnic Studies for its supposed parochialism:

> Studying one ethnic group, or even a collection of ethnic groups, in isolation can easily obscure . . . and rob the study of ethnicity (as well as of the United States more generally) of some of its most profound complexities. The simplification of American culture can become especially dangerous when assessing a particular work of art, literature, or music. Is it not fallacious to believe that any cultural artifact, from a symphony to a folk painting, is representative of an entire social category, let alone one as diverse as an ethnic group? Is it not equally fallacious to believe that individual artists or writers are beholden only to their specific ethnic or racial backgrounds?[8]

While refusing to confront the lack of diversity among Princeton's faculty and academic programs, Wilentz pretends that the American Studies program at Princeton will be among the first academic units in the nation to do comparative studies and cross-cultural analysis. Princeton's solution is to require students "to study other aspects of American life" besides their own ethnicity, while requiring those with "more-traditional interests" to "rigorously study the many varieties of American culture"—a practice long-established in Ethnic Studies programs around the country. While it is easy to dismiss this elitist perspective, it is important to analyze more carefully the total mischaracterization of Ethnic Studies by the director of an American Studies program at one of the most prestigious institutions in the country. Indeed, how can "integration now"—a call Wilentz uses to begin and end his article—proceed in American Studies, if Ethnic Studies is so belittled? More importantly, why do some in American Studies seem to feel the need to diminish Ethnic Studies in order to incorporate the study of race and ethnicity?

Indeed, white scholars of American labor history like Wilentz have been among the most prominent supporters of this new attempt to corral the "excesses" of Ethnic Studies—often equated with a turn to "identity politics" since the 1960s—within American Studies because of their overdetermined need to understand the way that race has, in their interpretation, circumvented a full discussion of class in American society. Largely emerging from the shadow of mentor Herbert Gutman, these new labor historians have been particularly concerned about the ways in which culture and community promote or forestall alliances around labor and class issues in the United States. Moving beyond Gutman's classic work on the European radical tradition and its intersection with American labor movements, historians have shown how, while immigrants contributed to various radical movements, it was in their assimilation to a common left tradition in the United States that social activism came to fruition, particularly under the New Deal.[9]

In this historiographical tradition, race continues to be seen as a legacy from Old World traditions, and, in the case of African Americans—usually the only non-white racial group of significance in this highly East Coast–centric history—as an intractable problem unlikely to go away without major alliances with the left and a diminution of nationalist claims by Afrocentrists. What has yet to enter in full dialogue in this labor history tradition is the important work of scholars such as David Roediger, Robin D. G. Kelley, Michael Honey, and George Lipsitz—all labor historians who stress the centrality of African American history in American labor—of how the identity of white American laborers has been decidedly shaped by a white racial identity formed in opposition to black Americans. In short, rather than taking a development on race in their own field seriously, these scholars have instead continued to marginalize the study of race in their version of American labor history.[10]

There are fundamental reasons why this development marks a central crisis in American Studies today, not only in American labor history. What I am arguing is that much of this generation of white New Left scholars who have now assumed positions of power in the academy and who are at the forefront of shaping much of the new reconfiguration of American Studies today continue to struggle with their own racial identity and the history of racial discourse since the 1960s. In their attempt to understand why the New Left fell apart after 1968, they have often placed the blame squarely on the so-called "identity politics" of the 1970s and 1980s and what they perceive to be overzealous advocates for race-based power in the academy and in society. Rather than come to terms with the appeal of the New Right to the white, working-class population of the United States, they have framed a scenario which sees "white flight" as a result of unjust appeals for benefits to nonwhites. In the 1990s, this generation has increasingly made a call for a new American community that "goes beyond race," imagining a national community that can overlook its differences and return to the "real issues" of class equity. In short, this generation now calls

for a new "liberal nationalism" which can reassert itself into national prominence by controlling those issues that split the nation—like race and gender—while calling for equality for all.

What is most interesting to me about this intellectual development is
how closely it mirrors a previous intellectual tradition that gave rise to
American Studies in the 1950s—that of a stress on a consensual society
drawn together by a set of core American values, and differentiated from
other national societies by cohesion amidst diversity. An eloquent
spokesperson for this tradition is Gary Nash, prominent early American historian, whose academic work has focused on diverse societies of the revolutionary period, labor agitation, and the social history of Philadelphia. Attempting to insure that the new social history made its way into the
teaching of history in elementary and secondary education, Nash was
thrown into national prominence when his National Center at the University of California, Los Angeles (UCLA), was awarded a grant by the Reagan
administration to develop national standards for the teaching of history in
the schools. Clearly a left historian trying to do his craft in conservative
times, Nash increasingly had to adjust his own perspective toward that of
national unity stressed by the Reagan administration, particularly by Lynne
Cheney, who attacked the National Standards when originally presented
for being left-leaning and U.S.-bashing.

At the same time, Nash's own attempt to put forward a history series for
the state of California came under attack by black nationalists, some ethnic
scholars, and the Oakland public school board for trivializing and sometimes stereotyping racial and ethnic contributions to world history and ignoring other groups, despite a claim of presenting a comprehensive history. Despite the fact that these textbooks were clearly more inclusive than
anything else on the market, Nash's work was often viciously and unfairly
attacked on racial grounds. Nash himself recounted his hurt:

> As the history author of a multicultural series of books for children from
> kindergarten to eighth grade now in use throughout California's public
> schools, I have been told on many occasions in recent months by self-
> professed Afrocentrists that I cannot write African American history because
> only someone who is African American can understand it and is entitled to
> speak or write on the subject. However, none of those who have told me this
> has been prepared to tell me what they find wrong or insensitive about the
> last three scholarly books I have published.[11]

Not surprisingly, Nash defended himself. Interestingly, however, he often makes that defense on particularly nationalist grounds, stressing the
need for "core American values" in any attempt to intellectually move forward with a study of diversity:

If multiculturalism is to get beyond a promiscuous pluralism that gives every-thing equal weight and adopts complete moral relativism, it must reach some agreement on what is at the core of American culture. The practical goal of multiculturalism is to foster mutual respect among students by teaching them about the distinct cultures from which those who have come to the United States derive and the distinctive historical experiences of different racial, eth-nic, religious, and gender groups in American history. . . . But nurturing this mutual respect and an appreciation of cultural diversity can only be main-tained if parents, teachers, and children reach some basic agreement on some core set of values, ways of airing disputes, conducting dialogue—in short, some agreement on how to operate as members of a civic community, a democratic polity. . . . The *pluribus* in *e pluribus unum* can be upheld in all manner of cultural, religious, and aesthetic forms—from the clothes an indi-vidual or group chooses to wear, to their cuisine, their artistic preferences and styles, the dialect and linguistic constructions of their internal social life, their religious beliefs and practices, and so forth. But *pluribus* can flourish in these ways only if *unum* is preserved at the heart of the polity—in a common commitment to core political and moral values.[12]

At UCLA, efforts to develop Ethnic Studies departments were stymied for over thirty years, despite numerous student protests, faculty initiatives, and overwhelming needs in the city of Los Angeles. By combating what was per-ceived as academic separatism, traditional academic departments could move forward with "all deliberate speed" to hire (or not hire) minority fac-ulty, but the power and prestige of traditional disciplines could never be confronted with viable interdisciplinary alternatives in Ethnic Studies. As an Ethnic Studies scholar and a historian, I know full well that the history of the last thirty years indicates that without the political pushing and intel-lectual reconceptualization forced upon the academy by Ethnic Studies, none of the developments in the *pluribus* would have occurred. Indeed, I am not as convinced as Nash that these "gains" could not be turned back, and recent California history—especially as embodied in Propositions 187, 209, and 227—seems to back up my concerns.

This new version of American exceptionalism has also found its way into academic and journalistic writings which purport to reject the old di-visiveness of racial positioning on political questions in the call for a new recognition of what binds us together as a nation. In the 1990s, a veritable cottage industry has been created by publishers producing social com-mentary which purports to contain the newest answer on how to move past our supposedly current morass on issues of race and nationhood.[13] I will concentrate on a new triad of works on this subject—Michael Lind's *The Next American Nation*, Todd Gitlin's *The Twilight of Common Dreams*, and David Hollinger's *Postethnic America*—which come closest to representing some of the central issues confronting American Studies scholars as they attempt to deal with diversity while asserting a need for a new vision for the future. Unlike previous attempts to call into question our multicultural America, such as Arthur Schlesinger's *The Disuniting of America* and the racist *Alien Nation* by Peter Brimelow, the works which concern me all come from the liberal/left side of the political spectrum. As such, they all try to understand the ascendancy of the political and religious right in the country and, in different ways, lay the blame for the failure of the vision of the 1960s squarely on the divisiveness of battles over race and equality in the last thirty years.

But each of these books also reflects a new preoccupation with nationalism on the left, and a hope that America's supposed unflinching commitment to multiculturalism may lead the way toward a new reconceptualization of American society. While our research group discussed and debated the future of an American Studies which moved beyond nationalism, these works indicate that nationalism is undergoing a resurgence in some circles of American Studies, often hidden behind notions of an "American community" moving beyond race. In short, these writers collectively reflect the intellectual position in which American Studies finds itself in the mid-1990s, attempting to acknowledge the strength and veracity of multiculturalism while continuing a commitment to understand the American nation as a whole. This essay will explore these and similar dilemmas of race and nation in American society.

Michael Lind's work, whose subtitle is *The New Nationalism and the Fourth American Revolution,* tries to place our current contemporary moment in a broader historical context. Lind, a staff writer at the *New Yorker* and former senior editor at the *New Republic* and *Harper's,* argues that the United States has had three cultural "republics" since the War for Independence: (1) Anglo America (1789–1861), which celebrated an exclusively Anglo-Saxon national community; (2) Euro America (1875–1957), which accommodated European immigrants into this national community; and (3) our current Multicultural America (beginning in 1972), born of the revolutionary turbulence of the civil rights movement, but mostly characterized by what he describes as "the triumph of group-consciousness and racial preference programs."[14]

For Lind, this "third republic" of the United States, product of racial preferences and a "fivefold, race-culture-political bloc scheme," has failed to gain legitimacy in the eyes of most Americans. One central problem with this era of American democracy, according to Lind, is that "there is no generally agreed upon account of what the American community is, or how its place in the world or history should be conceived."[15] Critical to this confusion is the inclusion of the "pseudo-race of Hispanics" into the racial preference spoils system, as well as the favoring of "white overclass feminists" over "working class and middle-class white ethnics," a civil rights strategy that, according to Lind, destroyed the New Deal coalition and doomed any possibility of a biracial black-white coalition to defeat white conservative Republicanism.[16] Lind ties the growing inequality of the American class structure and the Republican ascendancy to a racial/gender system that he argues consistently favors tokenism over substantial economic transformation.

Not surprisingly, Lind argues that it is critical for the United States to emerge quickly out of this new "third republic" into a fourth, crafted by what he calls a "liberal nationalism" built around a "trans-American melting pot." After rejecting notions that the United States could be reconstructed on the basis of democratic universalism, cultural pluralism, or a new nativism, Lind argues that our already transracial America needs simply to recognize the cultural commonality which already binds us as a people.

Unlike most of the scholarly work on race by scholars of color, Lind's work has garnered attention across a broad range of popular journals and newspapers, including basically positive reviews from several scholars intimately associated with American Studies. Michael Kammen, in a review in the *Los Angeles Times Book Review,* positioned the book as particularly appealing to "liberals and moderate centrists," claiming particularly that "those who feel that insufficient progress has been made in human relations since the civil rights legislation of 1964 and 1965 . . . may welcome *The Next American Nation* as a well-informed, passionate attempt to think anew about our changing composition as a society."[17] Gary Gerstle goes further in his review of Lind's work in *Tikkun,* calling the book an "erudite and engrossing work" that "offers a sweeping reinterpretation of American history and a bold, imaginative program to revive the promise of American life."[18] While admitting that Lind romanticizes New Deal liberalism and underemphasizes its reliance on white supremacy, Gerstle agrees that the presence of affirmative action has had the effect of undermining class politics. For evidence, Gerstle turns to his "own profession of history, where a preoccupation with race and gender has driven questions of class from the main field of study." For Gerstle, "Lind's bold analysis of class privilege," despite its faulty historical reasoning on issues of race and class, makes this seminal work an important call to draw working-class Americans "out of their cultural bunkers" and toward a much-needed "vigorous common culture."[19]

Clearly part of Lind's appeal to liberal academics is his own intellectual journey from a neoconservative Wunderkind—he is a former editor of *The National Interest* and a protegé of William F. Buckley—to a "centrist extremist" willing to directly attack the white overclass. But at least one reviewer, Ellen Willis in *The Nation,* points out that Lind is simply a "warmed-over Daniel Bell," one whose intellectual position is similar to that of pre-1968 Cold War liberals who called for a strong central state but were decidedly authoritarian in culture.[20] While other neoconservatives jumped on the Reagan bandwagon, Lind's appeal is the same one that had practitioners of the 1950s version of American Studies interpreting "the end of ideology" and the extreme consensus of the American population under a "culture of plenty."[21] It is harder to understand why much of Lind's analysis mirrors the recent work of New Left academic poster child Todd Gitlin, whose beginnings as an SDS radical seem far removed from those Johnson Cold War liberals whom SDS so forcefully challenged in the 1960s. But Gitlin's work on the contemporary cultural scene, *The Twilight of Common Dreams: Why America Is Wracked by Culture Wars,* is full of much the same racial and class analysis which marks Lind's post- (or pre-?) neocon tract.[22]

Gitlin, not surprisingly, does provide quite a different emphasis in explaining developments in the 1960s which created an America full of cultural tension. Unlike Lind, whose white overclass thoroughly manipulated nationalists and those on the Left to insure the hegemony of a concentrated elite, Gitlin searches for the moment in which the New Left itself, of whom he was intimately part, abandoned a politics of commonality and therefore played a critical role in the unraveling of America. In short, Gitlin gives agency to segments of the New Left in his narrative while continuing to play out the disagreements that he was clearly in the middle of during that decade.[23] For Gitlin, central to this transformation was the distinction between the early and later New Left:

> Growing numbers in the civil rights and antiwar movements began by rejecting American practices, went on to reject American ideals, and soon, since America was its ideals, rejected the conventional versions of American identity altogether. The early New Left rejected the American political consensus as hypocritical: the country was in default on its promise to recognize equal rights. The later New Left and the black liberation movement rejected the promise as well: the American political consensus was cursed by original sin, it was and had ever been racist and imperial, it had long been making its way to napalm in the defense of freedom; the very idea of a common America came to feel like a pernicious defense of unwarranted and injurious privilege. . . . With an eerie suddenness, virtually before anyone noticed how drastically their terms had changed, American identity was at stake.[24]

As members of the antiwar movement abandoned rhetoric that emphasized that their opposition to the war was the height of patriotism from 1965 to 1968, "the anti-American outrage of Malcolm X and the Black Panthers became far more appealing."[25] For Gitlin, the abandonment of a desire to speak to a common American identity led directly to the failure of the New Left movement.

Compared to his emphasis on solidarity with the oppressed and participatory democracy, which characterized the best of the early New Left, Gitlin's analysis of the later years of the Left in the 1960s focuses on a futile search for useful theory that finally gave way to calls for separatism in which "one grouping after another insisted on the recognition of difference and the protection of their separate and distinct spheres."[26] Though having some sympathy for the potential universality of environmentalism, feminism, and gay rights, Gitlin characterizes most of the leftist politics which has emerged from this time as separatism, "a politics built on identity taken for granted."[27] For Gitlin, it is the "politics of race" that has taken central stage and robbed the Left of its capacity to appeal to the wider American community. Claims based on race have led directly to "the break-up of ideas of a whole Left [which] throws the contest to the Right."[28]

While many historians of the New Left, especially in the new revisionist wave of writing on the 1960s, might disagree with the stark dividing line Gitlin proposes between the early 1960s and the late 1960s, others would take issue with the notion that the New Left would have appealed to a broader, class-based coalition of Americans had not the Left splintered into various separatist factions.[29] Indeed, new scholarship on racial developments in the post–World War II era indicates strongly that white supremacy was solidly entrenched within the northern labor movement, as well as throughout suburban America.[30] In other words, the white backlash toward racial politics had begun well before the late 1960s, already finding expression in George Wallace's 1964 campaign for the presidency and the ascendancy of Goldwater to the Republican nomination.[31] Yet Gitlin's narrative, despite its inattentiveness to actual political developments in the 1970s and 1980s, is one that serves as the underpinning for most descriptions of racial politics since the 1960s in this new wave of scholarship which seeks to move "beyond race."

Gitlin's contemporary analysis is no less problematic, for he concentrates on focusing disparagingly on the attention that multiculturalists have paid to transforming the curriculum ("Marching on the English Department While the Right Took the White House"), while ignoring the appeal that the Right has made to the white working-class constituency he believes would have moved politically left, had it not been for this "disintegration" into racial separatism. His answer for the end of the twentieth century is a call to reembrace the Enlightenment and its universal principles, whatever history (and politics) has taught us about the fiction of Enlightenment universality. To Gitlin, "the Enlightenment is self-correcting."[32] For someone who so attentively calls on lessons to be learned from the ideological missteps in the New Left, his call for a reinvigoration of Enlightenment philosophy among the Left in the 1990s is both intellectually limited and politically unsatisfying. As Robin D. G. Kelly has pointed out, Gitlin ignores labor movements of the past thirty years which have organized workers across racial boundaries, while disregarding scholarship which shows "that the tragedy of most progressive movements in the United States has been white racism."[33]

Indeed, Gitlin's narrative of the New Left's demise as a result of an ideology of racial separation and his opening section framing "the problem" of contemporary politics through the lens of the travails faced by the previously mentioned historian Gary Nash as he confronted the parochial Oakland School Board over his multicultural textbooks indicate to me that part of Gitlin's analysis rests on a much-underdiscussed form of "identity politics": the personal victimization felt by many white male academics when forced to confront their own privilege. Gitlin captures this form of identity politics when he observes that, "if not an oppressor, the white male is a blank, made to feel he lacks roots, culture, substance."[34] But he does not follow that insight up with any sustained analysis. Instead, while spending some time recounting his own disgust with minority student activists at Berkeley, Gitlin joins a host of other tenured academics who have framed their political outlook from personal confrontations with those without much power on their campuses.[35] Unlike others, however, Gitlin is willing to denounce any focus on the campus as a "true" site for political empowerment, all the while using campus politics to define the trajectory of the left in the last two decades.

In the end, Gitlin proposes a politics of commonality which seeks to construct a democratic majority that will face "the necessary discussion," one he hints at as concerning control of multinational corporations by national states, especially the United States. For him, it is only "the obsession with difference [which] stands in the way of asking the right questions."[36] Unlike Lind, who unabashedly calls for a "liberal nationalism" to shape this democratic majority, Gitlin calls for an American "community"—a weak politics of "common moral obligations" in which class itself is elided through populist rhetoric of the "common man." I would argue that Gitlin indeed calls for an American nationalism, grounded around support for "majoritarian" values, that falls short of confronting both the U.S. population's tortured history with race and difference and its contradictory future in leading an international revolt against the very multinational corporate structure it has cultivated.[37] Just as in the movie *Independence Day*, in Gitlin's position America's role as world leader goes unquestioned, even though how international leadership can be developed from such an unabashedly nationalist project remains unexplored.

While both Lind and Gitlin call for a reduction of claims for affirmative action and are adamant about the need to reduce immigration to the United States in order to insure that multiculturalism remains palatable for American citizens, David Hollinger's approach to these questions in *Postethnic America: Beyond Multiculturalism* is quite different and, in many ways, more challenging to those involved with the project of American Studies.[38] Hollinger, as a former director of the Program in American Culture at the University of Michigan, introduces us to several ideological and political currents quite central to the American Studies enterprise today. In particular, his important concept of "cosmopolitanism" helps us understand the motivation of many American Studies practitioners to move beyond national parochialism and toward a more inclusive sense of belonging. Yet, it also contains a problematic relationship with American nationalism, particularly because of what it ignores: power, shaped between American groups and between the U.S. citizenry and other citizens of the world.

Among the many strengths of *Postethnic America* is its attention to the wider spectrum of ideas, what Hollinger refers to as "a larger transition from species to ethnos," that marks the intellectual terrain in which multiculturalism in the United States is but one trend.[39] Unlike Gitlin's self-correcting Enlightenment, Hollinger does not minimize the extent to which previous claims of universalism, particularly in the 1950s, were grounded in a specific American generation's tendency "to conflate the local with the universal."[40] He also recognizes the intellectual advance in acknowledging the "historicity" of our beliefs and values, that allow us to "shy away from essentialist constructions of human nature, from transcendentalist arguments about it, and from timeless rules for justifying claims about it."[41] While the key issue for Hollinger is the future of the American civic community, as it is for Gitlin and Lind, Hollinger problematizes the relationship of the individual to the nation by asking a fundamental question: "How wide is/should be the circle of we" to truly have an American community of racial and ethnic equality? Hollinger goes further than others in answering this question by introducing the concept of "cosmopolitanism" as a goal.

Hollinger begins by demonstrating how similar cosmopolitanism is to other varieties of universalism, especially pluralism. Like other universalisms, Hollinger's cosmopolitanism has "a profound suspicion of enclosures," but unlike others is defined by the "recognition, acceptance, and eager exploration of diversity." In his definition, "cosmopolitanism urges each individual and collective unit to absorb as much varied experience as it can, while retaining its capacity to advance its aims effectively."[42] So far, virtually every member of the American Studies community nationwide at the moment would qualify as "cosmopolitan." Moreover, given the unequal nature of intellectual exchange in American higher education, any faculty members or students of color at a predominantly white university would by definition be a "cosmopolitan," since they have placed themselves in an institutional setting in which they are a minority "absorbing" a higher degree of "varied experience" than almost all of their white counterparts.

Where we disagree revolves around issues of power and history in play with questions of diversity, which are more clearly drawn by Hollinger in his distinction of cosmopolitanism from pluralism. To Hollinger,

> Pluralism differs from cosmopolitanism in the degree to which it endows with privilege particular groups, especially the communities that are well established at whatever time the ideal of pluralism is invoked. While cosmopolitanism is willing to put the future of every culture at risk through the sympathetic but critical scrutiny of other cultures, pluralism is more concerned to protect and perpetuate particular, existing cultures . . . . If cosmopolitanism can be casual about community building and community maintenance and tends to seek voluntary affiliations of wide compass, pluralism promotes affiliations on the narrower grounds of shared history and is more quick to see reasons for drawing boundaries between communities.[43]

Hollinger's concept of cosmopolitanism, in my reading, therefore needs to ignore differences in power, both in the present and in the past, in order to achieve cultural interaction. While this might be fine for those who need not fear putting the very presence of their culture at risk, it would be a ridiculous posture for anyone who believes that power is distributed unequally to various cultural groups, thereby making some affiliations more "voluntary" than others.[44] If one believes, as I do, that collective action has been critical to the survival of certain racial and ethnic groups in U.S. society, and is, indeed, the only way that individuals in those groups have had choice, then cosmopolitanism is not a viable option for most with a commitment to Ethnic Studies.

In short, I remain skeptical that anyone but those with racial and economic power in American society can truly be "postethnic." When Hollinger notes that "a truly postethnic America would be one in which an ethno-racial component in identity would loom less large than it now does in politics as well as culture, and in which affiliation by shared descent would be more voluntary than prescribed in every context," and then goes on to say that "many middle-class Americans of European descent can now be said to be postethnic in this sense," I wonder mightily about its applicability for a society that continues to be riveted and committed to racial and class hierarchies.[45] It is, indeed, the power to affiliate as white, as much as the desire to "move beyond multiculturalism" which fostered the turning-back of affirmative action in California via Proposition 209, for example. And it is exactly this "power to affiliate" which shapes the very academic departments that remain quite un-diverse throughout the University of California system with which Hollinger and Gitlin have both been associated. As with the question posed by the film *Independence Day*, we need to ask ourselves whether a "post-nationalist" American Studies actually hopes to break down these national boundaries of inquiry or whether they will be repackaged under a new rubric of difference controlled.

For me, it is critically important to understand why—for American liberal academics—it is "separatist" and dangerous for scholars who study race and ethnicity, or one particular racial-ethnic group, to organize themselves into an academic department. Clearly Ethnic Studies departments should meet the same rigorous demands of scholarship and teaching implicit in any university department. And clearly, one cannot call "separatist" any intellectual discipline which seeks its place among others at the table of intellectual inquiry. Indeed, the proliferation of departments which have focused on one nation or one linguistic group seems never to have threatened before the "unity" of scholarly inquiry at the university.

The work of literary scholar Chris Newfield and sociologist Avery Gordon points toward an answer to these questions through the advent of "managerial democracy"—developed often in the corporate business world's attempt at diversity management—in the world of academia, particularly in the humanities.[46] They have stressed that this newfound interest in managing multiculturalism on college campuses has its roots in a larger discourse at the heart of the University of California system. Former University of California President Clark Kerr memorialized this version of postwar university management philosophy when he wrote thirty years ago, "To make the multiversity work really effectively, the moderates need to be in control of each power center, and there needs to be an attitude of tolerance between and among the power centers, with few territorial ambitions. When the extremists get in control of the students, the faculty, or the trustees with class warfare concepts, then the 'delicate balance of interests' becomes an actual war."[47] Is this what is going on? Does moving American Studies to the forefront of the study of race ensure that moderates will remain in positions of power—moderates being the newly tenured members of the New Left, rather than the "tenured radicals" predicted by the New Right?

Or is this impulse combined with an underexplored form of identity politics—that of white males of the left, whose own concept of the American nation requires a department of diversity to lay claim to a "new American future?" In some academic conversations, I often feel as if my own scholarship, if not my very body, is just a leg of a scaffold being built which allows these pronouncements of an "exceptional America" to be professed. Do I threaten this delicate scaffold when I ask to surround myself with scholars from the field which I know nurtures best my own intellectual interests?

I say all of this as someone committed to participating in the future of American Studies. I do not believe that my voice in this conversation carries any less weight because it emerges from the fields of Chicano Studies and

American history. But I also know that if a true conversation is to exist between Ethnic Studies and American Studies, we must collectively fight off the tendency to collapse difference into some new nationalist paradigm, even if "multicolored."

A post-nationalist American Studies must find a way to incorporate the various intellectual traditions in a multicultural United States and the specific histories at individual campuses without assuming a position of ideological control over the study of race and ethnicity. Moreover, few ethnic faculty want to face the age-old question, "Are you American?" by having to decide to contribute to either an overarching American Studies program or a marginalized Ethnic Studies program. And very few American Studies faculty believe that a multicultural curriculum can be sustained without advances in the hiring and promotion of faculty of color who specialize in the study of specific racial/ethnic groups in the United States.

In short, American Studies programs and departments are unable to transcend the very divisions of race and power that shape American institutions and society as a whole. Acknowledging our discomfort with our power and privilege because of our citizenship, I call on American Studies scholars to re-examine notions of nationhood which presume that the health of the nation should be equated with the absence of conflict and questioning. Indeed, if American Studies and Ethnic Studies are to exist together in a positive relation in academia, those involved must accept conflict and compromise as a function of the continued marginalization of ethnic scholarship and scholars by their institutions. Rather than simply considering conflict as debilitating for academic discourse, American Studies scholars must see themselves at the forefront of a truly multicultural university, willing to struggle with the consequences of continued inequality while pushing forward for a new reconfiguration of power and a sharing of privilege in American society.

NOTES

1. The film *Independence Day* was directed by Roland Emmerich (Twentieth Century Fox, 1996).

2. For a further exploration of these issues, see Michael Rogin, *Independence Day, or, How I Learned to Stop Worrying and Love the Enola Gay* (London: British Film Institute Publishing, 1998).

3. For our collective group's own debates over the meaning of the terms *post-national* and *post-nationalist*, see the introduction to this volume.

4. Mary Helen Washington, " 'Disturbing the Peace: What Happens to American Studies If You Put African American Studies at the Center?': Presidential Address to the American Studies Association, 29 October 1997," *American Quarterly* 50: 1 (March 1998), p. 6.

5. Ibid., p. 3.

6. Indeed, the analysis which follows is a result of being invited as an outside re-

viewer of or consultant to at least eight different American Studies programs over the past four years. From this vantage point, similar tensions seemed to exist across campuses, although the problems encountered and possible solutions varied dramatically depending on specific institutional histories between the areas.

7. Quoted in Sean Wilentz, "Integrating Ethnicity into American Studies," *Chronicle of Higher Education,* 29 November 1996, p. A56.

8. Ibid.

9. See Lizbeth Cohen, *Making A New Deal: Industrial Workers in Chicago, 1919–1939* (Cambridge: Cambridge University Press, 1990); Gary Gerstle, *Working-Class Americanism: The Politics of Labor in a Textile City, 1914–1960* (New York: Cambridge University Press, 1989); and Michael Denning, *The Cultural Front: The Laboring of American Culture in the Twentieth Century* (London: Verso, 1996).

10. One exception is Gary Gerstle, who struggles with these questions in "Liberty, Coercion, and the Making of Americans," *Journal of American History* 84: 2 (September 1997), pp. 550–70.

11. Gary Nash, "The Great Multicultural Debate," *Contention: Debates in Society, Culture, and Science* 1: 3 (Spring 1992), p. 17.

12. Ibid., p. 24.

13. Michael Lind, *The Next American Nation: The New Nationalism and the Fourth American Revolution* (New York: The Free Press, 1995); Todd Gitlin, *The Twilight of Common Dreams: Why America Is Wracked by Culture Wars* (New York: Metropolitan Books, 1995); David Hollinger, *Postethnic America: Beyond Multiculturalism* (New York: Basic Books, 1995). See also Arthur M. Schlesinger, Jr., *The Disuniting of America* (New York: W. W. Norton, 1992); Peter Brimelow, *Alien Nation: Common Sense about America's Immigration Disaster* (New York: Random House, 1995); Dinesh D'Souza, *The End of Racism* (New York: The Free Press, 1995); Richard Bernstein, *Dictatorship of Virtue: Multiculturalism and the Battle for America's Future* (New York: Knopf, 1994); Michael Tomasky, *Left for Dead: The Life, Death, and Possible Resurrection of Progressive Politics in America* (New York: The Free Press, 1996); Jim Sleeper, *The Closest of Strangers: Liberalism and the Politics of Race in New York* (New York: W. W. Norton, 1990); Robert Hughes, *Culture of Complaint: The Fraying of America* (New York: Oxford University Press, 1993); and Paul Craig Roberts and Lawrence M. Stratton, *The New Color Line: How Quotas and Privilege Destroy Democracy* (Washington, D.C.: Regnery, 1995).

14. Lind, *Next American Nation,* p. 12.

15. Ibid., p. 98.

16. Ibid., pp. 116–17.

17. Michael Kammen, "On Colorblindness: A Rational Argument from the Extreme Center," *Los Angeles Times Book Review,* 2 July 1995, pp. 2, 9.

18. Gary Gerstle, "Class-Conscious Patriot," *Tikkun* 10: 5 (September/October, 1995), p. 90.

19. Ibid., pp. 92, 93.

20. Ellen Willis, "A Neocon Goes Back to Class," *The Nation,* 28 August/4 September 1995, pp. 211–14.

21. Daniel Bell, *The End of Ideology* (Glencoe: Free Press 1960); and David Potter, *People of Plenty* (Chicago: University of Chicago Press, 1954).

22. Gitlin, *Twilight of Common Dreams.*

23. For an account of Gitlin's involvement in SDS, see Todd Gitlin, *The Sixties: Years of Hope, Days of Rage* (New York: Bantam Books, 1987); and James Miller, *Democracy Is in the Streets: From Port Huron to the Siege of Chicago* (Cambridge: Harvard University Press, 1987).

24. Gitlin, *Twilight of Common Dreams,* pp. 68–69.

25. Ibid., p. 70.

26. Ibid., p. 100.

27. Ibid., p. 101.

28. Ibid., p. 103.

29. David Farber, *The Age of Great Dreams: America in the 1960s* (New York: Hill & Wang, 1994); Doug Rossinow, "The New Left in the Counterculture: Hypotheses and Evidence," *Radical History Review* 67 (Winter 1997), pp. 79–120.

30. See, for example, Thomas Sugrue, *The Origins of the Urban Crisis: Race and Inequality in Postwar Detroit* (Princeton: Princeton University Press, 1996); Arnold Hirsch, *Making the Second Ghetto: Race and Housing in Chicago, 1940–1960* (Cambridge: Cambridge University Press, 1983); and George Lipsitz, *The Possessive Investment in Whiteness: How White People Profit from Identity Politics* (Philadelphia: Temple University Press, 1998).

31. Dan T. Carter, *From George Wallace to Newt Gingrich: Race in the Conservative Counterrevolution, 1963–1994* (Baton Rouge: Louisiana State University Press, 1996).

32. Gitlin, *Twilight of Common Dreams,* p. 215.

33. Robin D. G. Kelley, *Yo Mama's Disfunktional!: Fighting the Culture Wars in Urban America* (Boston: Beacon Press, 1997), p. 119. See especially chapter 4, "Looking Extremely Backward: Why the Enlightenment Will Only Lead Us into the Dark," pp. 103–24, for a thorough repudiation of the "enlightenment" perspective, and chapter 5, "Looking Forward: How the New Working Class Can Transform Urban America," pp. 125–58, for a description of various post-sixties movements which have embodied a transracial organizing strategy without ignoring race.

34. Gitlin, *Twilight of Common Dreams,* p. 125.

35. Ibid., pp. 151–59.

36. Gitlin, *Twilight of Common Dreams,* p. 236.

37. Much the same point is made by Kelley, *Yo Mama's Disfunktional!,* pp. 118–19.

38. Hollinger, *Postethnic America.*

39. Ibid., p. 65.

40. Ibid., p. 54.

41. Ibid., p. 60.

42. Ibid., p. 84.

43. Ibid., pp. 85–86.

44. The same critique is made by Gerstle in "Liberty, Coercion, and the Making of Americans," pp. 554–57.

45. Hollinger, *Postethnic,* p. 129.

46. Avery F. Gordon and Christopher Newfield, "Introduction," and "Multiculturalism's Unfinished Business," in *Mapping Multiculturalism* (Minneapolis: University of Minnesota Press, 1996).

47. Clark Kerr, *The Uses of the University* (Cambridge: Harvard University Press, 1963), p. 39.

Syllabus INTRODUCTION TO AMERICAN STUDIES AND ETHNICITY
University of Southern California

Instructor: George J. Sánchez

This course explores a variety of themes, theoretical influences, and methodological approaches currently alive in American Studies, and its related disciplinary fields. My aim is to introduce you, at the graduate level, to a wide array of ongoing "conversations" in the field of American Studies and Ethnicity with the hope of promoting active engagement in those discussions from you. Particular emphasis is placed on the current controversies and scholarship surrounding the area of cultural studies and scholarship focused on race, ethnicity, and gender.

After providing a general mapping of the current intellectual terrain in the field, this course is organized around four sections, each designed to explore a particular direction in American/Ethnic Studies. "Origins in Place" will explore some of the historical origins of American Studies, centered around regional/spatial issues in a variety of subfields. "Immigration and Response" will examine interdisciplinary approaches to understanding the entry of newcomers to American society, as well as the ability of the United States to change as a result of immigration. "Performing Identity" will explore various approaches to the relationship between the individual and the larger community, focusing on cultural arenas of performance where difference is expressed. "One Nation, Many Peoples" examines the historical and contemporary sites of ethnic interaction, as well as the hierarchies of race which continue to shape American society.

Schedule

Week 1: Introduction to Course

Week 2: New Directions and Old Issues in American Studies

Mary Helen Washington, " 'Disturbing the Peace: What Happens to American Studies If You Put African American Studies at the Center?': Presidential Address to the American Studies Association, 29 October 1997," *American Quarterly* 50 (March 1998), pp. 1–23.

Amy Kaplan, " 'Left Alone with America': The Absence of Empire in the Study of American Culture," in *Cultures of United States Imperialism*, ed. Amy Kaplan and Donald E. Pease (Durham, N.C.: Duke University Press, 1993), pp. 3–21.

Allen F. Davis, "The Politics of American Studies," *American Quarterly* 42: 3 (September 1990), pp. 353–74.

Gene Wise, " 'Paradigm Dramas' in American Studies: A Cultural and Institutional History of the Movement," *American Quarterly* 31 (1979), pp. 293–337.

ORIGINS IN PLACE

Week 3: Slavery and the South

Saidiya Hartman, *Scenes of Subjection: Terror, Slavery, and Self-Making in Nineteenth-Century America* (New York: Oxford University Press, 1997).

Alexander O. Boulton, "The American Paradox: Jeffersonian Equality and Racial Science," *American Quarterly* 47 (September 1995), pp. 467–92.

Priscilla Wald, "Terms of Assimilation: Legislating Subjectivity in the Emerging Nation," in *Cultures of United States Imperialism*, pp. 59–84.

Week 4: Conquest and the West

Frieda Knobloch, *The Culture of Wilderness: Agriculture as Colonization in the American West* (Chapel Hill: University of North Carolina Press, 1996).

Brad Evans, "Cushing's Zuni Sketchbooks: Literature, Anthropology, and American Notions of Culture," *American Quarterly* 49 (December 1997), pp. 717–45.

Richard Slotkin, "Buffalo Bill's 'Wild West' and the Mythologization of the American Empire," in *Cultures of United States Imperialism*, pp. 164–81.

Week 5: Power and the City

Mike Davis, *Ecology of Fear: Los Angeles and the Imagination of Disaster* (New York: Metropolitan Books, 1998).

Sean McCann, "Constructing Race Williams: The Klan and the Making of Hard-Boiled Crime Fiction," *American Quarterly* 49 (December 1997), pp. 677–716.

William Sharpe and Leonard Wallock, "Bold New City or Built-Up 'Burb?: Redefining Contemporary Suburbia," *American Quarterly* 46 (March 1994), pp. 1–30.

IMMIGRATION AND RESPONSE

Week 6: Acting as Immigrants

Lisa Lowe, *Immigrant Acts: On Asian American Cultural Politics* (Durham, N.C.: Duke University Press, 1996).

K. Scott Wong, "The Transformation of Culture: Three Chinese Views of America," *American Quarterly* 48 (June 1996), pp. 201–32.

Roger Rouse, "Mexican Migration and the Social Space of Postmodernism," *Diaspora* 1 (Spring 1991), pp. 8–23.

Week 7: Anti-Immigrant Nativism

Michael Peter Smith and Joe R. Feagin, eds., *The Bubbling Cauldron: Race, Ethnicity, and the Urban Crisis* (Minneapolis: University of Minnesota Press, 1995).

George J. Sánchez, "Face the Nation: Race, Immigration, and the Rise of Nativism in Late Twentieth-Century America," *International Migration Review* 31 (Winter 1997), pp. 1009–30.

William H. Katerberg, "The Irony of Identity: An Essay on Nativism, Liberal Democracy, and Parochial Identities in Canada and the United States," *American Quarterly* 47 (September 1995), pp. 493–524.

Week 8: Moving Beyond Multiculturalism?

David Hollinger, *Postethnic America: Beyond Multiculturalism* (New York: Basic Books, 1995).

Robert James Branham, " 'Of Thee I Sing': Contesting 'America,' " *American Quarterly* 48 (December 1996), pp. 623–52.

Christopher Newfield and Avery F. Gordon, "Multiculturalism's Unfinished Business," in *Mapping Multiculturalism,* ed. Avery F. Gordon and Christopher Newfield (Minneapolis: University of Minnesota Press, 1996), pp. 76–115.

PERFORMING IDENTITY

Week 9: Performing Race, Performing Gender

Dorinne Kondo, *About Face: Performing Race in Fashion and Theatre* (New York: Routledge, 1997).

Pamela Fox, "Recycled 'Trash': Gender and Authenticity in Country Music Autobiography," *American Quarterly* 50 (June 1988), pp. 234–66.

Chela Sandoval, "U.S. Third World Feminism: The Theory and Method of Oppositional Consciousness in the Postmodern World," *Genders* 10 (1991) pp. 1–24.

Week 10: Cultural Politics in Exhibition

Alicia Gaspar de Alba, *Chicano Art Inside/Outside the Master's House: Cultural Politics and the CARA Exhibition* (Austin: University of Texas Press, 1998).

Kristine C. Kuramitsu, "Internment and Identity in Japanese American Art," *American Quarterly* 47 (December 1995), pp. 619–58.

James Clifford, "On Collecting Art and Culture," in *The Predicament of Culture: Twentieth-Century Ethnography, Literature, and Art* (Cambridge: Harvard University Press, 1988), pp. 215–51.

Week 11: Watching Race, Watching Culture

Herman Gray, *Watching Race: Television and the Struggle for Blackness* (Minneapolis: University of Minnesota Press, 1995).

George Lipsitz, "Listening to Learn, Learning to Listen: Popular Culture, Cultural Theory, and American Studies," *American Quarterly* 42 (1990), pp. 615–36.

Lynn Spigel, "High Culture in Low Places: Television and Modern Art, 1950–1970," in *Disciplinarity and Dissent in Cultural Studies,* ed. Cary Nelson and Dilip Parameshwar Gaonkar (New York: Routledge, 1996), pp. 313–46.

ONE NATION, MANY PEOPLES

Week 12: American Studies Association conference, Seattle, Washington

Week 13: Thanksgiving

Week 14: The Politics of Cultural Interaction

Neil Foley, *The White Scourge: Mexicans, Blacks, and Poor Whites in Texas Cotton Culture* (Berkeley: University of California Press, 1997).

Robert Orsi, "The Religious Boundaries of an Inbetween People: Street *Feste* and the Problem of the Dark-Skinned Other in Italian Harlem, 1920–1990," *American Quarterly* 44 (September 1992), pp. 313–47.

Laura Pulido, "Multiracial Organizing among Environmental Justice Activists in Los Angeles," in *Rethinking Los Angeles,* eds. Michael J. Dear, H. Eric Shockman, and Greg Hise (Thousand Oaks: Sage, 1996), pp. 171–89.

Week 15: Reexamining Whiteness

George Lipsitz, *The Possessive Investment in Whiteness: How White People Profit from Identity Politics* (Philadelphia: Temple University Press, 1998).

Eric Lott, "White Like Me: Racial Cross-Dressing and the Construction of American Whiteness," in *Cultures of United States Imperialism,* pp. 474–95.

Shelley Fisher Fishkin, "Interrogating 'Whiteness,' Complicating 'Blackness': Remapping American Culture," *American Quarterly* 47 (September 1995), pp. 428–66.

Rethinking (and Reteaching) the Civil Religion in Post-Nationalist American Studies

Jay Mechling

Several years ago I inherited from my good friend and colleague, David S. Wilson, an undergraduate course entitled "Religion in American Lives." I had been teaching an undergraduate course on "Technology, Science, and American Culture," which examines science as a belief system and compares that belief system with other systems of belief and practices, including religion. Murphey's essay "On the Relation between Science and Religion," which argues that the culture critic has no meaningful grounds for making a distinction between the two systems, governs my perspective in teaching the science and technology course, so taking on the religion course meant teaching the same idea, but entering the network of systems through another door.[1]

The title of the course, "Religion in American Lives," wonderfully captures the William Jamesian approach begun by my colleague and continued in my teaching. Just as James was interested in the multiple "varieties of religious experience," from the ordinary to the extraordinary, I am interested in students' understanding the broad range of experiences we should count as "religious."[2] The sociology of knowledge and belief provides the theoretical base for the course, represented (for example) by the work of sociologist Peter L. Berger, but also by folklorists and others who do the ethnographic, microsociological study of the ways people construct and maintain knowledge and practices that the people consider religious. The goals of the course reflect this orientation as well as my view that American Studies should be defined as a way of thinking about American materials rather than as a field defined by the materials. I do not aim to "cover" American religion(s) through some checklist of facts the students must acquire. Being clear on the goals of a course goes a long way toward imagining how to make selections about course readings, nonverbal texts, writing assignments, and other learning activities.

The interdisciplinary study of religious experiences has had an uneven history within American Studies scholarship and teaching. While historians of American religion were instrumental in founding the field at schools like Yale and in the pages of the *American Quarterly*, only a relatively small cadre of teachers and scholars continues the tradition in the 1990s. Many American Studies teachers largely ignore a cultural system of beliefs and practices that the majority of Americans testify is the most important thing in their everyday lives. Nor is the rising stock of cultural studies within American Studies very promising for the study of religion. The absence of religion in most cultural studies is all the more puzzling when one realizes that a central question in postcolonial, post-nationalist American Studies is the viability of "the nation" itself as the proper category for understanding world cultures. Perhaps the same Marxian roots that lead cultural critics to look at global capitalism as a transnational engine of culture also lead to the purposeful neglect or, worse, disdain of religion as mere superstructure to the more important base of the political economy. Still, one would think that the transnational nature of most major religions would make their study an appropriate topic for a post-nationalist American Cultural Studies. Actually, there is a growing body of scholarship on the ways particular religions cross borders, but most of this work does not ask some of the synthetic and integrative questions that American Studies scholars are inclined to pose.[3]

My aim in this essay is to place the study of religion at the heart of the emerging post-nationalist American Studies. I propose here a conceptual map for organizing work on religion from several disciplines. A workable notion of the "civil religion" in the United States and in other societies needs to be at the center of our thinking about religion in a post-nationalist, postmodern world. A post-nationalist notion of the American civil religion sets aside the older, nationalist understandings of American "exceptionalism" but is not afraid to ask whether there are some "religious" aspects of the narratives that dominate public discourse in the United States. The scholar searching for a post-nationalist understanding of the civil religion also might look for certain ideas shared across the particular religious systems practiced in the United States. A post-nationalist notion of the civil religion also recognizes that religious communities often are transnational, crossing borders and interrupting all sorts of generalizations the scholar might want to make about "national" cultures.[4]

My narrative moves from the most private to the most public experiences of religion, but (of course) even the most private experiences are fashioned in many ways by social experiences. I shall discuss relatively briefly the first few steps away from the most private experiences, even though they get more substantial treatment in the syllabus, which follows this essay. Our thinking about civil religion must address its public nature and the relationship between private and public cultures in the United

States, so I devote the bulk of my discussion to those matters. Still, we begin with the individual's experience of religion as subjective reality.

RELIGION AS SUBJECTIVE REALITY

The phenomenological approach to religion stresses the individual's actual experiences. We all have unique and privileged knowledge of our "subjective reality."[5] William James's definition of religion, for example, privileges the individual: "The feelings, acts, and experiences of individual men in their solitude, so far as they apprehend themselves to stand in relation to whatever they may consider the divine."[6] In this Jamesian mode, Peter L. Berger's definition of religion stresses the "supernatural," what James meant by "the divine." Berger observes that the term "supernatural . . . denotes a fundamental category of religion, namely, the assertion or belief that there is *an other reality,* and one of ultimate significance for man, which transcends the reality within which our everyday experience unfolds."[7]

Each of us has access to our own experiences (including emotions, moods, and so on) with a transcendent reality, with a "sacred" reality posed against the "profane," ordinary, everyday reality. This is not to say that every person has such experiences or that a person having such experiences would label them in this way. The phenomenological position asserts simply that all people have experiences that we might call "ecstatic" (as Berger notes, "in the literal sense of *ek-stasis*—standing or stepping outside reality as commonly defined") and that for many people this ecstasy gives them a glimpse of a reality that transcends our own.[8]

A focus on ecstasy suggests a relationship between the experience of transcendent reality and the experience of play. Handelman, for example, shows how the play frame and the ritual frame both resemble and differ from one another.[9] Taking another tack, Csikszentmihalyi has spent several years studying "flow," "the holistic sensation that people feel when they act with total involvement," and examining the many sorts of frames that induce the experience of "flow."[10] All these theories share with William James an interest in understanding those conditions under which a person steps outside the ordinary, commonsensical, "taken-for-granted" reality of everyday life and experiences a different reality.

We still must confront James's problem, of course. If we want to study religious experiences, how do we gain access to the subjective realities of others? People make their subjective realities "intersubjectively" available through discourses, narratives both verbal and nonverbal. Sometimes the person offers such narratives as a purposeful act, and we can imagine a range of such testimony, from personal experience narratives to formal autobiographies, poetry, and novels to the visual and performing arts. Sometimes it is an interviewer who prompts the discourse. Rorty wisely points to

our ethnographers and our novelists as the two sorts of intellectuals whose
narratives provide the most insight into both the particularities and univer-
salities of human experience, so novels and ethnographies are natural texts
for our phenomenological study of religious experience.[11]

Berger proposes an interesting goal for the ethnography of religious experiences. Having mustered all of his sociology of knowledge to demonstrate the social construction of reality, of all human affirmations, he still
asks, "Which affirmations are true and which are false?" He proposes a move
he calls "relativizing the relativizers," which grounds theology in anthropology by examining ethnographically the everyday lives of people in search of
"prototypical human gestures" that he takes as "signals of transcendence," as
signs of the sacred.[12] His list includes order, play, hope, damnation, and hu-
mor, all of which can be the topic of novelistic or ethnographic narrative.[13]

We must keep in mind that we approach religious experience phenom-
enologically because we want to understand the nature of this experience
and its relation to other cultural experiences. James was attracted to religion for the passion and sense of freedom it offers. "Like love, like wrath,
like hope, ambition, jealousy, like every other instinctive eagerness and impulse," he writes, "religion adds to life an enchantment which is not rationally or logically deducible from anything else. . . . Religious feeling is thus
an absolute addition to the Subject's range of life. It gives him a new sphere
of power. When the outward battle is lost, and the outer world disowns
him, it redeems and vivifies an interior world which otherwise would be an
empty waste. . . . This sort of happiness in the absolute and everlasting is
what we find nowhere but in religion."[14]

I detect in the students who take my "Religion in American Lives" course
something of these motives and attractions. On the first day of class I ask
the students to write anonymously about why they are taking the course and
what they expect to get out of it. The brief essays seem to cluster around two
reasons—the one representing students who count themselves religious
and want to broaden their understanding of religion, and the other representing those who are not religious but are envious (some even use this
word) of the passion they see in friends and family members who have religious faith. In part, then, the study of religion in American lives must begin
with this phenomenological, subjective reality which has so much power
and, even from the outside, seems so empowering or liberating.

RELIGIOUS EXPERIENCE IN COMMUNITIES OF MEMORY

As private as religious experiences and as personal as ecstasy may be, nar-
rating these individual experiences makes them social. Most people have
and narrate religious experiences in the context of a face-to-face group.
This is the "folk group," but I like and have adopted the phrase "commu-

nity of memory" that Bellah and his colleagues invented in *Habits of the Heart*. These are the face-to-face groups in which people learn their "practices of commitment."[15] A person experiences a religion not as an abstract doctrine or as a formal organization but as a set of experiences shared with a group of people in a face-to-face setting, even if that face-to-face reality is mass-mediated. "Memory" is an apt word to attach to "community" because people become a folk group not only by sharing a significant set of experiences but also by "remembering" those shared experiences and their shared identity through shared narratives, ceremonies, and the like. Thus, a community of memory recreates itself constantly through its practices. We level our ethnographic gaze at this sort of community.

The move from the intensely private and personal religious experience to the social requires an expanded definition of religion, and I like the one offered by anthropologist Clifford Geertz. Religion is, he writes, "(1) a system of symbols which acts to (2) establish powerful, persuasive, and long-lasting moods and motivations in men by (3) formulating conceptions of a general order of existence and (4) clothing these conceptions with such an aura of factuality that (5) the moods and motivations seem uniquely realistic."[16] Geertz then elaborates each of his numbered points in the definition, raising such issues as the relationship between social action and symbolization, culture patterns as both models "of" and models "for" reality, three sorts of chaos (bafflement, suffering, evil) threatening order, and the role of ritual in reinforcing the concepts, moods, and motivations of the religious system. Geertz's anthropological definition slights the personal experiences so important to James and Berger, but we can easily subsume their notion of a divine, sacred, transcendent reality under Geertz's "general order of existence."

What constitutes a "good ethnography," a "good account" of a religious community of memory? Earlier ethnographies of religious communities worked out of the positivist, realist paradigm which ethnographers abandoned in poststructuralist thinking about the politics and poetics of the act of writing about others' ways of seeing the world.[17] Most scholars would now agree that a "good" ethnography works out of a sense that the ethnographic encounter is a dialectical event with dynamic rather than fixed relations between the subject and object positions. Barbara Myerhoff's *Number Our Days* is a favorite of mine for both the literary grace of its narrative and the power of Myerhoff's sense that she is writing reflexive ethnography, but there are many others from which to choose.[18]

Many issues complicate our ethnographic practices or our readings of ethnographies. First, we make a mistake if we see the figurative "center" of a community of memory as the focus of the ethnography, as if there were some sort of authentic reality to the religious beliefs and practices that bring together the group. The center/periphery metaphor in Cultural

Studies has some problems, but we are well advised to study the periphery, the hot border zones where folk groups meet and interact. Thus, an ethnography of a specific Muslim community, for example, must take into account the other communities with which this one interacts, ever watchful for the effects of those interactions on the Muslim group of worshippers.

Second, making the dynamic borders our focus requires a rich understanding of the syncretism or creolization that occurs in that dialectical process. Older notions of "assimilation" or Americanization—in this case, the view that a religion from elsewhere becomes Americanized on our soil and that these assimilated religions come to resemble one another—must give way to a more complex model of syncretism, in which the elements of all the interacting religious systems modify one another to create a new, syncretic system.[19] Moreover, the religious syncretism or creolization that we see in the United States can be compared across cultures and contexts. Worldwide diasporas provide a sort of living laboratory for understanding the post-nationalist dynamics of syncretism.[20] The Church of Jesus Christ of Latter Day Saints (the Mormons), for example, is a "very American" religion; along with Christian Science, Scientology, and a few other examples, it is a religion invented in the United States rather than imported to these shores from elsewhere. But the Mormons also have a highly successful worldwide mission, and it would be interesting to see how this very American religion enters into syncretic relationships with other cultures. Similarly, Scientology has been spreading internationally, alarming the German government enough to launch a controversial crackdown on the church in 1997.

Of course, the Roman Catholic church provides a much earlier version of this transnational process, and the Cuban-based religion known as Santería, a syncretic blend of the Catholicism of the Spanish colonists and the African religions the slaves brought to Cuba, makes a good case study for post-nationalist American Studies. The Cuban diaspora brought this complex of religious beliefs and practices to the United States, primarily to Miami, Los Angeles, and New York, and already there is some fine ethnographic scholarship on Santería in the United States.[21] The role of African-based music in Santería helps make the syncretism point, as the evolution of Cuban music demonstrates the ways Europeans and Africans affected each other in the dynamic creation of a wholly new thing.[22]

Finally, an important goal for the ethnography of communities of memory is that of understanding whether and how the community works as a "mediating structure." A large scholarly project created by Peter L. Berger, Richard John Neuhaus, and others in the 1970s elaborated the idea that there are "mediating structures"—"those institutions standing between the individual in his private life and the large institutions of public life"—that play a crucial role in "mediating" between private and the most public, impersonal values of liberal democratic society.[23] Religious institutions are among the most important mediating structures, and if they are performing the mediating function, then these institutions are the site for citizens to work through the negotiations between private and public values.

Because mediating structures stand between the more private and the more public institutions in society, their study belongs in both this section of the course syllabus and in the next. In the first instance we study mediating structures ethnographically in order to see how they help people bring more private, home values into more diverse public settings; and, in the second, we study mediating structures ethnographically in order to understand these institutions as sites in the public sphere. So let me turn, now, to this site, which we might call "the public square."[24]

PRIVATE RELIGION IN THE PUBLIC SQUARE

Understanding religious communities of memory as mediating structures leads naturally to considering the ever-larger public settings into which people carry their religious beliefs and practices. In liberal democracies with traditions of religious pluralism and tolerance, the public square becomes one of those "hot" zones where cultural differences meet. How people negotiate these border encounters is a crucial topic for a post-nationalist American Studies.

The last two decades have seen an escalation of the "culture wars" in the public square, and religious beliefs and practices lie behind many of the battles in the public square over some basic issues of reality, authority, moral absolutism/relativism, and so on.[25] There may be both sorts of positions within a single religious denomination, so these cultural/political categories cut across the traditional religious ones. Gender, race, ethnicity, and sometimes social class seem to be the focus of attention as progressives, liberals, and neoconservatives debate multiculturalism and nationalism (see George Sánchez's essay in this volume), but religious beliefs underlie a great many of these differences, so that what we commonly call the ethnic "politics of identity" might have more to do with the politics of religious identity. Again, the public sphere is the site where people work out the relationships between their private cultures, values, and identities, on the one hand, and the norms of the public sphere on the other. The map of identity choices in the public sphere is very complex, but to neglect religion in the discussion is to miss a great deal of the complexity.

Social movement activities by religious mediating structures have a history older than the rise of the 1980s culture wars, of course. Recent attention to the "religious right" sometimes makes us forget the role of religious communities of memory in earlier struggles by marginalized people against oppression. The role of "the black church" in the Civil Rights movement of the 1950s and 1960s, for example, shows how communities of memory can become mediating structures that force a conversation about the relationships between religious values, democratic values, and public policy.

As always, we learn a great deal more about the dynamics of private religion in the public square if we compare the United States with other societies. In some cases, the religious pluralism has a different form, and the public square does not have as strong a tradition of liberal democratic norms as ours. In other cases, we look at societies that draw their norms of the public culture from the same Enlightenment ideas as ours. Habermas's theory of the public sphere, after all, speaks largely to the condition of Western democracies.[26] Glendon's comparison of the ways the United States, Great Britain, France, and Germany draw conclusions about the nature of "rights" from different Enlightenment traditions nicely shows how different liberal democracies handle conflicting rights claims in the public sphere.[27] Comparisons between the United States and Canada, with its dramatic confrontations between French and English versions of being Canadian, for example, provide yet another way to put our public sphere into national perspective.[28]

Still another way to look comparatively at the public sphere is to understand that there might be more than one public sphere in the United States. Fraser's socialist-feminist critique of Habermas's concept, for example, points to the work of historians who document the presence of alternative, nonbourgeois public spheres not sanctioned by the hegemonic, masculinist public sphere described by Habermas. Women, workers, and others create what Fraser calls "subaltern counterpublics," a multiplicity of "public" spaces and public spheres that deserve attention for their democratic and utopian possibilities. Fraser's argument for preferring a plurality of competing publics serves well the post-nationalist American Studies we are developing here, though I am disappointed that she, too, neglects (maybe even fears) religion in rethinking the relationships between strong publics and the state.[29]

The clash between conflicting rights claims frequently ends in the courts, and the religious clauses (regarding "free exercise" and "establishment") of the First Amendment make certain that a good proportion of Constitutional law cases involve religion. The 1996–97 session of the Supreme Court, to take just one recent year, saw significant cases establishing just what are the proper relationships between private religious beliefs and practices on the one hand and the practices of public institutions on the other. That Court, for example, struck down the Religious Freedom Restoration Act of 1993. Previous Supreme Court cases and issues dealt with such questions as the rights of parents to withhold medical treatments for their minor children based on religious beliefs (e.g., Christian Science), the rights of worshippers of Santería to sacrifice live animals in their religious services, the rights of children to wear religious head covering to public schools, and so on.

All of this discourse and negotiation occurs in the larger public institutions of the courts and the mass media. But the same processes also occur a bit less publicly and more informally in mediating structures, which (at their best) serve as living laboratories for working out similar dilemmas arising out of conflicting rights claims within the group. Millions of Americans spend eight or more hours a day in their workplaces, for example, where the people in the face-to-face setting must work out somehow such thorny issues as how to respect one another's religious holidays, or how religious requirements of clothing or headwear might be exempted from the dress code, or how free speech might be abridged in favor of a more civil workplace. An understanding of the workings of private religion in the public square needs to look at both the large and mediating structure scales of "public" settings.

THE CIVIL RELIGION

We arrive finally at the topic that must undergo the most revision from the older American Studies to the new, post-nationalist American Studies. It would be possible to stop short of this step, that is, to move from examining religion as a subjective reality, to seeing it as a shared reality in a community of memory, and finally as a source of private values adding to the mix of the public square, ending with the observation that this multicultural, dynamic public culture is the plural reality we must recognize and respect.

But we need to entertain a further question. Is it possible to detect a "public religion" shared to some extent by very large numbers of people in the United States? This was the question posed by Robert Bellah in his classic 1967 essay entitled "Civil Religion in America." Bellah's notion seems to belong to the older, "consensus" view of American history which marked American Studies for decades and which came apart in the late 1960s. Its 1967 publication date would seem to make Bellah's essay a last, desperate attempt to save the consensus paradigm; but maybe not. In any case, by the 1970s the "conflict" view of American history and society came to replace the consensus view, making obsolete such concepts as the "civil religion." Then some prominent historians in the mid-1980s began to exhort their colleagues to return to writing synthetic histories. As George Sánchez (this volume) shows, the 1990s version of this return to synthetic history shows up in the books by "liberal nationalist" scholars who are trying to recover a narrative of American national identity that provides a satisfactory, progressive alternative to the nationalist narratives being offered by neoconservatives and by more troubling nativists.

The question, therefore, is whether the notion of a "civil religion" in the United States can be resuscitated in a form that returns to the American

Studies agenda of generalizing about American experience and, at the same time, avoids the errors of the nationalist, "consensus" view that Americans share some basic, distinctive, and unique national culture and character (i.e., American "exceptionalism"). Is there a satisfactory way for us to talk about the American civil religion in post-nationalist American Studies? Toward answering this question, I shall review briefly the original idea of the civil religion and then examine the recent scholarship on the public or civil sphere, in order to suggest ways to reconceive the civil religion in the United States.

Robert Bellah's "Civil Religion in America" was the lead essay in the winter, 1967, issue of *Daedalus* devoted to "Religion in America." "While some have argued that Christianity is the national faith," begins Bellah, "and others that church and synagogue celebrate only the generalized religion of 'the American Way of Life,' few have realized that there actually exists alongside of and rather clearly differentiated from the churches an elaborate and well-institutionalized civil religion in America." The separation of church and state, notes Bellah,

> has not denied the political realm a religious dimension. Although matters of personal religious belief, worship, and association are considered to be strictly private affairs, there are, at the same time, certain common elements of religious orientation that the great majority of Americans share. These have played a crucial role in the development of American institutions and still provide a religious dimension for the whole fabric of American life, including the political sphere. This public religious dimension is expressed in a set of beliefs, symbols, and rituals that I am calling the American civil religion.[30]

One of these beliefs, for example, regards "the obligation, both collective and individual, to carry out God's will on earth." Bellah acknowledges that the idea of the civil religion is old. The phrase is Rousseau's, and it is not difficult to find the idea (though not the phrase) in the Enlightenment political and religious ideas of the founding fathers. "Though much is selectively derived from Christianity, this religion is clearly not itself Christianity." This God is unitarian, and he (no doubt about the gender) resembles the God of the Hebrew testament more than the God of the Christian testament. "Even though he is somewhat deist in cast," writes Bellah, "he is by no means simply a watchmaker God. He is actively interested and involved in history, with a special concern for America."[31] The analogy to Israel's covenantal relationship with God is explicit.

Bellah acknowledges critics who see the potential for nationalist abuses of this exceptionalist notion of a special covenant with God. "Against these critics," replies Bellah, "I would argue that the civil religion at its best is a genuine apprehension of universal and transcendent religious reality as seen in or, one could almost say, as revealed through the experience of the

American people. Like all religions, it has suffered various deformations and demonic distortions." But its genius, in Bellah's view, is that the civil religion "borrowed selectively from the religious tradition in such a way that the average American saw no conflict between the two," thereby permitting the civil religion to symbolize "national solidarity and to mobilize deep levels of personal motivation for the attainment of national goals."[32]

I have quoted at length from Bellah's original essay, because it is easy to simplify and miss his point. Bellah is not claiming that all Americans practice some sort of general, Protestant religion. His claim, simply, is that public discourse generated by certain powerful people backed by certain powerful institutions articulates the notion that the people of the United States have a covenantal relationship with God to create a society that embodies God's will. To be sure, this notion of a covenant belongs most clearly to a Judeo-Christian tradition not shared by every American. But we are talking about the power of some groups to control the discourse in the public sphere of culture, an understanding common in the radical critique of consensus history. Recognizing that there is religious pluralism in a multicultural United States does nothing to weaken Bellah's claim.

Returning to civil religion in 1975, Bellah makes clear his acute awareness of a declining sense of moral obligation in favor of "individual freedom."[33] The affinity between capitalism and a utilitarian morality has taken us down a path that is not the only option, given other religious and moral traditions in American experience, and he seeks to call Americans back to a concept of covenant and virtue central to the civil religion. By 1985 Bellah had another change in mood and strategy. Still worried that utilitarian morality and individualism were threatening democracy, Bellah and his coauthors of *Habits of the Heart* announce that their goal is to search for the American traditions that might counteract the destructive trajectory of selfish individualism. Using in-depth interviews with everyday Americans around issues of success, freedom, and justice, the authors identify four main sources for everyday languages of American individualism—the Biblical, republican, utilitarian, and expressive strands—and they affirm the importance of "communities of memory" (i.e., folk groups) as the sites where Americans learn and perform these languages.[34]

This brief summary of the argument does not do justice to the complex argument in *Habits of the Heart,* and there are many problems with generalizing from the sample (the informants were all white and middle class). But I am most interested in the shift toward understanding the civil religion in relationship to "the market" and to "materialism" in American culture. I believe that the most interesting possibilities for rethinking and reteaching the civil religion in a post-nationalist American Studies lie in this direction.[35]

As I indicated in the previous section, the culture wars have prompted renewed scholarly discourse on the nature, importance, and health of the civil or public sphere of culture apart from the government and crucial to the health of liberal democracy. This civil, public sphere includes institutions like print and electronic journalism, the mass-media entertainment industry, the university, the advertising industry, and so on. The three spheres—the state, the market, and the civil society—maintain important checks on each other's power in a liberal democratic state. "The paradox of liberalism," as Glendon puts it, "seems to be that the strong state, the free market, and a vital civil society are all potential threats to individual citizens and to each other, yet a serious weakness in any one of them puts the entire enterprise in jeopardy."[36] Glendon and others who lean toward the communitarian position against classic liberalism worry that a hyperindividualistic "rights talk" has weakened the institutions in the civil society. Renewed discourse about the public, civil sphere necessarily considers religious institutions as important elements of that sphere. Religious beliefs provide legitimacy to all three spheres, for example.

Two important books, one by a neoconservative and the other by a progressive, show the trajectory of this thinking. Michael Novak argues that we understand our culture as a system of "democratic capitalism," which he sees as "three dynamic and converging systems functioning as one: a democratic polity, an economy based on markets and incentives, and a moral-cultural system which is pluralistic and, in the largest sense, liberal."[37] The system works only when all three are healthy. "The invention of democratic capitalism," he continues, "was aimed at the discovery of practical principles that would make such common life possible, while holding sacred the singular sphere of each human person. . . . Its aim is to establish the practical substructure of cooperative social life."[38] The market provides many conditions necessary to the health of democracy, but the "commercial values are not . . . sufficient to their own defense. A commercial system needs taming and correction by a moral-cultural system independent of commerce" (121). Thus, "the moral-cultural system is the chief dynamic force behind the rise both of a democratic political system and of a liberal economic system. . . . Neglect of it bodes ill" (185). Novak musters the neoconservative "New Class" argument to warn of the dangers of permitting the journalists, academics, and filmmakers to define the tenets of the moral-cultural system. He calls upon religious thinkers to formulate a new discipline, a "theology of economics," that will "put into words the actual moral and theological presuppositions of democratic capitalism as it now exists" (241), and as an invitation to debate, he lays out his own tenets of a "theology of economics." I don't see much evidence that American Studies folks (or anyone else outside the neoconservative ranks) accepted Novak's invitation, though one easily can read *Habits of the Heart* as an inquiry into the moral-cultural system of Americans.[39]

Robert Wuthnow, coming from a political stance different from Novak's, asks similar questions. Wuthnow is interested in seeing the ways Americans understand their economic commitments and economic behavior within moral frameworks. The "American dream" is just such a moral framework. The American dream, he writes,

> supplies understandings about why one should work hard and about the value of having money, but it does so in a way that guards against money and work being taken as ends in themselves. It creates mental maps that allow distinctions to be drawn between economic behavior and other commitments. It draws deeply on implicit understandings about the family, community, and the sacred. It comes in many varieties, reflecting different ethnic, religious, regional, and occupational subcultures. But its core assumptions transcend these subcultures.[40]

Like the authors of *Habits of the Heart* and unlike Novak, Wuthnow gathers the actual discourse of a sample of Americans to describe "the ways in which people already think about their work, their money, their consumer behavior, and the relationships between these commitments and other parts of their lives."[41] Wuthnow charts the strategies people use to deal with the tensions between their worry that "the United States is too materialistic" (as nine in ten Americans agreed in a poll cited by Wuthnow, 246) and their deep commitments to economic well-being. Wuthnow's argument is too complex and provocative to summarize in this brief space, so I shall say simply that I like putting the Novak and Wuthnow books into a conversation with each other and both into a conversation with *Habits of the Heart*. Together, they point to a new line of inquiry about American civil religion, a line that understands religious, spiritual ideas and practices in relation to economics and materialism.

Rethinking the civil religion in terms of narratives struggling with the tensions between commodity capitalism and some sort of public system of moral values offers plenty of dangers if we are not careful. The Novak and Wuthnow conversation echoes the one held a hundred years ago as thinkers like Charles Graham Sumner created an ideology out of the mix of Protestant Christianity, free market economics, and Darwin's theory of natural selection, an ideology that legitimated American exceptionalist ideas of Manifest Destiny and mission and the Spanish-American War. But we are experiencing a different stage of capitalism in the 1990s, and I think we can steer a course through these issues and questions without recapitulating the "American liberal democratic internationalism" (as one scholar calls it) that has marked so much American exceptionalist thinking since 1898.[42]

For the post-nationalist American Studies scholar and teacher, this new line of inquiry leads us to precisely those sorts of texts that Novak thinks are under the dangerous influence of the socialist-influenced New Class— namely, mass-media narratives in film, television, music, and popular fiction. To take a rich example that I think cuts quickly to the issues raised by

Novak, Wuthnow, and others, the mass-mediated discourses about Christmas in the United States provide some very interesting materials for thinking about the civil religion.

It is nearly impossible for a person of any faith or skepticism to avoid the celebration of Christmas as a public performance in the United States. There are many ways to account for the power of Christmas. Many of the central symbols of Christmas are pagan, pre-Christian, drawing their power from natural symbols, like the winter solstice. Present-day Christmas symbolism and custom are richly syncretic, drawing upon a range of pre-Christian, Christian, and non-Christian sources.[43]

In consumption-driven "late capitalism," a primary topic of public discourse about Christmas has been the felt tension between spirituality and materialism. The films appearing every year on network television as "Christmas classics" explore this cultural contradiction, and the viewing public never seems to tire of these films' rehearsal of the problem and its solution. These are so familiar to the reader that I hardly need recount the stories; but briefly: the various film versions of Dickens's *A Christmas Carol,* from the 1938 version starring Reginald Owen and the 1951 version starring Alastair Sim, to Richard Donner's *Scrooged* (1988), starring Bill Murray, recount the story of a man who becomes so attached to his wealth that he neglects all human relationships (family, employees, loved ones) until he has an epiphany about what really counts in life. These are all variations on what we might call the "Yuppie redemption films" of the Reagan-Bush era (e.g., *Baby Boom,* 1987; *Regarding Henry,* 1991; *Grand Canyon,* 1991; *The Doctor,* 1991; *Doc Hollywood,* 1991; *City Slickers,* 1991; up through *Jerry Maguire,* 1996), wherein a highly materialistic character learns what really counts in life. In *Miracle on 34th Street* (1947, with remakes in 1973 and 1994), it is a woman who is so consumed with "making it" that she neglects her daughter's and her own need for redeeming love. Perhaps the definitive Christmas film is Frank Capra's *It's a Wonderful Life* (1946), where (with the help of an angel named Clarence) Jimmy Stewart learns that it is the love of family and friends, not wealth, that sustains our lives. Of more recent vintage, *Home Alone* (1990), a television Christmas "classic" already, features as a crucial subplot the reconciliation of an old neighbor with his son and his family, and the subplot echoes a major theme of the film— namely, that family and love matter most. Only time will tell whether *The Santa Clause* (1994, starring television sitcom comic Tim Allen) becomes another "Christmas classic," but its theme of the redemption of a divorced man who neglects his children until he is forced to become Santa Claus's replacement has all the elements of a narrative resolving tensions around materialism, family, and sentiment (if not spirituality).

Other mass-media narratives appearing in the holiday period between

Thanksgiving and Christmas collaborate in working against materialism. This is a charity season, but beyond the usual stories about giving there are usually more dramatic stories about the triumph of values of the human spirit over materialist values. Every season in the San Francisco Bay area media, it seems, there is a fire or a theft resulting in the loss of toys and food gathered by an organization for distribution to "the underprivileged" families for Christmas. Just as predictably, people respond to the loss with even greater giving. In the 1996 season, a particular instance of this formula concerned the "Tickle Me Elmo" doll fad, which made the doll especially difficult to find in stores. Local radio and television stations were auctioning the dolls for charities. Amidst this swirl, a family's house fire destroyed all the belongings, including a Tickle Me Elmo doll, that the single mother had for her daughter. A person who had bought the doll (for over $500, as I recall) in a media auction made the doll a gift to this heartbroken little girl.

All these public stories of charity provide possible narrative solutions to the felt contradictions between materialism and morality in American culture. So do the various texts of the "angel" phenomenon of the late 1980s and 1990s. Jerry Zucker's immensely successful film, *Ghost* (1990), is the most notable early text in this 1990s wave, which includes *Always* (1989), *Heart and Soul* (1993), and *Michael* (1996). The television series *Highway to Heaven* (Michael Landon) and *Touched By an Angel* testify to the lasting interest in the idea that guardian angels (latter-day Clarences) live in our midst to help us effect our redemption. So prevalent is this new phenomenon that the cover story for the March 29–April 4, 1997, issue of *TV Guide* was a special report on "God and Television."

Thinking beyond the example of Christmas, we find many other public rituals and celebrations in which spiritualism and materialism accommodate one another and ecstasy becomes a valued element of an otherwise commercial experience. Novak makes this argument for sports, and others have shown where religion pops up in the most unlikely places in American experience.[44] The sacralization of nature in the United States may mean that some encounter a transcendent reality high in the mountains or out on the desert, but even these experiences inevitably make their meaning against the commercial civilization left behind.

CONCLUSION

My goal has been to persuade the scholars and teachers of the new postnationalist American Studies to include the study of religion in their shared project. The study of religion opens up every sort of question characteristic of the new perspective, including issues of American exceptionalism and of transnational cultural systems. Students make wonderful ethnographers of religious beliefs and practices, so that they can become full partners with other scholars in creating some understanding, however piecemeal and tentative, about the ways particular religions interact with other cultural systems. Many things will disappear with the new millenium, but we can be certain that religion will not be among them.

NOTES

1. Murray G. Murphey, "On the Relation between Science and Religion," *American Quarterly* 20 (1968), 275–95.

2. William James, *The Varieties of Religious Experience* (1902; New York: Penguin, 1982).

3. Steve Brouwer, Paul Gifford, and Susan D. Rose, *Exporting the American Gospel: Global Christian Fundamentalism* (New York: Routledge, 1996). See also José Casanova, *Public Religions in the Modern World* (Chicago: University of Chicago Press, 1994).

4. Jane C. Desmond and Virginia R. Domínguez, "Resituating American Studies in a Critical Internationalism," *American Quarterly* 48 (1996), 475–90.

5. Peter L. Berger and Thomas Luckmann, *The Social Construction of Reality* (Garden City, NY: Anchor/Doubleday, 1967).

6. James, *Varieties of Religious Experience*, 31.

7. Peter L. Berger, *A Rumor of Angels: Modern Society and the Rediscovery of the Supernatural* (Garden City, NY: Anchor/Doubleday, 1969), 2. See Jay Mechling, "The Jamesian Berger," in *Making Sense of Modern Times: Peter L. Berger and the Vision of Interpretive Sociology*, ed. James Davison Hunter and Stephen C. Ainlay (London: Routledge and Kegan Paul, 1986), 197–220.

8. Peter L. Berger, *The Sacred Canopy: Elements of a Sociological Theory of Religion* (Garden City, NY: Anchor/Doubleday, 1967), 43.

9. Don Handelman, "Play and Ritual: Complementary Frames of Meta-Communication," in *It's a Funny Thing, Humour*, ed. Anthony J. Chapman and Hugh C. Foot (Oxford: Pergamon, 1977), 185–91.

10. Mihaly Csikszentmihalyi, *Beyond Boredom and Anxiety: The Experience of Play in Work and Games* (San Francisco: Jossey-Bass, 1975), 36. See also his *Flow: The Psychology of Optimal Experience* (New York: Harper & Row, 1990).

11. Richard Rorty, *Contingency, Irony, and Solidarity* (New York: Cambridge University Press, 1989), 94.

12. Berger, *Rumor of Angels*, 45, 59.

13. See also Kathleen M. Sands, "Ifs, Ands, and Butts: Theological Reflections on Humour," *Journal of the American Academy of Religion* 64: 3 (1996), 499–523; Jay Mechling, "Peter L. Berger's Novels of Precarious Vision," *Sociological Inquiry* 54 (1984), 359–81.

14. James, *Varieties of Religious Experience*, 47–48.

15. Robert N. Bellah, William M. Sullivan, Ann Swidler, and Stephen Tipton, *Habits of the Heart: Individualism and Commitment in American Life* (Berkeley: University of California Press, 1985), 54.

16. Clifford Geertz, "Religion as a Cultural System," in *The Interpretation of Cultures* (New York: Basic Books, 1973), 90.

17. See James Clifford and George Marcus, *Writing Culture: The Poetics and Politics of Ethnography* (Berkeley: University of California Press, 1986); Ruth Behar and Deborah A. Gordon, eds., *Women Writing Culture* (Berkeley: University of California Press, 1995).

18. Barbara Myerhoff, *Number Our Days* (New York: Simon & Schuster, 1978).

19. See, for example, Mechal Sobel, *The World They Made Together: Black and White Values in Eighteenth-Century Virginia* (Princeton: Princeton University Press, 1987).

20. Stephen R. Warner and Judith G. Wittner, eds., *Gatherings in Diaspora: Religious Communities and the New Immigration* (Philadelphia: Temple University Press, 1998).

21. See, for example, Joseph M. Murphy, *Santería: An African Religion in America* (Boston: Beacon Press, 1988); and Joseph M. Murphy, *Working the Spirit: Ceremonies of the American Diaspora* (Boston: Beacon Press, 1994).

22. Ray Allen, "Unifying the Disunity: A Multicultural Approach to Teaching American Music," *American Studies* 37 (Spring 1996), 135–47; Charles Keil and Steven Feld, *Music Grooves* (Chicago: University of Chicago Press, 1994); and George Lipsitz, *Dangerous Crossroads: Popular Music, Postmodernism, and the Poetics of Place* (London: Verso, 1994).

23. Peter L. Berger and Richard John Neuhaus, *To Empower People: The Role of Mediating Structures in Public Policy* (Washington, DC: American Enterprise Institute, 1977); Jay Mechling, "Mediating Structures and the Significance of University Folk," in *Folk Groups and Folklore Genres: A Reader*, ed. Elliott Oring (Logan: Utah State University Press, 1989), 339–49; and Jay Mechling, "Myths and Mediation: Peter Berger's and Richard John Neuhaus's Theodicy for Modern America," *Soundings* 62 (1979), 338–68.

24. Richard John Neuhaus, *The Naked Public Square* (Grand Rapids, MI: Eerdmans, 1989).

25. James Davison Hunter, *Culture Wars: The Struggle to Define America* (New York: Basic Books, 1991), and *Before the Shooting Starts: Search for Democracy in America's Culture Wars* (New York: Free Press, 1994).

26. Jürgen Habermas, *The Structural Transformation of the Public Sphere: An Inquiry into a Category of Bourgeois Society*, trans. Thomas Burger, with Frederick Lawrence (1962; Cambridge, MA: MIT Press, 1989).

27. Mary Ann Glendon, *Rights Talk: The Impoverishment of Political Discourse* (New York: Free Press, 1991).

28. Richard M. Merelman, *Partial Visions: Culture and Politics in Britain, Canada, and the United States* (Madison: University of Wisconsin Press, 1991).

29. Nancy Fraser, "Rethinking the Public Sphere: A Contribution to the Critique of Actually Existing Democracy," in *The Phantom Public Sphere*, ed. Bruce Robbins (Minneapolis: University of Minnesota Press, 1993), 1–32. See also her excellent *Unruly Practices: Power, Discourse, and Gender in Contemporary Social Theory* (Minneapolis: University of Minnesota Press, 1989), but look in vain for a discussion of religion.

30. Robert N. Bellah, "Civil Religion in America," *Daedalus* 96: 1 (1967), 1, 3–4.

31. Ibid., 7.

32. Ibid., 12–13.

33. Robert N. Bellah, *The Broken Covenant: American Civil Religion in Time of Trial* (New York: Seabury, 1975).

34. Bellah et al., *Habits.*

35. See Casanova, *Public Religions.*

36. Glendon, *Rights Talk,* 138.

37. Michael Novak, *The Spirit of Democratic Capitalism* (New York: Simon & Schuster, 1982), 14.

38. Ibid., 65; page numbers hereafter cited parenthetically in the text.

39. A related issue is the ways religion and business are tangled in American society, from church ownership of real estate to media ownership to business enterprises owned and operated by religious organizations. See, for example, R. Laurence Moore, *Selling God: American Religion in the Marketplace of Culture* (New York: Oxford University Press, 1994).

40. Robert Wuthnow, *Poor Richard's Principle: Recovering the American Dream through the Moral Dimensions of Work, Business, and Money* (Princeton, NJ: Princeton University Press, 1996), 4.

41. Ibid., 10.

42. Tony Smith, *America's Mission: The United States and the Worldwide Struggle for Democracy in the Twentieth Century* (Princeton, NJ: Princeton University Press, 1994).

43. Jack Santino, *All Around the Year: Holidays and Celebrations in American Life* (Urbana: University of Illinois Press, 1994). See also Leigh Eric Schmidt, *Consumer Rites: The Buying and Selling of American Holidays* (Princeton, NJ: Princeton University Press, 1995); Stephen Nissenbaum, *The Battle for Christmas* (New York: Knopf, 1996); and Stephen M. Feldman, *Please Don't Wish Me a Merry Christmas: A Critical History of the Separation of Church and State* (New York: New York University Press, 1997).

44. Michael Novak, *The Joy of Sports: End Zones, Bases, Baskets, Balls, and the Consecration of the American Spirit* (New York: Basic Books, 1976); James B. Gilbert, *Redeeming Culture: American Religion in an Age of Science* (Chicago: University of Chicago Press, 1997).

Syllabus (RE)TEACHING THE CIVIL RELIGION
    Religion in American Lives

    Instructor: Jay Mechling

The following syllabus describes only one of several possible ways to translate the foregoing ideas into a concrete course. I teach this course in a ten-week quarter, but I present here a twelve-week design that can be expanded or contracted to fit terms of different lengths.

The course design moves from the individual's most private experience ("Religion as Subjective Reality") to the social construction of religious experiences in the face-to-face group ("Religious Experience in Communities of Memory") to the meeting of home-world religions in still more public, cultural spheres ("Private Religion in the Public Sphere") to the most "public religion" that might organize public thinking about virtue, morality, ethics, and so on ("The Civil Religion"). The class schedule follows.

WEEKS 1–3: I. RELIGION AS SUBJECTIVE REALITY

In this unit we shall establish a set of concepts and vocabulary for approaching religion as a cultural system of beliefs and practices. Our focus is on religious experience as a "subjective reality" for the individual. Through lectures and discussion, we shall acquire concepts of the social construction of reality, of the ways people "frame" experiences, and of the experience of "flow."

Required Reading

    Peter L. Berger, *A Rumor of Angels* (Garden City, NY: Anchor/Doubleday, 1969) and a novel drawn from the list distributed in class.

Writing Assigment

    Write a 1,000–1,500-word essay using the ideas and language from the lectures/discussions and in *A Rumor of Angels* to analyze the religious experiences described in the novel you read. There are many possible ways to write this paper—remember, the key is that I want to see you intellectually engage Berger's argument. Counts 20 percent of term grade.

WEEKS 4–6: II. RELIGIOUS EXPERIENCE IN COMMUNITIES OF MEMORY

In this unit we move beyond the individual's subjective religious experience to consider the social construction of religious experiences in groups. We are interested in the folk cultures of religious groups, that is, the actual face-to-face culture created by the community. Santería will provide a case study of syncretism. We also want to understand the idea of "mediating structures."

Required Reading

Barbara Myerhoff, *Number Our Days* (New York: Simon & Schuster, 1978).

Writing Assignment

Write a 2,000–2,500-word essay analyzing a religious community of your choice (approved by instructor). This essay should be based on firsthand experience with the group, either as a member or as an outsider ethnographer. In so short an ethnographic essay, you might want to focus on a smaller group of people within the larger group and on a single event or theme. Does this religious group function as a mediating struture for its members? Counts 40 percent of term grade.

WEEKS 7–9: III. PRIVATE RELIGION IN THE PUBLIC SQUARE

The family, education, arts, law, and electoral politics as fields of conflict in the culture wars; moral pluralism and the democratic ideal; comparison of the United States with other societies, especially with other liberal democracies; democratic possibilities.

Required Reading

James Davison Hunter, *Culture Wars: The Struggle to Define America* (New York: Basic Books, 1991).

Writing Assignment

Write a 750–1,000-word essay analyzing the uses of religion in the public discourse of the election campaigns this fall. You might find this discourse in newspapers, magazines, journals of opinion, or in printed campaign or social movement materials. Perhaps the discourse you want to analyze is in the electronic media (radio or television). It is better to focus on one theme or even one text, if it is a rich one, rather than to attempt a survey. Your goal is to write a well-organized essay with a thesis and examples to support your ideas. I expect you to use the Hunter book (Myerhoff, too, if it works), as well as class lectures and discussions, in writing your essay. Your goal is to write a cogent piece of culture criticism. Counts 20 percent of term grade.

WEEKS 10–12: IV. THE CIVIL RELIGION

The "civil religion" (or "public religion"), from its earliest formulations to the present, with emphasis on the relationship between public religion, liberal democracy, and the late capitalist ecomomy. Evidence of this civil religion in public discourse, including political discourse, civic rituals, popular amusements (e.g., sports), advertising, and mass-mediated narratives. Patriotism and nationalism as expressions of civil religion. Christmas as a case study in the civil religion.

Required Reading

Robert N. Bellah, "Civil Religion in America," *Daedalus* 96: 1 (1967), 1–21.

Robert Wuthnow, *Poor Richard's Principle* (Princeton, NJ: Princeton University Press, 1996).

Writing Assignment

Write a 1,000–1,500-word essay analyzing the elements of a civil religion you find in an American theatrical film of your choice (have me approve the choice). Counts 20 percent of term grade.

Foreign Affairs
Women, War, and the Pacific

Katherine Kinney

Near the end of Joan Didion's novel *Democracy*, the main character, Inez Victor, the wife of a Kennedyesque senator, is waiting in Hong Kong in April of 1975 while her lover, Jack Lovett, searches for her daughter in Saigon. Lovett tells Inez to listen to the shortwave radio for the final evacuation order from the American embassy in Saigon. "Mother wants you to call home," the American Service announcer would say and then play Bing Crosby singing "I'm Dreaming of a White Christmas." This secret signal is no less absurd for the way in which it uncannily articulates Inez's personal desire to find her daughter. But listening to it, she comes to a conclusion which reverses typical expectations. Rather than allowing her concern for her daughter to individualize and privatize her understanding of that convulsive historical moment, Inez comes to realize that after twenty years "she was not particularly interested in" the members of her family.

> They were definitely connected to her but she could no longer grasp her own or their uniqueness, her own or their difference, genius, special claim.
> . . . What difference did it make in the long run whether any one person got the word, called home, dreamed of a white Christmas? The world was full that night of people flying from place to place and fading in and out and there was no reason why she or [her husband] Harry or [her son] Adlai or [her daughter] Jessie . . . should be exempted from the general movement.
> Just because they believed they had a home to call.
> Just because they were Americans. (208)[1]

Within the traumatic context of the fall of Saigon, Inez comes to reject both the belief in a home separate from the convulsions of history and her own constitutive place within it as wife and mother. By refusing to accept the primacy of domestic, familial relationships, Inez "gives up the American exemption" and comes to see the world and her place within it with new, "post-national" eyes.

The sharp demarcation between domestic U.S. history, defined within the boundaries which became the lower forty-eight states, and "foreign affairs" is a key tenet of the exceptionalist conception of American Studies. The boundaries of the continental United States are naturalized as domestic space, and the domestic is naturalized, in turn, as woman's sphere. The relationship between national and familial conceptions of the domestic becomes particularly acute in times of war; and war, hot and cold, has held a privileged place in the construction of U.S. nationality in the twentieth century. World War II consolidated the primacy of consensus models of American culture, society, and politics, and the Cold War coercively enforced that consensus. Post-nationalist American Studies are more than coincidentally a product of the post–Cold War era, an injunction to re-imagine the nation in a new global narrative.

The gendered distinction between the foreign and the domestic and its inscription through war has been mapped across the Pacific with a particular intensity. As one of the oldest and most conspicuous sites of American imperial expansion, the Pacific throws certain features of American exceptionalism into bold relief. In its most basic sense, American exceptionalism testifies to (or searches for) the difference of the United States not simply from the nations of Europe but from their history. The absence of feudalism, of class difference, of empire, even of war have all at various times defined the American exception from history. In cultural understanding (and often in the tradition of American Studies) American exceptionalism has functioned in deeply idealized and mythic terms. "The city on the hill" is one of the most resonant expressions of the idealism of American exceptionalism, an image of a nation above borders, separate and inviolate, righteous and exemplary.

The Pacific holds an almost irresistibly mythic appeal in this context. It is quite simply the end of the West, a phrase which is so powerful because its claims seem simultaneously literal and mythic. The phrase "post-nationalist American Studies" likewise suggests the end of something, what comes after, the going beyond. In a very real sense, the end of the West is one of the ideas which a post-nationalist American Studies must supersede if its purpose is to re-imagine the United States as something other than the separate, inviolate, and exceptional "city on the hill." The Pacific is a powerful place to engage such a re-imagining.

In the twentieth century, the United States has gone to war in the Pacific five times: in the war with Spain, followed by the long war in the Philippines to suppress resistance to U.S. rule, World War II, Korea, and Vietnam. Mao's Revolution marks in many ways a sixth war—the "loss of China" which was one of the crucial "battles" of the Cold War. Typically, the differences among these wars are seen as crucial. World War II, with its dramatic and self-justifying victory, vanquishes the memory of the openly imperialist moment of the turn of the century, and measures the failure of the United States to win in either Korea or Vietnam. This twentieth-century litany of wars has a long prehistory—dating to Lewis and Clark if not Christopher Columbus, in which the dream of the China trade was promoted through military agency.[2] I want to rethink the significance of this history through what may seem oblique means, by focusing on the place of women in war. The phrase "women and war" doubles a series of oppositions—domestic and foreign, the United States and Asia, present and past—which are far more than parallel; they are mutually dependent, sustaining and naturalizing the logic of American national narratives.

I am interested in a group of novels published by women in the 1980s which share a sophisticated interest in plotting these vexed and contradictory relationships across the Pacific: Joy Kogawa's *Obasan* (1981), Joan Didion's *Democracy* (1984), Jayne Ann Phillips' *Machine Dreams* (1984), and Maxine Hong Kingston's *China Men* (1989). My interest in the commonalities among these novels grew out of my research on American narratives of the Vietnam War. I was struck by the very different conception of World War II in these works as compared to that found in the most well-known works by Vietnam veterans. In works such as Ron Kovic's *Born on the Fourth of July,* Philip Caputo's *A Rumor of War,* Tim O'Brien's *Going After Cacciatto,* or journalist Michael Herr's *Dispatches,* it is precisely the failure of Vietnam to be World War II which animates the profound, often enraged, sense of loss and disillusionment for which these works are known. Why, I wondered, did these women write about the Pacific and World War II in such radically different terms? The novels I am interested in here were all written after the U.S. withdrawal from Vietnam and the final victory of the North. Most of these works appeared during the period of intense popular interest in the Vietnam War, marked most immediately by the dedication of the Vietnam Veterans Memorial in 1982 and Hollywood's subsequent rediscovery of the war. Much of this cycle of Vietnam War representations was conspicuously marked by what Susan Jeffords has called the "remasculinization of America," valorizing the masculine collectivity of war and banishing women from the narrative.[3]

In this context it is easy to assume that women will tell a different story, barred as they have been historically from the role of the soldier. The category of the "women's novel" carries a particularly heavy burden in relationship to the domestic, one which has long been used to limit the scope of its appeal and address. One sign of this limit is the traditional understanding of the "women's novel" and the "war novel" as mutually exclusive categories. These works by Kogawa, Didion, Phillips, and Kingston openly dispute the traditional place of women in war and the power of war to determine the boundaries of home and nation. Even so, white and Asian American women engage such categories from radically different perspectives and locations. As Lisa Lowe has forcefully argued, it is crucial to understand "the *contradictions* of Asian immigration, which at different points in the last century and a half of Asian entry into the United States have placed Asians 'within' the U.S. nation-state, its workplaces, and its markets, yet linguistically, culturally, and racially marked Asians as 'foreign' and 'outside' the national polity."[4] According to Lowe, "the American of Asian descent remains the symbolic 'alien,' the *metonym* for Asia who by definition cannot be imagined sharing in America."[5] The patterns of immigration, labor, and citizenship have been historically both culturally and legally gendered: " 'the Chinese immigrant' . . . was legally presumed to be male."[6] Nineteenth-century laws openly banned the immigration of Chinese women, creating the famous "bachelor society." World War II brought changes to the Chinese exclusion acts, recognizing in small numbers the Chinese refugees of the Pacific War and the "war brides" of American servicemen. Chinese Americans were rewarded for military service with the right to "bring back" a wife from China. War thus intensifies the implications of Asian exclusion and its gendered structure, even as it displaces people and motivates immigration.

I want to consider briefly two of the most famous images of World War II in American culture by way of establishing traditional assumptions about women, war, and the Pacific. When it first appeared on the front pages of American newspapers in February 1945, Joe Rosenthal's photograph of the flag-raising on Iwo Jima promised a victory not yet assured, one being bought at horrific and much-protested costs. Fifty years later, the image of six Marines bracing the weight of the standard atop the broken terrain of battle as the flag unfurls against a bright sky continues to compel attention. Even in retrospect, when it is all but impossible to suspend knowledge of ultimate victory, it is the dynamic quality of the image, the vivid effort of raising the flag which makes it so memorable. Uniformed bodies, faceless beneath helmets, lean forward with bent knees and braced legs, arms stretched forward. The active, embodied labor of the image testifies to Elaine Scarry's observation that war is "the most unceasingly radical and rigorous form of work."[7] Yet the image simultaneously demonstrates the sublimation of that labor into the national symbolic. The very action of the bodies carries the eye up toward the flag, an effect intensified in the Iwo Jima monument where the massive bronze figures are forever frozen but the flag is "real," flying whenever the wind blows. The human, embodied labor of the image all the more effectively masks even as it enhances the image's mythic quality. We seem to see quite literally the nation being built, freedom being preserved, and the solitary supremacy of the victorious American nation. The city on the hill is consecrated yet again on the crest of Mount Suribachi.

But what does it mean for the nation to be thus made by men through war in the Pacific? Battle is traditionally understood to be a male space and a male activity. Iwo Jima and other World War II battles for Pacific atolls mark the rare and extreme case in which this was absolutely true. There were no women on Iwo Jima and no civilian population. There were only soldiers who fought to an unprecedented degree to the death, literalizing another truism of war.[8] The carnage of Iwo Jima marks what John Dower has called "war without mercy," in which racialized propaganda in the United States and Japan worked together to intensify war's violent alterity "into an obsession with extermination."[9] As Dower demonstrates, American "race words" had long been "war words."[10] The first American war in the Pacific, in the Philippines at the beginning of the twentieth century, was fought by the same troops who had previously fought Native Americans, including those troops led by Arthur MacArthur. "That his son (Douglas MacArthur) commanded U.S. forces in the Pacific in World War Two is as good a reminder as any of how close in time the Indian Wars, the war in the Philippines, and World War Two really were."[11] "Indian fighting," the metaphor so often used to mark the movie-fed surrealism of the Vietnam War, in fact names the very material heritage of the American military push to and then across the Pacific.

If both the enemy and the remote, annihilated landscape of Iwo Jima, just visible at the bottom of the frame in Joe Rosenthal's photograph, marked an absolute otherness, home and country were imagined and marketed as the white American woman. In many ways the symbolic twin of the Iwo Jima image is the Betty Grable pin-up. Equally ubiquitous, some five million copies of Grable's image were distributed to servicemen during the war, a sign of both popularity and official sanction. As Richard Westbrook has argued, the pin-up marks a parallel, if less immediately obvious exchange between embodied identity and the national symbolic. While acknowledging that "pin-ups functioned as surrogate objects of sexual desire," Westbrook argues that they were also understood as a symbol of the private obligation which both soldiers and the state recognized as the crucial motivating factor in American mobilization.[12] Betty Grable offers a significant justification for "why we fight."

In the Pacific theater Grable's iconic whiteness became an increasingly self-conscious part of her appeal. According to *Time* magazine, Grable's popularity over other pin-ups rose "in direct ratio to [soldiers'] remoteness from civilization."[13] Two "Sad Sack" cartoons from the war clearly illustrate the equation of the Pacific with such remoteness.[14] In the first, Sad Sack, the luckless G.I., is aboard ship; an unlikely sign in the ocean reads "Pacific." He starts dreaming of a white-skinned beauty dancing before a palm tree. When he disembarks, a white woman stands waiting. In the last frame she and two other women, USO inscribed on their bags, wave good-bye as they board the ship he has just left. The second cartoon has the same basic structure, except that the last frame finds Sad Sack trudging past a dark-skinned, bare-breasted, large-lipped "native." The Pacific is defined by the absence of white women, who in turn define home, a site of private obligation which stands in for the political nation. In a critical symbolic sense, the Pacific thus becomes where and what the United States is not, in the same way that the Pacific ocean marks the naturalized "end" of American narratives of westward expansion and nation-building. Ironically, the long history of the U.S. quest for hegemony in the Pacific is most fully repressed at its moment of ultimate triumph in World War II.

The empty landscape and masculine agon of the Iwo Jima flag-raising seems to demand what Elaine Tyler May has called the "homeward bound" quality of postwar American culture, the logical return to Betty Grable from "over there."[15] The United States is one of a very few nations for whom this distance between home and battle held true during World War II. Removed from the devastating violence of the war, even as it mobilized for war production, domestic American society emerged as an idealized space, a safe home. This idealization continues to shape American cultural imagination. The brilliantly crafted images of Americanness which saturated American visual culture during the war, from Betty Grable's girl next door to Norman Rockwell's "Four Freedoms," are always close at hand when politicians make contemporary appeals to family values.[16] As Michael Rogin has argued, "the grip of the 'good war' " on American politics and culture follows from its morally self-justifying narrative in facing the terrible evil of Nazism, specifically freeing American culture from the stigma of racism.[17] But equally important is the concurrent domestic narrative, the propaganda of everyday life promoted in advertising and Hollywood.

The atomic bomb literally annihilated such distinctions. In the opening pages of his journalistic account, *Hiroshima*, John Hersey describes Mrs. Hatsayo Nakamura sitting at her kitchen window while her children sleep on the morning of August 6, 1945, watching the man next door "tearing down his home, board by board," to make way for a fire lane in anticipation of incendiary raids. The pathos of the neighbor's action testifies to war's traditional power to displace people and destroy homes, but the scale of power shifts radically in the next instant:

> As Mrs. Nakamura stood watching her neighbor, everything flashes whiter than any white she had seen. She did not know what happened to the man next door; the reflex of a mother set her in motion toward her children. She had taken a single step (the house was 1,350 yards, or three quarters of a mile, from the center of the explosion) when something picked her up and she seemed to fly into the next room, over the raised sleeping platform, pursued by parts of her house.[18]

Hersey depicts the atomic blast as an assault on domesticity, attacking women and children, homes and churches. The violence is undeniably material, but it simultaneously destroys the logic of the domestic, turning the house against the housewife as Mrs. Nakamura is "pursued by parts of her house."

The shift I have just made from American domestic narratives to the bombing of Hiroshima remains deeply controversial. The battle over the exhibit of the *Enola Gay* at the Smithsonian demonstrated this quite clearly. Veterans' groups and their congressional supporters specifically objected to plans to include photographs of Japanese victims and to present the *Enola Gay* and Hiroshima as the beginning of the Cold War as opposed to the ending of World War II.[19] Such an exhibit would deeply compromise not only the reverential particularity of World War II, its perceived difference from all other moments, but the boundaries between women and war, foreign and domestic, which structured the consensus memory of World War II. At the same time, Hiroshima vividly reminds us that American women, culturally and often legally denominated as white, and Asian women inhabit radically different domestic spaces in the logic of war. Asian American women, to return to Lisa Lowe's formulation, embody the historical "contradictions" of the gendered geography of war in the Pacific, challenging the absolute distance between here and there.

It is precisely the distance between white and Asian American women's locations in the narrative of foreign and domestic which makes it valuable to read their novels side by side. The novels of Joy Kogawa, Joan Didion, Jayne Ann Phillips, and Maxine Hong Kingston plot precisely these connections and contradictions, even as they engage them from significantly different class, national, regional, and racial positions. There is no natural or even strategic alliance to be found here; none of these novels describe more than a passing acquaintance between white and Asian American women. So, too, Japanese-Canadian, and Chinese-American narratives of war's legacy attest to the historical contradictions and differences within Asian American identity as well. For all their radical differences in style and subject, these novels share a number of specific features which deconstruct the traditional framing of World War II, not simply in order to challenge the memory of that period, but to understand the deep continuities between the Pacific wars. All of these works insist on a double framing of time, remembering the past from an increasingly unstable present. But even more critically, these novels are narrated not only by women, but by women self-consciously placed in the roles of daughter and sister. War is traditionally told both as the story of brothers in arms and as a story of fathers and sons, in which either the son goes off to war to earn the father's approbation and respect or old men send young men off to die. This genealogy not only represents but perpetually renews the nation. Women enter the narrative of war and nation under male coverture, as either mothers, wives, or sweethearts. Sisters and daughters are the domestic excess of such narratives and thus offer these writers literal and symbolic positions of counternarrative which are post-nationalist.

Furthermore, I want to claim more for the novel as a site for such discussions than simply the accident of my training as literary critic. Anne McClintock has argued that "National progress (conventionally the invented domain of male, public space) was figured as familial, while the family itself (conventionally the domain of private, female space) was figured as beyond history."[20] As a form, the novel exists at precisely the point of delineation between private and public, enacting the gendered dialectic between familial and national domains. Edward Said has argued that the classical novelistic beginning can be understood as an act of "fathering."[21] In *Beginnings* Said traces the decline of the "novel's paternal role—to author, father, procreate a rival reality," which he finds so powerful in the eighteenth and nineteenth centuries. This "rival reality" is a signature mark of the spread of print capitalism, which Benedict Anderson argues is fundamental to modern nationalism itself.[22] In the classical novel, Said argues, textual unity and integrity are "maintained by a series of genealogical connections: author-text, beginning-middle-end, text-meaning, reader-interpretation" which are undergirded by "the imagery of succession, of paternity, of hierarchy."[23] In Modernism the dynastic "familial analogy [of] fathers and sons" gives way to the "brother," the figure of "complementarity and adjacency."[24] Such beginnings do not descend from and succeed a revered and authorized origin, but stand next to other beginnings, other possibilities.

Said's brother is almost certainly the brother of a brother. His "figure of complementarity and adjacency" doubles the metonymic male role in nationalism in which "men are continuous with each other and the national whole."[25] Anne McClintock cautions that "not all men enjoy the privilege of political contiguity with each other in the national community."[26] The bonds of American national brotherhood are typically drawn within racial lines; in war stories it is the difference between American and Asian which remains the most constant. The uniform of the American G.I. (the abbreviation stands for General Issue) is the most compelling sign of the principle of male contiguity. Popular narratives of both World War II and the Vietnam War turn critically on the discovery of brotherhood across ethnic and racial lines. In films from *Bataan* (1943) to *Full Metal Jacket* (1987) the differences between Americans are subsumed first by the uniform ("All my pukes are army green" roars the drill sergeant in *Full Metal Jacket*), then by the utterly alien Pacific landscapes of war. Asians remain forever alien— Asian Americans are very rarely figured as part of the symbolic platoon.[27] Sisters do not share this same principle of contiguity in the nation, a fact made most obvious in times of war. At the structural core of each of these novels is a prototypical nuclear family: mother, father, sister, brother. In the ideology of the Cold War such families promised the perfect reproduction of the "American way of life." Read alongside each other, these novels suggest instead the fault lines between the familial and the national, the profound differences that race, class, and history make in the creation of domestic space and its nationalist incorporation.

Joy Kogawa's *Obasan* offers the most immediate connections between women's lives and the violence of World War II. At the same time *Obasan*, as a Japanese-Canadian novel, transgresses the neat alignment of America with the United States, demonstrating that the interlocking patterns of Asian immigration to "America" and war in the Pacific are not delimited by the national boundaries of the United States. *Obasan* connects the wartime expulsion of Japanese Canadians from British Columbia with the dropping of the bomb at Hiroshima. Racism motivates and shapes the violence directed at the Nakane family at every turn, but gender is the crucial agent of Kogawa's plotting of this history. Set in Alberta in 1972, *Obasan* tells the story both of the Nakane family's violent separation during World War II and of the adult Naomi Nakane's confrontation with the terrible loss of her parents during the war. Naomi is haunted by the memory of the family and home she once had.

The impossible relation of the personal and the political is embodied by Naomi's two aunts: Obasan, who raised her and now lives in a world of powerful silence, and her Aunt Emily, "the word warrior," a scholar dedicated to remembering what happened to Japanese Canadians during World War II.[28] Near the beginning of the novel Naomi receives a package from Emily, a box containing documents related to the forcible eviction of the Nakanes from British Columbia during World War II. They include correspondence between Emily and a satirically named bureaucratic, "B. Good"; instructions for her uncle to be registered as an "enemy alien"; a scrapbook of newspaper clippings; a notebook which Emily had dedicated to "THE STORY OF THE NISEI IN CANADA: A STRUGGLE FOR LIBERTY"; and Emily's diary from 1941, with the entries addressed to "Nesan," her older sister, Naomi's mother. With this box Kogawa testifies to the complexity of history, the variety of its sources and languages. Naomi is overwhelmed by Emily's command to read everything at once, but she is also pointedly aware of all that the box does not contain. At the same time, it is critical that Emily claims the language of history and citizenship. *Obasan* is structured by maternal and domestic bonds, but it yields no territory to a privileged male sphere of power.

At the bottom of the box are two letters, written in Japanese, which Naomi cannot read. Those letters will not be read until novel's end, telling the terrible story of the fate of Naomi's mother, who had sailed for Japan with her mother to care for Naomi's great-grandmother just before the war began. As the boat sails in the fall of 1941, Naomi wonders: "In what marketplace of the universe are the bargains made that have traded my need for my great-grandmother's?" (80). Kogawa's maternal genealogy suggests the complicated nature of the domestic even before war intervenes, strained by the competing responsibilities of mother and daughter and the distance between the familial homes of Japan and Canada. These are personal, not nationalist, loyalties. Naomi's mother and grandmother seem to move within a continuous domestic space, from family home to family home at a gendered remove from the nationalist discourse of borders and war. But the letters tell of the ultimate obliteration of this understanding of the domestic: " 'Though it was a time of war,' Grandma writes, 'what happiness there was to hear from my niece Setsuko in Nagasaki' " (282). The happy narrative of visiting Setsuko and the birth of a baby girl who looks like Naomi is overshadowed by the terrible promise of the name "Nagasaki." The sustaining narrative of birth and familial continuity is obliterated with the blast. Amid the wrecked homes of her niece's neighborhood, Naomi's grandmother does not at first even recognize the naked, "utterly disfigured" woman with the maggot-filled wounds as her own daughter (286). Naomi had long imagined her mother trapped in Japan after the war by either a faceless government bureaucracy or an ailing mother. The bomb combines political coercion and personal obligation with its inhuman force and its indiscriminate violence. Naomi's mother and grandmother stay in Japan, with the baby girl, now four and dying of leukemia, but also clearly unwilling, even if they were able, to return home with the war's violence written so graphically on their bodies.

Naomi's own experience testifies to the fact that North America was not as separate from the war's violence as her mother might have hoped or most histories assume. The violence of the atomic bomb is of a scale that defies comparison. But Kogawa's complicated narration of war's intrusion into domestic space makes such connections meaningful. When Naomi first asks Obasan about the letters in Japanese, her aunt offers her an old picture of Naomi as a child of two or three holding onto her mother's leg. "Here is the best letter." As she looks at the picture, Naomi animates its images, recalling her mother's touch, the intimate bodily connection to her grandmother, and an intense feeling of loss, which she invests in the memory of the house in which her family lived. "The house then—the house if I must remember it today, was large and beautiful" (60). The comfort of the Vancouver house stands in vivid contrast to Obasan's house, filled with old newspapers, cracked teacups, underwear pinned and repaired over and over again. "It is more splendid than any house I have lived in since. It does not bear remembering. None of this bears remembering" (60).

Emily presses Naomi to remember Slocan, the ghost town they were sent to when exiled from British Columbia. "[I]t must have been hell in the ghost towns," Emily sympathizes, but she was not there, having been able to move to Toronto instead (220). Slocan certainly marks a place of impoverishment, in which Naomi grows up confused by the continuing absence of her parents, but there is still a sense of family and community. Emily does not seem to understand that the worst time was after the war when Naomi's family and the other "evacuees" were barred from returning to British Columbia and sent to work in the beet fields of Alberta, "our exile from our place of exile" (236). In Emily's box Naomi finds a grotesque newspaper clipping featuring a photograph of a "Grinning and Happy" family. The article attests that "Jap Evacuees Best Beet Workers." In this headline the "race words," which John Dower notes are also "war words," show their third critical feature as "labor words." "There is a word for it," Naomi asserts in anger: "Hardship" (232). Postwar life in a chicken coop with no insulation from the cold or the heat, no protection from bugs, and covered with dust offers no "home" and obliterates the distinctions between public and private, between men and women, as surely as the bomb, if less suddenly.

It is only in the realm of the domestic that the political and economic, as well as intensely personal implications of this history can be fully registered. The home left behind, the home built, the home destroyed: this is the true history of immigration and war. *Obasan* is exemplary in its voicing of what Homi Bhabha has called the "unhomely," in which "the border between home and the world becomes confused; and, uncannily, the private and public become part of each other, forcing upon us a vision that is as divided as it is disorienting. . . . The unhomely is the shock of recognition of the-world-in-the-home and the-home-in-the-world."[29]

Set in a small West Virginia town, Jayne Ann Phillips' *Machine Dreams* is the farthest removed of these novels, geographically and culturally, from the Pacific coast. War sends the men west; the father Mitch serves in the Pacific in World War II and son Billy goes to Vietnam where he is lost, "missing in action." The war experiences of father and son are presented as structurally parallel, in chapters of "War Letters" in which each man writes home from the alien landscape of the Pacific. Phillips underscores the similarity of the two wars by beginning each chapter with an excerpt from army propaganda, first about the treacherous Japanese enemy and then about the superiority of American firepower in Vietnam. Official racism and faith in technology come together, as *Obasan* demonstrates, in the bombing of Hiroshima and Nagasaki. The "machine dreams" motif which runs throughout the novel does not explicitly invoke the atomic bomb, but it combines the destructive and optimistic elements of Cold War culture in fantasies that recast home and family into the landscape of war. Structurally and symbolically, Phillips builds the narrative continuity between World War II and Vietnam, even while the parents, Mitch and Jean, voice the familiar understanding of the wars as inherently different.

The most important historical and symbolic connection predates World War II. Amid the farmers and miners of rural West Virginia, Mitch is raised by an aunt whose husband has a "good job" working for the railroad: "A railroad uniform in the '20s had almost as much respect as military dress."[30] The railroad forges the critical link between the American heartland of small-town life and the distant Pacific, joining as well the narrative of domestic settlement and war in the Pacific. In the 1940s Mitch rides the railroad to California when shipping out to war. But during the twenties the railroad brings the Pacific to West Virginia in the person of Li Sung, a Chinese railroad employee who is found to have leprosy. The B&O railroad finally places Li Sung on a plot of isolated land near Mitch's home and advertises for "a widow" to bring meals out to the leper. Mitch's aunt Ava takes the job. Although not a widow, she has just lost a child and has been unable to keep house, lost in grief and depression. The plight of the leper speaks to Ava, and finally her husband "signed a paper saying he allowed the endangerment of his wife and family and would not hold the railroad accountable" (36). A fragile relationship between Ava and Li Sung is forged. Across the barriers of language and the distance they enforce because of the disease, they share their individual losses. Leprosy forms a vivid symbol of the distance between Li Sung and the American domestic life which Ava embodies. Yet, her world is not as naturally isolated and removed from the larger world as the ideology of separate spheres would claim. Her yard is bounded by the railroad, and her house shakes each time a train passes by, making her fear for her children. Her freedom to work outside the house is granted by a contract between her husband and the railroad. Again, the scale of her isolation does not compare to Li Sung's, but their relationship is another unhomely "shock of recognition of the world-in-the-home and the home-in the-world," and of the Pacific as a crucial site of that interpenetration.[31] Only by seeing her loss, the death of her child, mirrored in the larger world that Li Sung represents can Ava reclaim her own domestic role.

The implications of this personal, domestic connection expand profoundly when Li Sung dies and the men of the town go to bury him and burn the shack. Ava had given Li Sung some of her husband Eban's old clothes, but no one had ever seen him wear them. When Eban enters the cabin he is startled by the image of his clothes carefully sewn onto Li Sung's blankets, "the sleeves of the shirts and the trouser legs spread out like one body on top of another" (41). Eban's uncanny recognition of himself layered over the alien Chinese figure of Li Sung makes visible the repressed dependency of his role as a "railroad man" on Chinese labor. This link is destroyed once again when the shack burns, but it begets another uncanny return twenty years later when Mitch is stationed in the Pacific. Mitch dreams of Li Sung "walking toward me on the tarmac strips we laid in New Guinea" (53). The dream of Li Sung and building the landing strip becomes, in turn, intermixed with the terrible memory of using a bulldozer to bury the decaying bodies of Japanese soldiers. The vulnerability of flesh and the power of machines are at the heart of the various dreams that all the characters have in the novel. The United States and the Pacific, at home and at war, the body at labor and at war become confused. Mitch tries to end this confusion and put it all right by taking what he learned about construction in the war and building a business, a home, and a family. None of this offers the permanence promised by the spectacle of total victory. His marriage finally ends when Jean refuses to give him money out of her teacher's salary to build a bomb shelter. Ten years later Billy jumps out of a helicopter in Vietnam, never to be seen again. As Li Sung learned during the harsh winter, there is no safe place, no home separate from violence and dislocation.

With Billy gone, this legacy passes to his sister Danner, but it has really been hers, as sister, all along. When Billy is drafted, Danner urges him to resist the war and leave the country, to flee to Canada. She actively works in the antiwar movement and with veterans' groups. She measures the comfort of American life against the deprivations of the Vietnamese people. Danner seizes the forms of political protest associated with Aunt Emily in *Obasan,* but once again, "getting out of the house" cannot on its own save the home under threat. Whereas Billy's machine dreams attach themselves to planes and cars, to apparent signs of real power and possibility, Danner's are invested in the radio and the uncanny possibility of disembodied travel across long distances. She recognizes the seductive fantasy of the machine and acknowledges at some level that she is doomed to sit, watch, and listen as Billy runs too close to its inhuman power. Danner ultimately leaves home, literally and figuratively rejecting the traditions of domesticity and patriotism inherited from World War II, but she recognizes the Pacific as the boundary which continues to shape her life: "My parents are my country, my divided country. By going to California, I'd made it to the far frontiers, but I'd never leave my country. I never will" (386). The novel ends on this implicit note of challenge to reimagine home and nation, domestic and foreign, and the war stories which define their boundaries.

The connection suggested in *Machine Dreams* between the history of Chinese labor in the United States and war in the Pacific is at the heart of Maxine Hong Kingston's *China Men.*[32] Kingston likewise insists on the recurrent connections between World War II and the Vietnam War, but makes explicit the much longer history of war in the Pacific. As the narrator surmises at the beginning of the book's final chapter, "The Brother in

Vietnam," "There was always a war whether I knew it or not" (264). The narrator pronounces this fact while rehearsing her earliest memories, beginning with her panicked confusion as a young child at a war movie. It is hardly surprising that "The Brother in Vietnam" begins with the spectacle of World War II movies—many if not most memoirs of the war begin figuratively or literally with them. But unlike the Vietnam War memoirs of Ron Kovic or Philip Caputo, Kingston's novel presents World War II movies not as the ideological opposite of Vietnam, but as its violent and senseless prefiguration.

It is telling that not only the last chapter, "The Brother in Vietnam," but the first, "The Father from China," begins with memories of World War II. "Father," she begins, "I have seen you lighthearted." These opening memories are taken from the summers of "The War," when the father amused his children by turning captured dragonflies into airplanes and killing "Hitler moths"—games played on a front porch reached after walking through the Chinatown of Stockton, California, past "the Japanese's house, nobody home for years, and the Filipino Lodge" (12). Kingston's memory of playing war games echoes even as it recasts the nostalgic glow of World War II in the Cold War childhoods described by Kovic and Caputo. For Kingston and her father, however, killing Hitler does not offer the same promise of an identity centered in a moral and global order. At the beginning of the book, Kingston renarrates World War II as a story of fathers and daughters enacted within a neighborhood in which the geography of American military and economic hegemony in the Pacific is carried home—a history powerfully suppressed by the narrative of killing Hitler.

This choice of a beginning, the when and where which will lead to the brother in Vietnam, is critical. *China Men* offers a deeply canny countertext, in both form and substance, to the progressive, westward-moving narrative of American history. Just as the China men move backwards across the geography of American history, traveling east to the American West, so Kingston insistently challenges the naturalized relation of events across time. The popular American narrative of "killing Hitler" begins and ends in the Pacific, moving from Pearl Harbor to Hiroshima, but the centrality of Asia is curiously displaced by the spectacular evil of Nazism which emblematizes the fascism held to be the cause of World War II. In *China Men*, however, the war in Asia never ends. " 'The War,' I wrote in a composition, which the teacher corrected, 'Which war?' There was more than one" (276).

"The War" in *China Men* is continuous across space as well as time. The "home front" quite literally crosses the Pacific. The narrator's VJ-day souvenir photo of the atomic bomb is juxtaposed with the return of the "one family of AJA's, Americans of Japanese ancestry, on our block" (273). The narrator and her siblings suspect the family of hidden crimes, like those of wartime propaganda, but understand her parents' acts of generosity toward them: "We would want them to be nice to us when the time came for us Chinese to be the ones in camps" (274). Stated in the terms of childish misunderstanding, Kingston here marks the schizophrenic terms in which the narrator is made to understand her difference from and connection to other Asians. That this sense of connection derives equally from racist coercion and the communal bonds of experience only intensifies the paradoxical place Kingston narrates through irony. Growing up as a Chinese-American girl during the Cold War, the narrator becomes increasingly aware of the fraught relation between public and private, us and them, here and there. "For the Korean War, we wore dog tags. . . . our dog tags had *O* for religion and *O* for race because neither black nor white. Mine also had *O* for blood type. Some kids said *O* was for 'Oriental,' but I knew it was for 'Other,' because the Filipinos, the Gypsies, and the Hawaiian boy were *O*'s" (276). As the Cold War "comes home," the coercive categories of American identity continue to reinforce the alienated status of Asian Americans.

When the brother is drafted into the Vietnam War, these conflicted terms of identification come to crisis. Ironically, the antiwar movement's critique of the imperial nature of American economic as well as military power seems to diminish her brother's sense of possibility. "In a country that operates on a war economy, there isn't much difference between being in the Navy and being a civilian. When we ate a candy bar, drank grape juice, bought bread (ITT makes Wonder bread), . . . we were supporting the corporations that made tanks and bombers, napalm, defoliants, and bombs. . . . Everything was connected to everything else and to war" (284). As both an American and the child of Chinese immigrants, the brother is always already connected to the war in Vietnam. Burdened by this recognition that the war is everywhere and everything, the brother joins the Navy, retracing the routes of immigration and war, making port in the Philippines, Korea, Taiwan, and Hong Kong. The brother maps with heavy heart the imperial history which binds him to his impossibly compromised place. His story becomes one of deferment and denial, resolutions about what he will not do rather than what he will. "He would not shoot a human being; he would not press the last button that dropped the bomb" (285). He rationalizes that in the Navy he was "only coming a few miles physically closer to Vietnam, and his job of flipping switches and connecting circuits and typing was the same as on land, the numbers and letters were almost the same" (296).

The narrator is both understanding and critical, I believe, of her brother's plight and place. The complex interconnection of past and present, Asia and the United States, war and everyday life is one of the fundamental lessons of *China Men*. While this understanding of the imperial nature of American society as radically diffuse should involve the brother and sister equally, it does not. The brother is literally conscripted into his impossible place in history. The narrator's "I" disappears from the chapter once she drops her brother off for induction. The dispassionate account of her brother's internal struggles both respects the particularity of his place and subtly marks his failure to either voice or enact his opposition to the war. But, more important, the narrator does not write herself back into the war story. She does not describe her place on the "home front": writing letters, following the news, supporting her family, or performing any of the other typical duties of women during war. Kingston refuses to place women in the recuperative place of home which gives meaningful shape to both war and empire. In naming the last of the China men "brother" rather than "son," Kingston transforms the shape of this history, bringing the concept of genealogy, as Said argues, to a critical rather than coercive end. But in having the sister tell the brother's story, Kingston, like Phillips, insists on challenging the role that gender plays. In *China Men* the "unnaturalized" relation of family and nation tremendously complicates the ability to locate the boundaries of the American empire, even as the history of exclusion and citizenship, immigration and war becomes the narrative's recurrent text and context.

Joan Didion's *Democracy* is written out of the moment which most radically counters the victorious narrative of World War II, the fall of Saigon. As Didion warns the reader, "This is a hard story to tell" (15). *Democracy* is a story of privileged, wealthy, powerful people who are actively engaged in politics and business across the Pacific. The main character, Inez Christian Victor, is the daughter of an old colonial family in Hawaii, whose corporation, "Chriscorp," continues to wield great influence across the Pacific. She is married to a senator, Harry Victor, who is dedicated to becoming president. Her lover, Jack Lovett, is a CIA or CIA-connected operative who is very busy in the spring of 1975 flying in and out of Southeast Asia. Inez lives at, or at least very near, the center of power which the characters of the other novels never see. The fall of Saigon, however, marks a vivid loss of power for such men and institutions—a loss they try to deny. Didion brings this loss home by plotting instead the loss of familial control. Two crucial, and largely inexplicable, events form the central action of the novel: the murder of Inez's sister Janet by their apparently insane father, and Inez's daughter Jessie's trip to Saigon in the spring of 1975. The two events are and are not meaningfully connected. Jessie goes to Vietnam instead of going to Janet's funeral, but she does not go to Vietnam because Janet was shot. The relation between these events is neither causal nor simply coincidental. It is, as Didion maintains all human behavior to be, "circumstantial" (186)—confined by the possibilities of time and place; in other words, subject to history. Didion's focus on women characters, specifically women enacting roles as wives, mothers, and daughters, deepens this understanding of the "circumstantial." The presence of Inez, her sister Janet, or daughter

Jessie at historically significant places and times is quite literally "beside the point." They are not in Jakarta, or Saigon, or Kuala Lumpur to shape events the way their husbands and lovers and fathers are. But neither is their presence purely coincidental. It is the adjacency of events, the fact that Janet's murder and Jessie's disappearance make headlines alongside the fall of Saigon, that Didion forces to our attention. The perversity of these events frustrates our novelistic desire for cause and effect even as it challenges us to imagine the meaning of their relation.

Didion presses this point by making Harry and Inez's daughter Jessie rather than Jack Lovett the literal point of connection between the Christian and Victor families and the collapse of South Vietnam. Jessie, Didion tells us, is "the crazy eight in this narrative," the sign that as narrator, she, like Jack Lovett shuttling across the Pacific, no longer has "time for the playing out" (164). The day after Janet is shot, eighteen-year-old Jesse checks herself out of a drug rehabilitation program in Seattle, talks her way onto a transport flight and then through customs in Saigon with a driver's license and a fake press card, looking for one of the "cinchy jobs" a guy from Boeing had told her about. She finds one at the American Legion club. As "crazy eight" Jessie figures the peculiar randomness of the American evacuation from Saigon, a randomness which resulted from an entrenched disbelief that it would happen. But the logic of the Seattle/Boeing/Vietnam connection is anything but random. Jessie is attaching herself to a very real "trade route." This is part of the reason that Jessie's perverse escapade is not figured with the same dismissive irony as is her twin brother Adlai's "vigil for peace." There is a certain respect in the novel for Jessie's radical disengagement from her family and the world's preoccupations.

Inez comes to a more self-conscious but equally radical sense of disengagement while reading news stories "about Harry Victor's relatives" in the reception room of the American embassy in Hong Kong:

> In the *South China Morning Post* she read that Harry Victor's wife had not been present at the funeral of Harry Victor's sister-in-law, a private service in Honolulu after which Senator Victor declined to speak to reporters. In the Asian edition of the *International Herald-Tribune* she read that Harry Victor's father-in-law had required treatment at the Honolulu City and County Jail for superficial wounds inflicted during an apparent suicide attempt with a Bic razor. In the international editions of both *Time* and *Newsweek* she read that Harry Victor's daughter was ironically or mysteriously missing in Vietnam.
>
> "Ironically" was the word used by *Time,* and "mysteriously" by *Newsweek.*
> (191–92)

At stake is not simply the insufficient rationale for Jessie's actions, but the presumption that Harry Victor's daughter should not be part of the "playing out" of American policy in Vietnam, a policy which Harry both failed to significantly shape and capitalized on in his career as a politician. In the U.S.-centered view of the media, it is "ironic" or "mysterious," that is, completely unexpected, that Jessie should be subject to "the convulsions of history" in Southeast Asia. The stories presume that Jessie and her mother should be at her father's side. But as Janet's fate suggests, the father is no guarantee of safe haven. As daughter, Jessie marks this immersion in history more powerfully than, for example, a differently plotted novel might have done by making her twin brother Adlai subject to the draft. Jessie's plot is less about the hypocrisy of politicians who either waged or allowed a war in which privilege disproportionately exempted their own children, than about the more fundamental presumption of a home which is not subject to imperatives beyond individual—specifically the father's—control.

Inez becomes increasingly detached from her family while reading about them in the third person from Hong Kong. Gender is crucial to appreciating the hollowness of Harry Victor's claim to centrality, but so is geography. From Asia, Harry and his presidential aspirations to lead the free world appear increasingly irrelevant as a context for rendering events meaningful. But it is Inez's understanding of familial rather than more properly political relations which ultimately transforms her view of the world. When Inez hears the final evacuation message from Saigon, the playing of "White Christmas" and the message to phone home, she comes to the intensely personal understanding that none of the people in her family should "be exempted from the general movement. Just because they believed they had a home to call. Just because they were Americans" (208). Inez finds herself unable to "grasp her own or their uniqueness, her own or their difference, genius, special claim" which should differentiate them from the rest of the world which on that night "was full of people flying from place to place and fading in and out" (208). The loss of the "special claim" of family and nation erodes the naturalized assumptions of an "us" and a "them" on which the logic of war, empire, and racism all crucially depend.

Inez's response is to "give up the American exemption" and move to Kuala Lumpur, where she goes to work as director of a refugee camp. Inez and the novel end in a space that "existed only as the flotsam of some territorial imperative," a space at best tangentially connected to the maps and plots of the United States (228). The overlapping sense of narrative and political containment which Inez exceeds with this move is quite literal. She is inaccessible to the narrator's attempts to bring her into the story. "I could not call Inez and say that I just happened to be in Kuala Lumpur" (215–16). Geography, more than character, determines narrative in *Democracy*, the plausibility of being in a given place at a given time. Like Jessie's trip to Vietnam or Paul's murderous visit to Janet's home, from a certain familiar perspective it is both ironic and mysterious that "a woman who had once thought of living in the White House was flicking termites from her teacup and telling me about landing on a series of coral atolls in a seven-passenger plane with a man in a body bag" (228). That events in the White House can effect the dislocations of hundreds of thousands of people in Southeast Asia is a commonplace acknowledgment. Didion's strategy of using a privileged American woman to make that connection is not.

There are no "real" refugees in *Democracy:* no depictions of displaced Vietnamese, Cambodians, Montagnards, or Hmong. Didion does not humanize the refugees' plight by imagining an individual character to represent the unimaginable numbers: 1.5 million Southeast Asian refugees over twenty years.[33] Didion eschews this liberal gesture, presenting instead the structural accommodation of mass displacement: refugee camps situated "en route nowhere," worthy only of the occasional sidebar news item. Indeed, it is Inez rather than the plight of the refugees who brings Didion as narrator and character to Kuala Lumpur to search out the end of the story. Although Inez is described as "having many of the traits of a successful refugee," she does not stand in for the displaced peoples of Southeast Asia. Rather, Inez's self-exile marks war and empire as narratives and realities which exceed the domesticated patterns of American lives. Inez remains a figure of privilege, but she has recentered that privilege within the global realities of "having and not having" rather than in the self-satisfied presumption of American dominion (211).

The trajectory of these readings has moved insistently beyond the boundaries of the domestic as both familial and national space, to increasing levels of engagement with Asia. In conclusion I want to look briefly at Anna Deavere Smith's performance piece *Twilight: Los Angeles, 1992* for the ways in which it explicitly reframes the classic domestic (that is, black and white) problem of American race relations in the multi-ethnic, multi-racial, explicitly international and Pacific landscape of contemporary Los Angeles. In *Twilight* Smith performs a series of monologues drawn from her interviews with people about the urban unrest which rocked Los Angeles when four white policemen were acquitted in the beating of black motorist Rodney King. Most pointedly, Smith deals with the looting of Korean-owned businesses and the violence between African Americans and Korean Americans as a new feature of the racial landscape of Los Angeles.

In her preface Smith argues that "few speak a language about race that is not their own."[34] Language about race takes many forms. Smith notes that each character involves an embodied presence which is far greater than the words alone. Gesture, tone, diction, and pitch all inflect "language about race." In some ways the concept of a foreign language seems too simple a metaphor for something as illusory as race. But when Smith speaks in the

voice of Chung Lee, President of the Korean-American Victims Association, her phonetically rendered Korean makes all language uncanny. One
wonders if this language is understandable to Korean speakers and thus to
anyone? In the printed text Lee's speech is accompanied by a translation:

> gunyang da ijen, o,
> p'okttong-i nassunikkani,
> mulgoni gocchok waitta goredo urin
> gogi-e dehan-gon hanna
> miryonhanna an-gajottagu

> Well now, uh. . . .
> I realized then that the riot had begun,
> so even though our stuff was thrown out there,
> we decided to give up
> any sense of attachment to our possessions. (83–84)

Language becomes one of the "attachments" Smith must give up here. Even
if through a perfect phonetic repetition she could be understood to be
speaking Korean, she cannot herself understand what she is saying except
in the translation. A nationalist attachment is given up here as well—she is
pressing her "search for American character," the subtitle of her larger project, outside those safe domestic boundaries of knowing, having, and being.

But it is critical to realize that it is not only in Korean drag that Smith is
forced out across the Pacific in order to re-imagine the landscape of home.
Many of the monologues contain such crossings, but two are particularly striking. One is Elaine Brown, the former head of the Black Panther Party, who returns again and again to the history of American "interventions" in foreign
countries to frame the possibilities for armed resistance in the United States:

> But if you are talking about a war
> against the United States government,
> then you better talk to Saddam Hussein
> and you better talk to the Vietnamese people
> and the Nicaraguans
> and the El Salvadorans
> and the people in South Africa
> and people in the other countries in Southeast Asia
> and ask those motherfuckers about
> what this country is capable of doing. (230)

Here the line between foreign and domestic is dissolved by force of arms.
Brown passionately insists that it is only in relation to these past wars, particularly in Asia and Central America, wars which sent thousands of
refugees into Los Angeles, that the place of African Americans in that city
can be understood.

One last voice could not be more different, that of a wealthy white Hollywood agent, who struggles to explain the sense of panic and guilt which swept through the privileged enclave of Beverly Hills when word of the rioting reached there. Struggling to explain the competing sense of danger and unreality, the agent hits upon the perfect metaphor:

The vision of all these yuppies
and aging or aged yuppies,
Armani suits,
and, you know,
fleeing like
wild-eyed . . .
All you needed was Godzilla behind them,
you know,
like this . . .
Chasing them out of the building,
that's really it. (138)

Here Godzilla serves as the trivialized metaphor for race panic. This is a highly ironic return of the American atomic violence against Japan which gave birth to the monster. It is also an unconsciously canny metaphor for white self-victimization. But only in a world in which the United States is understood to be as isolated as Beverly Hills can such presumptions operate with impunity. Godzilla is a perfect emblem of the "unhomely," the displacement of home and world "in an unhallowed place."[35] So too, Smith's performances, which cross gender, ethnic, racial, linguistic, and class boundaries, refuse to stay comfortably at home. The expansive domestic novels of Kogawa, Phillips, Kingston, and Didion chart similarly transformed geographies, discovering an America in which Asia not only can but must be imagined as partaking.

NOTES

1. Joan Didion, *Democracy* (New York: Vintage, 1984). All further references are cited in the text.

2. See M. Consuelo Leon W., "Foundations of the American Image of the Pacific," *boundary* 2 21 (Spring 1994), 17–29; and John Carlos Rowe, "Melville's *Typee*: U.S. Imperialism at Home and Abroad," in *National Identities and Post-Americanist Narratives*, ed. Donald Pease (Durham, NC: Duke University Press, 1994), 255–78.

3. Susan Jeffords, *The Remasculinization of America: Gender and the Vietnam War* (Bloomington: Indiana University Press, 1989).

4. Lisa Lowe, *Immigrant Acts: On Asian American Cultural Politics* (Durham, NC: Duke University Press, 1996), 8.

5. Ibid., 6.

6. Ibid., 11.

7. Elaine Scarry, *The Body in Pain* (New York: Oxford University Press, 1985), 82.

8. Of the 25,851 Americans who fought on Iwo Jima, 6,821 were killed, died of wounds, or were missing at the end of the thirty-six days of battle. Of the estimated 22,000 Japanese soldiers on the island, only 1,083 survived. Bill Ross, *Iwo Jima* (New York: Vintage Books, 1986), xiii–xiv.

9. John Dower, *War Without Mercy: Race and Power in the Pacific War* (New York: Pantheon Books, 1986), 11.

10. Ibid., 148.

11. Ibid., 152. See also Richard Slotkin's reading of the Custer myth just before and during World War II, *Gunfighter Nation: The Myth of the Frontier in the Twentieth Century* (New York: HarperCollins, 1993), 313–43.

12. Robert Westbrook, " 'I Want a Girl, Just like the Girl That Married Harry James': American Women and the Problem of Political Obligation in World War II," *American Quarterly* 42 (December 1990), 595.

13. Ibid., 599.

14. Westbrook includes these illustrations but offers no readings of them (560).

15. Elaine Tyler May, *Homeward Bound: American Families in the Cold War Era* (New York: Basic Books, 1988).

16. See George H. Roeder, Jr., *The Uncensored War: American Visual Experience During World War II* (New Haven: Yale University Press, 1993), 43–66. Kaja Silverman's reading of *It's a Wonderful Life* underscores the disjunctions which had to be minimized between the traumatic male narrative of war and the female narrative of domesticity; see *Masculinity at the Margins* (New York: Routledge, 1992), 90–106.

17. Michael Rogin, " 'Make My Day!' Spectacle as Amnesia in Imperial Politics" *Representations* 29 (Winter 1990), 108.

18. John Hersey, *Hiroshima* (1946; New York: Vintage Books, 1989), 8.

19. See Edward T. Linenthal and Tom Engelhardt, eds. *History Wars: The Enola Gay and Other Battles for the American Past* (New York: Henry Holt, 1996), 9–62.

20. Anne McClintock, " 'No Longer in a Future Heaven': Gender, Race, and Nationalism," in *Dangerous Liaisons: Gender, Nation, and Postcolonial Perspectives*, ed. Anne McClintock, Amir Mufti, and Ella Shohat (Minneapolis: University of Minnesota Press, 1997), 93.

21. Edward Said, *Beginnings: Intention and Method* (Baltimore: Johns Hopkins, 1975), 48.

22. Benedict Anderson, *Imagined Communities: Reflections on the Origin and Spread of Nationalism* (New York: Verso, 1991), 25–36.

23. Said, *Beginnings,* 152, 162.

24. Ibid., 66.

25. McClintock, " 'No Longer,' " 90.

26. Ibid., 90.

27. For a discussion of the significance of race and ethnicity in *Bataan,* see my "Cold Wars: Black Soldiers in Liberal Hollywood," forthcoming, in *War, Literature, and the Arts.* Susan Jeffords argues that the interracial bond is integral to the "remasculinizing" function of Vietnam War narratives. See *The Remasculinization of America,* 54–58. Two exceptions to the rule that Asian Americans are not included in the symbolic platoon are Samuel Fuller's iconoclastic film of the Korean War, *The Steel Helmet,* which features a Nisei medic, and the television show *Tour of Duty,* which also includes an Asian-American medic. *Go for Broke,* the film about the

442nd, the Japanese-American unit that fought in Europe, suggests how crucial the experience of the internment of Japanese Americans was to this absence from popular representations of the war.

28. Joy Kogawa, *Obasan* (New York: Anchor Books, 1994), 39. All further references are cited in the text.

29. Homi K. Bhabha, "The World and the Home," in *Dangerous Liaisons,* ed. McClintock, Mufti, and Shohat, 445.

30. Jayne Ann Phillips, *Machine Dreams* (New York: Simon and Schuster, 1984), 34. All further references are cited in the text.

31. Bhabha, "World and the Home," 445.

32. Maxine Hong Kingston, *China Men* (New York: Vintage Books, 1989). All further references are cited in the text.

33. Lily Dizon, "For Thousands of Refugees, Return to Vietnam Looms," *Los Angeles Times* (June 26, 1996), A9.

34. Anna Deavere Smith, *Twilight: Los Angeles, 1992: A Search for American Character* (New York: Anchor Books, 1994), xxv. All further citations appear in the text.

35. Bhabha, "World and the Home," 445.

Syllabus PACIFIC AMERICA
>   War, Memory, and Imagination
>   *Instructor: Katherine Kinney*

This class considers the importance of the Pacific and Asia in twentieth-century American conceptions of nationalism and culture, particularly in relationship to war. For the first half of the course we will consider a variety of historical moments and cultural icons—Captain Cook, Madam Butterfly, the atomic bomb, and war memorials—which mark the frequently militarized place of Asia in American national memory and imagination. In the second half of the course, we will turn to the war novel as a national form, moving from Norman Mailer's classic World War II work, *The Naked and the Dead,* to four novels by women which challenge the gendered boundaries of war narratives and the nation. We will consider how these novels plot the imagined relationship of home to battle, the U.S. to Asia and the Pacific, domestic to foreign, and past to present. We will end with Anna Deavere Smith's performance piece about civil unrest in Los Angeles, *Twilight,* which "searches for American characters" within a multiracial, multinational, and Pacific-American landscape.

Each student will be asked to complete a midterm "Image Project" in which they will trace the repetition of a single image of Asia and/or the Pacific in American popular culture. Each student must consult at least five different *kinds* of sources. These could include the Internet, your local shopping mall, a grocery store, travel brochures, magazines, newspapers, toys, movies, television, or maps. The project can take the form of a collage, a visual essay, a website, or any other visual format. Other requirements will include frequent informal writing exercises, midterm and final exams, and a ten-page final essay.

HISTORICAL MOMENTS AND CULTURAL ICONS

Week 1   Across the Pacific: The United States and Asia

We will read short selections from the following:

John Ledyard, *The Journal of Captain Cook's Last Voyage to the Pacific in Quest of the Northwest Passage*

Thomas Jefferson on the China Trade

Alfred Thayer Mahan, *The Influence of Sea Power on History* (1890; reprint Dover, 1987)

William B. Gatewood, ed., *"Smoked Yankees" and the Struggle for Empire: Letters from Negro Soldiers, 1898–1902* (letters from the Philippines; University of Illinois Press, 1971)

Walt Whitman, "Facing West from California's Shores," and "Passage to India," in *Leaves of Grass*

Joan Didion, "Letter from Paradise, 21° 19' N., 157° 52' W." in *Slouching Towards Bethlehem* (Farrar, Straus, and Giroux, 1990), 187–204

Week 2   War Memorials: Iwo Jima; the Vietnam Veterans Memorial; the *Enola Gay;* The Vietnam Women's Memorial; The Other Vietnam Memorial

Karal Ann Marling and John Wetenhall, from *Iwo Jima: Monuments, Memories, and the American Hero* (selections; Harvard University Press, 1991)

Beyond the Wall (CD ROM on Vietnam Veterans Memorial; Magnet Interactive Studios, 1995)

Maya Lin: A Clear Strong Vision (dir. Freida Lee Mock, 1994)

James Tatum, "Memorials of the American War in Vietnam," *Critical Inquiry* 22 (summer 1996): 634–78

Philip Nobile, ed., *Judgment at the Smithsonian* (Marlowe and Co., 1995)

David Yoo, "Captivating Memories: Museology, Concentration Camps, and Japanese American History," *American Quarterly* 48 (December 1996): 680–99

Week 3   Bikinis and Great Balls of Fire: The Bomb and Popular Culture

The Atomic Cafe (dir. Kevin Rafferty, Jayne Loader, and Pierce Rafferty, 1982)

Elaine Tyler May, *Homeward Bound: American Families and the Cold War* (Basic Books, 1998)

Robert Westbrook, " 'I Want a Girl, Just Like the Girl That Married Harry James': American Women and the Problem of Political Obligation in World War II," *American Quarterly* 42 (December 1990): 587–615

Weeks 4 and 5   *Madam Butterfly* as National Narrative

David Belasco, *Madam Butterfly*

David Henry Hwang, *M. Butterfly* (Penguin, 1989)

China Gate (dir. Samuel Fuller, 1958)

Alain Boublil and Claude-Michel Schonberg, *Miss Saigon* (sound recording; Geffen, 1990)

Selections from Gina Marchetti, *Romance and the "Yellow Peril"* (University of California Press, 1993); Dorrine Kondo, *About Face: Performing Race in Fashion and Theater* (Routledge, 1997); Traise Yamamoto, *Masking Selves, Making Subjects: Japanese-American Women, Identity, and the Body* (University of California Press, 1999); John Dower, *War Without Mercy: Race and Power in the Pacific War* (Pantheon, 1986)

THE WAR NOVEL AND THE IMAGINED NATION

Week 6   Men without Women

Norman Mailer, *The Naked and the Dead* (Henry Holt, 1998)

Week 7   Women and Children First
   Joy Kogawa, *Obasan* (Anchor Books, 1994)

Week 8   The Nuclear Family
   Jayne Ann Phillips, *Machine Dreams* (Simon and Schuster, 1984)

Week 9   "Everything was connected to everything else, and to war."
   Maxine Hong Kingston, *China Men* (Vintage Books, 1989)

Week 10   Reimagining the Nation
   Anna Deavere Smith, *Twilight: Los Angeles, 1992: On the Road: A Search for American Character* (Anchor Books, 1994)

Making Comparisons

First Contact, Ethnocentrism, and Cross-Cultural Communication

Steven Mailloux

Despite all his efforts, Kirk's scorn broke through, "And you consider yourself Plato's disciples!"

The comment amused Parmen. "We've managed to live in peace and harmony for centuries, Captain."

Spock's voice was icy. "Whose harmony? Yours? Plato wanted beauty, truth and, above all, justice."

"Plato's Stepchildren," *Star Trek*

"That's rhetorical nonsense."

Zefram Cochrane on the legendary story about his invention of warp drive, *Star Trek: First Contact*

The new American Studies is going radically comparativist. In John Rowe's words, it combines two models, one which "stresses the 'comparative American cultures' within the multiculture of the United States and another that allows us to situate domestic 'multiculturalism' within international, transnational, and potentially post-national contexts."[1] That is, the two dimensions of this new Comparative American Studies are internal and external to the cultural practices located within the geopolitical boundaries of the United States. Internally comparativist: such an interpretive project displaces traditional American exceptionalism and replaces misleading tropes of national homogeneity with an analytic framework comparing not only separate ethnic U.S. cultures but different versions of cultural hybridity.[2] Externally comparativist: this project includes examinations of "views from abroad," comparing domestic American Studies with its foreign "translations" throughout the world, focusing on both the interpretive content and the political function of American Studies as a research field and pedagogical subject outside the U.S. Finally, any post-nationalist American

Studies emerging out of this doubly comparativist model will redefine the nation-state as a factor in cultural production and reception; it will relocate this explanatory category in comparative relation to the intersection of other categories such as race, class, generation, religion, ethnicity, and gender.[3]

In this essay I examine the theoretical problem of *comparison* that is so central to this future American Studies and address the topic of making comparisons within and across different cultures. I am especially interested in questions of transcultural comparison related to attempts at cross-cultural communication. I begin with the problematic neopragmatism of Richard Rorty, especially suspect in its renewed American exceptionalism yet quite useful for describing comparisons made within cultural politics. His theoretical talk of how to interpret and evaluate alien practices leads me to some specific rhetorical analyses of intercultural contacts. The issue of making comparisons between cultures raises the question of the hermeneutic status of such comparisons and the political position of any future comparativist. My examples throughout are chosen more to clarify a theoretical problem than to illustrate a critical or historical practice. That is, I offer here an argument for theorizing cultural comparison rather than a model for doing Comparative American Studies.[4]

I

In "Cosmopolitanism without Emancipation," Rorty writes as a confident (some would say self-satisfied), Euro-American, liberal pragmatist:

> We look forward, in a vague way, to a time when the Cashinahua, the Chinese, and (if such there be) the planets which form the Galactic Empire will all be part of the same cosmopolitan social democratic community. . . . The Chinese, the Cashinahua, and the Galactics will doubtless have suggestions about what further reforms are needed [in our institutions], but we shall not be inclined to adopt these suggestions until we have managed to fit them in with our distinctively Western social democratic aspirations, through some sort of judicious give-and-take.[5]

There are two aspects to Rorty's particular brand of ethnocentrism—political and hermeneutic—and though they are logically separable, they intersect in significant ways. A useful theoretical take on the inevitably ethnocentric nature of comparison cannot be easily distanced from a certain questionable political attitude toward that inevitability. Indeed, as I will later show, Rorty's political attitude is partially constitutive of the comparisons he makes. But first we must distinguish more clearly between Rorty's political and hermeneutic ethnocentrisms.

On the one hand, Rorty reinstates a certain American exceptionalism by expanding his earlier claim that Western political institutions are the best we humans have been able to come up with in the history of the world.[6] He now combines this political ethnocentrism with a rather blatant and nonironic nationalist championing of U.S. patriotism.[7] That is, Rorty began with a Deweyan story about how continued reform of our social democratic institutions offers the best hope for humanity's future, but he has transformed this heartening tale into a scolding rebuke of the academic left for being too negative in demanding further reforms of these same institutions. In the face of a widening gap between rich and poor, recent retrenchments in welfare state policy, attacks on affirmative action, promotion of anti-immigrant legislation, evacuation of public support for higher education and the arts, and continued criticism of "tenured radicals," progressive U.S. intellectuals might find it hard to agree with Rorty's new American exceptionalism, worrying instead that it might give unintended support to those cultural forces in our nation that do not see or would rather not address the deep political injustices and social inequities enabling the progress Rorty celebrates. In fairness to Rorty, I should note that he is not one of those who fails to acknowledge these national and global problems. However, what I'm calling his political ethnocentrism can easily be seen as contributing to the problems rather than to their solutions. The pragmatic question is which cultural politics would be most strategically useful right now in achieving reforms within U.S. society: intensive critique and constant pressure for improvement or Rorty's optimistic political ethnocentrism that can be easily appropriated to resist systemic change?[8]

In contrast to his problematic political ethnocentrism, I find more valuable Rorty's neopragmatist arguments for the inevitability of what might be called hermeneutic ethnocentrism. This form of ethnocentrism lies behind Rorty's claim that we will evaluate any suggestions made by the Cashinahua, the Chinese, and the Galactics from within our own web of beliefs, desires, and practices. Intercultural comparisons of value develop as intracultural negotiations among members of our own community. When we meet up with alien practices, verbal and nonverbal, we ultimately interpret and evaluate such foreign practices domestically by troping and arguing within our own culture as we name, describe, and compare these practices. I can test the viability of this hermeneutic ethnocentrism by comparing these claims to cases involving those beings Rorty here declares as "other."

Some preliminary considerations will ease the way. Who is the "we" in Rorty's formulations? At least one answer to this often-asked question is that "we" (in contradistinction to "them") refers to those who at particular times and places self-identify as such. For example, the Cashinahua of Eastern Peru sometimes identify themselves with the Brazilian Cashinahua as a "we" across national boundaries, despite the isolation of their individual villages and regardless of their very different histories. It is the "we" of the Cashinahua that speaks when a villager uses the words *huni kuin* ("real man, Cashinahua") as opposed to *huni betsa* ("other man, outsider").[9] But the use of such identifiers—for example, the "we" assumed in kinship groupings—varies in relation to social context, cultural domain, and historical circumstance (Kensinger 142–46, 283, n. 1). Similarly, the "we" in Rorty's ethnocentrisms must always be understood as sociohistorically specific and politically contingent. Especially in the multiculture that is the United States, this "we" needs to be specified in each claim made about the politically or hermeneutically ethnocentric act under discussion.

To specify a "we" contextually on a case-by-case basis is to acknowledge its potential heterogeneity and historical fragility. Any "we" is potentially a temporary construction, the result of immediate, negotiated, or even imposed identifications. But the same is true of the "they" that each "we" posits. Others may be read as belonging to homogeneous groups, even as "they" disidentify and refuse the unity or otherness imposed upon them. These historical inclusions and exclusions defining a community illustrate another point often raised against Rorty: Where is his recognition of uneven power relations among participants in his inter- and intra-cultural conversations? It now seems rather uncontroversial to acknowledge that any identification preceding or during an interpretive act necessarily involves power relations among interpreting agents and between interpreters and the subjects interpreted. The new American Studies is especially adept at foregrounding these relations in its various multicultural, intersectional, and global analyses.

II

In the "Captain's Holiday" episode of *Star-Trek: The Next Generation,* the captain of the USS *Enterprise,* Jean-Luc Picard, demonstrates how comparative studies are alive and well in the twenty-fourth century. On Stardate 43745.2, Picard takes along various books for "light reading" during his vacation on the pleasure planet Risa; these include James Joyce's *Ulysses* and Ving Kuda's *Ethics, Sophistry, and the Alternative Universe.* Picard's comparativist interest in reading texts written in languages different from his own first one (French) and his possible intention to compare literature and philosophy are symptoms of his larger comparativist perspective: comparing the differences among alien cultures. As the Captain's voice-over opening each episode explains: "Space. The final frontier. These are the voyages of the Starship *Enterprise.* Its continuing mission: to explore strange new worlds, to seek out new life and new civilizations, to boldly go where no one has gone before." And what is it that one does with these new worlds, new forms of life, new civilizations, if not at first compare them?

This is a kind of Galactic Comparative Studies, a grander version of the kind of the Comparative Cultural Planetology practiced briefly by Immanuel Kant in his early treatise, *Universal Natural History and Theory of the*

Heavens.[10] Eschewing "levity" and "free flights of fancy," Kant included an essay of "comparison, based on the analogies of nature, between the inhabitants of the various planets" (Kant 182–83). Here he speculated that "thinking natures . . . become more excellent and perfect in proportion to the distance of their habitats from the sun" on the "planets from Mercury to Saturn, or perhaps even beyond" (Kant 189–90). Comparative American Studies is a more limited version of this planetary and galactic comparativism, a local, terran variety that has a long and distinguished ancestry in Western civilization.

The title of Picard's second book of "light reading" reminds us of one ancient group within this comparativist lineage. During the late fifth century B.C.E., there prospered in Athens some well-paid aliens, travelers among the Greek city-states, practitioners of sophistry. The most famous of these was Protagoras, a self-proclaimed Sophist, whose teachings derived from the comparisons he made of the differences among the alternative communities he had visited. His treatise *On Truth* (or *Refutations*) might appropriately be called his version of *Ethics, Sophistry, and an Alternative Universe.* The first sentence of this treatise, all that has survived, translates into English as: "Humans are the measure of all things, things that are that they are, things that are not that they are not." This human-as-measure maxim was a theoretical statement generalizing from Protagoras' observations that different communities he visited had different customs, laws, indeed, different ethical systems and views of truth. That is, his Sophistic view was that the values of truth, goodness, justice, and so forth are completely relative to particular communities. There are no absolutes. Protagoras was a contemporary of Socrates, whose student Plato passionately opposed the relativism of the Sophists. Plato's antirelativist position is summarized perhaps most clearly in a passage from his last work, *Laws* (716c): "In our view it is God who is pre-eminently the 'measure of all things,' much more so than any 'human,' as some say."

The question relevant here to any comparative cultural studies can be stated as follows: Is the comparative measure of all things (like truth and justice) found in some transcendental domain outside every human community and historical contingency; or, as the Sophist Protagoras would have it, is humanity, particular historical communities or even individuals, the measure of all things? Are cross-cultural comparisons (of truth, goodness, justice, beauty) transcendentally absolute or sociohistorically relative? One might say that the opposed answers to this question separate two long traditions of Western thought, which have been characterized in various ways: good philosophy that defends absolute truth versus bad rhetoric that relativistically argues for many truths. That is, Western intellectual history has continually restaged this conflict between relativism and absolutism, mere opinion and true knowledge, sophistry and platonism, antifounda-tionalist rhetoric and foundationalist philosophy.[11] The economic and po-litical stakes of this intellectual conflict become vividly manifest at different times and places, such as in the United States during the so-called Culture Wars of the nineties.[12]

Moreover, understanding the intellectual traditions manifest in these cul-tural battles reveals the shape of our particular hermeneutic ethnocentrism, demonstrating how our ongoing theoretical disputes are themselves part of the more general set of Western beliefs limiting and enabling our under-standing of non-Western philosophical traditions. Take the third group posited as other in the Rorty passage quoted above: the Chinese. In *The De-velopment of the Logical Method in Ancient China,* Hu Shih brings his Western education to bear on the early history of Chinese philosophy, referring to the sixth century B.C.E. as the "age of the Sophists." He uses the word *Sophists* "merely for lack of a better term" and because this group of early Chinese thinkers "resembles . . . closely those Greek Sophists with whom we have been made familiar through the Platonic Dialogues."[13] Teng Shih, for ex-ample, "taught the doctrine of the relativity of right and wrong, and em-ployed inexhaustible arguments."[14] Hu Shih describes the "founder" of Tao-ism, Lao-Tze, as "the greatest of all the Sophists . . . the Protagoras of Ancient China" (13). This Western analogizing of Eastern thought illus-trates the way comparisons are hermeneutically ethnocentric, but it also sug-gests the complicated relation between the "us" and "them" of cross-cultural interpretation, as Chinese-born Hu Shih's "we" appears to refer to those Western-educated readers of Plato who were trained, as he was at Cornell and Columbia, in the European philosophical tradition. Indeed, it is not too much of a stretch to say that, despite differences in national identification and generational affiliation, Hu Shih and Richard Rorty speak, in the in-stances I have quoted, the same "we" of Western philosophy, even down to the fact that both were powerfully influenced by the work of John Dewey.[15]

Any comparison of differing truth claims, ethical values, philosophical traditions—that is, any comparison of cultural productions from different communities—inevitably faces the questions of who is right?/who is wrong? or what is better?/what is worse? To answer these questions of com-parative value necessarily involves measuring the couple to be evaluated against something else called a standard or criterion. Comparing two de-mands a third, a measure against which or according to which the two are compared. On this requirement, the necessity of having a standard against which two things are measured, both Protagoras and Plato were agreed. They simply, and significantly, disagreed over the status of the measure: for the Protagorean Sophist the measure is relative to community; for the Pla-tonic philosopher it is absolute. For the relativist, the value of any person, action, or text is measured by communal standards; for the absolutist, the standard of value transcends any historical community.

Some postmodernists would challenge the need (or currently the possibility) of any preexistent measure guiding comparative judgment. Lyotard argues, for example, that judgments must now take place without prior criteria, with judges developing standards as their judgments proceed on a case-by-case basis.[16] Furthermore, judges can at times simply fail to rule justly, not only because rules are violated within the relevant language game but also because of the incommensurability of the parties' phrases. When radically different phrases, or language games, or cultures come into conflict, judgments cannot always be made on the model of litigation, in which the competing claims of two parties can be fairly compared and adjudicated. Instead, sometimes a *differend* is produced: "A case of differend between two parties takes place when the 'regulation' of the conflict that opposes them is done in the idiom of one of the parties while the wrong suffered by the other is not signified in that idiom."[17] Lyotard's claim for the differend—the incommensurability of phrases—has been extended by some into a claim for the radical incommensurability of cultures. In this extension of the differend notion, some cultures simply cannot be comparatively evaluated, and certain cultures cannot in principle ever communicate with each other because of their incommensurable beliefs and practices. At first Rorty might be expected to agree with this take on incommensurability, given his stand on hermeneutic ethnocentrism; that is, if communities are delimited by their ethnos in making interpretive comparisons, wouldn't a culture completely alien to that ethnos be incomprehensible, comparatively incommensurable, and thus impossible to communicate with? In fact, Rorty rejects such inevitable failure in communication, even in cases of contact between radically different cultures, as I will attempt to explain in the next section.

III

A Comparative American Studies could usefully employ cultural rhetoric as an interpretive focus. Studies of cultural rhetoric trace the movement of figural, suasory, and narrative energies across different sites of (what this essay might call) the cultural space-time continuum.[18] But I'm most interested here in those rhetorical exchanges that meet resistances across boundaries, borders that are difficult to traverse, especially those hermeneutic barriers between radically different cultures.

I will approach the special problems of cross-cultural communication by once again citing that twenty-fourth century comparativist, Captain Jean-

Luc Picard. In the "Samaritan Snare" episode, Stardate 42779.1, Picard is traveling by shuttle craft with young Ensign Wesley Crusher, who is on his way to take entrance exams for Starfleet Academy:

Picard: Did you read that book I gave you?
Wesley: Some of it.
Picard: That's reassuring.
Wesley: I just don't have much time.
Picard: There's no greater challenge than the study of philosophy.
Wesley: But William James won't be on my Starfleet exams.
Picard: The important things never will be. Anyone can be trained in the mechanics of piloting a starship. . . . It takes more. Open your mind to the past—art, history, philosophy—and all this may mean something.

William James is an excellent reading recommendation for any comparativist to have made. James's *Pragmatism* argues that when we read, measure, make sense of new things, alien worlds, our interpretations always involve in a very deep way the making of comparisons: comparisons of what we know with what we don't know. As James puts it, "New truth is always a go-between, a smoother-over of transitions. It marries old opinion to new fact so as ever to show a minimum of jolt, a maximum of continuity."[19] Establishing any new truth depends on a required traffic between old opinion and new experiences: facts, desires, contradictions, reflections, and so forth. Any new idea adopted as a true one "preserves the older stock of truths with a minimum of modification, stretching them just enough to make them admit the novelty, but conceiving that in ways as familiar as the case leaves possible." An entirely new explanation, one "violating all our preconceptions," not comparable to anything we already know, would, according to James, "never pass for a true account of a novelty" (35). All this is to say that the measure of all things new and old is indeed the human, and human measuring is from first to last comparative: it was in Plato's time, it is today, and it will be when our human ancestors boldly go where no one has gone before.

Rorty, then, is clearly following James in his own hermeneutic ethnocentrism, which might be rephrased as a claim that at any point in the space/time continuum, our own web of vocabularies, beliefs, and desires—the communal and individual subject/agents that we are—comprise the delimiting and enabling conditions of our comparative activities. We can never stand completely outside all cultural positions objectively comparing our ethnos with another alien one, but neither are we free to actualize any position whatsoever or convincingly make any comparisons we want through some imagined freedom of absolute relativism. We are "we" because of being positioned within a culture in a particular set of practices that empowers and constrains acts of interpretive and evaluative comparison. Recognition of this positionality is what I'm calling Rorty's hermeneutic ethnocentrism, which he sees as "an inescapable condition" that is "roughly synonymous with 'human finitude'."[20] Again, this recognition does not short-circuit comparative acts both inside and outside our culture; rather, it simply acknowledges that we all are comparativists from within our particular ethnos—a geographically and historically situated network of beliefs and desires, the contour of our particular version of "human finitude."

This network can and does change as various cultural comparisons are made within intra- and inter-cultural contacts. The specific shape of our hermeneutic ethnocentrism can be transformed; it always has a history and a future. Part of that shape includes sets of beliefs about and practices involving those understood as alien, not one of "us." As Rorty points out, many Western intellectuals now view with regret their communities' past military imperialism and with suspicion any current and future contacts that might result in cultural imperialism. This belief in prohibiting the forceful imposition of one culture's beliefs on another currently forms a significant defining characteristic of today's liberal democratic ethnos in the West. It is part of what Rorty admires about this ethnos, and thus it constitutes an aspect of his political ethnocentrism.

As Rorty recognizes, there is something quite circular about his version of this ethnocentrism. He criticizes cruder forms of politically ethnocentric activity that force our beliefs on other cultures. He values this anti-imperialist stance where he finds it within our Western culture and admits that this critical stance constitutes part of his story about why the Western democracies offer the best future for humanity. In other words, Rorty's political ethnocentrism in favoring his own culture consists partly of a belief that his culture's political ethnocentrism compares favorably to that of other cultures, but he realizes that this comparative judgment is a function of his own culture's hermeneutic ethnocentrism, its set of comparative practices that include the valuing of persuasion over force, verbal contest over physical conflict, rhetoric over war. Some might see this circularity as invidious, but Rorty sees it as necessary and unavoidable, and thus as simply to be accepted.

I happen to think that Rorty is theoretically correct—such ethnocentricity is, in some form, unavoidable—but that his attitude toward such inevitability is potentially dangerous, as I noted above. Progressive reform requires a more critical stance toward the political progress defining Rorty's story of the West. But there is another point to make here: Rorty's story assumes a difference between his culture and others that is difficult to support. Is the liberal West unique in valuing persuasion over force? Not according to many accounts of alien cultures. The Cashinahua, for instance, value influencing others primarily through example and indirect persuasion within their communities as much as Rorty's Western liberals and are even more adverse to aggressive behavior in general, whether verbal or physical (Kensinger, 46, 175–76).

Still, Rorty is right to argue that part of our own culture's history involves development of a greater and greater sensitivity to forms of military and cultural imperialism (at least in certain segments of our community), even if that sensitivity—as a version of valuing persuasion over force—is not unique to the liberal West.[21] Our ethnocentric beliefs now include a strong condemnation of certain cruder brands of political ethnocentrism. In the twenty-fourth century of the Star Trek universe, this ethnocentric wariness has evolved into the Prime Directive, Starfleet General Order #1 prohibiting interference in the normal evolution of alien cultures less technologically developed than the United Federation of Planets. Of course, what counts as "normal" or "less developed" is itself an interpretation based on a comparison made by the Federation within its own unavoidable hermeneutic ethnocentrism. This can be seen as another way in which political and hermeneutic ethnocentrisms are inextricably related.

The Prime Directive does not outlaw communication with life forms and civilizations considered equal to or more developed than the Federation. Indeed, first contact to establish such communication is a major aim of Federation starships exploring the galaxy. In what follows, I want to consider briefly an episode of first contact to make some final points about cross-cultural comparison and communication.

Stardate 45047.2: Captain Picard explains that "the *Enterprise* is en route to the uninhabited El-Adrel System. Its location is near the territory occupied by an enigmatic race known as the Children of Tarma." The Tarmarians, it seems, have been sending a subspace signal toward Federation space, and Starfleet has determined that this is an attempt at communication. The *Enterprise* has been sent to make first contact.

Well, not exactly first contact. According to Commander Data, the resident android historian and third in command of the *Enterprise,* "Federation vessels have encountered Tarmarian ships seven times over the past one hundred years. . . . However, formal relations were not established because communication was not possible." Why? "The Children of Tarma were called incomprehensible by Captain Sylvestrie of the Shikamaroo. Other accounts were comparable."

But Captain Picard is optimistic. He asks, "Are they truly incomprehensible? In my experience communication is a matter of patience, imagination. I would like to believe that these are qualities that we have in sufficient measure." The *Enterprise* then makes contact with a Tarmarian ship, and over the telescreen we see and hear the Tarmarian captain. He says to Picard: "Rai and Jiri at Lungha. Rai of Lowani. Lowani under two moons. Jiri of Ubaya. Ubaya of crossed roads. At Lungha. Lungha, her sky gray."[22] The *Enterprise* crew members respond with blank stares. The Tarmarian begins again: "Rai and Jiri at Lungha." Data observes: "The Tarmarian seems to be stating the proper names of individuals and locations." Picard asks bewildered: "Yes, but what does it all mean?" Data: "I'm at a loss, sir." Picard speaks back to the Tarmarian captain offering a "mutual non-aggression pact between our two peoples, possibly leading to a trade agreement and cultural interchange." Now the Tarmarians don't understand. "Shaka, when the walls fell," sighs the Tarmarian captain.

After being involuntarily transported to a nearby planet with the Tarmarian captain, Picard struggles to interpret the actions and sounds of the alien. Finally, after many failed attempts at communication and a few more Tarmarian expressions of "Shaka, when the walls fell," Picard's patience pays off as he uses his imagination to produce a rhetorical theory to make sense of the Tarmarian's actions and sounds. Picard: "That's how you communicate, isn't it? By citing example. By metaphor." Simultaneously, Data and Councillor Troi have come up with a fuller and more rhetorically exact account after viewing and reinterpreting a video replay of their unsuccessful first contact. Data summarizes: "The Tarmarian ego structure does not seem to allow what we normally think of as self-identity. Their ability to abstract is highly unusual. They seem to communicate through narrative imagery, a reference to the individuals and places which appear in their mytho-historical accounts." Councillor Troi adds: "It's as if I were to say to you 'Juliet on her balcony.' " Dr. Crusher: "An image of romance." Troi: "Exactly. Imagery is everything to the Tarmarians. It embodies their emotional states, their very thought processes. It's how they communicate and how they think." The crew's theory about the Tarmarians' language coincides with that of Picard's interpretation on the surface, where he uses that theory to accomplish what the crew cannot. Isolated with the Tarmarian captain on the planet, he is able "to learn the narrative from which the Tarmarians draw their imagery." Having said his last "Shaka, when the walls fell," the Tarmarian acknowledges Picard's interpretive breakthrough: "Sokath, his eyes uncovered," just before he gets mauled by the killing Beast of the planet and eventually dies.

Now, what exactly happened in this cross-cultural communication? Though I have probably not given enough details to establish my case, I suggest that Rorty's ethnocentric account works quite well here. In this view there is no absolute incomprehensibility between alien cultures, no impassable boundary permanently separating one culture from another's (at least partial) understanding. No community can be so different from another that cross-cultural communication is in principle forever doomed to fail. With every community that we recognize as a community, our form of life always overlaps significantly, for it is only against such a background of commonality that we can perceive radical difference. As Rorty puts it, adopting Donald Davidson's notion of radical interpretation, "this overlap in effect reduces the intercultural case to an intracultural one—it means that we learn to handle the weirder bits of native behavior (linguistic and other) in the same way that we learn about the weird behavior of atypical members of our own culture."[23] This is exactly the way the *Enterprise* crew figures out the rhetorical acts of the Tarmarians. Indeed, Picard's call for patience and imagination in intercultural communication is analogous to Davidson's comment rejecting the utility of formal theories of language in such contacts: "We cannot expect . . . that we can formalize the considerations that lead us to adjust our theory to fit the inflow of new information. . . . There is no saying [beforehand] what someone must know who knows the language; for intuition, luck, and skill must play as essential a role here as in devising a new theory in any field; and taste and sympathy a larger role."[24]

Patience, imagination, intuition, luck, taste, and skill are all used by the *Enterprise* crew and especially Picard to make sense of the Tarmarian speech acts. But, interestingly, part of the skill they employ is that of a cultural rhetorician, using a rhetorical vocabulary and theory from within their own culture to make sense of a foreign language and to enable them to translate it (at least partially) into their own idiom. Successful communication takes place by the development of a theory and its refinement in very much the way Davidson would have it, but in this case with an explicitly rhetorical twist.

My analysis here does not question that cross-cultural communication can be difficult; quite the contrary. But it does challenge certain notions about the incommensurability of cultures and rejects general claims that cross-cultural communication can ever be endlessly futile in principle. Differends are indeed possible, even probable, between radically different communities; but the existence of differends between discursive genres is not the same thing as the incommensurability of cultures necessarily and permanently preventing communicative success. Still, I must admit that Lyotard's differend analysis using the Cashinahua does imply a different account of the contact case I have just described, an account that questions both Picard's confident understanding of his communicative success and my own Davidsonian explanation of that success.

What if the Tarmarians were actually more like the Cashinahua than the *Enterprise* crew? What if Starfleet was wrong in interpreting the Tarmarians as attempting to communicate in the way that the *Enterprise* was always trying to do (in order to establish diplomatic relations, make economic and cultural treaties, etc.)? Lyotard suggests that the purpose of the Cashinahua's story-telling is just for the sake of telling a story. Any Cashinahua "having heard a story is bound to retell it, because to refuse to retell it would mean that he does not want to share, which is something that has a very derogatory name in Cashinahua and is a great abomination to them. In other words, someone speaks to me; he places me under an obligation. . . . The obligation to retell."[25] Perhaps the Tarmarians were not trying to communicate to achieve some later goal but were communicating, telling their stories, simply to fulfill their obligation to share, to tell their stories.

Furthermore, and perhaps Rorty would agree with Lyotard on this point, the very "we" of the ethnocentric act (of trying to communicate to make a treaty, of telling a story for its own sake, or of interpreting and eval-uating either attempt) is the "we" constituted and supported by the narra-tive told. "The Cashinahua narrator derives his authority from telling sto-ries in his name. But his name is authorized by his stories, and especially by those which recount the genesis of names." The "we" told and telling is the same "we" interpreting and evaluating the Other. Indeed, according to Ly-otard, "Narrative is authority itself. It authorizes an unbreakable *we*, outside of which there can only be *they*" ("Universal History" 321).[26] But we also can and do tell stories about the others outside, and the roles given them and the narrated events exemplify the hermeneutic ethnocentrism involved in first and subsequent contacts between different cultures. Again the Cashinahua provide a useful example when they interpret their first con-tact with Brazilian traders in terms of their traditional Inka mythology (Kensinger, 261).

The hermeneutic ethnocentrism of first contact narratives also applies to the narratives told about our own ancestors and descendants, including the stories that articulate our political hopes and fears. Here we return one final time to the relationship between hermeneutic and political ethnocen-trisms in Rorty's thought. A liberal narrative of the West's progress (includ-ing the desire to include more and more people within the "we") is one of Rorty's strong beliefs, and the narrative's positive evaluation (compared to other stories and desires) constitutes Rorty's political ethnocentrism.[27] But the valued story also functions as a strand in the web of beliefs, desires, and practices in and through which Rorty comparatively judges those who are not yet part of his ever-expanding "we"; that is, Rorty's own political ethno-centrism—and that of his community—is part and parcel of his hermeneu-tic ethnocentrism. This fusion of the two occurs in theory and practice. Theoretically speaking, ethnocentrism is unavoidable in cross-cultural comparisons. Practically, the particular shape any comparison takes in a specific case depends on the particulars of that case, including whether the cultural practices involved are those of Euro-American liberals, Peruvian Cashinahua, Taoist Chinese, or Tarmarian Galactics.

NOTES

1. John Carlos Rowe, "A Future for 'American Studies': The Comparative U.S. Cultures Model," in *American Studies in Germany: European Contexts and Intercultural Relations*, ed. Günter H. Lenz and Klaus J. Milich (New York: St. Martin's Press, 1995), p. 265.

2. See, for example, Lisa Lowe, *Immigrant Acts: On Asian American Cultural Politics* (Durham, NC: Duke University Press, 1996).

3. Examples of intersectional studies within U.S. cultural criticism are proliferating. For just one illustration within the new American Studies, see Robyn Wiegman, *American Anatomies: Theorizing Race and Gender* (Durham, NC: Duke University Press, 1995).

4. Of course the examples are not arbitrary; they emerge directly out of the same subject matter preoccupying a Comparative American Studies. Furthermore, the theory/practice split suggested here is overstated. I have elsewhere argued for a slogan that seems applicable to certain sections of the present essay: Use rhetoric to practice theory by doing history. See my *Reception Histories: Rhetoric, Pragmatism, and American Cultural Politics* (Ithaca, NY: Cornell University Press, 1998).

5. Richard Rorty, "Cosmopolitanism without Emancipation: A Response to Jean-François Lyotard," in *Objectivity, Relativism, and Truth* (Cambridge: Cambridge University Press, 1991), p. 212.

6. See, for example, Rorty, "On Ethnocentrism: A Reply to Clifford Geertz," in *Objectivity, Relativism, and Truth*, pp. 203–210.

7. Richard Rorty, "The Unpatriotic Academy," *New York Times*, 13 February 1994, p. E15. Also see his *Achieving Our Country: Leftist Thought in Twentieth-Century America* (Cambridge, MA: Harvard University Press, 1998).

8. But my either/or question here undoubtedly suggests a misleadingly simple picture not only of Rorty's coalition politics but also of its various possible receptions across the ideological spectrum. See, for example, Bruce Robbins, "Sad Stories in the International Public Sphere: Richard Rorty on Culture and Human Rights," *Public Culture* 9 (Winter 1997): 209–32; Mark Reinhardt, "Classless and Casteless," *The Nation* (27 April 1998): 29–32; and Richard J. Ellis, "Achievement Gap," *National Review* (22 June 1998): 60–61.

9. Kenneth M. Kensinger, *How Real People Ought to Live: The Cashinahua of Eastern Peru* (Prospect Heights, IL: Waveland Press, 1995), pp. 91, 260; hereafter cited in text. See also Susan Montag, *Diccionario Cashinahua*, 2nd ed. (Yarinacocha, Perú: Instituto Lingüístico de Verano, 1981), p. 158.

10. Immanuel Kant, *Universal Natural History and Theory of the Heavens*, trans. Stanley L. Jaki (Edinburgh: Scottish Academic Press, 1981). I coin this term for Kant's cosmological speculations by modeling it on the developing contemporary field of Comparative Planetology, the systematic study of similarities and differences among planets in our solar system—a field most recently in the news during the 1997 Mars Pathfinder mission. For the rhetorical context of Kant's cosmology, see Steven J. Dick, *Plurality of Worlds: The Origins of the Extraterrestrial Life Debate from Democritus to Kant* (Cambridge: Cambridge University Press, 1982); and Michael J. Crowe, *The Extraterrestrial Life Debate, 1750–1900: The Idea of a Plurality of Worlds from Kant to Lowell* (Cambridge: Cambridge University Press, 1986).

11. See Samuel Ijsseling, *Rhetoric and Philosophy in Conflict: An Historical Survey,* trans. Paul Dunphy (The Hague: Martinus Nijhoff, 1976); and Stanley Fish, "Rhetoric," in *Doing What Comes Naturally: Change, Rhetoric, and the Practice of Theory in Literary and Legal Studies* (Durham, NC: Duke University Press, 1989), pp. 471–502.

12. For just one example in which Platonic philosophy and Sophistic rhetoric are explicitly cited in the Culture Wars between traditional universalist humanism and cultural critique/poststructuralist theory, see the public statements made by Lynne V. Cheney, chair of the National Endowment for the Humanities under Presidents Reagan and Bush: Cheney with Bernard Knox, "A Conversation with Bernard Knox," *Humanities* (May - June 1992): 36; cf. Lynne V. Cheney, *Telling the Truth: Why Our Culture and Our Country Have Stopped Making Sense—and What We Can Do About It* (New York: Simon & Schuster, 1995). For more general background, see John K. Wilson, *The Myth of Political Correctness: The Conservative Attack on Higher Education* (Durham, NC: Duke University Press, 1995); and Steven Mailloux, ed., *Rhetoric, Sophistry, Pragmatism* (Cambridge: Cambridge University Press, 1995).

13. Hu Shih, *The Development of the Logical Method in Ancient China* (1922; reprint New York: Paragon, 1963), pp. 10–11; subsequently cited in text.

14. *Lieh Tze,* 6, quoted in Hu, *Logical Method,* p. 12.

15. See Hu Shih, "Hu Shih," in *Living Philosophies* (New York: Simon and Schuster, 1933), p. 252; and Richard Rorty, "Trotsky and Wild Orchids," *Common Knowledge* 1 (Winter 1992): 146–47.

16. Jean-François Lyotard and Jean-Loup Thébaud, *Just Gaming,* trans. Wlad Godzich (Minneapolis: University of Minnesota Press, 1985), pp. 26–29. In light of my essay's own comparisons, I'd like to note in passing an interesting analogy that Lyotard implies in this section of *Just Gaming.* It goes something like this: In ethics and politics, the Sophists' notion of opinion-based judgments challenges Plato's theory of the model Idea just as the Cashinahua's heteronomous narrativity challenges Kant's theory of the autonomous will.

17. Jean-François Lyotard, *The Differend: Phrases in Dispute,* trans. Georges Van Den Abbeele (Minneapolis: University of Minnesota Press, 1988), p. 9.

18. On cultural rhetoric studies, see William E. Cain, ed., *Reconceptualizing American Literary/Cultural Studies: Rhetoric, History, and Politics in the Humanities* (New York: Garland Publishing, 1996).

19. William James, *Pragmatism: A New Name for Some Old Ways of Thinking* (1907; reprint Cambridge, MA: Harvard University Press, 1978), p. 35. Hereafter cited in text.

20. Richard Rorty, "Introduction: Antirepresentationalism, Ethnocentrism, and Liberalism," in *Objectivity, Relativism, and Truth,* p. 15.

21. There is also the issue of whether Rorty's story of Western progress remains convincing when the distinction between physical force and verbal persuasion gets challenged. See the brief exchange between Lyotard and Rorty, which follows the original French publication of their essays cited in notes 5 and 26: "Discussion entre Jean-François Lyotard et Richard Rorty," *Critique* 41 (May 1985): 581–84. (I am grateful to Brook Thomas for reminding me about this problem with Rorty's story.)

22. My transcription of the Universal Translator's translation of the Tarmarian language has been checked against the helpful "Darmok Dictionary" compiled by Raphael Carter (http://www.wavefront.com/~raphael/darmok/darmok.html).

23. Richard Rorty, "Inquiry as Recontextualization: An Anti-Dualist Account of Interpretation," in *Objectivity, Relativism, and Truth,* p. 107.

24. Donald Davidson, "Communication and Convention," in his *Inquiries into Truth and Interpretation* (Oxford: Oxford University Press, 1984), p. 279.

25. Lyotard and Thébaud, *Just Gaming,* 35.

26. Jean-François Lyotard, "Universal History and Cultural Differences," trans. David Macey, in *The Lyotard Reader,* ed. Andrew Benjamin (Oxford: Basil Blackwell, 1989), p. 321. Lyotard notes the gendered roles of the Cashinahua narrator and audience: "All males and prepubertal girls can listen," but "only men can tell stories" (p. 320). Such gendering, of course, complicates further the constitution of the ethnocentric "we."

27. See Richard Rorty, "Solidarity or Objectivity?" in *Objectivity, Relativism, and Truth,* pp. 21–34, and his *Contingency, Irony, and Solidarity* (Cambridge: Cambridge University Press, 1989), p. 198.

Syllabus MAKING COMPARISONS

Instructor: Steven Mailloux

The new American Studies has made a strong comparativist turn. This course examines several of the theoretical issues surrounding the practice of making comparisons in such a revisionist field. In particular we will look at comparisons made within and across different geopolitical communities, cultural traditions, professional disciplines, and historical periods. We will begin with an overview of a Comparative American Studies and then focus on the theoretical and political problems of comparison such a study might face as it develops. We will then move through a series of examples of making comparisons that simultaneously attempt several tasks: highlighting the theoretical problems we have raised about comparative interpretations and evaluations (incommensurability, ethnocentrism, relativism); suggesting various American Studies topics pertinent to a comparative focus (first contact and cross-cultural communication); and examining several comparativist practices, borrowing from strategies of comparative method within different disciplines.

TOPICS AND READINGS

Comparative American Studies

John Carlos Rowe, "A Future for 'American Studies': The Comparative U.S. Cultures Model." In *American Studies in Germany: European Contexts and International Relations*, ed. Günter H. Lenz and Klaus J. Milich (New York: St. Martin's Press, 1995), pp. 262–78.

Günter H. Lenz, "Toward a Dialogics of International American Culture Studies: Transnationality, Border Discourses, and Public Culture(s)," *Amerikastudien/American Studies* 44 (1999): 5–23.

Cultures of United States Imperialism, ed. Amy Kaplan and Donald E. Pease (Durham, NC: Duke University Press, 1993).

Theorizing Comparisons

Frederick Douglass, *Narrative of the Life of Frederick Douglass*.

Jean-François Lyotard, "Universal History and Cultural Difference." In *The Lyotard Reader*, ed. Andrew Benjamin; trans. David Macey (Oxford: Basil Blackwell, 1989), pp. 314–23.

Richard Rorty, "Cosmopolitanism without Emancipation: A Response to Jean-François Lyotard." In *Objectivity, Relativism, and Truth* (Cambridge: Cambridge University Press, 1991), pp. 211–22.

Comparative Anthropology I: Cross-Cultural Communication

Between Languages and Cultures: Translation and Cross-Cultural Texts, ed. Anuradha Dingwaney and Carol Maier (Pittsburgh: University of Pittsburgh Press, 1993).

Frances Karttunen, *Between Worlds: Interpreters, Guides, and Survivors* (New Brunswick: Rutgers University Press, 1994).

Comparative Anthropology II: A Case Study

Bartolomé de Las Casas, *Very Short Account of the Destruction of the Indies.*

Lewis Hanke, *Aristotle and the American Indians: A Study in Race Prejudice in the Modern World* (Bloomington: Indiana University Press, 1959).

Anthony Pagden, *The Fall of Natural Man: The American Indian and the Origins of Comparative Ethnology* (Cambridge: Cambridge University Press, 1982).

Philosophical Anthropology

E. E. Evans-Pritchard, *Witchcraft, Oracles, and Magic Among the Azande* (Oxford: Oxford University Press, 1937).

Peter Winch, "Understanding a Primitive Society," *American Philosophical Quarterly* 1 (October 1964): 307–24.

Charles Taylor, "Rationality." In *Philosophy and the Human Sciences* (Cambridge: Cambridge University Press, 1985), pp. 134–51.

Multiculturalism: Examining the Politics of Recognition, ed. Amy Gutmann (Princeton: Princeton University Press, 1994).

Comparative Philosophy and Rhetoric

Plato, *Protagoras, Gorgias.*

David A. Dilworth, *Philosophy in World Perspective: A Comparative Hermeneutic of the Major Theories* (New Haven: Yale University Press, 1989).

George A. Kennedy, *Comparative Rhetoric: An Historical and Cross-Cultural Introduction* (New York: Oxford University Press, 1998).

Comparative Cultural Planetology

Steven J. Dick, *Plurality of Worlds: The Origins of the Extraterrestrial Life Debate from Democritus to Kant* (Cambridge: Cambridge University Press, 1982).

Mark Rose, *Alien Encounters: Anatomy of Science Fiction* (Cambridge, MA: Harvard University Press, 1981).

"Plato's Stepchildren" (*Star Trek*); "Darmok" (*Star Trek: The Next Generation*).

Comparative History

George M. Fredrickson, *Black Liberation: A Comparative History of Black Ideologies in the United States and South Africa* (New York: Oxford University Press, 1995).

Comparative Literature

Comparative Literature in the Age of Multiculturalism, ed. Charles Bernheimer (Baltimore: Johns Hopkins University Press, 1995).

Comparative Cultural Politics I: Multiple Public Spheres

The Phantom Public Sphere, ed. Bruce Robbins (Minneapolis: University of Minnesota Press, 1993).

The Black Public Sphere: A Public Culture Book, ed. The Black Public Sphere Collective (Chicago: University of Chicago Press, 1995).

Lisa Lowe, *Immigrant Acts: On Asian American Cultural Politics* (Durham, NC: Duke University Press, 1996).

Comparative Cultural Politics II: Culture Wars and the University

PC Wars: Politics and Theory in the Academy, ed. Jeffrey Williams (New York: Routledge, 1995).

After Political Correctness: The Humanities and Society in the 1990s, ed. Christopher Newfield and Ronald Strickland (Boulder: Westview Press, 1995).

English Studies/Culture Studies, ed. Isaiah Smithson and Nancy Ruff (Urbana: University of Illinois Press, 1994).

Race, Nation, Equality

Olaudah Equiano's Interesting Narrative and a Genealogy of U.S. Mercantilism

David Kazanjian

After I had been sailing for some time with [Capt. Thomas Farmer, an English-man], I at length endeavoured to try my luck and commence merchant. . . . Thus was I going all about the islands upwards of four years, and ever trading as I went, during which I experienced many instances of ill usage, and have seen many injuries done to other negroes in our dealings with whites.

> Olaudah Equiano, *The Interesting Narrative of the Life of Olaudah Equiano, or Gustavus Vassa, the African*

I take the liberty, Mr. Chairman, at this early stage of the business, to introduce to the committee a subject . . . that requires our first attention, and our united exertions. No Gentleman here can be unacquainted with . . . the impotency which prevented the late Congress of the United States from carrying into effect the dictates of gratitude and policy. The union, by the establishment of a more effective government, having recovered from the state of imbecility that heretofore prevented a performance of its duty, ought, in its first act, to revive those principles of honor and honesty that have too long lain dormant. The deficiency in our Treasury has been too notorious to make it necessary for me to animadvert upon that subject. Let us content ourselves with endeavouring to remedy the evil. To do this a national revenue must be obtained; but the system must be such a one, that, while it secures the object of revenue, it shall not be oppressive to our constituents. Happy is it for us that such a system is within our power; for I apprehend that both these objects may be obtained from an impost on articles imported into the United States.

> James Madison, *Annals of Congress*

On July 4, 1789, four months into its first session, the U.S. Congress celebrated thirteen years of formal U.S. independence by passing its first tariff bill. The bill placed duties of 5–15 percent on approximately thirty different goods, ranging from nails to carriages, with the highest rates reserved for "articles of luxury."[1] When James Madison proposed this "endeavour"

with the first nonprocedural words uttered in the new Congress,[2] he represented the tariff as a means of restoring the lost unity of the nation, as my
epigraph to this essay indicates.[3] For Madison, "The deficiency in our Treasury" threatens the "union" with disintegration into the implicitly plural
and antagonistic realm of the Representatives' "constituents." In response,
he calls the Representatives' "first attention" and "united exertions" to a national economic policy. However, Madison suggests that this tariff will do
more than fill the treasury; it is precisely a *national* policy because it
promises to transform these potentially plural and antagonistic "constituents" into united subjects abstracted from their particularities and antagonisms and represented as formally equivalent units of a national population—units he elsewhere calls "citizens" who will engage in lively
economic exchange.[4]

In the words of Massachusetts Representative Fisher Ames, as he con-
curred with Madison on the floor of the House: "Good policy and sound wis-
dom demonstrate the propriety of an interchange between the different
States of the Union: to procure this political good, some force was necessary.
Laying a small duty upon foreign manufactures must induce . . . one fellow
citizen to barter with, or buy of another, what he had long been accustomed
to take from strangers."[5] These "fellow citizens" are, as with Madison, equated
on the formal and abstract basis of rational economic exchange. That is, the
fellowship of these citizens only exists to the extent that they are rationally abstracted from their particularities and antagonisms. According to Ames, the
tariff will help "force" that rational abstraction, and forge that equivalence.

Yet Ames also discloses that one particularity is, paradoxically, a precon-
dition for such abstract equivalence: a nationally particular "union" differentiated from "strangers" and the "foreign." Pennsylvania Representative
Thomas Fitzsimons, another Madison ally in April of 1789, echoes Ames:

> The merchants of this country have . . . succeeded in discovering one [chan-
> nel] that bids fair to increase our national importance and prosperity, while
> at the same time it is lucrative to the persons engaged in its prosecution. I
> mean, sir, the trade to China and the East Indies. I have no doubt but what
> it will receive the encouragement of the general government for some time
> to come. There is scarcely any direct intercourse of this nature, but what re-
> quires some assistance in the beginning: it is peculiarly necessary in our
> case, from the jealousy subsisting in Europe of this infant branch of our
> commerce.[6]

Fitzsimons argues for the tariff as a way to raise money to aid U.S. merchants in their battle with European merchants for colonial markets. Aid-
ing U.S. merchants with funds from the tariff becomes a way of securing
both the particularity of the United States as an aspiring imperial power
and, in turn, formal and abstract equality among increasingly empowered
and enriched U.S. citizens. Thus the formal and abstract equality among

citizens to which Madison, Ames, and Fitzsimons refer is itself dependent upon the differentiation of "America's" national particularity from the rest of the globe.

Since 1781, tariffs had been part of the economic policy of many of the States united under the Articles of Confederation, and before that they had been part of the economic policy of the British-American colonies.[7] As such, they were just one manifestation of an extensive system of economic nationalism known as "mercantilism." As I will discuss later in this essay, "mercantilism" refers to a system of political and economic policies and discourses, most popular in Europe and North America between the sixteenth and nineteenth centuries, meant to regulate trade within a territorially specific economy. Mercantilism can be thought of as a set of discourses and practices that gave a *national* shape to merchant capital at the beginnings of historical capitalism. Thus, as merchant capital flooded the Atlantic theater after the sixteenth century, European mercantilist measures emerged almost immediately to regulate that flood, to give it social and political shape. The Tariff of 1789 was simply the first such measure enacted by the Congress of this new territorial dominion known as the United States in response to the more recent flood of merchant capital into the North American theater in the late eighteenth century.

Less than one month after the passage of the Tariff of 1789, on August 1, 1789, Olaudah Equiano published *The Interesting Narrative of the Life of Olaudah Equiano, or Gustavus Vassa, the African* in London.[8] An account of his life from his birth in West Africa in 1745 to his experiences of capture, middle passage, slave labor, manumission, "free" labor, and antislavery agitation, the *Narrative* traces Equiano's attempts to tie fragments of his African past to the Euro-U.S. present forced upon him, and thereby to constitute a new identity. And yet each of those attempts proves fleeting, for each persistently threatens to collapse, to recoil on him and recode him as slave, as raced property. Persistently transgressing fixed or established institutional identities, Equiano just as persistently finds the space of transgression an unfixed and unstable one, a space occupiable for only a brief moment, if at all. Of these attempts, one of the most important, given the tenacity with which Equiano pursues it, has escaped sustained analysis.[9] This is his engagement in the transatlantic merchant marine trade; as he puts it in the passage given in my epigraph, "I at length endeavoured to try my luck and commence merchant" (E, 116; 84). Equiano's "endeavour" is precipitated by his exclusion from the very national "endeavour" that Madison, Ames, and Fitzsimons call forth. That is, many African diasporans like Equiano, who were racially barred from national citizenship, either left or refused to enter emerging racial nations such as the United States and sought freedom in the relatively mobile and ambiguously national space of the Atlantic.[10]

However, like many other black men who entered or were forced to enter the merchant marine trade in the late eighteenth and early nineteenth centuries, Equiano encountered an increasingly hostile terrain, signified by the "many instances of ill-usage" and "injuries done to other negroes in our dealings with whites" quoted in my epigraph. In the *Narrative,* when Equiano's transatlantic mercantile endeavors repeatedly confront such "instances" and "injuries," we begin to see the complex, *mutually constitutive* relationship among discourses and practices of abstract equality, racialization, and nationalism that marked the beginnings of capitalism in the Northern Atlantic (E, 116; 84).

In this essay I argue that Equiano's "instances" and "injuries" repeatedly bring him to a *racial-national limit* of mercantile capitalism and its promise of formal, abstract equality. That is, though he does deploy the practices of mercantile capitalism sufficiently to buy his freedom from slavery, and he does become relatively socially and financially secure, Equiano also encounters a definite point at which his access to formal and abstract equality is ritually barred, a point which he represents in national and racial terms. Equiano's repeated "instances" and "injuries" in the ambiguously national spaces of the Atlantic zone suggest that the iteration of a racial-national limit is actually constitutive of mercantile capitalism and its logic of formal, abstract equality. Equiano's text reveals that, rather than simply being excluded from this capitalist calculation of "freedom," black merchant mariners had to be ritualistically invoked as the limit of mercantile exchange for that exchange to maintain a racial-national coherence, and for formal and abstract equality to be sustained.

Furthermore, it is mercantil*ism* that Equiano encounters during these "instances" and "injuries." That is, mercantilist discourses and practices, such as the debate over the Tariff of 1789, as well as the tariff itself, had the cumulative effect of ritually invoking black merchants as the limit of mercantile exchange. Consequently, Equiano's text suggests that mercantilism can be understood as a set of discourses and practices that articulated formal and abstract equality with racial and national codification in the northern Atlantic during the late eighteenth and early nineteenth centuries. Finally, racial and national codification was neither an aberration from, nor a contradiction of, the principle of formal and abstract equality that animated modern citizenship under capitalism; rather, that principle was produced and sustained by the systematic iteration of hierarchically codified racial and national identities.

Such an argument is only possible, however, if we combine the literary-historical terms in which Equiano's narrative has been understood with the economic-historical terms in which mercantilism has been understood. In this essay, I offer one such hybrid interpretation of this textual and historical conjuncture. It is my hope that this interpretation is a specific, if lim-

ited, example of the interdisciplinary practice of American Studies that is
so important to a critical movement beyond the exceptionalist paradigm.

In the first part of this essay, I suggest that Equiano's text urges us to
consider how mercantilism worked to produce and to conjoin discourses
and practices of "equality," "race," and "nation" in the late-eighteenth-
century United States. In the second part, I consider how Marx's theory of
value opens up a critique of mercantilism's articulation of formal and abstract equality with racial and national codification. Finally, I return to
Equiano's text and examine its representation of this articulation in the
mercantilist conjuncture of the late-eighteenth- and early-nineteenth-
century Atlantic zone.

I. ON MERCANTILISM AND NATION FORMATION

In *Blues, Ideology, and Afro-American Literature—A Vernacular Theory,* Houston
A. Baker, Jr., inaugurates his epochal call for a "new American literary history" with an astute reading of the political economics of Olaudah Equiano's
Narrative.[11] Baker eschews the "traditional" guiding perspectives or, in Fou-
cauldian terms, "governing statements" of U.S. literary study—statements
such as "religious man," "wilderness," "migratory errand," "increase in store,"
and "New Jerusalem"—as well as the traditional canon of U.S. literary history.[12] Reading under a set of "new governing statements" such as the "economics of slavery" and "commercial deportation," Baker performs the work
of both critiquing the "traditional" perspective by exposing its veneer of self-
evidence, and displacing that perspective by pursuing another.[13] He summarizes his reading as follows: "[The *Narrative*'s] middle section represents an
active, inversive, ironically mercantile ascent by the propertied self from the
hell of 'commercial deportation' [i.e., the slave trade]. It offers a graphic 're-
invention' of the social groundings of the Afro-American symbolic act par
excellence. It vividly delineates the true character of Afro-America's historical origins in a slave economics and implicitly acknowledges that such economics *must be mastered* before liberation can be achieved."[14] Baker allows us
to see the *Narrative* not simply as a narrative of religious or existential self-
discovery and personal development, but rather as a text about the dynamic
and historically specific relationship between race and capital.[15]

Yet Baker's untroubled representation of the *Narrative* as an "Afro-
American" text imposes some crucial limits on his perspectival shift. While
William L. Andrews has called the *Narrative* an "Afro-English" text on the
grounds that Equiano spent much more time in England than he did in
the United States, other critics have stressed the national ambivalencies of
the text.[16] As Chinosole argues, "As a man who is marginal to many countries and cultures, including West African, West Indian, American, and
British, but as a man, most accurately, of the 'high seas,' Equiano assumes a

variety of voices for a variety of audiences. . . . Critics trying to decide which national literary canon owns Equiano's work miss his international importance."[17] Baker's challenge to the traditional canon of American literary history does not address the "Afro-English" aspects of the *Narrative* or the "international importance" to which Chinosole refers, and thus leaves the "American" in "American literary history" at least partially in its traditional place.

Paul Gilroy's "black Atlantic" framework has encouraged the study of such national ambivalencies. In the spirit of Baker's call, Gilroy proposes his own set of new governing statements or, in his words, "intermediate concepts, lodged between the local and the global, which have a wider applicability in cultural history and politics precisely because they offer an alternative to the nationalist focus which dominates cultural criticism."[18] Of particular importance to Equiano's text is Gilroy's emphasis on the under-examined role of "sailors, moving to and fro between nations, crossing borders in modern machines that were themselves micro-systems of linguistic and political hybridity."[19] Read in the context of Gilroy's project, Baker's representation of the *Narrative* as an exclusively "Afro-American" text would thus seem to be determined by the national framework of his project to refigure "*American* literary history."

In fact, on closer consideration even Baker's salutary reframing of the *Narrative* in political-economic terms is limited by his subtly nationalist perspective.[20] Throughout his reading, Baker uses the terms *mercantile* and *mercantilism* interchangeably. For instance, expanding on Equiano's "ironically mercantile ascent," Baker writes, "It is, ultimately, Vassa's[21] adept mercantilism that produces the conflation of a 'theory' of trade, an abolitionist appeal, and a report of African conjugal union that conclude *The Life of Olaudah Equiano*."[22] Baker seems to mean that Equiano's *mercantile*—that is, *commercial* in a general sense—endeavors can be read as complex, more-than-economic blendings of racial, sexual, and political "statements." However, Baker's use of the word *mercantilism* as if it meant mercantile trade in general obscures mercantilism's historically specific role in the formation of nations in the eighteenth and nineteenth centuries and, in turn, occludes much of the economic and historical specificity of the *Narrative*. Baker's failure to consider how Equiano narrates his mercantile encounters with mercantil*ism*—a political-economic system that helped to form nations—thus mirrors his failure to consider the *Narrative* not only as part of an African American literary canon, but also as a text about the interdependent emergence of "nation" and "race."[23]

Alerted by Baker to the *Narrative*'s political-economic import, reminded by critics such as Chinosole of the text's "international importance," and pushed to consider a transatlantic framework by Gilroy, we can begin to see that Equiano's mercantile endeavors are striking and precarious precisely because they confront capitalism at the moment of the emergence of modern racial and national formations—an emergence made possible in part by the discourses and practices of mercantilism.

But what was "mercantilism" in late-eighteenth- and early-nineteenth-century North America? Let us start with a current, somewhat traditional, economic and historical answer to this question. Beginning in the sixteenth century, in order to unify and increase political power and monetary wealth within their dominions, the European powers forged varying degrees of centralized governmental regulation of territorially specific economies. This regulation was achieved through policies designed to accumulate bullion, to effect a favorable balance of trade, to develop a diversified and more or less self-sufficient balance of agriculture and manufacture, or simply to manage a range of economic crises. Examples of such policies include protectionist policies such as tariffs and other import restraints, preferential treaties, and monopolies for joint-stock or chartered companies, as well as encouragement policies, including export subsidies such as bounties and drawbacks, and state-funded infrastructural development. These policies make up the extensive systems of economic nationalism now called "mercantilism."[24]

As the white settler colonization of the Americas accelerated in the eighteenth century, merchant capital flooded into North America along channels of commerce carved by a complex British mercantilist structure. Writes Richard B. Sheridan, summarizing the vast historical research on British-American colonial economies:

> One stereotypical view of early American history is that the colonists revolted against political and economic tyranny imposed by the British government with the goals of establishing a small property-owning democracy and a system of competitive enterprise free from intervention by government. Countering this laissez-faire myth is the view that within their restricted sphere of influence, colonial governments sought to control, regulate, restrain, and stimulate activity and thus to guide economic and social development. Colonial governments responded to popular demand by establishing public markets and regulating the price of country produce entering towns and cities. They enacted laws to fix wages . . . to license such quasi-public functionaries as porters, draymen, millers, smiths, and gravediggers; to fix wharfage and storage rates and fares on ferries, to set prices on . . . basic commodities. . . . [C]olonial authorities laid down standards of quality and measure for commodities . . . [and] able-bodied males were required to work a certain number of days in the year on . . . public-works projects. By means of compulsory or statute labor and tax revenues, Indian trails and bridle paths were upgraded to wagon roads that served as arteries of trade. . . . In sum, political establishments sought to foster development.[25]

After U.S. independence, and despite the complaints of U.S. revolutionaries in the Declaration of Independence about aspects of Britain's oppressive mercantile system, merchant capital expanded in North America as an effect of U.S. mercantilism.[26] The Annals of the first U.S. Congress and Alexander Hamilton's *Report on Manufactures* (1791) testify to the initially moderate U.S. mercantilist policies that began with the Tariff of 1789 and then steadily expanded, especially after the end of the War of 1812.[27] Marshaled first to hold the North American colonies in the economic orbit of Britain, the very same mercantilist policies, with minor alterations, were by the late eighteenth century marshaled to structure a North American orbit of its own. Global economic expansions, upturns, and downturns thus took the particular "shapes" of imperial nation (Britain), white settler colony (British North America), and emerging imperial nation (United States), in part through remarkably similar mercantilist policies instituted and controlled by changing political centers. The United States was not simply founded by a community of enterprising merchants; U.S. "enterprise" was founded and sustained by a concerted, mercantilist management of merchant capital.

This mercantilist production of U.S. "enterprise" can also be set within the more global context of the emergence of historical capitalism. There is a strong case to be made that mercantilist policies have been a necessary (though not sufficient) historical condition for the rapid development of capitalist productive efficiency. Mercantilist policies have facilitated the successive rise of the United Provinces, Britain, and the United States to hegemonic status in the capitalist world system. Though such policies may have been advocated for different and contradictory reasons, the policies nonetheless had the effect of facilitating the rise of the mercantilist states to hegemonic status.[28]

However, in "The Nation Form: History and Ideology," Etienne Balibar helps us to think of mercantilism as more than just a technical set of state policies. Why, he asks, have "non-national state apparatuses aiming at quite other (for example, dynastic) objectives . . . progressively produced the elements of the nation-state or, if one prefers, [why have they] been involuntarily 'nationalized' and . . . begun to nationalize society"? Searching for an answer, he argues that, while the "development of market structures and class relations specific to modern capitalism" certainly helped to create nation-states, "it is quite impossible to 'deduce' the nation form from capitalist relations of production," for "in the history of capitalism, state forms other than the national have emerged and have for a time competed with it before finally being repressed or instrumentalized." It is only the immense power of nineteenth-century, Euro-U.S. nationalist historiographies that has taught us to perform such a deduction by rote, to see in every non-national social formation a "pre-national formation." Rather, Balibar continues, there was not "a single inherently 'bourgeois' political form, but several"—the seventeenth-century Dutch United Provinces being one crucial example. "The nascent capitalist bourgeoisie seems to have 'hesitated',," Balibar writes, "between several forms of hegemony. Or let us rather say that there existed different bourgeoisies, each connected to different sectors of exploitation of the resources of the world-economy. If the 'national bourgeoisies' finally won out, even before the industrial revolution," we need to examine more closely the discourses and practices that worked to transform "social formations into national formation."[29]

For Balibar, capitalism emerged and even thrived under a variety of political forms. To understand how the nation form became the dominant, if not exclusive, political form for capitalism, we need to examine the discourses and practices that articulated capitalism with nationalism. Both Balibar and Giovanni Arrighi suggest that mercantilism was one such set of discourses and practices.[30] We are thus confronted by two questions. Exactly *how* did mercantilism articulate capitalism with emerging conceptions of "race" and "nation"? I address this question in the next section. In turn, how do Equiano's precarious mercantile endeavors confront this articulation? I address this question in the final section.

II. MARXIAN VALUE THEORY AND THE "RACIAL GRAFT"

In the first volume of *Capital,* Karl Marx describes "protectionism," or mercantilism, as having "the objective of manufacturing capitalists artificially in the mother country," adding in a footnote to this passage that mercantilism's "artificial manufacturing" eventually "became a temporary *necessity* in the international competitive struggle" (emphasis mine).[31] Marx here suggests that mercantilism is one of the central ways capitalism worked to control and to manage the development of capital for the nation, to make capital make sense nationally. But precisely how does this "artificial manufacturing" take place? Marx persistently reminds us that when capitalism first emerged as an economic and political force, it worked to break down current ways of making sense of and giving value to social relations, while simultaneously instituting a new way of making sense of or giving value to social relations. Marx describes the process of breaking down in part 8 of *Capital* (vol. 1) in economic terms as "a process which divorces the worker from the ownership of the conditions of his own labour" through expropriation, so-called "bloody legislation," the agricultural and industrial revolutions, and colonization.[32] In turn, Marx calls the new, capitalist way of making sense of social relations, or the form in which social relations are valued under capitalism, the "value form." If mercantilism makes capital make sense nationally, that making sense, or "artificial manufacturing," involves the establishment of the value form.

How, then, does this devaluing and revaluing process proceed? That is, how is the value form established? In the first chapter of *Capital* (vol. 1),

Marx describes this process by using the commodity, or "the product of labor," as an exemplary (but not exclusive) instance of social relations "manufactured" under capitalism.[33] He explains that two materially different objects, such as a coat and linen, are equated with each other—their differences are suppressed—on the basis of a third commodity shared by the coat and the linen. That third commodity is abstract labor, or labor which has been abstracted from its particular qualities. Explains Marx,

> By equating, for example, the coat as a thing of value to the linen, we equate the labour embedded in the coat with the labour embedded in the linen. Now it is true that the tailoring which makes the coat is concrete labour of a different sort from the weaving which makes the linen. But . . . weaving too, in so far as it weaves value, has nothing to distinguish it from tailoring, and, consequently, is abstract human labor . . . [or] human labour in general.[34]

In effect, the value form transforms the particularistic aspects of social relations into the universal and abstract form of "human labour in general." In the next paragraph, Marx further explains that the value form actually recreates or reforms particularity:

> However, it is not enough to express the specific character of the labour which goes to make up the value of the linen. Human labour-power in its fluid state, or human labour, creates value, but is not itself value. It becomes value in its coagulated state, in objective form. The value of the linen as a congealed mass of human labour can be expressed only as an "objectivity" [*Gegenständlichkeit*], a thing which is materially different from the linen itself and yet common to the linen and all other commodities.[35]

The exchange of the coat and the linen gives a formal, abstract, and universal meaning to what were the "fluid," particular human actions of weaving or tailoring. The value form expressed in the commodity actually creates, or gives a determinate value to, previously indeterminate social relations. What is more, the determinate value of abstraction has a substantiality here—it is "coagulated," "congealed," and "objective." The value form produces a universal abstraction with substantiality.[36]

In addition, as Marx explains in "The Chapter on Capital" from the *Grundrisse*, under capitalism this abstract labor is represented not only as the basis for the economic *equality* of commodities, but also as the basis for the economic *freedom* of the laborer. The valuing of abstract labor over particular labor allows each laborer to sell his or her labor on the market and to receive wages for it. The wage-laborer, or the laborer who sells his or her abstract labor, is the *free* economic subject of capitalism, because he or she is said to be formally and abstractly *equal* to all other laborers. The laborer's freedom is his or her abstraction from particularity; he or she is freed from particularity. "Freedom" thus acquires meaning through the logic of abstract equivalence. The very substance of sociality—that which "stipulates" subjects "not only in an equal, but also in a social relation" to one another, as Marx writes—is the active valuation of "freedom" as equality or formal and abstract equivalence.[37]

What is more, Marx argues that the process is not confined merely to the social relation of commodity production and exchange: "The exchange of exchange values is the productive, real basis of all *equality* and *freedom*. As pure ideas they are merely the idealized expressions of this basis; as developed in juridical, political, social relations, they are merely this basis to a higher power."[38] For Marx, another significant "juridical, political, and social relation" animated by the value form under capitalism is the institution of modern citizenship. In *Capital* and especially in the *Grundrisse,* he illustrates this by repeatedly comparing the value of the commodity to the value of the citizen. To be representable as a citizen, a subject must be abstracted from its particularities just as a coat and tailoring or linen and weaving are abstracted from their particularities. This formally abstract citizen-subject is thus brought into a relationship of formal and abstract *equality* with its fellow citizen-subjects, and this relationship is represented as *freedom.* That is, subjects in capitalist civil society become citizens to the extent that they understand themselves as formally and abstractly equivalent to other subjects.

The value form thus represents subjects as rational abstractions, formally equivalent and legally free, in order to be representable as constituent members of civil society. The theory of value thus functions as a critique not only of commodity exchange, but also of the logic of freedom and equality in civil society "as developed in juridical, political, social relations." What is more, Marx alerts us that the logic of abstract equivalence does not simply *reflect* the ideals of freedom and equality. Rather, the embodiment of the value form in complex social and cultural relations actually *generates* those very ideals; the value form animates, substantializes, and materializes "juridical, political, social relations" through universal abstraction.[39]

Marx does not pay much attention to the question of what happens to the social particularities abstracted by the value form, particularities such as the differences among a coat, linen, corn, and gold, or the differences among subjects before they are transformed into citizens.[40] Are those particularities abstracted away completely, or are they re-formed? If abstraction has a substantiality, if it remakes and revalues substance from a "fluid" and indeterminate state to a "coagulated" and "congealed" state, what happens to the particularities that marked labor power in its "fluid state"? Do they reemerge, revalued and in some relation to universal equality and freedom? Since new "particularities," such as "race" and "nation," vigorously emerge precisely at the historical moment in which the value form abstracts subjects and commodities from their particularities, and in which capitalism represents this abstraction as "freedom," we would seem to need an account of "particularity" under the value form.

Marx's failure to consider carefully this question has resonated throughout the Marxian tradition, leaving many critics to argue that the value form progressively destroys or erases all particularities.[41] Yet Marx's emphasis on the substantiality and materiality of universal abstraction—its "coagulated" and "congealed" character—begs the question of the manner or form of this relationship between universal abstraction and substantialized, naturalized particularity.

In fact, in his rarely read letters and passages on slavery in the Americas, Marx does furtively attempt to think about what happens to social particularities such as "race" and "nation" when formal, abstract equality becomes the reigning way of rendering economic and political freedom.[42] Although always critical of slavery as an unjust practice, Marx was unable to account fully for what he considered a feudal or even prefeudal form of labor in the midst of the United States, which he called "the most modern form of existence of bourgeois society."[43] He often argues that universal free wage-labor is the *sine qua non* of capitalism; as he writes in the *Grundrisse,* "Capital ceases to be capital without wage-labor."[44] Consequently, he tends to understand slavery in the Americas as an incidental atavism because it was not wage-labor. This allows him to suggest, and generations of Marxists after him to argue explicitly, that racialization simply accompanied slavery, that both were residues of premodern, precapitalist modes of production, and that both would simply dissipate in the face of the bourgeois revolution, after which the "real" struggles for freedom from wage-labor would begin.[45]

However, Marx is also at times uncomfortable with this dogmatic position. In Notebook 4 of the *Grundrisse,* for example, he writes cryptically in parentheses, "(The fact that slavery is possible at individual points within the bourgeois system of production does not contradict [my argument about the exchange relation]. However, slavery is then possible there only because it . . . appears as an anomaly opposite the bourgeois system itself)."[46] When Marx writes that slavery "*appears* as an anomaly," he suggests that from the perspective of classical liberalism itself, slavery is anomalous; that is, liberalism makes itself make sense by anomalizing slavery. Thus a *critique* of liberalism would need to offer another *interpretation* of "the anomalous"—another interpretation, that is, of the relationship between the abstract value form and the particularistic logic of racial slavery.

Marx does occasionally hint at an interpretation of this "anomalous" status in the U.S. context. For example, in *Theories of Surplus Value,* he writes that in southern U.S. plantations,

> [W]here commercial speculations figure from the start and production is in-
> tended for the world market, the capitalist mode of production exists, al-
> though only in a formal sense, since the slavery of Negroes precludes free
> wage labor, which is the basis of capitalist production. But the business in
> which slaves are used is conducted by *capitalists*. The mode of production
> which they introduce has not arisen out of slavery but is grafted on to it. [*Die
> Produktionsweise, die sie einführen, ist nicht aus der Sklaverei entsprungen, sondern
> wird auf sie gepfropft.*][47]

Marx wavers between two perspectives in this passage and ultimately offers
a hybrid of both perspectives with the figure of the graft. From the perspective of production, he still insists in this passage on a mode-of-production
narrative that makes "the slavery of Negroes" an atavistic vestige of the past.
Slavery "precludes free wage labor," and thus production on southern U.S.
plantations could only be capitalist "in a formal sense." Yet even this grudg-
ing acceptance of U.S. plantation slavery as "formal" capitalism belies another, less explicit perspective: that of *trade*—"production . . . *intended for
the world market.*" The perspective of trade shifts Marx into a consideration of capitalism as a world system; that is, he shifts his frame of analysis
from the production perspective, which assumes the nation as a given unit
of analysis and posits a linear and uniform narrative of development, to the
perspective of trade, which can consider multiform and uneven development.[48] It is this shift that allows him, at the end of the passage, to consider
how the specificity of slavery could be factored into an analysis of capitalism. That is, he is able to consider slavery as "grafted onto," rather than necessarily anterior to, outside of, or contradictory to capitalism. This suggests
that when "nation" is taken as a self-evident category, slavery and racialization are occluded or dismissed as incidental, whereas when the question of
the nation form is raised, slavery and, implicitly, "race" become social relations whose precise relationship to capitalism needs to be articulated.

Marx's figuration of this relationship as one of "grafting" is rich indeed
here. This passage opposes a necessary or even natural development
(*entspringen* as "to arise from," "to derive from") to an actively forced transformation (*pfropfen* means "to cork" or "to plug," even colloquially "to stuff"
something into something else, as well as "to graft" in an agricultural
sense). *Entspringen* would suggest that the mode of production of the plantation capitalists is derived from slavery and, while originally enabled by
slavery, will eventually advance beyond slavery or leave slavery behind. By
suggesting, with *pfropfen*, that plantation capitalism is "stuffed with" slavery
or "grafted onto" it, the passage insists both on a more forced and on a
more imbricated relationship between capitalism and racial slavery (*die
Negersklaverei*), deemphasizing any sense of capitalism leaving racial slavery
behind. The verb *pfropfen* urges us, I would suggest, to read this forced imbrication carefully.[49]

Let us remain with *pfropfen* in the sense of "to graft" for a moment, then. The graft, or that which is grafted onto a host, is neither strictly natural nor strictly artificial. It is at once secondary or foreign to the host, and, after some time and if successful, legibly one with that host to such an extent that the violent act of grafting itself becomes illegible. If, as the passage above suggests, grafting figures the relationship between national forms of racial slavery and capitalism, or racial and national codification and the abstract equality of the value form, then we need to consider how racial and national particularities are not *erased* under or *developed away* by the value form, but vigorously and actively *produced* at or *conjoined with* the moment of abstraction.

We can thus say that Marx's discomfort with the anomalous status of racial slavery under capitalism signals both the limit and the possibility of the Marxian critique of the value form and of classical liberal citizenship. By extending Marx, we can understand this moment of abstraction as the moment in which abstract equality and racial and national codification are actively produced and grafted or conjoined. The calculation of subjects *as* citizens could be said to *depend* upon the codification of racial and national particularity, and vice versa, such that the very categories of sameness and difference, or the universal and the particular, are produced together. We can only further specify this relationship of grafting, however, by considering historically specific instances of abstract citizenship actively produced with or grafted onto codified racial and national forms.[50]

We have seen how mercantilism helps to "manufacture" capitalism by establishing the value form, and how the value form "manufactures" citizenship as an institution of formal and abstract equality supplemented by codified particularities such as "race" and "nation." We can now read Equiano's "injuries" and "instances" as just such an historically specific instance of Marx's graft. As we will see, the *Narrative* discloses the fact that the transformation of "social formations into national formations" paradoxically involved *both* the "categorization of humanity into artificially isolated [racial] types"[51] *and* the emergence of modern egalitarianism, as embodied in the formal and abstract equality of national citizenship.[52]

III. "I AT LENGTH ENDEAVOURED TO TRY MY LUCK AND COMMENCE MERCHANT"

Equiano begins to learn the terms of the merchant marine trade and its productive potential over the course of the first five chapters of the *Narrative,* particularly when, after the horrors of the Middle Passage (E, 55–61; 32–37) and a brief but brutal period in Virginia slavery (E, 62–64; 38–40), he is sold to Michael Henry Pascal, a royal navy lieutenant and captain of a merchant ship called the *Industrious Bee* (E, 63; 40). Equiano represents his sale to Pascal as a blessing after the misery of the Middle Passage and Virginia, signaling that "industriousness" and mercantile capitalism accrue meaning in relative opposition to his past misery. From this point on he tries to gain access to mercantile capitalism, again and again attempting to make his way by forging equivalencies with traders. Trading eventually becomes one of Equiano's most persistent responses to both his violent entrance into what Wallerstein calls the European world-economy of the late eighteenth century, and his relentless subjection to the regimes of capitalist exchange, production, accumulation, and circulation.[53]

We know from chapters 4 and 5 that, throughout his early years of enslavement, Equiano engaged in "trifling perquisites and little ventures" in the interest of scraping together some form of sustenance (E, 94; 65). But with his formal declaration of "commenc[ing] merchant" in chapter 6 following his sale to Mr. Robert King, a Quaker merchant from Philadelphia who "hires" Equiano out to the English merchant mariner Captain Thomas Farmer, Equiano's trading changes character (E, 116; 84). No longer just pursuing sustenance within local economies, his declaration in chapter 6 marks his active engagement precisely with merchant capital and the world-economy's sphere of circulation. That is, chapter 6 marks the beginning of his attempt to "realize" commodity capital on the market by transforming it into money capital, which could in turn be reinvested in commodity capital and transformed once again into money capital, with profit.

In fact, throughout the text Equiano very carefully marks this transition from his involvement in local economies to his subjection to and increasingly active participation in the European world-economy. For example, in the somewhat controversial first two chapters of the narrative, he represents his homeland as based on subsistence economies.[54] As Joseph Fichtelberg notes, this is historically suspect, since "Benin had a thriving commerce, extensive markets, and widely circulating currency" at the time.[55] Nonetheless, Equiano's homeland was not yet extensively integrated into the orbit of Europe, a fact Equiano marks with his retrospective representation of, on the one hand, "the Kingdom of Benin" as "a country where nature is prodigal of her favours, our wants are few and easily supplied" (E, 36; 16), and, on the other hand, the ubiquity of European economic and cultural objects in the more coastal regions of West Africa (E, 53; 31).

Similarly, Equiano distinguishes his for-profit mercantile endeavors after chapter 6 from the more standard sustenance ventures practiced by slaves bound to the more restricted plantation unit (E, 108–9; 77–78). As he repeatedly remarks, Equiano "commences merchant" in the perverse and subversive interest of *freeing* himself. Most immediately, that is, he acts in the interest of saving enough money to buy his freedom, and thereby to extricate himself from the life-cycle of capital as a laboring object of exchange. But we can also hear in Equiano's use of the infinitive "to commence" an interest which is manifested in the scenes of trading he subsequently recounts. Just as the infinitive is a verb form that exposes itself to an open-ended futurity, a potentiality not fully figured but nonetheless anticipated, Equiano's declaration "to commence merchant" inaugurates an attempt to realize not just his material sustenance, not even just his economic independence, but also his freedom as an active social subject in this new world which has forced itself upon him. In other words, he is hoping to have free subjectivity conferred to him and to confer it upon himself through the action and logic of capitalist accumulation and exchange.

This is not just any subjectivity, however, but precisely subjectivity as it "means" in this new capitalist world: formal and abstract subjectivity, of the kind Madison and Ames invoke, and Marx critiques, above. As we saw earlier in this essay, the subjectivity of the economic and political actor in civil society under capitalism is supposed to be "freed" (i.e., abstracted) from material particularities, a freedom that renders all subjects in civil society formally interchangeable and thus formally and abstractly equal. The hope embedded in this phrase "to commence merchant," then, is that by mastering the mechanics of mercantile exchange, Equiano will accede to the ontological status he figures repeatedly in the narrative by signifying on the Christian humanist terms of the golden rule: " 'Do unto all men as you would men should do unto you' " (E, 61; 38). Equiano hopes to accede to the ontological status, that is, of a subject formally and abstractly equal to all the subjects around him, and therefore "free." "To commence merchant" signifies Equiano's attempt to use capitalist mercantile exchange as a *weapon* against capitalist slavery, as a *tool* that would solder freedom to formal and abstract equivalence, and as a *lever*, or *mochlos*,[56] that would propel him into that state of formal and abstract equality as freedom.[57]

Equiano's mercantile strategy is, on its grandest terms as well as in many of its details, a failure, although it is also a certain success. While many of Equiano's trading ventures end up with whites robbing or swindling him out of his capital, he nonetheless does eventually buy his freedom (E, 135–38; 101), get married (E, 235; 178), and become a transatlantic advocate of British missionary and capitalist development in Africa—development he represents as a means to abolish the slave trade and deliver Africa (he always writes of the continent as such) to European modernity (chapter 12). However, he never accedes to the radical freedom beyond racial oppression that he had envisioned. In other words, he attains particular financial, imperial, and gendered freedoms, but he fails to access the formal and abstract *equality* he had associated with freedom as such. How, then, do we make sense of Equiano's failures and his successes?

Let us consider in detail Equiano's first attempt to "try [his] luck and commence merchant." Upon landing at "Santa Cruz Island," or St. Croix in a British ship of his new master, a Quaker merchant from Philadelphia, he and a friend who is also a slave are robbed by "two white men" of three bags of fruit they had intended to trade (E, 117; 85). As these men run "to a house . . . adjoining the [island's] fort," Equiano and his friend plead for the return of their bags of fruit. As Equiano explains, these whites "not only refused to return them, but they swore at us, and threatened if we did not immediately depart, they would flog us as well" (E, 117; 85). When Equiano and his partner proceed to explain that "those three bags were our all, that we brought them with us to sell, and that we came from Montserrat, and shewed them the vessel," they get in even worse trouble:

> But this was rather against us as they now saw we were strangers as well as slaves. They still therefore swore, and desired us to be gone, and even took sticks to beat us. . . . We went to the commanding officer of the fort and told him how we had been served by some of his people; but we obtained not the least re-dress. He answered our complaints only by a volley of imprecations against us, and immediately took a horse-whip, in order to chastise us. (E, 117; 85)

The crucial phrases here are "they now saw we were strangers as well as slaves" and "how we had been served by some of his people," for they tell us that Equiano and his partner have stumbled into a nationalist conflict as well as a racial conflict in this scene. Initially, it seems as if "the two white men" express only a sense of racial superiority by so boldly robbing Equiano and his partner: Equiano names their whiteness, notes that the robbers declare their right to flog the two black men, and tells us that the robbers first understand Equiano and his partner only as slaves with the phrase "they *now* saw we were strangers *as well as* slaves." However, when the robbers see Equiano's and his partner's ship and hear their defense of themselves as merchants, these white men realize Equiano and his partner are not only Africans but also are trading under the British flag. Equiano marks this by distinguishing the term *strangers,* most often invoked to sig-nify national difference in the period, from the term *slaves.* Similarly, the commanding officer's assault on Equiano and his partner with "impreca-tions" and "a horse-whip" seems to figure only his understanding of them as slaves. But the text tells us that this officer grasps both the racial and na-tional difference between the two parties when Equiano and his partner present their case as a conflict between themselves and "some of [the com-mander's] people."

What does this emphasis on national difference as well as racial differ-ence tell us? At the time of this incident, in the mid-1760s, St. Croix was part of the Danish West Indies, together with St. Thomas and St. John. The Spanish, English, Dutch, French, and Danish had fought over these islands since the Spanish exterminated or enslaved the "Carib Indians" Columbus first encountered in 1493 during his second voyage. After Denmark took control of all three islands in 1733 (initially under the auspices of the Danish West Indies Company and then directly under the Danish Crown), it fought for decades against slave uprisings and British attempts to seize the islands. In fact, Britain took control of St. Thomas for ten months in 1801 and 1802, and held all three islands between 1807 and 1815.[58]

The islands emerged as a cauldron of colonial rivalry because Denmark struggled to assert its economic control, in part because of the islands' small size and the relative weakness of the Danish military. In addition, since the Danes left the islands open to settlement by any European subjects, the Danish West Indies Company and the crown found themselves in constant competition and confrontation with foreign residents and creditors. In fact, most Danish profits seem to have come from the smuggling trade in slaves and sugar when periods of war interrupted the trade of the British and French. The 1760s in particular found the Danes imposing mercantilist measures on St. Croix while opening St. Thomas to relatively free trade in a desperate if contradictory effort to assert economic control over the islands.[59]

Thus, in the everyday world of the St. Croix port where Equiano and his partner attempt to trade their "whole stock" (E, 117; 85), the Danish commanding officer and the two white men—perhaps themselves Danish or perhaps simply nationally allied with the Danes against the British—are actors in, and are immediately aware of, a complex set of racial and national antagonisms characteristic of the region's mercantilist conjuncture. The two white men are incited to violence, and the commanding officer invokes his authority, from a racism articulated with nationalism. In turn, Equiano and his partner are violently barred from the formal and abstract equality of mercantile exchange by this articulation. It is because Equiano frames this mercantile "endeavour" as a quest for freedom, and then traces the material manner in which that freedom is bound both to racism and nationalism, that we can glimpse mercantilist discourses and practices at work on Santa Cruz island.

Equiano's "injury" on Santa Cruz island is neither incidental nor unique. The *Narrative* recounts a series of incidents in which he is excluded from formal and abstract equality on the basis of its articulation with the codification of "race" and "nation." Immediately after the Santa Cruz incident, for example, Equiano rejects an offer of freedom from French merchantmen, choosing instead to remain a slave on a transatlantic merchant ship. As he explains,

> Had I wished to run away, I did not want opportunities . . . and particularly at one time, soon after this. When we were at the island of Guadaloupe there was a large fleet of merchantmen bound for Old France; and, seamen then being very scarce, they gave from fifteen to twenty pounds a man for the run. Our mate, and all the white sailors, left our vessel on this account, and went

on board of the French ships. They would have had me also gone with them, for they regarded me, and swore to protect me, if I would go: and, as the fleet was to sail the next day, I really believe I could have got safe to Europe at that time. However, as my master was kind, I would not attempt to leave him; still remembering the old maxim, that "honesty is the best policy," I suffered them to go without me. Indeed my captain was much afraid of my leaving him and the vessel at that time, as I had so fair an opportunity: but I thank God, this fidelity of mine turned out much to my advantage hereafter, when I did not in the least think of it; and made me so much in favour with the captain, that he used now and then to teach me some parts of navigation himself. But some of our passengers, and others, seeing this, found much fault with him for it, saying, it was a very dangerous thing to let a negro know navigation; thus I was hindered again in my pursuits. (E, 123; 90)

Though Equiano says "I really believe I could have got safe to Europe at that time" and thus become free under French auspices, his deep distrust of such nationally bound freedom keeps him from fleeing. By saying "However, as my master was kind," he makes clear that he is not choosing Britain over France, but rather transatlantic, mercantile slavery with his relatively (Equiano makes this qualification clear) trustworthy master over formal freedom in France. His decision positions him against both racism and nationalism, and holds out the hope of a radical equality beyond both. This hope found a certain realization in his relations with the white merchantmen while they too resided in the precariously national space of the merchant marine ship.[60] Though Equiano makes clear that his white shipmates "regarded" him and "swore to protect" him in France, his decision to stay behind suggests that he believed such fidelity would carry little weight within the confines of France. He thus decides that "honesty" to his master is more valuable than fleeing to freedom in France since his servitude allows him to remain a transatlantic merchant.

As the passage above suggests, this initially seems a wise decision to Equiano, for he learns more about the merchant marine trade. The reactions of the "passengers, and others," however, indicate that the figure of a black, transatlantic seaman was perhaps too successful at the business of "freedom." To them, Equiano tell us, "it was a very dangerous thing to let a negro know navigation" precisely because such knowledge carved out a certain space of "freedom," albeit a precarious one. The reactions of the passengers indicate that "navigation" knowledge might well escape the newly emerging mercantilist discourses and practices of racism and nationalism, and subjectify Equiano differently. Once again, in the passage above, Equiano indicates the self-evidence of the articulation of racial and national codification with equality by depicting the immediacy of the passengers' perception and interpretation of him: "But some of our passengers, and others, *seeing this,* found much fault with him for it." The passengers' relatively successful invocation of a prohibition against Equiano—"and thus I was hindered again in my pursuits"—indicates the pervasive, disciplinary power of this articulation.

The *Narrative*'s very next paragraph underscores the precariousness of Equiano's position, as his hoped-for, transatlantic, a-national space of freedom disintegrates even further, and he once again encounters the articulation of mercantile capitalism's formal and abstract equality with "race" and "nation":

> About the latter end of the year 1764, my master bought a larger sloop, called the Prudence, about seventy or eighty tons, of which my captain had the command. I went with him into this vessel, and we took a load of new slaves for Georgia and Charles Town. My master now left me entirely to the captain, though he still wished me to be with him; but I, who always much wished to lose sight of the West Indies, was not a little rejoiced at the thoughts of seeing any other country. Therefore, relying on the goodness of my captain, I got ready all the little venture I could; and, when the vessel was ready, we sailed to my great joy. When we got to our destined places, Georgia and Charles Town, I expected I should have an opportunity of selling my little property to advantage; but here, particularly in Charles Town, I met with buyers, white men, who imposed on me as in other places. (Equiano, 120; 90)

This incident throws Equiano back into national racialization. Attempting to maintain his ideal position of merchant marine freedom, he slips precipitously into the contradictions of being a slave attempting to trade on a slave ship in slave colonies with slave traders. His joy "at the thoughts of seeing *any other country*" is dashed precisely because such thoughts are increasingly impossible for a black subject at this historical moment. In the emerging capitalism of the Atlantic zone, subjects increasingly are free only to the extent that they are particular, racially and nationally codified subjects—white subjects working for a particular nation.

A few pages later, in an account of a trip he made to Charleston, South Carolina in 1766[61] as a slave on a British-American ship, Equiano underscores this articulation of "race," "nation," and "equality" by offering an interpretation of one of the turning points in the struggle for U.S. independence: the 1766 repeal of the Stamp Act. Many contemporary American historians represent the Stamp Act repeal as one of the key victories of the colonial American desire for freedom from British tyranny and thus as part of the struggle for equality culminating in U.S. independence. However, Equiano's account shows us that the most significant common thread between the Stamp Act repeal and the emergence of an independent United States was not a glorious desire for "freedom" and "equality," but rather an emerging understanding of "equality" as entirely consistent with, indeed constitutive of, the codification of racial and national identities. What is more, his account suggests that mercantilism played a role in articulating "equality" with "race" and "nation." Writes Equiano:

> We arrived at Georgia, and, having landed part of our cargo, proceeded to Charlestown with the remainder. While we were there I saw the town illuminated; the guns were fired, and bonfires and other demonstrations of joy shewn, on account of the repeal of the stamp-act. Here I disposed of some goods on my own account; the white men buying them with smooth promises and fair words, giving me, however, but very indifferent payment. There was one gentlemen particularly who bought a puncheon of rum of me, and gave me a great deal of trouble; and although I used the interest of my friendly [British] captain, I could not obtain anything for it; for, being a negro man, I could not oblige him to pay me. This vexed me much, not knowing how to act; and I lost some time in seeking after this Christian; and though, when the sabbath came (which the negroes usually make their holiday) I was inclined to go to public worship, but, instead of that, I was obliged to hire some black men to help me to pull a boat across the water to go in quest of this gentleman. When I found him, after much entreaty, both from myself and my worthy captain, he at last paid me in dollars, some of them, however, were copper, and of consequence of no value; but he took advantage of my being a negro man, and obliged me to put up with those or none, although I objected to them. Immediately after, as I was trying to pass them in the market amongst other white men, I was abused for offering to pass bad coin; and though I shewed them the man I had got them from, I was within one minute of being tied up and flogged without either judge or jury; however, by the help of a good pair of heels, I ran off and so escaped the bastinadoes I should have received. I got on board as fast as I could, but still continued in fear of them until we sailed, which, I thank God, we did, not long after; and I have never been amongst them since. (E, 128–129; 94–95)

The Stamp Act was one of the many mercantilist policies the British Parliament conducted in North America. Colonial American anger over the Act precipitated the 1765 Stamp Act Congress, held at New York City Hall. On October 19, the Congress published a Declaration of Rights and Grievances, which decried taxation without representation, and called for "boycotts" of British goods until the Act was repealed.[62] Though the Stamp Act Congress's Declaration certainly disturbed British authorities, it was the many petitions from English merchants, in which they complained about the impact of colonial "boycotts" on their businesses and themselves called for the repeal of the Stamp Act, that caused the greatest stir in Parliament. The *combined* force of the New York Declaration and the English merchants' petitions led Parliament to repeal the act. Yet, as Equiano's account suggests, in North America in 1766 this transatlantic aspect of the Stamp Act repeal was hardly noticed, as burgeoning American nationalism represented the repeal as simply an effect of colonial resistance.[63]

That is, by juxtaposing the celebrations over the Stamp Act repeal on the streets of Charleston with an account of being swindled by white American colonials, Equiano tells us that he has been barred from the formal and abstract equality of mercantile exchange which the repeal was supposedly recognizing. The market into which Equiano enters fails to confer equality upon him not just because he is passing "bad coin." Rather, the market fails because Equiano is understood *both* as black ("for, being a negro man, I could not oblige him to pay me," "he took advantage of my being a negro man") *and* as British ("although I used the interest of my friendly [*British*] captain, I could obtain nothing for it"). Equiano shows us that these American colonials are celebrating an equality irreducibly bound to, and consistent with, racial and national codification. They are joyously recognizing their mutual identity by hierarchically differentiating it from Britishness and blackness.

Paradoxically, when the Tariff of 1789 went into effect twenty-three years later, the duties it imposed were not unlike the British Stamp Act duties. The common "American" thread between the Stamp Act repeal celebrations and the first U.S. Congress was thus not "free trade" among all people. The 1766 repeal, as a move away from protectionism, and the 1789 Tariff, as a move toward protectionism, are entirely contradictory on that score. Rather, as Equiano's account makes clear, the common thread between these two events is the formal and abstract equality embodied by the Charleston market *articulated with* the racial and national codification Equiano encounters when he is swindled. We see this articulation both in Equiano's 1766 and in Madison's, Ames's, and Fitzsimons's 1789.

Even after Equiano buys his freedom, he encounters this articulation. In fact, Equiano acknowledges "that my first free voyage would be the worst I had ever made" (E, 142; 105). As he explains,

> During our stay at this place [Savannah, Georgia], one evening a slave belonging to Mr. Read, a merchant of Savannah, came near to our vessel, and began to use me very ill. I entreated him, with all the patience I was master of, to desist, as I knew there was little or no law for a free negro here; but the fellow, instead of taking my advise, persevered in his insults, and even struck me. At this I lost all temper, and fell on him and beat him soundly. The next morning his master came to our vessel as we lay alongside the wharf, and desired me to come ashore that he might have me flogged all round the town, for beating his negro slave. (E, 139; 102)

Though Equiano informs his Captain of his fight with Mr. Read's slave, and the Captain promises to take care of the matter, the conflict escalates: "The captain being on board when Mr. Read came and applied to him to deliver me up, he said he knew nothing of the matter, I was a free man. I was astonished and frightened at this, and thought I had better keep where I was, than go ashore and be flogged round the town, without judge or jury" (E,

139; 103). Equiano knows that his freedom will not be recognized in a slave state, but he is "astonished" to discover that his Captain will not assist him on the ship. He is "astonished," in other words, to discover that he does not fully understand the meaning of his newly obtained "freedom" even on his ship.

His initial response to this situation is an affective and principled one; he decides to insist on his freedom: "At that instant a rage seized my soul, and for a while I determined to resist the first man that should attempt to lay violent hands on me, or basely use me without a trial; for I would sooner die like a free man, than suffer myself to be scourged by the hands of ruffians, and my blood drawn like a slave" (E, 140; 103). But his Captain and shipmates preach caution, and finally agree to hide Equiano until they leave port. To hide, however, Equiano must leave the ship and go ashore, lest Mr. Read search for him on board. Paradoxically, then, Equiano's formal freedom leads him into a conflict that makes it necessary for him to leave the ship for a place where his freedom has no meaning. The text implies that, had Equiano still been a slave, the Captain would not have told Mr. Read that "he knew nothing of the matter" because Equiano "was a free man." Rather, Equiano's behavior would have necessarily been his *master's* responsibility, and thus the Captain would have acted in his own interest and protected his property, Equiano, from Mr. Read. Instead, Equiano's freedom is rootless, at home neither on ship nor in Savannah.

The loss of Equiano's newly formalized freedom on his ship at the hands of a slave owner "protecting" his slave underscores the loss of maritime spaces where black merchants could realize a freedom relatively detached from racial and national codification. In turn, this incident documents the way Equiano is persistently pulled toward a bounded, nationally defined space. His formal freedom actually increases the strength of that pull, such that the only way he can protect himself is to renounce his formal freedom and become a technically unfree subject by hiding in the nationally defined space of Savannah. His ploy works, but, as if to mark the impossibility of a freedom detached from racial-national codification, Equiano concludes with a difficult recognition of what awaits him back on board ship: "so I consented to slave on as before" (E, 141; 105).

The repetitive nature of Equiano's "incidents" and "injuries" suggests that his mercantile failures are neither incidental nor unique, but systematic and constitutive of the logic of formal and abstract equality. That is, Equiano does not simply encounter an exclusion from such equality, but a *constitutive* exclusion ritually iterated and reiterated in the Atlantic zone at least in part by a mercantilist system which, as we have seen throughout this essay, articulates "equality" with "race" and "nation." Equiano finds himself increasingly caught in this reiteration as he repeatedly seeks freedom "betwixt and between," in Paul Gilroy's phrase, nation-states, through the merchant marine trade. Eventually, Equiano abandons his efforts, offering a sharp condemnation of the merchant marine trade in the last chapter of his narrative: "I had suffered so many impositions in my commercial transactions in different parts of the world, that I became heartily disgusted with the seafaring life, and was determined not to return to it, at least for some time. I therefore once more engaged in service shortly after my return, and continued for the most part in this situation until 1784" (E, 220; 167).

As the final pages of the *Narrative* indicate, Equiano then began to pursue a different way of rendering freedom, though eventually he would abandon and condemn it also. In the early 1780s, Equiano became a missionary in Africa as well as an advocate of the British "colonization" of African diasporans—that is, their deportation from Britain and North America and resettlement to the colony of Sierra Leone.[64] Equiano's turn to colonization is a strikingly direct engagement in the very discourses of racial and national particularization that he had unsuccessfully tried to avoid with his transatlantic mercantile endeavours. In his embrace of colonization, Equiano accepts the racial-national codification of formal, abstract equality. Yet perhaps Equiano's eventual renunciation of colonization suggests that such a strategy was just as precarious for early-nineteenth-century black subjects as was the merchant marine trade in the face of mercantilism in the Atlantic zone.

NOTES

I would like to thank those who have generously commented on this essay, in its many forms: Dina Al-Kasim, Rakesh Bhandari, Katherine Clay Bassard, Emma Bianchi, Marianne Constable, Florence Dore, David L. Eng, Carolina Gonzales, Donna Hunter, Donna Jones, Miranda Joseph, David Lloyd, Colleen Lye, Nikhil Pal Singh, Tim Watson, Alys Eve Weinbaum, Michelle Wolfson, and the contributors to this volume. For her incisice comments and her inspiration, I thank Judith Butler. For her immeasurable contributions, I can hardly thank María Josefina Saldaña enough.

1. William Hill, "The First Stages of the Tariff Policy of the United States," *Publications of the American Economic Association* 8, no. 6 (1893): 564; F. W. Taussig, *The Tariff History of the United States* (New York: G. P. Putnam's Sons, 1931), pp. 14–15.

2. Joseph Gales, Sr., ed., *Annals of Congress, 1st Congress, 1789–90, Part 1* (Washington, DC: Gales and Seaton, 1834–1856), pp. 106–7.

3. In the *Annals* of the early years of Congress, only House debates are recorded in any detail. For more of this debate, see sections under "Collection of Duties" in *Annals of Congress, 1st Congress, 1789–90, Part 1*, pp. 106–867.

4. Ibid., p. 106.

5. Ibid., p. 164.

6. Ibid., p. 147.

7. Hill, "First Stages of the Tariff Policy," pp. 461–90; Harold U. Faulkner, "The Development of the American System," *The Annals of the American Academy of Political and Social Science* 141 (January 1929): 11; Taussig, *Tariff History*, p. 15.

8. Olaudah Equiano, *The Interesting Narrative and Other Writings*, ed. Vincent Carretta (New York: Penguin Books, 1995); Olaudah Equiano, *The Interesting Narrative of the Life of Olaudah Equiano, or Gustavus Vassa, the African*, ed. Henry Louis Gates, Jr. (New York: Penguin Books, 1987). Throughout this essay I quote from the ninth edition of Equiano's narrative, originally published in London in 1794. Vincent Carretta, editor of Penguin's 1995 republication of this edition, has made the case for the 1794 text (E, xxix). Textual citations give the page number of the Carretta edition first, followed by the equivalent page number from the widely available 1814 Leeds edition, edited by Henry Louis Gates, Jr. Subsequent parenthetical references in the text give page numbers preceded by E.

9. The exceptions are Houston Baker, whom I discuss below; Joseph Fichtelberg, "Word between Worlds: The Economy of Equiano's Narrative," *American Literary History* 5, no. 3 (1993): 459–80; and Susan M. Marren, "Between Slavery and Freedom: The Transgressive Self in Olaudah Equiano's Autobiography," *PMLA* 108 (January 1993): 94–105. Akiyo Ito's comparison of the subscriber lists of the only U.S. edition of the *Narrative* with the lists of the nine British editions shows that the *Narrative's* U.S. subscribers tended to be artisans, while its British subscribers tended to be elite merchants and aristocrats. Though for Ito this difference indicates the relative strength of abolitionism in Britain and the United States, it also offers intriguing clues to a reception study of Equiano's mercantile discourse. See "Olaudah Equiano and the New York Artisans: The First American Edition of *The Interesting Narrative of the Life of Olaudah Equiano, or Gustavus Vassa, The African*," *Eighteenth-Century Studies* 27 (Summer 1994): 82–101. On the publication history of the *Narrative*, see James Green, "The Publishing History of Olaudah Equiano's *Interesting Narrative*," *Slavery and Abolition* 16, no. 3 (1995): 362–75.

For studies, not mentioned elsewhere in this article, of the *Narrative's* shifting voices and its spiritual, autobiographical, and abolitionist components, see Henry Louis Gates, Jr., *The Signifying Monkey: A Theory of African-American Literary Criticism* (New York: Oxford University Press, 1988); Victor C. D. Mtumbani, "The Black Voice in Eighteenth-Century Britain: African Writers against Slavery and the Slave Trade," *Phylon*, 45, no. 2 (1984): 85–97; Geraldine Murphy, "Olaudah Equiano, Accidental Tourist," *Eighteenth-Century Studies* 27 (Summer, 1994): 551–68; Katalin Orban, "Dominant and Submerged Discourses in *The Life of Olaudah Equiano* (or Gustavus Vassa?)," *African American Review* 27, no. 4 (1993): 655–64; Adam Potkay, "Olaudah Equiano and the Art of Spiritual Autobiography," *Eighteenth-Century Studies* 27 (Summer 1994): 677–92; Wilfred D. Samuels, "Disguised Voice in *The Interesting Narrative of Olaudah Equiano, or Gustavus Vassa, the African*," *Black American Literature Forum* 19 (1985): 64–69; Valerie Smith, *Self-Discovery and Authority in Afro-American Narrative* (Cambridge: Harvard University Press, 1987).

After I wrote this essay, Elizabeth Jane Wall Hinds published "The Spirit of Trade: Olaudah Equiano's Conversion, Legalism, and the Merchant's *Life*" in *African American Review* 32, no. 4 (1998): 635–47. Hinds offers an important account of how Equiano's ambiguous engagement with capitalist enterprise interacts with his religious and legal engagements. Unfortunately, however, it replicates Baker's conflation of "mercantile" with "mercantilism" (636, 637–38, 639), and thus does not address the constitutive relationship among racial codification, national codification, and formal equality.

10. In the larger project to which this essay contributes, I examine the rise of black sailors on the Atlantic in the eighteenth century and their decline in the nineteenth century as illustrative of the increasingly constitutive relationships among discourses and practices of race, nation, equality, and gender. For excellent historical accounts of seafaring as a crucial avenue of employment for black men in the late eighteenth and early-to-mid-nineteenth centuries, see W. Jeffrey Bolster, " 'To Feel like a Man': Black Seamen in Northern States, 1800–1860," *The Journal of American History* 76 (March 1990): 1173–99, and *Black Jacks: African American Seamen in the Age of Sail* (Cambridge, MA: Harvard University Press, 1997); Philip S. Foner and Ronald L. Lewis, eds., *The Black Worker: A Documentary History from Colonial Times to the Present*, vol. 1, *The Black Worker to 1869* (Philadelphia: Temple University Press, 1978), pp. 196–241; Jesse Lemisch, *Jack Tar vs. John Bull* (New York: Garland, 1997); Peter Linebaugh, "All the Atlantic Mountains Shook," *Labour/Le Travailleur* 10 (Autumn 1982): 87–121; Peter Linebaugh and Marcus Rediker, "The Many-Headed Hydra: Sailors, Slaves, and the Atlantic Working Class in the Eighteenth Century," *Journal of Historical Sociology* 3 (September 1990): 225–52; Gary B. Nash, "Forging Freedom: The Emancipation Experience in the Northern Seaports, 1775–1820," in *Race, Class, and Politics: Essays on American Colonial and Revolutionary Society* (Urbana: University of Illinois Press, 1986); Martha S. Putney, *Black Sailors: Afro-American Merchant Seamen and Whalemen Prior to the Civil War* (New York: Greenwood Press, 1987); Marcus Rediker, *Between the Devil and the Deep Blue Sea: Merchant Seamen, Pirates, and the Anglo-American Maritime World, 1700–1750* (Cambridge: Cambridge University Press, 1987); Gladdis Smith, "Black Seamen and the Federal Courts, 1789–1860," in *Ships, Seafaring, and Society: Essays in Maritime History*, ed. Timothy J. Runyan (Detroit: Wayne State University Press, 1987), pp. 321–38

11. Houston A. Baker, Jr., *Blues, Ideology, and Afro-American Literature: A Vernacular Theory* (Chicago: University of Chicago Press, 1984).

12. Ibid., p. 19. In his reading of Foucault, Baker represents the "statement" as "the fundamental unit of discourse. [Foucault] defines the statement as a materially repeatable (i.e., recorded) linguistic function. A chart, graph, exclamation, table, sentence, or logical proposition may serve as a statement (pp. 79–87)." In turn, he represents the function of statements in a "discursive formation" as follows: "The distribution and combination of statements in a discourse are regulated, according to Foucault, by discoverable principles or laws (p. 56). These laws of formation are referred to as a 'discursive formation' (p. 38). They make possible the emergence of the notions and themes of a discourse" (Baker, 18). Baker's page references in this section refer to Michel Foucault, *The Archaeology of Knowledge* (New York: Pantheon Books, 1972). A "canon" in Baker's argument refers not simply to a selection of texts, but also to the logic of selecting, organizing, and representing those texts as a unified body of knowledge (see pp. 16–26). Baker takes Perry Miller's own epochal *Errand into the Wilderness* (Cambridge, MA: Harvard University Press, 1956) as exemplary of traditional U.S. literary study, and Robert Spiller's *A Literary History of the United States*, 4th rev. ed. (New York: Macmillan, 1974) as exemplary of traditional U.S. literary history.

13. Ibid., p. 26.

14. Ibid., p. 37.

15. Ibid., pp. 32–38.

16. William L. Andrews, "The First Fifty Years of the Slave Narrative, 1760–1810," in *The Art of the Slave Narrative: Original Essays in Criticism and Theory*, ed. John Sekora and Darwin T. Turner (Macomb, IL: Western Illinois University Press, 1982), pp. 6–24; Angelo Costanzo, *Surprising Narrative: Olaudah Equiano and the Beginnings of Black Autobiography* (Westport, CT: Greenwood Press, 1987), Chapter 4; Frances Smith Foster, *Witnessing Slavery: The Development of the Ante-bellum Slave Narratives* (Madison: University of Wisconsin Press, 1979), p. 15; Paul Gilroy, *The Black Atlantic: Modernity and Double Consciousness* (Cambridge, MA: Harvard University Press, 1993), p. 12; Marren, "Between Slavery and Freedom," p. 95.

17. Chinosole, "Tryin' to Get Over: Narrative Posture in Equiano's Autobiography," in Sekora and Turner, eds., *Art of the Slave Narrative*, p. 46.

18. Gilroy, *Black Atlantic*, p. 6.

19. Ibid., p. 12. Gilroy draws on the work of Bolster, Linebaugh, and Rediker (see note 10 above) to make this point.

20. See Fichtelberg, "Word between Worlds," pp. 459–80.

21. Gustavus Vassa is the name Equiano is forced to adopt by one of his masters.

22. Baker, *Blues*, p. 38.

23. Baker inadvertently indicates the source of this category mistake in a footnote: "I have relied heavily on the works of [Eugene] Genovese for my claims about slavery in the Old South" (p. 209)—namely, Genovese's *The Political Economy of Slavery* (Middletown, CT: Wesleyan University Press, 1989 [1961]) and his *The World the Slaveholders Made* (New York: Vintage, 1971). Baker thus selectively draws on just one side— Genovese's—of what has in fact been an extensive, multisided debate among economic historians over the relationships among slavery, mercantilism, and capitalism. The crucial texts for this debate are Elizabeth Fox-Genovese and Eugene Genovese, *The Fruits of Merchant Capital: Slavery and Bourgeois Property in the Rise and Expansion of Capital* (New York: Oxford University Press, 1983); Genovese, *Political Economy of Slavery;* Robert William Fogel and Stanley Engerman, *Time on the Cross: The Economics of American Negro Slavery*, vols. 1–2 (Boston: Little, Brown, 1974); Immanuel Wallerstein, "American Slavery and the Capitalist World-Economy," in *The Capitalist World-Economy* (Cambridge: Cambridge University Press, 1993). This debate can be read as the U.S. "spin-off" of an earlier debate over the global origin and status of capitalism, feudalism, and slavery, a debate staged most starkly between Robert Brenner and Ernesto Laclau, on one side, and André Gunder Frank and Immanuel Wallerstein, among others, on the other side. For a sampling of this debate, see Robert Brenner, "The Origins of Capitalist Development: A Critique of Neo-Smithian Marxism," in *The Brenner Debate*, ed. T. H. Aston and C. H. E. Philpin (New York: Cambridge University Press, 1985); André Gunder Frank, *World Accumulation, 1492–1789* (New York: Monthly Review Press, 1978); Immanuel Wallerstein, "The Rise and Future Demise of the World Capitalism System: Concepts for Comparative Analysis," in *The Capitalist World-Economy* (Cambridge: Cambridge University Press, 1979). For an excellent summary of this debate, its context, and its antecedents, see Jorge Larrain, *Theories of Development: Capitalism, Colonialism, and Dependency* (Cambridge: Polity Press, 1989).

24. Recent economic histories of mercantilism have accepted that the term itself was not used by many of the economic thinkers to whom it is attributed and that there were vast differences among and within the mercantilist arguments and poli-

cies of different countries and different economists. Nonetheless, they suggest that the term can be used analytically and nominally to indicate the emergence, beginning in early-seventeenth-century England and later developing in Europe and the United States, of a set of economic discourses and practices that had the effect of systematically creating economic wealth and power within nationally defined, territorially specific economies. On this account of mercantilism, see Giovanni Arrighi, *The Long Twentieth Century* (New York: Verso, 1994); Fernand Braudel, *Civilization and Capitalism, Fifteenth–Eighteenth Century*, vols. 1–3 (New York: Harper and Row, 1981–84 [1979]); Lars Magnusson, ed., *Mercantilist Economics* (Boston: Kluwer Academic Publishers, 1993), and *Mercantilism: The Shaping of an Economic Language* (London: Routledge, 1994); Immanuel Wallerstein, *The Modern World-System*, vol. 2, *Mercantilism and the Consolidation of the European World-Economy, 1600–1750* (New York: Academic Press, 1980); Wallerstein, *The Modern World-System*, vol. 3, *The Second Era of Great Expansion of the Capitalist World-Economy, 1730s–1840s* (New York: Academic Press 1989).

The term *mercantilism* has been extremely controversial among classical and neoclassical economists and economic historians, and I will offer only a thumbnail sketch of this controversy here. The term *systéme mercantile* was apparently first used by Marquis de Mirabeau in his *Philosophie Rurale ou Economie Générale et Politique de L'agriculture* (Amsterdam, 1763). Adam Smith offers the first extensive account of what he called, from Mirabeau, "the mercantile system" in book 4 of *An Inquiry into the Nature and Causes of the Wealth of Nations* (Chicago: University of Chicago Press, 1976 [1776]). Smith polemically and reductively defines this system as one based on a confusion of a nation's wealth with its supply of money and consequently as harmfully seeking to institutionalize a favorable balance of trade with extensive protectionist policies. He further insists that the mercantile system is the invention of devious and self-interested merchants, and that it runs counter to his own economic system. Although Smith's own system actually has many similarities with the mercantile systems of his day—he was by no means an opponent of significant protectionist or encouragement policies—subsequent economists and economic historians adopt his polemical account, further narrowing Smith's already narrow definition of mercantilism and further exaggerating the distinction between Smith's system and mercantilism. J. R. McCulloch in his 1828 introduction to *The Wealth of Nations* (Edinburgh: Adam Black and William Tait) and Richard Jones in his 1859 "Primitive Political Economy of England" (in *Literary Remains Consisting of Lectures and Tracts on Political Economy* [New York: Augustus M. Kelley, 1964]) begin this tradition. In the mid-to-late nineteenth century, economists such as Friedrich List and Gustav Schmoller in Germany, William Cunningham in England, and H. C. Carey in the United States revive and defend mercantilism as an economic system characterized by centralized state regulation of territorially specific economies in the interest of increasing the power and wealth of national economies (see List, *The National System of Political Economy*, Sampson S. Lloyd, trans. [London: Longmans, 1885]; Schmoller, *The Mercantile System and Its Historical Significance* [New York: Macmillan, 1896]; Cunningham, *The Growth of English Industry and Commerce* [Cambridge: The University Press, 1921]; Carey, *The Past, The Present, and The Future* [Philadelphia: Henry Carey Baird, 1869 (1847)]). In reaction to these arguments, neoclassical economists revive the McCulloch and Jones critique of mercantilism, thus further institutionalizing and exaggerating Smith's polemical account. In 1930, Jacob Viner furthers this neoclassical polemic against a straw-mercantilism ("Early English Theories of Trade," reprinted in his *Studies in the Theory of International Trade* [London: Allen and Unwin, 1937], 1–118). In 1931 Eli F. Heckscher, though critical of mercantilism, defines it much more broadly as an extensive system of economic thought and practice in *Mercantilism* (London: George Allen and Unwin, 1934 [1931]). A. V. Judges in 1939 and later D. C. Coleman respond that, in fact, mercantilism never even existed as a coherent system of economic thought or practice (see Judges, "The Idea of a Mercantile State," in D. C. Coleman, ed., *Revisions in Mercantilism* (London: Methuen, 1969); Coleman, "Mercantilism Revisited," *Historical Journal* 23, no. 4 (1980): 773–91). On the intellectual history of the term, see D. C. Coleman, "Introduction," in *Revisions in Mercantilism;* Magnusson, ed., *Mercantilist Economics;* Magnusson, *Mercantilism;* Robert Harry Inglis Palgrave, *Dictionary of Political Economy* (London: MacMillan, 1917) 727–28. Karl Pribram, *A History of Economic Reasoning* (Baltimore: Johns Hopkins University Press, 1983).

Many of these classical and neoclassical economic historians argue that mercantilist policies were based exclusively or primarily on the medieval theory (named bullionism or monetarism and often figured as the Midas fallacy) that a nation's money supply equals its wealth, and that there is a fixed supply of wealth in the world that consequently has to be fought over through the merchant trade. In fact, however, most mercantilists have been explicitly critical of such a theory, and have offered a diverse and much more complex range of justifications for their policies right up through the twentieth century. Consequently, mercantilism can hardly be reduced to an atavistic, medieval theory of wealth. For the range of theoretical justifications for mercantilism, see Braudel, *Civilization and Capitalism*, vol. 2, 542 ff.; Coleman, ed., *Revisions in Mercantilism;* Magnusson, ed., *Mercantilist Economics;* Magnusson, *Mercantilism*.

25. Richard Sheridan, "The Domestic Economy," in Greene and Pole, eds., *Colonial British America*, 70. For accounts of mercantilist policies and practices in North America, see Bernard Bailyn, *The New England Merchants of the Seventeenth Century* (Cambridge, MA: Harvard University Press, 1955). On the seventeenth and eighteenth centuries, see Carl Bridenbaugh, *Cities in the Wilderness: The First Century of Urban Life in America, 1625–1742* (New York: Knopf, 1955); Richard L. Bushman, *From Puritan to Yankee: Character and the Social Order in Connecticut, 1690–1765* (Cambridge, MA: Harvard University Press, 1967); Bruce C. Daniels, "Economic Development in Colonial and Revolutionary Connecticut: An Overview," *William and Mary Quarterly*, 3rd series, 37, no. 3 (1980): 429–50; Carville V. Earle, *The Evolution of a Tidewater Settlement System: All Hallow's Parish, Maryland, 1650–1783* (Chicago: University of Chicago Press, 1975); Carville V. Earle and Ronald Hoffman, "Staple Crops and Urban Development in the Eighteenth-Century South," *Perspectives in American History* 10 (1976): 7–78; Jack P. Greene, *Pursuits of Happiness: The Social Development of Early Modern British Colonies and the Formation of American Culture* (Chapel Hill: University of North Carolina Press, 1988); Clarence P. Gould, *Money and Transportation in Maryland, 1720–1765* (Baltimore: Johns Hopkins University Press, 1915); James A. Henretta and Gregory H. Nobles, *Evolution and Revolution: American Society, 1600–1820* (Lexington, MA: D. C. Heath, 1987), pp. 197–220; James T. Lemon, *The Best Poor Man's Country: A Geographical Study of Early Southeastern Pennsylvania* (Baltimore: Johns Hopkins University Press, 1972); Harry Roy Merrens, *Colo-*

nial North Carolina in the Eighteenth Century: A Study in Historical Geography (Chapel Hill: University of North Carolina Press, 1964); Isabel S. Mitchell, *Roads and Road-Making in Colonial Connecticut* (New Haven: Yale University Press, 1933); Robert D. Mitchell, *Commercialism and Frontier: Perspectives on the Early Shenandoah Valley* (Charlottesville: University Press of Virginia, 1977); Richard B. Morris, *Government and Labor in Early America* (New York: Octagon Books, 1965); Gary B. Nash, *The Urban Crucible: Social Change, Political Consciousness, and the Origins of the American Revolution* (Cambridge, MA: Harvard University Press, 1979); Curtis P. Nettels, "British Mercantilism and the Economic Development of the Thirteen Colonies," *Journal of Economic History* 12 (1952): 105–14; Edward G. Roberts, "The Roads of Virginia, 1607–1840," Ph.D. diss., University of Virginia, 1950; Mary McKinney Schweitzer, "Economic Regulation and the Colonial Economy: The Maryland Tobacco Inspection Act of 1747," *Journal of Economic History* 40 (1980): 551–69; John Flexer Walzer, "Transportation in the Philadelphia Trading Area, 1740–1755," Ph.D. diss., University of Wisconsin, 1968; William Earl Weeks, "American Nationalism, American Imperialism: An Interpretation of United States Political Economy, 1789–1861," *Journal of the Early Republic* 14 (Winter 1994): 485–95. See also a crucial essay, published after I wrote this essay, by Lawrence Peskin: "From Protection to Encouragement: Manufacturing and Mercantilism in New York City's Political Discourse, 1783–1795," *Journal of the Early Republic* 18 (Winter 1998): 589–615.

26. The Declaration of Independence complains about "cutting off our trade with all parts of the world" and "imposing taxes on us without our consent."

27. Leonard Gomes, *Foreign Trade and the National Economy: Mercantilist and Classical Perspectives* (London: Macmillan, 1987), p. 263; Taussig, *Tariff History.* More generally, see Hill, "First Stages of the Tariff Policy," pp. 455–614, for the tariff history of British-North America and the early United States. On the political contexts of this tariff history in the post-independence period, see also Fox-Genovese and Genovese, *Fruits of Merchant Capital;* James A. Henretta and Gregory H. Nobles, *Evolution and Revolution: American Society, 1600–1820* (Lexington, MA: D. C. Heath, 1987); Allan Kulikoff, *The Agrarian Origins of American Capitalism* (Charlottesville, VA: University Press of Virginia, 1992); David Montgomery, *Citizen Worker* (Cambridge: Cambridge University Press, 1993); Gordon S. Wood, *The Creation of the American Republic, 1776–1787* (New York: W. W. Norton, 1969).

28. Arrighi, *Long Twentieth Century* (New York: Verso, 1994), pp. 1–84, 58–84, 140–42, 223–24; Braudel, *Civilization and Capitalism,* vols. 2 and 3; Gomes, *Foreign Trade and the National Economy,* pp. 3–37, 258–64; Lars Mjoset, "The Turn of Two Centuries: A Comparison of British and U.S. Hegemonies," in *World Leadership and Hegemony,* ed. D. P. Rapkin (Boulder, CO: Lynne Reiner, 1990); Karl Polanyi, *The Great Transformation* (Boston: Beacon Press, 1957), pp. 36–42, 67–76, 278; Taussig, *Tariff History;* Immanuel Wallerstein, *The Modern World-System,* vol. 2, pp. 37, 56, 80–81, 98–99, 209, 236–41, 268–89, and vol. 3, pp. 66–71, 77–87, 97–100, 122, 170–71, 196–204, 247–50; Donald Winch, *Classical Political Economy and the Colonies* (Cambridge, MA: Harvard University Press, 1965), p. 97. A set of policies can be called "mercantilist," on these accounts, because it nationalizes an economy by strengthening the state so that it can enforce a temporary delinking from international trade and a concomitant expansion and diversification of agriculture and manufacture within a territorially discrete space.

29. Etienne Balibar and Immanuel Wallerstein, *Race, Nation, Class: Ambiguous Identities* (London: Verso, 1991), pp. 88–90.

30. Ibid., p. 88; Arrighi, *Long Twentieth Century,* p. 49.

31. Karl Marx, *Capital: A Critique of Political Economy,* vol. 1, trans. Ben Fowkes (New York: Vintage Books, 1977), p. 932.

32. Ibid., p. 874.

33. I will examine this process from the perspective of what Marx calls "the simple form of value." Marx argues that the value form can actually be broken down into four forms: "the simple, isolated, or accidental form of value" (ibid., pp. 139–54), "the total or expanded form " (pp. 154–57), "the general form" (pp. 157–62), and "the money form" (pp. 162–63). While he says that "we have to trace the development of the expression of value contained in the value-relation of commodities from its simplest, almost imperceptible outline to the dazzling money-form" (p. 139), it seems clear from the argument that this "development" is synchronic; that is, the value form is simultaneously all four of these forms. Analytically, the four forms are four different ways of representing the value form that offer different perspectives on its meaning and force in the world of commodities; synthetically, the four forms render the meaning and force behind social relations such as the commodity.

34. Ibid., p. 142.

35. Ibid.

36. This is also argued in the *Grundrisse,* when Marx renders the process of naturalizing the value form as a process, on one hand, of suppression, obfuscation, and forgetting and, on the other hand, of active re-creation; see his *Grundrisse: Foundations of the Critique of Political Economy,* trans. Martin Nicolaus (New York: Vintage Books, 1973), pp. 247–48. Thus an account of the "specificity of the value form" is not simply an account of an essence cloaked by a destructive and "false form of appearance;" rather, it is an account of the compulsive reformation of social relations.

37. Ibid., pp. 241–45.

38. Ibid., p. 245.

39. The work of the value form on citizenship can also be gleaned from the so-called early Marx, most strikingly from "On the Jewish Question" (1833) and the "Economic and Philosophical Manuscripts" (1844), in Karl Marx, *Early Writings* (New York: Vintage Books, 1975). For a fine reading of the former text as an analysis of universal abstraction in citizenship, see Wendy Brown, *States of Injury: Power and Freedom in Late Modernity* (Princeton: Princeton University Press, 1995), pp. 96–134. Lisa Lowe has also addressed this question in her important *Immigrant Acts: On Asian American Cultural Politics* (Durham, NC: Duke University Press, 1996). Whereas Lowe places great emphasis on the necessary or likely "contradiction" or "antagonism" between racial particularization and formal, abstract equality (see, for example, pp. ix, 2, 8, 9, 10, 13, 15, 20–24, 27, 28, 30, 32), my research suggests that, in eighteenth- and nineteenth-century North America, historically specific articulations of racial codification are more likely supplementary to—and thus often constitutive of—historically specific articulations of formal and abstract equality. Consequently, efforts to turn such a supplement toward a contradiction or an antagonism are at least as precarious as they are urgent.

40. Gayatri Chakravorty Spivak's work on value theory has been indispensable to my interpretation of Marx in this essay, as I explain explicitly in the larger project

from which this essay is culled. For further developments of Spivak's reading of value theory, see her "Scattered Speculations on the Question of Value," in *In Other Worlds: Essays in Cultural Politics* (New York: Routledge, 1985); "Speculations on Reading Marx: After Reading Derrida," in *Post-Structuralism and the Question of History*, ed. Derek Attridge, Geoff Bennington, and Robert Young (Cambridge: Cambridge University Press, 1987); "Poststructuralism, Marginality, Post-Coloniality and Value," in *Literary Theory Today*, ed. Peter Collier and Helga Geyer-Ryan (Ithaca: Cornell University Press, 1990); "Remembering the Limits: Difference, Identity, and Practice," in *Socialism and the Limits of Liberalism*, ed. Peter Osborne (London: Verso, 1991); "Limits and Openings of Marx in Derrida," in *Outside in the Teaching Machine* (New York: Routledge 1993), pp. 97–119. See also Noel Castree, "Invisible Leviathan: Speculations on Marx, Spivak, and the Question of Value," *Rethinking Marxism* 9, no. 2 (1996–97): 45–78. For a brilliant deployment of Spivak's work in the context of a feminist politics of reproduction, see Alys Eve Weinbaum, "Marx, Irigaray, and the Politics of Reproduction," *Differences: A Journal of Feminist Cultural Studies* 6, no. 1 (1994): 98–129.

41. The concept of "reification," elaborated classically by Georg Lukács, is the most prevalent reading; see his *History and Class Consciousness*, trans. Rodney Livingstone (Cambridge: MIT Press, 1988).

42. The complex developments of Marx's and Engels's positions on "the national question" in Europe, especially Ireland, and in India are other important sites for such furtive attempts. See Marx's articles in the *New York Daily Tribune* on India and China from 1853, in Karl Marx, *Political Writings*, vol. 2, *Surveys from Exile*, ed. David Fernbach (New York: Vintage Books, 1974), pp. 301–33; his letters and passages, some written with Engels, on Ireland, in Karl Marx and Frederick Engels, *Ireland and the Irish Question* (Moscow: Progress Publishers, 1971); "The Communist Manifesto" from 1847, in Karl Marx, *Political Writings*, vol. 1, *The Revolutions of 1848*, ed. David Fernbach (New York: Vintage Books, 1974), pp. 62–98; Marx and Engels's speeches on Poland from 1847–48 and their "The Demands of the Communist Party in Germany" from 1848, in Karl Marx, *Political Writings*, vol. 1, pp. 99–103 and 109–11; see also Engels's articles in *Rheinische Zeitung* on the Magyar struggle, and Bakunin's "Democratic Pan-Slavism" from 1849, in Karl Marx, *Political Writings*, vol. 1, pp. 213–45.

43. Karl Marx, *On America and the Civil War*, trans. Saul K. Padover (New York: McGraw-Hill, 1972), p. 104.

44. Marx, *Grundrisse*, p. 275.

45. Throughout the nineteenth-century United States, as David Roediger has argued, the trope of "wage-slavery" performed precisely this erasure of racialization under capitalism; see David R. Roediger, *The Wages of Whiteness: Race and the Making of the American Working Class* (New York: Verso, 1991), pp. 72–74, 176.

46. Marx, *Grundrisse*, p. 464.

47. Marx, *Collected Works*, vol. 31, *Karl Marx, 1861–63* (New York: International Publishers, 1989), p. 516. For the German, see *Werke*, Band 26.2 (Berlin: Dietz Verlan, 1967), p. 299.

48. Marx's perspectival shift between the production perspective and the world-market perspective lays down the terms of the debate, mentioned in note 23 above, over the origins of capitalism. Marxists such as Robert Brenner, Eugene Genovese,

and the early Ernesto Laclau take up the production perspective, whereas members of the world-system and *dependendista* schools take up the global perspective of trade.

49. I would like to thank Judith Butler and Katrin Pahl for discussing this passage from Marx with me.

50. For related theoretical accounts of the relationship between universalism and particularism under capitalism, see Etienne Balibar, "Ambiguous Universality," *Differences: A Journal of Feminist Cultural Studies* 7, no. 1 (1995): 48–74; Balibar and Wallerstein, *Race, Nation, Class,* pp. 1–27, 37–67, 86–105; Brown, *States of Injury,* pp. 96–134; Ernesto Laclau, *Emancipation(s)* (London: Verso, 1996), pp. 20–65; Miranda Joseph, "The Performance of Production and Consumption," *Social Text* 54 (Spring 1998): 25–61; Peter Osborne, *The Politics of Time: Modernity and the Avant-Garde* (London: Verso, 1995), p. 165; Moishe Postone, "Anti-Semitism and National Socialism," in *Germans and Jews Since the Holocaust: The Changing Situation in West Germany,* ed. Anson Rabinbach and Jack Zipes (New York: Holmes and Meier, 1986); Naoki Sakai, "Modernity and Its Critique: The Problem of Universalism and Particularism," *South Atlantic Quarterly* 87 (Summer 1988): 475–504; Joan W. Scott, "Universalism and the History of Feminism," *Differences: A Journal of Feminist Cultural Studies* 7, no. 1 (1995): 1–14, and *"Only Paradoxes to Offer": French Feminists and the Rights of "Man," 1789–1994* (Cambridge, MA: Harvard University Press, 1995).

51. Balibar and Wallerstein, *Race, Nation, Class,* p. 9.

52. On the "categorization" to which Balibar refers, see Theodore W. Allen, *The Invention of the White Race: Racial Oppression and Social Control* (New York: Verso, 1994); Balibar, "Ambiguous Universality"; Michael Banton, *Racial Theories* (Cambridge: Cambridge University Press, 1987); Robert E. Bieder, *Science Encounters the Indian, 1820–1880: The Early Years of American Ethnology* (Norman: University of Oklahoma Press, 1986); Jack D. Forbes, *Africans and Native Americans: The Language of Race and the Evolution of Red-Black Peoples* (Urbana: University of Illinois Press, 1993); David Theo Goldberg, ed., *Anatomy of Racism* (Minneapolis: Minnesota University Press, 1990), and *Racist Culture: Philosophy and the Politics of Meaning* (Oxford: Blackwell, 1993); Thomas F. Gossett, *Race: The History of an Ideal in America* (Dallas: Southern Methodist University Press, 1963); Colette Guillaumin, "The Specific Character of Racist Ideology," in *Racism, Sexism, Power, and Ideology* (New York: Routledge, 1995); Stephen Jay Gould, *The Mismeasure of Man* (New York: W. W. Norton, 1981); Sandra Harding, ed., *The "Racial" Economy of Science: Toward a Democratic Future* (Bloomington: Indiana University Press, 1993); Reginald Horsman, *Race and Manifest Destiny: The Origins of American Racial Anglo-Saxonism* (Cambridge, MA: Harvard University Press, 1981); Winthrop D. Jordan, *White Over Black: American Attitudes Toward the Negro, 1550–1812* (New York: W. W. Norton, 1977); Alden T. Vaughan, *The Roots of American Racism: Essays on the Colonial Experience* (New York: Oxford University Press, 1995). For accounts of the notion of "equality" in this period, see Celeste Michelle Condit and John Louis Lucaites, *Crafting Equality: America's Anglo-African World* (Chicago: University of Chicago Press, 1993); and Jack P. Greene, *Imperatives, Behaviors, and Identities: Essays in Early American Cultural History* (Charlottesville: University of Virginia Press, 1992), chaps. 10, 11, and 13.

53. See, for example, Wallerstein, *Modern World-System,* vol. 3, and "American Slavery and the Capitalist World-Economy."

54. There has been a debate over the authenticity of Equiano's representations of his West African homeland—see Catherine Obianuju Acholonu, *The Igbo Roots of*

Olaudah Equiano: An Anthropological Research (Owerri, Nigeria: AFA, 1989), and "The Home of Olaudah Equiano: A Linguistic and Anthropological Search," *The Journal of Commonwealth Literature* 22, no. 1, (1987): 5–16; S. E. Ogude, "Facts into Fiction: Equiano's Narrative Revisited," *Okike: An African Journal of New Writing* 22 (September 1982): 57–66.

55. Fichtelberg, "Word between Worlds," p. 469.

56. On the dynamic of the mochlos, see Jacques Derrida, "Mochlos; or, The Conflict of the Faculties," in *Logomachia: The Conflict of the Faculties*, ed. Richard Rand (Lincoln: University of Nebraska Press, 1992).

57. This formal, abstract equality is also a gendered form of freedom, for women were all but absent from the radically mobile form of labor conducted on merchant ships. In fact, Equiano is so intent upon mastering that form of labor that he is unable to consider its gendered specificity, and consequently is often unable to represent labor in general as other than masculine. For instance, accounts of the abuse of Africans as laborers in the *Narrative* are at times followed immediately by accounts of the sexual abuse of African women (E, 108–10; 77–79). While his representation of sexual violence brings to the fore the gendered specificity of racial exploitation and could be read as a critique of the exploitation of black women's reproductive labor, it is also part of the text's pattern of representing black men as laborers exploited in a public realm and black women as subjects exploited only in a "private," sexual realm. As studies of gender and labor under slavery have made clear, the sexual division of labor common to the free white world was not mirrored in slavery; see Angela Davis, *Women, Race, and Class* (New York: Vintage Books, 1983), pp. 5–6. While sharply critical of an aspect of gendered exploitation—sexual abuse—the *Narrative* nonetheless assumes a sexual division of slave labor, which has the effect of gendering the "public" formal and abstract equality held out by merchant capitalism as necessarily masculine.

I am currently working on the articulation of gender in the merchant marine conjuncture of the eighteenth and early nineteenth centuries. Increasingly during this period, as mercantilist regulations enclosed the North Atlantic, black mariners were pushed into shipboard jobs which were feminized because, at least in part, they resonated with forms of land labor that had already been vigorously feminized—stewards and cooks, for instance. See Bolster, *Black Jacks*, pp. 165–70, and " 'To Feel Like a Man,' " p. 1197; Margaret S. Creighton and Lisa Norling, eds., *Iron Men, Wooden Women: Gender and Seafaring in the Atlantic World, 1700–1920* (Baltimore: Johns Hopkins University Press, 1996).

58. On this history, see William W. Bower, *America's Virgin Islands: A History of Human Rights and Wrongs* (Durham, NC: Carolina Academic Press, 1983); Darwin D. Creque, *The U.S. Virgins and the Eastern Caribbean* (Philadelphia: Whitmore Publishing, 1968); Neville A. T. Hall, *Slave Society in the Danish West Indies: St. Thomas, St. John, and St. Croix*, ed. B. W. Higman (Baltimore: The Johns Hopkins University Press, 1992); *The Virgin Islands of the United States: A General Report by the Governor* (Washington: United States Government Printing Office, 1928).

59. See Robin Blackburn, *The Making of New World Slavery: From the Baroque to the Modern, 1492–1800* (New York: Verso, 1997), pp. 500–1; Hall, pp. 19–23; Svend E. Green Pedersen, "The Scope and Structure of the Danish Negro Slave Trade," *Scandinavian Economic History Review* 19 (1971): 149–97.

60. Bolster has found evidence for such cross-racial allegiances in his research on black seamen in the nineteenth century. Writes Bolster, "While by no means either color-blind or without internal frictions, Atlantic maritime culture created its own institutions and its own stratifications, which could work to the relative advantage of black men. One [nineteenth-century] observer summed it up by writing, 'The good will of "old salts" to negroes is proverbial' " (" 'To Feel Like a Man,' " p. 1179).

61. Equiano sets this scene in 1765, but as Carretta reminds us, the Stamp Act was repealed by Parliament on 18 March 1766 (E, 1995: 276).

62. The term *boycott* was, in fact, not coined until 1880. See "Boycott," in *The Compact Edition of the Oxford English Dictionary,* vol. 1 (New York: Oxford University Press, 1971), p. 260.

63. On the history of the Stamp Act, see Lawrence Henry Gipson, "The Great Debate," *Pennsylvania Magazine of History and Biography* 86 (1962): 10–41; Lemisch, *Jack Tar; New York Historical Society Quarterly* 49 (1965): 313–26; Edmund S. Morgan, *The Stamp Act Crisis: Sources and Documents* (Providence: reproduced from typewritten copy, 1952); Edmund S. Morgan and Helen M. Morgan, *The Stamp Act Crisis: Prologue to Revolution* (Chapel Hill: University of North Carolina Press, 1995); P. D. G. Thomas, *British Politics and the Stamp Act Crisis* (Oxford: Clarendon Press, 1975); Wood, *Creation of the American Republic.*

64. I examine the rhetoric of the early colonization movement in the United States in "Racial Governmentality: Thomas Jefferson and African Colonization in the United States before 1816," *Alternation: Journal of the Centre for the Study of Southern African Literature and Languages* 5, no. 1 (1998): 39–84.

Syllabus ENCLOSING THE "OPEN SEA"
    Race, Nation, Gender, and Equality in the Northern Atlantic
    Instructor: David Kazanjian

This class examines the confrontations of African diasporans who traveled
the Northern Atlantic during the late eighteenth and early nineteenth centuries with emerging Enlightenment conceptions of "race," "gender," "nation," and "equality." The readings will allow us to consider the relationships among central aspects of the period's Northern Atlantic cultures:
hierarchical codifications of racial, national, and gender identities, and a
liberal model of citizenship based on formal and abstract equality.

READINGS

Primary Material

Briton Hammon, *A Narrative of the Uncommon Sufferings, and Surprising
Deliverance of Briton Hammon, A Negro Man* (1760), in *A Collection of Writings by Negro Authors, 1760–1840* (Nendeln: Kraus Reprints, 1972).

James Albert Ukawsaw Gronniosaw, *A Narrative of the Most Remarkable
Particulars in the Life of James Albert Ukawsaw Gronniosaw, an African Prince*
(1770), in ibid.

Phillis Wheatley, "On Being Brought from Africa to America" (1773),
and "To a Lady on her coming to North America with her son, for the
Recovery of her Health," in *The Collected Works of Phillis Wheatley*, ed. John
Shields (New York: Oxford University Press, 1988 [1773]).

Quobna Ottobah Cugoano, "Thoughts and Sentiments on the Evil
and Wicked Traffic of the Slavery and Commerce of the Human
Species" (1787), in *Thoughts and Sentiments on the Evil of Slavery, and Other
Writings*, ed. Vincent Carretta (New York: Penguin Books, 1999).

Olaudah Equiano, *The Interesting Narrative of the Life of Olaudah Equiano,
or Gustavus Vassa, the African* (1789), in *The Interesting Narrative and Other
Writings*, ed. Vincent Carretta (New York: Penguin Books, 1995).

Venture Smith, *A Narrative of the Life and Adventures of Venture, a Native of Africa* (1798), in *Early American Imprints* (microprint), first series,
no. 34560.

Nancy Prince, *Narrative of the Life and Travels of Mrs. Nancy Prince*
(1850), in *A Black Woman's Odyssey through Russia and Jamaica* (New York:
Markus Wiener, 1990).

Adam Smith, Chapter 1, Book 4 of *An Inquiry into the Nature and Causes
of the Wealth of Nations* (Chicago: University of Chicago Press, 1976
[1776]).

Annals of Congress, 1st Congress, 1789–90, Part 1, ed. Joseph Gales, Sr.
(Washington, D.C.: Gales and Seaton, 1834).

Alexander Hamilton, "Report on the Subject of Manufactures," in *State Papers and Speeches on the Tariff,* ed. F. W. Taussig (Cambridge: Harvard University Press, 1892 [1791]).

Karl Marx, "On the Jewish Question" (1843), in *Early Writings* (New York: Vintage Books, 1975).

Secondary Material

Houston A. Baker, Jr., *Blues, Ideology, and Afro-American Literature: A Vernacular Theory* (Chicago: University of Chicago Press, 1984).

W. Jeffrey Bolster, *Black Jacks: African American Seamen in the Age of Sail* (Cambridge, MA: Harvard University Press, 1997).

Chinosole, "Tryin' To Get Over: Narrative Posture in Equiano's Autobiography," in *The Art of the Slave Narrative: Original Essays in Criticism and Theory,* ed. John Sekora and Darwin T. Turner (Macomb: Western Illinois University Press, 1982).

Margaret S. Creighton and Lisa Norling, *Iron Men, Wooden Women: Gender and Seafaring in the Atlantic World, 1700–1920* (Baltimore: Johns Hopkins University Press, 1996).

Angela Davis, *Women, Race, and Class* (New York: Vintage Books, 1983).

Paul Gilroy, *The Black Atlantic: Modernity and Double Consciousness* (Cambridge, MA: Harvard University Press, 1993).

Peter Linebaugh, "All the Atlantic Mountains Shook," *Labour/Le Travailleur* 10 (Autumn 1982): 87–121.

Peter Linebaugh and Marcus Rediker, "The Many-Headed Hydra: Sailors, Slaves, and the Atlantic Working Class in the Eighteenth Century," *Journal of Historical Sociology* 3, no. 3 (September 1990): 225–52.

Marcus Rediker, *Between the Devil and the Deep Blue Sea: Merchant Seamen, Pirates and the Anglo-American Maritime World, 1700–1750* (Cambridge: Cambridge University Press, 1987).

Elizabeth Fox-Genovese and Eugene Genovese, *The Fruits of Merchant Capital: Slavery and Bourgeois Property in the Rise and Expansion of Capital* (New York: Oxford University Press, 1983).

Immanuel Wallerstein, "American Slavery and the Capitalist World-Economy," in *The Capitalist World-Economy* (Cambridge: Cambridge University Press, 1993).

Etienne Balibar and Immanuel Wallerstein, *Race, Nation, Class: Ambiguous Identities* (London: Verso, 1991).

Joaquín Murrieta
and the American 1848

Shelley Streeby

1998 marked the 150th anniversary of the American 1848, the year that gold was discovered in California just before the signing of the Treaty of Guadalupe Hidalgo formally ended the war between the United States and Mexico. Eighteen forty-eight has been and continues to be, of course, a crucial date for Chicano Studies scholars and cultural workers. In the 1960s and 1970s writers and activists formulated theories of internal colonialism as responses to the events of 1848; more recently the violent break marked by the war has been central to work by Tomás Almaguer, Genaro Padilla, Beatrice Pita, José David Saldívar, Rosaura Sánchez, and many others.[1] Despite the significance of 1848 for Chicanos, however, many other Americans are unaware that the U.S.-Mexican War ever took place. While the Civil War is a major period marker in history and literature courses and is the subject of numerous popular movies and books, the U.S.-Mexican War is still scarcely mentioned in most college survey classes and rarely figures in mainstream, contemporary popular culture. Forgetting the U.S.-Mexican War, however, means eliding an influential early episode in imperialist U.S. nation-building, taking the national boundary-line between the United States and Mexico out of history, and naturalizing postwar redefinitions of the native and the alien. Today, as neo-nativisms play an increasingly large role in state and national politics, addressing the meanings of the American 1848 is clearly an important task for a post-nationalist American Studies.[2]

In what follows, I explore the ways that U.S. racial economies and class relationships were reshaped by the redrawing of boundaries that followed the U.S.-Mexican War and the Gold Rush. For if the war led to the remapping of national borders, the discovery of gold in California drew miners and other workers to the region from all over the world, but especially from Mexico, Hawaii, Chile, Peru, China, Ireland, Germany, France, the Eastern

United States, and Australia.³ While these shifts affected racial classifications in general, they dramatically influenced the racialization of former Mexican nationals and the construction of a transcontinental white national identity in particular.⁴ Far from serving as a safety valve for class pressures, the newly conquered land in the West remained a battlefield where race and nationalism decisively shaped class conflicts. These conflicts sometimes erupted as nativism, often pitted white workers against workers of color, and were always powerfully affected by the migratory movements of people across national boundaries and by the larger fields of hemispheric and global relations.

When Michael Rogin coined the periodizing phrase "the American 1848" in his excellent 1979 study of Herman Melville and nineteenth-century U.S. politics and culture, he compared the United States and Europe in order to argue that the U.S.-Mexican War ironically exposed the limits of republicanism and the contradictions within U.S. nationality at the very moment when both seemed unassailably triumphant.⁵ While other scholars, including Saldívar and Carolyn Porter, have subsequently resituated Rogin's American 1848 in relation to the history of U.S. imperialism in the Americas, a good deal of American Studies scholarship still subsumes all other meanings and consequences of the events of 1848 within a national narrative of slavery and freedom.⁶ For instance, Eric Lott argues in *Love and Theft* that "the minstrel show provided the soundtrack for the American 1848," revealing "the political unconscious of Manifest Destiny."⁷ The "racial repressed" that Lott uncovers, however, has little to do with U.S. imperialism, Mexico, immigrant workers, or international conflict. Instead, Lott focuses on "the sectional conflict western emigration not only failed to dispel but—in reopening the question of whether the occupied land would be slave or free—actually revivified."⁸ As a result, his brilliant analysis of the relationship between the formation of U.S. working-class whiteness and fantasies of blackness elides the important relationships between whiteness, blackness, and other racializations as they were elaborated during and after the U.S.-Mexican War in the borderlands and in the gold mines of California. Lott's analysis shows how the international dimensions of the U.S.-Mexican War and the non-binary race relations that it affected tend to disappear within national narratives that isolate domestic, sectional conflict from a larger global framework.

How might we explore the significance of the American 1848 more fully, giving more attention to the U.S.-Mexican War, inter-American relations, and the intersections of multiple class and racial formations? In this essay, I address this question by focusing on the international circulation of the story of Joaquín Murrieta, the California social bandit who supposedly terrorized California during the early 1850s. John Rollin Ridge's 1854 novel, *The Life and Adventures of Joaquín Murieta* is, at least in literature departments in U.S. colleges and universities, probably the most well-known version as well as the first novel written by an American Indian.[9] But the Murrieta story has also inspired an astonishing array of national and transnational textual fantasies, including one that was serialized in the *California Police Gazette;* a number of cheap novels; a 1936 Hollywood film; several widely circulated Spanish-language *corridos* or ballads; plays in both English and Spanish, including one written by Pablo Neruda; and revisions published in Mexico, Spain, France, and Chile.[10] Although Ridge's novel certainly provides an important point of departure for an investigation of the American 1848, I suggest that a focus on this narrative must be supplemented by an analysis of other revisions of the Murrieta story, especially the *California Police Gazette* version, which informed many of the Spanish-language adaptations, and the *corridos*. This supplementation is crucial because the dialogic interplay of all of these texts foregrounds the inter-American context of the American 1848 in ways that are not as apparent if only Ridge's text is consulted.

Finally, I hope to show that tracing the intersecting trajectories of the different revisions of the Murrieta crime narrative reveals the interdependent relationships among the mid-nineteenth century popularization of a fictive, transcontinental, white, American identity; the long, uneven postwar re-racialization of former Mexican nationals and other Spanish-speakers; and the articulation of a disjunctive, transnational, *mexicano,* cultural nationalism which introduces gaps and fissures into what too often passes for a seamless story of U.S. national belonging. The different versions of the Murrieta story suggest, in other words, how whiteness took hold as a unifying national and transcontinental structure of feeling and how its parameters began to shift decisively in the postwar period to include previously despised groups of Europeans and to exclude most of the newly conquered peoples in the West.[11]

This is only one side of the story, however. In *corridos* and other revisions of the Murrieta narrative, Latinos have challenged such exclusionary constructions of national identity by celebrating Murrieta's exemplary resistance to U.S. laws. While most U.S. citizens have naturalized the post-Treaty boundaries between Mexico and the United States, many border ballads refuse to accede to this mapping of the territory. Insisting that he is not a stranger (*extraño*), the Murrieta who tells his story in one of the most well-known of these *corridos* argues that "California is part of Mexico because God wanted it that way" ("De México es California/porque Díos así lo quizo"). Such a heroic narrative of resistance may in turn perform closures of its own: the sanctification of Mexican sovereignty elides the Spanish and creole subjugation of indigenous peoples, and Murrieta's insistence on his status as a "native" could imply a disdain for other immigrants such as the Chinese workers who are persecuted by his gang in the English-language versions of the story. What is more, figuring resistance to U.S. power as a paradigmatically masculine feat best accomplished by the *corrido* hero with a pistol in his hand marginalizes female agency, as many feminist critics have suggested.[12]

But if the *corridos* paradoxically try to locate a national community in transregional and transnational movements of male workers, during and after the war a good deal of popular U.S. sensational literature labors to redefine and restrict a white national identity by identifying a community of people of Mexican origin and other Spanish-speakers with a "foreign" criminality.[13] Postwar sensational crime literature, especially, continues the work of wartime representations by racializing this community as essentially alien in an early example of what Etienne Balibar calls "the immigrant complex": the "functioning of the category of *immigration* as a substitute for the notion of race and a solvent of 'class consciousness.' " This does not mean that pseudo-biological notions of race become irrelevant, but that they are supplemented by "culturalist" definitions of race which suggest that the differences between national cultures are natural and insurmountable but also perpetually endangered by the transnational movements and mixings of populations.[14] While I would dispute the claim that the category of immigration dissolves class consciousness rather than strongly shaping the latter's multiple manifestations, Balibar's theory of the immigrant complex is suggestive for an analysis of racialized criminality in the post-1848 period. To explore the ways that national cultural differences are recast as the difference between legality and illegality, I turn to the *California Police Gazette*'s sensational account of Murrieta's scandalous crimes and border crossings.

RACE WAR CRIMES

The criminal fait divers, *by its everyday redundancy, makes acceptable the system of judicial and political supervisions that partition society; it recounts from day to day a sort of internal battle against the faceless enemy; in this war, it constitutes the daily bulletin of alarm or victory. The crime novel, which began to develop in the broadsheet and in mass-circulation literature, assumed an apparently opposite role. Above all, its function was to show that the delinquent belonged to an entirely different world, unrelated to familiar, everyday life. . . . The combination of the* fait divers *and the detective novel has produced for the last hundred years or more an enormous mass of "crime stories" in which delinquency appears both as very close and quite alien, a perpetual threat to everyday life, but extremely distant in its origin and motives, both everyday and exotic in the milieu in which it takes place. . . . In such a formidable delinquency, coming from so alien a clime, what illegality could recognize itself?*

MICHEL FOUCAULT, *Discipline and Punish*

It is easy to recognize the basic outline of the *California Police Gazette*'s version of the Murrieta story in the pattern of the typical heroic *corrido*. As in the classic heroic *corrido,* in *The Life of Joaquin Murieta, the Brigand Chief of California,* a man with a "very mild and peaceable disposition" turns into a criminal after being violently persecuted by white Americans and the regimes of law and lawlessness they bring with them.[15] But these two types of popular crime narrative show how complex and divided the international field of popular knowledge about crime and criminality was during this period. For while *corridos* take the part of the criminal and question the justice of U.S. law, the *Police Gazette* disseminates ambivalent representations of criminals but ultimately upholds the law by striving to make its victory over criminality seem natural, inevitable, and best for the safety of the public. That is, even though both types of popular crime narrative respond to what Michel Foucault calls "the desire to know and narrate how men have been able to rise against power" and "traverse the law," *corridos* attack the legitimacy of the new forms of power and law that the *Police Gazette* ends up defending.[16] For as popular crime narratives, *corridos* and the *Police Gazette* are engaged in a discursive battle not over a generalized, abstract law or power as such, but over the violent transition from Mexican to U.S. law in the postwar period.

Even the title of the *California Police Gazette,* which was apparently modeled on the more successful and long-lived *National Police Gazette,* already implies a panoptic gaze leveled statewide, pulling together diverse incidents, crimes, and historical events into a field of visibility for the eye of police power.[17] Founded in 1845, the *National Police Gazette* was itself modeled on British police gazettes and "promised to publish descriptions of criminals and accounts of crime for the avowed purpose of revealing the identities of criminals and to supplement the work of the police."[18] During the U.S.-Mexican War the *National Police Gazette* even printed the names and descriptions of deserters from the U.S. ranks and the War Department "thereupon authorized a large subscription for distribution among the soldiers."[19]

The *California Police Gazette,* a weekly, four-page journal published in San Francisco that sold for twelve and a half cents per issue, or five dollars per year, was first issued in January 1859. The Murrieta story ran from September 3 to November 5 of that year, and was subsequently reissued as a pamphlet novel.[20] In the same issues of the *California Police Gazette* that contained installments of the Murrieta story, readers could find news of California prison escapes; an editorial advocating that the state take over the management of prisons, using convict labor to pay their costs; a story about the capture of 218 California Indians by a detachment of volunteers; and reprints of short crime stories from newspapers across the nation about the suicide of an unemployed ex-soldier, about a creature with the "form of a woman" and the head and arms of a pig, and about white people sold as slaves.[21] Each week, the paper ran a long profile of one in a series of "California Thieves," ending with a description of the criminal and speculations about his current whereabouts. Another weekly feature was the "City Police Court," a long column that listed the names, crimes, and often the race or nationality of those who had appeared before the San Francisco court that week. While these features inspired a range of responses in its readers, the paper's main business is stated succinctly in an ad for a special edition of a *Pictorial California Police Gazette,* which promised "Portraits and Lives OF ABOUT FIFTY OF THE Most Notorious Thieves, Felons and Desperadoes in the State, many of whom are now at large!" along with portraits of judges and other state officials, and views of the state prisons and jails. "This Pictorial SHOULD BE In the Hands of All," the ad states, "as by it many of the ESCAPED CONVICTS and DESPERADOES NOW AT LARGE Can be detected and brought to justice. It will also serve to put RESIDENTS OF THE REMOTE PORTIONS OF THE STATE UPON THEIR GUARD when visited by them."[22] Despite its sometimes ambivalent representations of criminals such as Murrieta, then, the *California Police Gazette* ultimately tried, in Foucault's words, to make "acceptable the system of judicial and political supervisions that partition society" by framing crime stories within a popular format that was strongly identified with the state and the police and was devoted to helping citizens detect and capture criminals.

In the territories newly acquired from Mexico, however, making the "system of judicial and political supervisions" seem natural and right was both a more difficult and a more urgent task. Thus the *California Police Gazette* imports sensational racial stereotypes from popular literature of the U.S.-Mexican War, which help, on the one hand, to make a hero out of a representative of the state—namely, Harry Love, the California Ranger and former U.S.-Mexican War soldier who leads the company of men who finally kill Murrieta—and, on the other, to racialize Mexicans by identifying them both as essentially foreign and as similar to so-called "savage" Indians. In this way, people of Mexican origin are represented as natural criminals, as part of what one contemporary writer called "the semi-barbarous hordes of Spanish America, whose whole history is that of revolution and disorder."[23]

The *California Police Gazette* makes crime both alien and familiar as it brings the story of the Sonoran immigrant bandit back into the homes of its readers. This version of the Murrieta crime narrative, which most of the Latin American versions seem to echo, follows Ridge's version closely, often word for word, but it mixes up the order of events, cuts or elides some passages and scenes, notably those which justify or excuse Murrieta's crimes, and adds new ones, especially flashbacks to the recent war, which most of the criminals and lawmen in this narrative are said to have fought in. War and crime are brought into an intimate and menacing relationship with each other as memories of war explode in the middle of different scenes. The *California Police Gazette* story is gorier and even more sensational than Ridge's, lingering over dripping blood, severed heads, and other body parts. It replaces Murrieta's mistress, Rosita, who survives a gang rape and a beating at the hands of lower-class, "false" Americans in the Ridge version, with a first wife, Carmela, who is raped and killed, and a second wife who, dressed in male drag, often rides along with Murrieta and survives to mourn his death. In both of these versions of the Murrieta story violence directed at women's bodies represents threats or violence to a larger community. In this and in innumerable other ways, Ridge's and the *Gazette* version are part of an international field of popular sensational crime literature, one that includes broadsides about crimes and criminals; pamphlets supposedly based on criminal confessions; novels about the crimes of the rich and about capitalism as crime; detective fiction; an array of ballads and tales about bandits, rogues, and criminals; articles in daily and weekly newspapers; and mass-produced papers devoted to crime, such as the police gazette.[24]

Beginning in the 1850s, the story of Joaquín Murrieta began to circulate in a variety of such popular forms, but daily and weekly newspapers in California were one of its most important early sources. In January of 1853, California newspapers such as the *San Francisco Herald,* the *Calaveras Chronicle,* the *San Joaquín Republican,* and the *Sacramento Union* started carrying lurid articles about the crimes of a gang of "Mexican marauders" led by a Mexican named Joaquín.[25] But only a year later, crime narratives about Murrieta were being published, including two that were serialized in relatively obscure weekly police gazettes and one novel, Ridge's *The Life and Adventures of Joaquín Murieta,* which appeared in San Francisco.[26] Although Ridge's story was published as a book instead of being serialized in a paper, his novel cannot be neatly separated from the daily and weekly newspaper accounts of Joaquín's crimes. Ridge's narrative is episodic, sometimes reading like a series of newspaper stories loosely pulled together, and many of the incidents he describes recall the contemporary newspaper reports that Ridge almost certainly read while he was living in Marysville and Yuba City, California, during those years. The narrative registers its place in this larger world of popular crime writing when Joaquín reads crime stories in the newspapers such as the *Los Angeles Star,* "which made a very free use of his own name in the account of these transactions and handled his character in no measured terms" (R, 30).

From the beginning of the narrative, Ridge also alludes to different types of crime literature, placing his novel within an international field of popular knowledge about crime by comparing Murrieta to the "renowned robbers of the Old or New World, who have preceded him" (R, 7). This body of crime literature about famous robbers not only "precedes" the crimes committed by Murrieta's gang, but also actively inspires them. Reyes Feliz, for instance, "had read the wild romantic lives of the chivalrous robbers of Spain and Mexico until his enthusiastic spirit had become imbued with the same sentiments which actuated them" (R, 17). So Ridge repeatedly registers his awareness of a larger body of crime narratives set in Spain and Mexico as well as in England, France, and the United States, which provide a framework within which his own text will inevitably be read.

If Ridge insists that Murrieta's story is a part of "the most valuable history of the State" (R, 7), and thereby suggests that this is a story from which all Californians can take a lesson, however, the *California Police Gazette* restricts the meaning of Murrieta's example by making the latter only a part of "the criminal history" of California (PG, 1). This revision of Ridge's language pathologizes Murrieta, making him an example of an alien, racialized criminality instead of an example of how "prejudice of color," in Ridge's words, may lead to "*injustice to individuals*" (R, 158) and the abrogation of moral law, which in turn provokes crimes such as Murrieta's.[27] In other words, while Ridge implies that the citizens of California need to think about how race prejudice turned Murrieta into a criminal, the *California Police Gazette* makes Murrieta into an example of an innate, alien criminality.

The *California Police Gazette* version of the Murrieta story gives crime a Mexican face, making it seem "very close" and yet still "quite alien"—an enduring stereotype which resurfaces today *ad nauseam* in debates about immigration, welfare, and citizenship. Indeed, it is the very combination of the "close" and the "alien" that makes the Mexican immigrant bandit seem especially threatening. Mexico is "close," first of all, because it is geographically adjacent to the United States, sharing a common border. In both Ridge's version and in the *Police Gazette,* Joaquín and the members of his gang repeatedly cross and recross national boundaries, mapping out transnational networks of migration and illegal activity. The gang is continually reconstituted through the departures and the arrivals of new members across the border, especially from Sonora, but also from Chile and Peru. Ridge suggests that the "ramifications" of Murrieta's "organization" "are in Sonora, Lower California, and in this State" (R, 74), while the *California Police Gazette* notes at the beginning that Murrieta's "powerful combination" was "steadily increasing by arrivals from Lower California and Sonora" (PG, 8). In both versions, Murrieta's "gang" is a sort of international army which both recruits and deploys soldiers across national boundaries. Much of their business involves moving stolen horses from the United States to Mexico. Again and again, the narratives expose secret connections between Mexico and the United States, as when the wife of a "wealthy ranch owner in Guadalajara, Mexico," travels to California to "urge [Joaquín] on in his bloody warfare against the Americans" (PG, 105); or when Murrieta repeatedly sends "remittances of money" to a "secret partner" in the state of Sonora (R, 32). In these ways, the novels incessantly link the cross-border movement of money and people to international crime networks, thereby suggesting that the "closeness" of the

United States to Mexico and the "openness" of adjacent national borders make the United States vulnerable to invasion by an alien race of lawless Mexicans who can easily move between nations.

This pattern of transnational movement is established in the beginning of the *California Police Gazette* version, when Joaquín initially travels to San Francisco in 1848 to look for his brother Carlos, "who had long been living in California, and had obtained a grant of four leagues of land from one of those excessively generous governors who flourished about that time" (PG, 3). Not finding Carlos, Joaquín "retraced his steps homeward" to Mexico (PG, 3). A year later, however, when a letter from his brother arrives, which also brings news of the Gold Rush in California, Joaquín and his wife set out on the journey back to San Francisco. When they arrive, Carlos is about to leave for Mexico City, because his land has "been taken from him by the Americans, by means of forged papers" (PG, 3), and he needs to go to Mexico to "see the grantor himself, and so recover the land" (PG, 3). In the opening chapter of the novel, these actual and anticipated journeys across the border make national boundary lines seem porous and insecure, given the spatial proximity or "closeness" of Mexico to the United States. They also imaginatively link up northern Mexico and California, as the story of Joaquín's brother, who is a Sonoran, is identified with the history of the Californios, many of whom were forced to become involved in costly litigation over land grants. Carlos even plans to take "a young native Californian named Flores" (PG, 3) to Mexico with him to serve as a witness.

The journey into the heart of Mexico that Carlos proposes activates the memory of another system of political supervision, an older set of Mexican laws and institutions (the land grants of the "excessively generous" Mexican governors), which were in the process of being replaced by the U.S. political and legal system. But this transition did not happen seamlessly, and the older order continued to clash with the new one. So the "Mexican period" still seemed close and yet alien to U.S. settlers in the sense that California had until very recently been a part of Mexico, and so had been governed by other laws and institutions. Mexico's property law, for instance, continued to be a factor in land disputes throughout the second half of the nineteenth century, when white immigrants squatted on land owned by Mexicans and went to court (sometimes with forged papers) to challenge land grants made by the old regime.[28] After California became a state within the U.S. system, the Mexican period was increasingly represented with both fear and nostalgia as a superseded stage of history, as a time which was historically close and yet alien, which was always already passing away, naturally giving way to Anglo-Saxon energy, institutions, and mastery of the "commercial principle." But as an earlier "stage" of California history, the period of Mexican rule continued to haunt, at times erupting from within that history to make national law and national boundary lines seem strange, new, and artificial rather than familiar, primordial, and natural.

For during the 1850s, U.S. boundaries, laws, and institutions were strange, new, artificial, unevenly in place, violently enforced, and violently abrogated. Instead of war giving way to peace and the rule of law, after 1848 war continued to be fought by other means as Spanish-speakers and other so-called foreigners confronted racist legislation, claim-jumping, vigilantism, and lynching at the hands of newly arrived immigrants from the Eastern United States, many of whom had fought on the U.S. side in the war. In San Francisco, for instance, the members of the nativist vigilante gang The Hounds, who were especially fond of persecuting Spanish-speakers, were mostly "disbanded soldiers from the regiment of the New York Volunteers."[29] The war, in other words, was very recent, raw history which continued to shape the present as many of those who fought it reencountered each other in California.

The *California Police Gazette* tries to close the wounds of war and to unify a heterogeneous society by defining a white American identity in opposition to what are constructed as the "savage" and therefore naturally criminal, essentially alien, even if native, bodies of Mexicans, Latin Americans, and Californios within the state. This effort to stabilize differences responds to a crisis in the boundaries of whiteness and national identity in mid-nineteenth-century California. While the Treaty of Guadalupe Hidalgo guaranteed "all the rights of citizens" to Mexicans who chose to remain in the new territories, and while the California State Constitution defined Mexicans as "white" and declared them, as opposed to Indians, eligible for citizenship, these legal provisions were unevenly enforced during the postwar period. The big wave of immigration from Mexico and South America during the Gold Rush years, especially, upset the system of racial meanings and classifications that were initially proposed in California.[30] Leonard Pitt suggests that whether "from California, Chile, Peru, or Mexico, whether residents of twenty years' standing or immigrants of one week, all the Spanish-speaking were lumped together as 'interlopers' and 'greasers.' . . . In essence then, the Latin-American immigrants were a sort of catalyst whose presence caused the sudden and permanent dissolution of the social elements."[31] The precarious whiteness of certain Spanish-speakers did not simply dissolve into thin air, however. Rather, during the postwar period, the racialization of different groups of Spanish-speaking people was a problem addressed through legislation like the Foreign Miner's Tax and the Federal Land Law of 1851, through violence, and through popular representations such as the crime literature I have been describing.

The racializations promoted by the Murrieta story must be understood in the context of what one historian has called "the great Sonoran migration of 1848–1856."[32] During these years, between ten and twenty thousand miners made the long journey across the desert and up the coast from

Sonora to the gold fields of California, bringing with them superior mining skills as well as "hard feelings toward Americans developed when the latter invaded their homeland."[33] They were joined by five thousand miners from Latin America, most of them from Chile, in the year 1849 alone.[34] From the beginning, the Americans who were moving west in large numbers loudly voiced their resentment of "foreigners" in the mines; they believed that their recent victory in the war with Mexico entitled U.S. citizens and only U.S. citizens to claim the prodigious amounts of gold that had been discovered. In January of 1849, General Persifor F. Smith, whose ship had stopped at Panama on the way to California, where he would take command of the U.S. army, issued a proclamation in response to this nativist hysteria, announcing his intention to fine and imprison "persons not citizens of the United States, who are flocking from all parts to search for and carry off gold belonging to the United States in California."[35] Xenophobic Americans violently turned foreigners away from Sutter's Mill in April, and other vigilantes drove Sonorans "out of the Tuolumne, Stanislaus, and Mokolumne River placers in the summer of 1849."[36] The Foreign Miner's Tax Law, which was enacted in 1850 and required all "foreigners" working in the mines to pay $20 a month for a permit, was thus only one example among many of the ways that U.S. citizens quickly naturalized the new national boundary lines and, in Josiah Royce's words, "turned upon foreigners as a class, and especially upon Sonorans and South Americans."[37]

Despite the efforts of many Californios to distinguish themselves from the new immigrants, most Americans included them within this newly revised "class" of foreigners.[38] While "local attachments and loyalties, class differences, and subtle variances in customs and language patterns" divided the different groups of Spanish-speakers from each other, many white Americans saw no significant differences among them.[39] In a discussion of the criminalization of the Spanish-speakers during this period, Josiah Royce scathingly exposes the essentialist logic that supported the classification of these diverse groups of people as a race:

> It was, however, considered safe by an average lynching jury in those days to convict a "greaser" on very moderate evidence, if none better could be had. One could see his guilt so plainly written, we know, in his ugly, swarthy face, before the trial began. Therefore the life of a Spanish-American in the mines in the early days, if frequently profitable, was apt to be a little disagreeable. It served him right, of course. He had no business, as an alien, to come to the land that God had given us. And if he was a native Californian, a born "greaser," then so much the worse for him. He was so much the more our born foe; we hated his whole degenerate, thieving, land-owning, lazy, and discontented race.[40]

The "denial, or flattening, of differences within a particular racially defined group," which Michael Omi and Howard Winant identify as a key feature of racial essentialism, can be seen in the pejorative epithet "greaser" that collapses the differences between the "native Californian" and the "alien" Mexicans, Chileans, and Peruvians.[41] The more neutral, but still homogenizing term "Spanish-American," which Royce chooses in order to distinguish himself from the nativist vigilantes, also covers over differences between those who had elected to become U.S. citizens, those who became citizens by default under the terms of the treaty, those who retained other national or regional allegiances and never hoped to become citizens, and those who were excluded from citizenship because they were considered Indian or mestizo. And while the nativists assume that all "greasers" are "aliens," even the qualifier "native" fails to protect the Californios from those who find a natural criminality, common to the native and alien alike, inscribed on their "swarthy" faces. Indeed, their "native" status makes them even more of a threat to the white settlers who covet their land; it is not surprising that Royce adds "land-owning" to the long list of racist adjectives that the white nativists use to vilify the native Californians.

Of course, many Californios were still legally considered "white" and were therefore in a much better position than the Chinese, Blacks, and Indians, who were absolutely excluded from citizenship on the basis of their race, as well as many other people of Mexican origin. But racial categories were swiftly being recreated, reinhabited, transformed, and destroyed during the 1850s.[42] In practice, access to white privilege was always severely stratified by class. As Tomás Almaguer suggests, while the ranchero elite were usually considered white, potentially assimilable, and worthy of intermarriage with other kinds of white people, working-class people of Mexican origin were "often denied their legal rights by being categorized as Indians."[43] Even members of the elite, however, could lose their white privilege if they were too dark-skinned. Almaguer tells the story of Manuel Dominguez, who had served as a delegate to the California State Constitution of 1849, but was barred from testifying in a San Francisco courtroom in 1857 because the judge ruled that he was an Indian. In the wake of the war, the increasing dispossession and proletarianization of the Californio ranchero class, and the influx of new immigrants, the hold of any of these Spanish-speakers on whiteness became increasingly tenuous as, more and more, they were all lumped together and were at best considered ambiguously white. In this strange new world, then, Spanish-speaking people were uncanny and therefore especially threatening, for what seemed to be familiar (at least marginally white) was now becoming disturbingly alien, positioned on the shifting border of whiteness.

The *California Police Gazette* version of the Murrieta story exploits this uncanny racial status but ultimately labors to unify and racialize these diverse groups, placing them precariously on the boundary of whiteness by identifying them with an innate, savage criminality. As we have seen, the novel initially focuses on postwar injustices inflicted on different groups of Spanish-speakers, linking these injuries together only to override them in favor of a crime narrative that justifies state-sponsored violence. I have suggested that the story of Joaquín's brother, Carlos, whose Mexican land grant is taken away from him "by means of forged papers," recalls the fate of the Californios, who were displaced during the postwar period through fraud, through the complicated and costly Land Law of 1851, and through frivolous lawsuits.[44] The ensuing scene in which Joaquín is prevented from working the mines on the Stanislaus River by a group of "lawless and desperate" Americans typifies a long, bloody history of Anglo claim-jumping and violence inflicted on Sonoran miners during the Gold Rush. Finally, the existence of an extensive, hidden network of Californios, Mexicans, and Latin Americans who help Joaquín avenge his injuries implies that all of these groups have suffered similar injuries and injustices at the hands of the Americans. The opening frame, then, suggests that Joaquín's injuries are representative of injuries suffered by Californios, Sonorans, and Latin Americans as a group, and that the criminality of the group is to some degree a legitimate or at least understandable response to these postwar injuries. If the novel's opening emphasizes the constructedness of Joaquín's criminality, however, the narrative ultimately overrides this explanation in favor of one which suggests that this criminality is rooted in the dark recesses of his nature—a "savage" impulse that takes hm outside the pale of white civility.

This redrawing of boundaries around whiteness depends upon the importation of stereotypes from U.S.-Mexican War–era sensational literature that define American, Anglo-Saxon heroism by opposing it to Mexican "savagery." One flashback in particular, which fleshes out Captain Love's U.S.-Mexican War encounter with a "hideous-looking fellow, half Indian, half Mexican," suggestively indicates the larger project of this version of the Murrieta story. Echoing Ridge's language, the *California Police Gazette* sets up Love as a point of identification for white readers early on by characterizing him as a "hardy pioneer" who "during the Mexican war had performed valuable service as an express rider, carrying dispatches from one military post to another, over the wildest and most dangerous parts of Mexico" (PG, 14). But the police gazette embroiders with lurid and telling details a scene that Ridge only hints at as it interjects a long description of Love's victory over a band of guerrillas led by a "half Indian, half Mexican" warrior. The threat represented by this mestizo soldier, "whose face was marked with a deep scar across his right cheek . . . urging his animal on with such savage fury, that its sides were covered with gore" (PG, 15) haunts the narrative, which opposes white representatives of the racial state to "savage," lawless Mexicans by reinserting both within the theater of the recent war.

The novel repeatedly describes the gangs' crimes as the continuation of war by other means. At night, the members of Murrieta's gang sit around the campfire remembering the war by telling gory, sensational stories about the battles they fought with "the guerrilla chief and priest, Padre Jurata [*sic*]" (PG, 8). The brutal Three-Fingered Jack, in particular, who is closely identified with Jarauta and who lost his finger while fighting the war, is a character straight out of U.S.-Mexican War–era pulp fiction. A long story about Jarauta in combat, "sheathing his dripping blade in the bodies of the dead as well as the living, and in a perfect frenzy of excitement severing the neck-joints and casting the gaping heads into the rushing water" (PG, 21), is framed by multiple accounts of Jack's murderous abandon. Indeed, when one of the bandits suggests that Jack "takes rather too much delight in drawing blood," another replies, "Not half so much as old Padre Jurata whom some of us had for a leader in Mexico" (PG, 20). As Jack satisfies "his brutal disposition" by "discharging three loads from his revolver into the head" of a corpse, tortures Chinese miners, and exults in "the luxurious feast of blood" (PG, 23), the police gazette implies that Mexican "savagery" has migrated from the battlefields of the U.S.-Mexican War to the California goldfields.

If early on the novel suggests that Joaquín is an "exceptional" Mexican who is *made* into a criminal by un-American Americans, by the end it identifies him with the essentially depraved and bloodthirsty Jack. Even in the opening chapters of the novel, however, Joaquín is more brutal than in Ridge's version. For instance, Joaquín's first vengeful murder, which is briefly described after the fact by Ridge, becomes a full-blown, bloody scene in *The Life of Joaquin Murieta, the Brigand Chief of California.* Joaquín's eyes glare "with the fury of an enraged tiger," and his body seems to "quiver with excitement" as he plunges his knife again and again "into the body, until the latter was almost hacked to pieces, for the demon of revenge possessed the soul of Joaquin and urged him to excess" (PG, 6). And when Joaquín and his gang later meet up with the men who killed Carmela, Joaquín, who has intermittently tried to control Jack's sadistic behavior, commands him to exercise his "natural propensity," an order which encourages Jack to disembowel them and cut out their hearts. As the narrative proceeds, Joaquín's desire for revenge is thus figured, more and more, as savage, innate, and out of control, as something which links him to the utterly savage Jack, who indiscriminately hacks people to pieces because his "heart to its very core is black with evil" (PG, 29). In this way, the wild, brutal Jack is figured as Joaquín's inner "truth": Jack is an indispensable part of Joaquín's organization that Joaquín cannot control, and ultimately does not want to control, as long as the "demon of revenge" spawned by postwar California possesses him.

By identifying Joaquín's gang and the extended network of people who support them with an innate, savage criminality linked to the U.S.-Mexican

War, the narrative implicitly redraws the boundary lines around the white nation, collapsing the differences between diverse peoples of Mexican origin and other Spanish-speakers, whether they are "natives" or "foreigners," and classifying them as an inassimilable body within the nation-state. When, after a day of adventure, the bandits sit around the fire singing a song called "Our Home Is Mexico," which they claim was "a favorite with the padre Jurata" (PG, 64), this vision of an insurgent alien nation within the white republic is even supported by a cultural nationalist anthem, albeit one which is sung to the tune of "The Maid of Monterey." In this fantasy of postwar cultural hybridity, the *California Police Gazette* has Joaquín's men proclaim their eternal allegiance to Mexico (the novel includes a full set of lyrics) to the tune of a song which is about interracial, "south of the border" romance. While the novel's representation of this musical interlude says a lot more about the work of postwar national fantasy than it does about Mexican culture, the *Gazette* does get one thing right when it insists upon the importance of music in disseminating a nationalist sentiment across borders and in defiance of official national jurisdictions.[45] This transnational national sentiment transmitted by *mexicano* songs is the subject of the concluding section.

JOAQUÍN MURRIETA AND THE CHICANA/O COUNTERCULTURES OF MODERNITY

It could be argued that diverse forms of twentieth-century cultural production, from barrio murals to Rodolfo "Corky" Gonzales's nationalist epic poem "I Am Joaquín" to versions of the Murrieta *corrido* sung by Los Madrugadores, Lalo Guerrero, and Lydia Mendoza, among many others, have made Joaquín Murrieta an important and pervasive symbol of resistance for people of Mexican origin in the United States. Stories about Murrieta's severed head, which was exhibited in mining camps throughout California, seem to have stimulated many Chicana/o responses, including Luis Valdez's play *The Shrunken Head of Pancho Villa*, Richard Rodriguez's essay, "The Head of Joaquín Murrieta," and Cherríe Moraga's *Heroes and Saints*. Moraga's play, which focuses on a woman who is born without a body because of her mother's exposure to pesticides in the fields of the Central Valley, might be read as a radical revision of the many male-authored accounts of displacement and loss provoked by Murrieta's head. Rodriguez's essay offers one such account, albeit one which is unusual in that it ultimately recoils from, rather than celebrates, Murrieta as a symbol of the larger community. Rodriguez writes in a half-satirical, half-serious way about his travels around the state with a Jesuit priest named Alberto Huerta in search of the head, which he describes as a symbol of California's violent, gothic past. But the more Huerta urges Rodriguez to help him pursue various leads and thereby calls him "to come to terms with California," the more Rodriguez anxiously "pull[s] back" in order to return to "the California of Fillmore Street, of blond women and Nautilus-educated advertising executives, this California of pastels and pasta salad ... where I live."[46] These very different examples suggest that whether the myth of Murrieta as symbol of a larger Chicano community has been enthusiastically endorsed, implicitly criticized and imaginatively transformed, or nervously relegated to a dead past, many Chicana/o cultural producers have felt compelled to come to terms with it.

Accounts of the transmission of the Murrieta story that focus exclusively on Ridge's novel obscure this important history of Chicana/o responses to the legend. Critics often privilege Ridge's narrative as a literary point of origin, implicitly distinguishing it from the subliterary newspaper accounts that preceded it in the 1850s, as well as from the mass cultural texts, such as the *California Police Gazette* and the dime novels, that followed it.[47] I have suggested that such an analysis elides a larger, violently divided, inter-American field of popular knowledge about crime that responded to and helped to reshape class and racial formations in the wake of the American 1848. But if the low or mass-cultural world of cheap sensational literature and the crime gazette comprises one important part of that field, the ballads and legends produced by diasporic *corrido* communities are surely another.

Neither the police gazette nor the *corrido* versions of the Murrieta story can be attributed to an individual author, as Ridge's novel can, and this may be one of the reasons, aside from the fascinating set of issues that his text raises, that many discussions of Murrieta focus only on Ridge. While the "author" of the *California Police Gazette* version is unknown, the text's close relationship to Ridge's novel, to the newspaper stories, and to the conventions of U.S.-Mexican War–era cheap fiction make traditional notions of individual authorship untenable anyway. On the other hand, *corridos* also challenge such notions of authorship because they are extremely formulaic, influenced substantially by oral traditions, and because their producers are usually anonymous, so that rather than reflecting the views of an individual author, *corridos* offer, in Ramón Saldívar's words, "a heightened, reflexive analysis of the mutual values and orientations of the collective."[48] In the case of the Murrieta *corrido,* we could go even further, for its migratory movements call into question notions of a stable, unitary community. The formulaic nature of the *corrido,* as well as its sensational, body-grabbing qualities, doubtless facilitated its transmission across widely dispersed sites. As José Limón suggests, "the sheer music, the strict predictable measured poetics, the Spanish language of the *corrido,*" and its "strong sensory quality" may well have "constituted a point of resistance" to U.S. capitalist modernity at "the level of form."[49]

Attempts to fix the literary origin of the Murrieta story miss the important point that the latter was from its inception a profoundly intercultural construction. While Ridge's novel, which itself depends heavily on newspaper accounts, forces a consideration of intercultural relationships in postwar California, it is but one of many texts, articulated from different social locations, that contributed to the construction of the Murrieta story and to the debate about law, race, and criminality which took place after 1848. To these newspaper accounts and novels, we must add the *corridos* that circulated about Murrieta, beginning at some point—no one knows exactly when—during the nineteenth century. Because *corridos* are usually transmitted orally, it is difficult to confidently fix their point of origin. Luis Leal has suggested that the Murrieta *corridos* are based on a song about Indian warfare from nineteenth-century Zacatecas, which gives the date of the events it describes as 1853, and he concludes that there was probably an earlier prototype for both *corridos* which is lost today.[50] According to Víctor Sánchez, a member of the group that first recorded it in 1934, "The *corrido* was written before I was born; it is from the last century. I heard it as a child in Mexico, sung during the time of the Revolution, and later in Arizona."[51] As this sensational crime story moves across regional and international boundary lines, it exposes the violence of U.S. empire-building and incessantly registers shifts in racial and national boundaries, thereby foregrounding the historical contingency of changing definitions of the native and the alien.

The *corrido* recorded during the 1930s must be understood in relation to the virulent nativism of the period and to the English-language versions of the story that were published during these years. Novels such as Ernest Klette's *The Crimson Trail of Joaquin Murieta* (1928), Dane Coolidge's *Gringo Gold* (1939), and especially Walter Noble Burns's *The Robin Hood of El Dorado* (1932) look back upon an earlier era of immigration and state formation and try to exorcise the ghosts of race wars past, or rather to argue that racial injustice and the violence of conquest are part of the dead past, which has given way to equality and the rule of law. They also labor to make the post-1848 boundary between the United States and Mexico seem natural and right by representing Spanish-speakers and especially people of Mexican origin as outlaws who threaten the state, in part because they easily move between nations. But the dead past is reanimated, the border becomes uncanny, and the alien and the native become hopelessly entangled in these narratives, which invoke ghosts that they cannot possibly lay to rest. To follow the ghosts in these Murrieta narratives means, then, as Avery Gordon puts it, to be startled into a recognition of the animating force of "what seems dead, but is nonetheless alive," to confront "whatever organized violence has repressed and in the process formed into a past, a history, remaining nonetheless alive and accessible to encounter."[52]

In the final part of this essay I argue that the Murrieta *corridos* still have the power to reanimate history and to make the familiar seem strange, for the circulation of Murrieta stories across regional and national boundaries during the 1930s made different mappings of America a haunting presence at a time when the policing of the border between United States and Mexico was being intensified. As debates over nativism and immigration grew more heated during the Depression years, and as the 1930s began to resemble uncannily Murrieta's California, the ghosts of California's so-called past clamored noisily in the present, troubling claims that acts of racist injustice had been superseded by democracy and the rule of law.

More than a million Mexican immigrants crossed the border and resettled in the United States between 1890 and 1920.[53] As David Gutiérrez suggests, "Mexican immigrants filled a wide variety of occupations, ranging from agricultural labor, mine work, and railroad construction and maintenance, to common day labor on innumerable construction sites throughout the Southwest." In California, workers of Mexican origin comprised almost 17 percent of unskilled construction workers and almost 75 percent of the state's farm labor force.[54] During prosperous times the immigrants were welcomed by California agribusiness and other employers and were more or less uneasily tolerated by most white workers, who generally benefited from their better position within the racially segmented labor market. But after the stock market crash of 1929 and the onset of the Great Depression, Mexican workers became convenient scapegoats for white nativists. The American Federation of Labor, the Veterans of Foreign Wars, and the American Legion, to name just three groups, supported the Immigration Service's intensified efforts to deport so-called illegal and undesirable Mexican immigrants, and between 1930 and 1939 Mexicans comprised "46.3 percent of all of the people deported from the United States."[55] During the early 1930s, U.S. Secretary of Labor William Doak specifically targeted labor organizers and strikers for deportation, and Southern California in particular became "the focal point of the deportation frenzy."[56] In August of 1931, the California state legislature also passed the Alien Labor Act, which made it illegal for companies to hire aliens for public works projects such as construction, highways, schools, and government office buildings, a policy which often meant that workers who "looked" Mexican were presumed to be illegal aliens.[57] Finally, repatriation programs were established that, according to Camille Guerin-Gonzalez, "made no effort to distinguish between immigrants and U.S.-born Mexicans and, in fact, set numerical goals that included both groups."[58] In all of these ways, nativists insisted that people of Mexican origin were fundamentally alien despite the promise of abstract equality enshrined in the rhetoric of liberal democracy.

For many writers, this context made the Murrieta story newly relevant.

For instance, in Walter Noble Burns's 1932 novel, *The Robin Hood of El Dorado*, which inspired the Hollywood movie, racial injustice is deplored, but it is also relegated to the dead past, represented as part of an older age of terror and lawlessness that has been superseded by "an era of law and order."[59] In the early chapters of the novel, as Burns rehearses the racist acts of white nativist terrorism that turned Murrieta into a criminal, he explains that nativists contravened the Constitution and the laws of the United States:

> As California had fallen into American hands as spoils of war, the American miners were imbued with the idea that the gold of California was rightfully theirs and theirs only. But as selfishly human as the idea may have been, it was legally without justification. According to the constitution and laws of the United States, Mexicans and all other foreigners had as much right to mine in California as Americans themselves. But the legality of the position of the Mexicans had no effect in mitigating American hostility towards them. The feeling between the two races grew more and more embittered. (44)

Here, Burns extends some sympathy to the Mexican immigrant, who is treated unfairly by the Americans. But as we shall see, he also mitigates this criticism of the nativists by calling their behavior "selfishly human," and he justifies state intervention after Murrieta becomes an outlaw.

In Murrieta's California, according to Burns, the "law was a dead letter. Citizens were helpless and dared not defend themselves. The marauders came and went as free as the winds with reckless bravado but they left no clews behind. Their trails were red with blood but from the scenes of their crimes they vanished like phantoms" (129). Inevitably, then, in Burns's account law must be enforced by the state, which, as he imagines it, rightfully unleashes its "crushing power" to end what he sees as Joaquín's reign of terror. In Burn's narrative of state formation, an age of lawlessness and terror must give way to an age of law. As he puts it in the novel's concluding chapters, the "age of law was dawning in 1853. For more than three years, the state had endured Joaquin Murrieta's reign of rapine and devastation. Now the Days of the Terror were drawing to a close. The state had grown weary of the red nightmare; and the weariness of the state was a menace of death. Heretofore communities, countrysides, counties, had fought Murrieta. For the first time he was to feel the crushing power of the state as a state" (256). Here Burns animates the state, endowing it with a kind of moral agency as it awakens from the "red nightmare" and crushes resistance. For Burns, the death of the Mexican immigrant outlaw coincides with the dawn of a new age. "As the outlaw died, the sun rose over the distant Sierras, and plains and mountains were bathed in the radiance of the morning. For California, a new era came with the sunrise—an era of law and order" (275). By concluding in this way, Burns suggests that the ghosts that haunted Murrieta, and the legally unjustified acts of nativist terrorism that provoked him, have been safely quarantined in the past, so that now they are no more than part of a "tale told in the twilight or a song sung to a guitar" (304).

If Burns labors to make the age of lawlessness and racial terror part of the dead past, however, there are several places in the text where his allusions to the present open up a wider, contemporaneous frame of reference for the Murrieta story. For instance, even as Burns tries to distance this story from his contemporary moment by making it, in the opening frame, a sort of gothic story told by an old-timer, a second-generation forty-niner who mourns the death of the old mining towns like a "mourner standin' by an open grave," he still yokes the past to the present as he comments on the fate of the succeeding generations of white Californians. "The Forty-Niners dipped up a fortune casual-like from some nameless creek in a tin washpan," the old-timer suggests, "but their children have had to scratch mighty hard for a livin' " (1). Here, this reference to economic hard times and perhaps to agricultural labor almost, but not quite, brings into view the scenes of nativist terrorism, labor competition, and white supremacist retrenching that were taking place in California during the early 1930s. Instead, this context eerily looms on the margins of Burns's story, only to be repressed by a temporal shift of the setting back to the California of the 1850s, which Burns tries to place securely in the past.

Burns's efforts to use a narrative of development to separate an age of terror from an age of law fail in part because the context of the 1930s keeps resurfacing on the margins of his text, but also because, in spite of his manifest intentions, his revision of the story also shows how law and racial terror frequently accompanied rather than worked against each other. In other words, the laws to which Burns appeals often supported nativism and white supremacy. This point is made even more forcefully in the Joaquín Murrieta *corrido*, "a song sung to a guitar," which is also a product of 1930s California, a time when laws often enabled racial terror rather than prohibiting it.

Luis Leal suggests that the earliest, most complete surviving version of the Murrieta *corrido* was recorded in 1934 in Los Angeles by Los Hermanos Sánchez y Linares, otherwise known as Los Madrugadores, or the Early Risers. According to Chris Strachwitz, Los Madrugadores "were one of the first groups to make an impact via Spanish language radio as well as via recordings in the Los Angeles area during the early thirties." Jesús and Víctor Sánchez, the original members of the group, grew up in Sonora, Mexico, where their father worked as a miner. When the two were teenagers, the family came to the United States as contract laborers, and eventually Jesús and Víctor worked in the fields in the Fresno area. In 1930, the brothers went to Los Angeles, and for several years they, along with Pedro González, developed an extremely successful radio program which aired from four to six in the morning, "because it was cheaper to buy air time, and it was the time when farm workers got up to go to work." The radio show mixed music and community activism as González, its host, provided important job information to laborers and spoke out against the mass deportations of both "native" and "alien" Spanish-speakers that were taking place in Los Angeles.[60] In 1934, the same year that Los Madrugadores recorded the Joaquín Murrieta *corrido,* González was sent to San Quentin on trumped-up statutory rape charges.[61] If, as "an exceptionally flexible musical genre," in George Sánchez's words, the *corrido*'s "relation to the working-class Mexican immigrant audience in Los Angeles" was "critical to its continued popularity," then the story of the unjust treatment and criminalization of a Mexican immigrant in the United States must have taken on new and tragic resonances for that working-class audience during these years of intensified nativism and forced repatriation, especially in light of Gonzalez's harsh experiences with the law.[62]

But although the version of the Murrieta *corrido* recorded by Los Madrugadores in 1934 undoubtedly responded to the particular conjunction of post-Revolution immigration, Anglo-American nativism, and *mexicano* cultural nationalism in Los Angeles, it also continued to transmit countermemories of the American 1848. For while a fictive, precariously unified, white national identity was reformulated in the cheap sensational literature that was moving west along with the Americans who were rushing for gold and land, the U.S.-Mexican War also provoked other forms of national fantasy in the *décimas, corridos,* and other songs which accompanied the Spanish-speaking people who were migrating north to California during the postwar period. Although the apex of the heroic *corrido* tradition comes, according to Américo Paredes, during the Mexican Revolution, the post–U.S.-Mexican War era marks a crucial transitional time for Mexican folk music, as songs about the war, in particular, relied more upon narrative and thereby became more *corrido*-like. Paredes argues, for example, that "*décimas* about Jarauta, the fighting priest who was a guerrilla against Scott's forces and who was executed because he refused to recognize the Treaty of Guadalupe, are more purely narrative than most others of their time. Jarauta himself is cast in the pattern of the *corrido* hero."[63] We last encountered Jarauta, you will recall, in Ridge's novel and in the *California Police Gazette,* where he was instead cast in the role of the bloodthirsty, savage leader of many of the members of Murrieta's band during the U.S.-Mexican War. If in the English-language versions, the evil Padre Jarauta prefigures the monstrous Three-Fingered Jack, whose viciousness justifies the imposition of U.S. laws despite Murrieta's appeal, Paredes implies that the *décimas* underline the injustice of U.S. law by celebrating Jarauta's doomed resistance to it.

María Herrera-Sobek and other *corrido* scholars have suggested that there was a "renaissance" in *corrido* production during the middle of the nineteenth century, when ballads dealing with conflicts between Anglos and Mexicans began to proliferate.[64] These songs helped to disseminate an uneven, contradictory national sentiment. As Paredes puts it, the "blaze stirred up by the daily conflict" between Mexicans and Anglo-Americans meant that a "nationalist feeling" arose in the borderlands before one was strongly and widely articulated in greater Mexico. While "Mexican nationalist feeling does not define itself until the last third of the nineteenth century," Paredes argues, in "the northern frontiers, however, and in the parts of the United States recently taken from Mexico, nationalism begins to be felt toward the end of the 1830s, if we may take the folklore of these regions as an indication."[65] In the face of a conquest that was often figured as the dismemberment of Mexico, the postwar producers of *décimas* and *corridos* struggled to re-member a truncated national body, reasserting its integrity by constructing a nationalist sentiment that was in many ways a defensive response to Anglo-American racism and the violence of U.S. nation-building.

I am arguing that, despite their different relationships to literacy, orality, and national languages, *corridos* and sensational crime literature such as the English-language Murrieta novels are intersecting, hybrid forms. But this hybridity does not magically dissolve differences or reconcile warring interpretations of the conquest and its consequences. Instead, the cultural syncretism of these popular texts forces us to confront the unequal power relations and the larger sphere of inter-American conflict that mutually shaped them.[66]

As popular forms, *corridos* and U.S. sensational literature might initially seem to belong to incommensurate worlds. *Corridos* are, after all, closely linked to oral traditions, while sensationalism signals the emergence of a U.S. mass culture marked by industrialized modes of cultural production and enabled by improvements in literacy rates, changes in print technology, and the development of transportation networks. This does not mean, however, that *corridos* were produced by a thoroughly premodern folk or that sensational literature is simply the corrupted, debased result of the incursions of capital into the sphere of popular culture, because there are many folkloric motifs and patterns in sensational literature and many links between *corridos*, the spread of print capitalism, and the uneven modernization of social space. Although they were inevitably transformed as they moved from one context to another, *corridos* were frequently printed as broadsides or in newspapers, for instance, and they are sometimes based on newspaper stories;[67] their dissemination was facilitated by the growth of railroad networks throughout Mexico and the United States in the last quarter of the nineteenth century;[68] and they often register the dislocating effects of U.S./capitalist restructuring. For even though some *corridos* were produced and performed by people who had lived in the border regions for years and were now being encroached upon by Anglo immigrants, *corrido* communities from at least the mid–nineteenth century on have more often been multiple and heterogeneous; marked by displacements and movements; stratified by differences of gender, generation, and regional origin; and composed of both immigrants and "natives." All of this suggests that *corridos* negotiate the forces of modernity along with those who produce and perform them, traveling along routes which are inevitably shaped and constrained by the "political disciplines and economic pressures" of that modernity.[69]

While *corridos* and popular sensational literature mark different paths through modernity, however, both expose the ways that modern nationalisms have, as Cynthia Enloe suggests, "typically sprung from masculinized memory, masculinized humiliation, and masculinized hope."[70] Sensational U.S.-Mexican War literature and postwar crime narratives most often focus on violent encounters between men; nation-building is represented as a patrilineal enterprise; and women are usually figured as the spoils of war or as mediators whose bodies facilitate or threaten national unity. Similarly, nineteenth-century *corridos* frequently valorize a violent masculine hero who steadfastly resists U.S. expansion and depredation, avenging a series of humiliations.

In the version of the Murrieta *corrido* recorded by Los Madrugadores, for instance, cowardly Americans murder his brother and kill Joaquín's wife, Carmelita, after making her suffer ("Carmelita tan hermosa / Cómo la hicieron sufrir"). The *corrido* omits the third humiliation that is presented as decisive in the English-language texts: the public whipping that Murrieta is forced to endure at the hands of the Americans. In the *corrido,* the violence done to Carmelita seems to stand in for the physical punishment that Murrieta himself withstands in the other versions, for the outrage done to his wife is the occasion ("Vengo a vengar a mi esposa") for his transformation into a Robin Hood–style social bandit who robs from the rich, takes his hat off to the humble and poor, and is only called a bandit because U.S. laws are so unjust. The writer of the *California Police Gazette* version, who suggests that Murrieta's wife, Carmela, is "ravished" and then killed, is more explicit about her suffering than the *corrido* is, or than Ridge is about Rosita's fate, who in his version is raped but not killed. Despite their differences, however, all three versions still figure violence to the woman's body as the ultimate outrage which prefigures or stands in for, depending on the version, violence done to Murrieta's own body and to the larger community. By making the woman a victim rather than an actor in this drama, and by provoking nationalist affect through a patriarchal narrative of rape, masculine humiliation, and violent homosocial revenge, the *corrido,* like Ridge and the police gazette, identifies masculinity with resistance and makes emasculation and the violated female body the signs of conquest. Thus all three versions appeal to so-called natural gender differences in order to stabilize the ruptures of a violent, migratory, inter-American modernity.

It could be argued that the Murrieta *corrido* evokes, in Julie Skurski's words, "ideas of undisputed origins, original creation, and sustained tradition" in order to suggest that people of Mexican origin "share an original identity which can be liberated or restored through the rejection of colonialism's pervasive influence."[71] In other words, in response to U.S. imperialism, the *corrido* strives to make Murrieta the bearer of an originary, authentic "Mexican" identity, reasserting the wholeness and reintegration of the Mexican nation as a way of dealing with the trauma of the war and the losses imposed by the Treaty. What is more, by naturalizing the connection between the soil and the Mexican nation ("I'm neither a Chilean nor a stranger on this soil which I tread. California is part of Mexico because God wanted it that way"), the *corrido* constructs a national sentiment that conceals its own constructedness.[72] An insistence on the integrity of the Mexican national body despite the ruptures of war is also signaled by the *corrido*'s conclusion, which omits any mention of Murrieta's severed head, so important in Ridge's and the *Police Gazette* texts, in favor of a first-person assertion of Murrieta's *mexicano* identity ("Yo soy ese Mexicano / de nombre Joaquín Murrieta"). While most *corridos* are narrated in the impersonal third person and end with a reflexive return to the metanarrative that frames the main story, the voices of the singers of this *corrido* must ventriloquize the first-person voice that dominates it from beginning to end. As the distinction between the impersonal third-person voice of the performer and the voice or dialogue of the *corrido* protagonist disappears, the singers become much more closely identified with the protagonist, who represents the Mexican nation, thus embodying more directly the values he champions.

But if the *corridos* circulate a cultural nationalism that may seem to be equivalent to the white, nativist nationalism of 1850s and 1930s California promoted in the crime gazette and the sensational novel, the different relationships that these nationalisms have to the U.S. nation-state significantly affect their meanings. In other words, while nationalisms as such may be inherently exclusionary, the different material and political histories of U.S. and Chicano nationalisms suggest that their identity can only be affirmed at the cost of an extremely high level of abstraction. Although the nationalism of the migrants who called themselves Anglo-Saxon usually supported the white-supremacist U.S. state, the nationalist sentiments invoked by the members of *corrido* communities were both at odds with official U.S. nationalism and at a distance from and irreducible to an emergent nationalism associated with the Mexican nation-state. Thus while the *corridos* can support exclusionary forms of nationalism, they also disseminate memories of another America and thereby challenge narratives of U.S. national identity that require the interiorization and naturalization of the external borders of the state.[73] For the process of internalizing national boundaries allows only some of us to, as Balibar suggests, "inhabit the space of the state as a place where we have always been—and always will be—'at home.' "[74]

Even when the *corridos* seek to disseminate exclusionary national sentiments, they underline the impossibility of a unitary national identity as they incessantly register the disruptions, displacements, and movements that provide the unstable ground for asserting it. The very facts that we can only guess about the *corrido*'s origins and that we have no access to a complete, unfragmented, certifiably nineteenth-century Murrieta *corrido* suggests that the folk tradition that transmits national identity is in this case manifestly synthetic, unavoidably responding to capitalist modernity even when resisting it. As Víctor Sánchez remembers, "We had many requests for this *corrido*, at parties, and then after we began to sing it on the radio, people would send us cards to the station and ask that we record it so they could have the disc. Felipe Valdéz Leal added three or four verses to make it fit both sides of the record—I don't remember which ones but possibly the one about coming from Hermosillo."[75] In other words, the national sentiment preserved in the Murrieta *corrido* was not only disseminated through mass cultural media such as records and the radio, but was also decisively shaped by these cultural technologies, since additions were made so it would "fit" the record. What is more, according to Luis Leal, the earlier Zacatecan *corrido* that the Murrieta *corrido* seems to be echoing asserts a strong regional identity rather than a national identity ("I am *zacatecano* because God wanted it that way" instead of "California is part of Mexico because God wanted it that way") and thereby decenters claims to an originary Mexican identity by preserving a countermemory of a time when regional or local identities were more powerful than national identity. Finally, the transregional and often transnational trajectories of those who have performed this *corrido*—from Zacatecas to Sonora, from Sonora to Arizona, from Sonora/Arizona to California, and maybe back again, to name just a few possible routes—problematize any appeal to the idea of a static, unfragmented national community. These singers, musicians, field laborers, miners, and other workers have preserved memories of the American 1848 and of a postwar crisis in the racial state that continues to haunt the U.S. "home" in an age of law and racial terror that has not ended.

NOTES

1. See Tomás Almaguer, *Racial Fault Lines: The Historical Origins of White Supremacy in California* (Berkeley: University of California Press, 1994); Genaro

Padilla, *"My History Not Yours": The Formation of Mexican American Autobiography* (Madison: University of Wisconsin Press, 1993); María Amparo Ruiz de Burton, *The Squatter and the Don,* ed. and intro. Beatrice Pita and Rosaura Sánchez (Houston: Arte Público Press, 1992); José David Saldívar, *Border Matters: Remapping American Cultural Studies* (Berkeley: University of California Press, 1997); and Rosaura Sánchez, *Telling Identities: The Californio Testimonios* (Minneapolis: University of Minnesota Press, 1995). See also the documentary *U.S.-Mexican War, 1846–1848,* produced by Paul Espinosa and directed by Ginny Martin.

For examples of the internal colonialism model in Chicano Studies, see Rodolfo Acuña, *Occupied America: A History of Chicanos,* 3rd ed.(New York: HarperCollins, 1988); and Mario Barrera, "The Barrio as Internal Colony," in *People and Politics in Urban Society,* ed. Harlan Hahn (Beverly Hills: Sage, 1972), and *Race and Class in the Southwest: A Theory of Racial Inequality* (Notre Dame, IN: University of Notre Dame Press, 1979). For a critique of that model, see Tomás Almaguer, "Ideological Distortions and Recent Chicano Historiography: The Internal Model and Chicano Historical Interpretation," *Aztlán* 18, no. 1 (Spring 1987): 7–28.

2. For an analysis of the historical roots and contemporary examples of U.S. nativism, see the essays in Juan F. Perea, ed., *Immigrants Out! The New Nativism and the Anti-Immigrant Impulse in the United States* (New York: New York University Press, 1997).

3. Malcolm Rohrbough, *Days of Gold: The California Gold Rush and the American Nation* (Berkeley: University of California Press, 1997), pp. 216–29. See also Almaguer, *Racial Fault Lines,* pp. 26–29; and Jay Monaghan, *Chile, Peru, and the California Gold Rush of 1849* (Berkeley: University of California Press, 1973).

4. On the reconstruction of whiteness in this period, see Reginald Horsman, *Race and Manifest Destiny: The Origins of American Racial Anglo-Saxonism* (Cambridge, MA: Harvard University Press, 1981); Noel Ignatiev, *How the Irish Became White* (New York: Routledge, 1995); Eric Lott, *Love and Theft: Blackface Minstrelsy and the American Working Class* (New York: Oxford University Press, 1993); David Roediger, *The Wages of Whiteness: Race and the Making of the American Working Class* (London: Verso, 1991); and Alexander Saxton, *The Rise and Fall of the White Republic: Class Politics and Mass Culture in Nineteenth-Century America* (London: Verso, 1990).

I understand the process of racialization in Michael Omi's and Howard Winant's terms, as "occurring through a linkage between structure and representation. Racial *projects* do the ideological 'work' of making these links. *A racial project is simultaneously an interpretation, representation, or explanation of racial dynamics, and an effort to reorganize and redistribute resources along particular racial lines.* Racial projects connect what race *means* in a particular discursive practice and the ways in which both social structures and everyday experiences are racially *organized,* based upon that meaning." See Michael Omi and Howard Winant, *Racial Formation in the United States from the 1960s to the 1990s,* 2d ed. (New York: Routledge, 1994), p. 56.

5. Michael Rogin, *Subversive Genealogy: The Politics and Art of Herman Melville* (New York: Alfred A. Knopf, 1983), pp. 102–3.

6. See Saldívar, *Border Matters,* pp. 170 and 177; and Carolyn Porter, "What We Know That We Don't Know: Remapping American Literary Studies," *American Literary History* 6 (Fall 1994): 518–19. Porter suggests that we should view 1848 "not only as a moment in U.S. history, but also as a moment in Pan-American history" (519).

7. Lott, *Love and Theft,* pp. 210, 203.

8. Ibid., p. 170.

9. See Cheryl Walker, *Indian Nation: Native American Literature and Nineteenth-Century Nationalisms* (Durham, NC: Duke University Press, 1997), p. 111. According to Walker, although Ridge was of Cherokee descent, he was "a metropolitan, acculturated Indian who migrated from Indian territory to California and upheld views repugnant to those who wished to maintain traditional Indian cultural practices" (111). Nonetheless, Walker suggests that Ridge "speaks as much as an Indian as he does as a voice of white culture" (112).

10. See John Rollin Ridge, *The Life and Adventures of Joaquín Murieta* (Norman: University of Oklahoma Press, 1955); and the *California Police Gazette* version of the story, which was published as a book under the title *Joaquin Murieta, the Brigand Chief of California* (Fresno, CA: Valley Publishers, 1969; reprint of 1932 Grabhorn Press edition). The latter includes a bibliography listing some of the different versions of the Murrieta story (pp. 117–20). For some of the *corrido* versions, see Luis Leal, "El Corrido de Joaquín Murieta: Origen y Difusión," *Mexican Studies/Estudios Mexicanos* 11, no. 1 (Winter 1995): 18–23; and Philip Sonnichsen, "Joaquin Murrieta," liner notes, *Corridos and Tragedias de la Frontera*, Mexican-American Border Music, vols. 6 and 7, Arhoolie Records 7019/7020, 1994, pp. 38–40. Subsequent citations from the two novels appear in parentheses in the text. Citations from the Police Gazette version are preceded by PG, and those from the Ridge version are preceded by R. All quotations from the Murrieta *corrido*, whether in Spanish or in the English translation, are from the Arhoolie Records liner notes, and will also appear parenthetically in the text.

11. On "structures of feeling," see Raymond Williams, *Marxism and Literature* (New York: Oxford University Press, 1977), pp. 133–34.

12. See JoAnn Pavletich and Margot Gayle Backus, "With His Pistol in *Her* Hand: Rearticulating the Corrido Narrative in Helena María Viramontes's 'Neighbors,' " *Cultural Critique* (Spring 1994): 127–52; Rosa Linda Fregoso and Angie Chabram, "Chicana/o Cultural Representations: Reframing Alternative Critical Discourses," *Cultural Studies* 4, no. 3: 208; Angie Chabram-Dernersesian, "I Throw Punches for My Race, but I Don't Want to Be a Man: Writing Us—Chica-nos (Girl, Us)/Chican*as*—into the Movement Script," in *Cultural Studies,* ed. L. Grossberg, C. Nelson, and P. Treichler (New York: Routledge, 1992), pp. 81–95. For an analysis of female soldiers in *corridos*, see María Herrera-Sobek, *The Mexican Corrido: A Feminist Analysis* (Bloomington: Indiana University Press, 1990), pp. 84–116.

13. See Carl Gutiérrez-Jones, *Rethinking the Borderlands: Between Chicano Culture and Legal Discourse* (Berkeley: University of California Press, 1995). Gutiérrez-Jones's important study of the "process by which Chicanos have become institutionally and popularly associated with criminality" (1) has significantly influenced my argument about the construction of a post–Mexican War racialized criminality.

14. Etienne Balibar, "Is There a Neo-Racism?" in Balibar and Immanuel Wallerstein, *Race, Nation, Class: Ambiguous Identities* (London: Verso Press, 1991), p. 20. Balibar further defines the immigrant complex as "a racism whose dominant theme is not biological heredity but the insurmountablity of cultural differences, a racism which, at first sight, does not postulate the superiority of certain groups or peoples in relation to others but 'only' the harmfulness of abolishing frontiers, the incompatibility of life-styles and traditions" (21).

15. On the epic heroic *corrido*, see John McDowell, "The Corrido of Greater

Mexico as Discourse, Music, and Event," in *"And Other Neighborly Names": Social Process and Cultural Image in Texas Folklore,* ed. Richard Bauman and Roger D. Abrahams (Austin: University of Texas Press, 1981); Américo Paredes, *"With His Pistol in His Hand": A Border Ballad and Its Hero* (Austin: University of Texas Press, 1958); José Limón, *Mexican Ballads, Chicano Poems: History and Influence in Mexican-American Social Poetry* (Berkeley: University of California Press, 1992), pp. 16–77.

16. Michel Foucault, ed. *I, Pierre Rivière, having slaughtered my mother, my sister, and my brother . . . ,* trans. Frank Jellinek (Harmondsworth: Penguin, 1978), p. 206.

17. See Frank Luther Mott, *A History of American Magazines, 1850–1865* (Cambridge, MA: Harvard University Press, 1938), pp. 186–87, 325–37; Alan Nourie and Barbara Nourie, eds., *American Mass-Market Magazines* (Westport, CT: Greenwood Press, 1990), pp. 284–91; and Gene Smith and Jayne Barry Smith, eds., *The Police Gazette* (New York: Simon and Schuster, 1972).

18. Daniel Straubel, "National Police Gazette," in Nourie and Nourie, *American Mass-Market Magazines,* p. 285. See also Saxton, *Rise and Fall of the White Republic,* pp. 207–9.

19. Mott, *American Magazines,* pp. 326–27.

20. See H. H. Bretnor, *The California Police Gazette, a brief description* (typescript in Bancroft Library, Berkeley, CA, #88305, 1955); and Francis P. Farquhar, "Notes on Joaquin Murrieta," in *Joaquin Murrieta, the Brigand Chief of California.*

21. *California Police Gazette,* September 24, October 8, and October 15, 1859.

22. *California Police Gazette,* September 24, 1859.

23. Alonzo Delano, *Life on the Plains and Among the Diggings,* p. 157. Quoted in Winifred Storrs Hill, *Tarnished Gold: Prejudice During the California Gold Rush* (San Francisco: International Scholars Publications, 1995), p. 10.

24. See Pedro Castillo and Albert Camarillo, eds., *Furia y Muerte: Los Bandidos Chicanos* (Los Angeles: Aztlán Publications, UCLA, 1972); Daniel Cohen, *Pillars of Salt, Monuments of Grace: New England Crime Literature and the Origins of American Popular Culture, 1674–1860* (New York: Oxford University Press, 1993); Michel Foucault, *Discipline and Punish: The Birth of the Prison,* trans. Alan Sheridan (New York: Vintage Books, 1979); Karen Halttunen, "Early American Murder Narratives: The Birth of Horror," in *The Power of Culture: Critical Essays in American History,* ed. R. W. Fox and T. J. J. Lears (Chicago: University of Chicago Press, 1993); Eric Hobsbawm, *Bandits* (New York: Pantheon Books, 1969); Simon Joyce, "Resisting Arrest/Arresting Resistance: Crime Fiction, Cultural Studies, and the 'Turn to History,' " *Criticism* 37 (Spring 1995): 309–35; Peter Linebaugh, *The London Hanged: Crime and Civil Society in the Eighteenth Century* (Cambridge: Cambridge University Press, 1992); and Américo Paredes, "The Mexican Corrido: Its Rise and Fall," in *Folklore and Culture on the Texas-Mexican Border,* ed. Richard Bauman (Austin: CMAS Books, 1993), pp. 129–41.

25. James Varley, *The Legend of Joaquín Murrieta: California's Gold Rush Bandit* (Twin Falls, ID: Big Lost River Press, 1995), pp. 48–65.

26. Ibid., p. 138.

27. In a longer version of this essay, I explore in much more detail Ridge's negotiation of the shifting field of racial classifications in postwar California. For other approaches to this topic, see Peter G. Christensen, "Minority Interaction in John Rollin Ridge's *The Life and Adventures of Joaquín Murieta," MELUS* (Summer 1991–92): 61–72; Karl Kroeber, "American Indian Persistence and Resurgence,"

boundary 2 (Fall 1992): 5–11; James Parins, *John Rollin Ridge: His Life and Works* (Lincoln: University of Nebraska Press, 1991); John Carlos Rowe, "Highway Robbery: 'Indian Removal,' the Mexican-American War, and American Identity in *The Life and Adventures of Joaquín Murrieta,*" *Novel: A Forum on Fiction* (Spring 1998): 149–73; and Walker, *Indian Nation*, pp. 111–38.

28. Sánchez, *Telling Identities*, pp. 275–79; and John Hittell, "Mexican Land Claims in California," in *California Controversies*, ed. Leonard Pitt (Atlanta: Scott, Foresman, 1968).

29. Hill, *Tarnished Gold*, p. 40. See also Donald C. Biggs, *Conquer and Colonize* (San Rafael, CA: Presidio Press, 1977), pp. 202–6.

30. Almaguer, *Racial Fault Lines*, 9.

31. Leonard Pitt, *The Decline of the Californios: A Social History of the Spanish-Speaking Californians, 1846–90* (Berkeley: University of California Press, 1970), p. 53. See also Almaguer, *Racial Fault Lines*, p. 55; and Ramón Gutiérrez, "Unraveling America's Hispanic Past: Internal Stratification and Class Boundaries," *Aztlán* 17, no. 1: 89.

32. Sister Mary Colette Standart, "The Sonoran Migration to California, 1848–1856: A Study in Prejudice," in *Between Two Worlds: Mexican Immigrants in the United States*, ed. David G. Gutiérrez (Wilmington, Delaware: Scholarly Resources, 1996), pp. 3–21.

33. Douglas Monroy, *Thrown Among Strangers: The Making of Mexican Culture in Frontier California* (Berkeley: University of California Press, 1990), p. 206. For the figure on Sonoran migration, see David Gutiérrez, *Walls and Mirrors: Mexican Americans, Mexican Immigrants, and the Politics of Ethnicity* (Berkeley: University of California Press, 1995), p. 19.

34. Pitt, *Decline of the Californios*, p. 52. See also Monaghan, *Chile, Peru, and the California Gold Rush.*

35. Cited in Monaghan, *Chile, Peru, and the California Gold Rush*, p. 114. See also Pitt, *Decline of the Californios*, pp. 55–56.

36. See Pitt, *Decline of the Californios*, p. 56; and Standart, "Sonoran Migration," p. 7.

37. Josiah Royce, *California from the Conquest of 1846 to the Second Vigilance Committee in San Francisco* (Boston: Houghton-Mifflin, 1886), p. 361.

38. See Pitt, *Decline of the Californios*, p. 53; Royce *California*, p. 277; and Standart, "Sonoran Migration," p. 10.

39. David Gutiérrez, "Introduction," in *Between Two Worlds*, ed. Gutiérrez, p. xx.

40. Royce, *California*, p. 364.

41. Omi and Winant, *Racial Formation*, p. 72.

42. In *Racial Formation*, Omi and Winant define racial formation "as the sociohistorical process by which racial categories are created, inhabited, transformed, and destroyed" (55).

43. Almaguer, *Racial Fault Lines*, p. 57.

44. Ibid., pp. 65–68.

45. I borrow the term *national fantasy* from Lauren Berlant, *The Anatomy of National Fantasy: Hawthorne, Utopia, and Everyday Life* (Chicago: University of Chicago Press, 1991). I elaborate on popular U.S.-Mexican War romances as fantasies of international heterosexual union in my manuscript, *American Sensations: Class, Empire, and the Production of Popular Culture*, forthcoming from the University of California Press.

46. See Richard Rodriguez, *Days of Obligation: An Argument with My Mexican Fa-

ther (New York: Viking, 1992), p. 140. Thanks are due to Barbara Brinson Curiel for telling me about this essay.

47. Many of the Spanish-language versions of the story, including a novel published in Los Angeles in 1919, seem to be based on the *California Police Gazette* adaptation. See Raymund F. Wood, "Supplementary Notes on Joaquin Murieta," in *Joaquin Murieta, the Brigand Chief of California*, x.

48. See Ramón Saldívar, *Chicano Narrative: The Dialectics of Difference* (Madison: University of Wisconsin Press, 1990), pp. 32, 36; and McDowell, "Corrido of Greater Mexico," pp. 45–46.

49. Limón, *Mexican Ballads, Chicano Poems*, p. 34.

50. Leal, "El Corrido de Joaquín Murrieta," pp. 1–23.

51. Liner notes, "Joaquín Murrieta," p. 37.

52. Avery Gordon, *Ghostly Matters: Haunting and the Sociological Imagination* (Minneapolis: University of Minnesota Press, 1997), p. 65–66.

53. Gutiérrez, *Walls and Mirrors*, p. 40.

54. Ibid., p. 45.

55. Francisco Balderrama and Raymond Rodriguez, *Decade of Betrayal: Mexican Repatriation in the 1930s* (Albuquerque: University of New Mexico Press, 1995), p. 53.

56. Ibid., p. 55.

57. George Sánchez, *Becoming Mexican American: Ethnicity, Culture and Identity in Chicano Los Angeles, 1900–1945* (New York: Oxford University Press, 1993), p. 211.

58. Camille Guerin-Gonzales, *Mexican Workers and American Dreams: Immigration, Repatriation, and California Farm Labor, 1900–1939* (New Brunswick, NJ: Rutgers University Press, 1994), p. 78.

59. Walter Noble Burns, *The Robin Hood of El Dorado: The Saga of Joaquin Murrieta, Famous Outlaw of California's Age of Gold* (Albuquerque: University of New Mexico Press, 1999; reprint of 1932 Coward-McCann edition), p. 275. Subsequent citations will appear in parentheses in the text.

60. Chris Strachwitz, liner notes, *Corridos and Tragedias de la Frontera*, Arhoolie Records, 1994, pp. 16, 18. See also Sánchez, *Becoming Mexican American*, p. 183.

61. Sánchez, *Becoming Mexican American*, p. 184. According to Sánchez, District Attorney Burton Fitts, who "believed that only English should be heard on the radio and that only American citizens should have the right to broadcast" (184), was responsible for the arrest.

62. See Sánchez, *Becoming Mexican American*, pp. 178, 183–85, and Gutiérrez-Jones, *Rethinking the Borderlands*, pp. 2–3, 50–56. I agree with the latter that González's example shows how "the stereotypical ascription of 'criminality' to Chicanos must be read in the context of larger U.S. institutional aims, including the maintenance of Chicanos and Mexicanos as a malleable, productive underclass" (3).

63. Paredes, "Mexican Corrido," p. 135.

64. María Herrera-Sobek, *Northward Bound: The Mexican Immigrant Experience in Ballad and Song* (Bloomington and Indianapolis: Indiana University Press, 1993), xxiii.

65. Américo Paredes, "The Folklore of Groups of Mexican Origin," in *Folklore and Culture on the Texas-Mexican Border*, p. 9. According to Paredes' logic, a "nationalist sentiment" would first be strongly articulated in Texas because of the battles there in the 1830s. In general, nationalist feeling was weak in the borderlands areas after Mexican independence in 1821, especially in California, which was so far re-

moved from greater Mexico. See also Gutiérrez, *Walls and Mirrors,* p. 30. According to Gutiérrez, "In the quarter century before annexation, many, if not most, Spanish-speaking residents of Mexico's northern provinces did not even identify themselves as Mexicans and instead probably thought of themselves first as Nuevomexicanos, Tejanos, or Californios" (30).

66. My understanding of hybridity has been influenced by Lisa Lowe's discussion of this concept in the Asian-American context in *Immigrant Acts: On Asian American Cultural Politics* (Durham, NC: Duke University Press, 1996). Lowe suggests that "Hybridization is not the 'free' oscillation between or among chosen identities. It is the uneven process through which immigrant communities encounter the violences of the U.S. state, and the capital imperatives served by the United States and by the Asian states from which they come, and the process by which they survive those violences by living, inventing, and reproducing different cultural alternatives" (82).

67. See Paredes, "The Mexican Corrido," 137–8 for information about *décimas, corridos,* and the Mexican broadside press.

68. See Sánchez, *Becoming Mexican-American,* pp. 21–22.

69. James Clifford, "Traveling Cultures," in *Cultural Studies,* ed. Grossberg, Nelson, and Treichler, p. 107.

70. Cited in Ann McClintock, " 'No Longer in a Future Heaven': Nationalism, Gender, and Race," in *Becoming National,* ed. Geoff Eley and Ronald Suny (New York: Oxford University Press, 1996), p. 260.

71. Julie Skurski, "The Ambiguities of Authenticity in Latin America," in *Becoming National,* ed. Eley and Suny, p. 375.

72. In Spanish, the lines are as follows: "No soy chileno ni extraño / en este suelo que piso. / De México es California, / porque Díos así lo quizo."

73. Citing Fichte, Balibar suggests in "The Nation Form" that for nationalism to take hold of subjectivities, "the 'external frontiers' of the state have to become 'internal frontiers' or—which amounts to the same thing—external frontiers have to be imagined constantly as a projection and protection of an internal collective personality, which each of us carries within ourselves and enables us to inhabit the space of the state as a place where we have always been—and always will be—'at home.' " See Balibar and Wallerstein, *Race, Nation, Class,* p. 95. Hence the *unheimlich* qualities of the *corridos,* which haunt the U.S. home and make its borders unfamiliar. For a strong analysis of nationalism and the uncanny, see Priscilla Wald, *Constituting Americans: Cultural Anxiety and Narrative Form* (Durham, NC: Duke University Press, 1995), pp. 4–13.

74. Balibar, "The Nation Form," p. 95.

75. Liner notes, "Joaquín Murrieta," p. 37.

Syllabus 1848
> Empire, Amnesia, and American Studies
> *Instructor: Shelley Streeby*

This course complicates the conventional periodization of nineteenth-century U.S. history and culture that makes the Civil War the pivotal event in a narrative that moves from sectional conflict to national consolidation and then to imperialism at the end of the century. By examining the early history of U.S. empire-building in Mexico as well as the filibustering attempts in Cuba and Latin America in the years that followed, we will think about how the events of 1848 established patterns for subsequent U.S. imperialist policies in 1898 and beyond. Topics to be addressed include the relationship between Indian Removal and the U.S.-Mexican War; the war and mass culture; cultural nationalism and Young America; the Revolutions of 1848; the complicated politics of anti-imperialism; slavery, resistance, and colonization schemes in the Americas; and migration and racial formation in the wake of the Gold Rush. The premise of this course is that U.S. class and racial formations throughout the nineteenth century were decisively shaped by international conflict and both the internal and the global dynamics of empire-building.

PRIMARY TEXTS

Alcaraz, Ramón, et al., eds., "Preface" and "Origin of the War" from *The Other Side: Or Notes for the History of the War between Mexico and the United States.* Trans. Albert C. Ramsey. New York: Burt Franklin, 1850; reprint, 1970. Selections.

Alcott, Louisa May. "An Hour." In *Louisa May Alcott on Race, Sex, and Slavery,* ed. Sarah Elbert. Boston: Northeastern University Press, 1997, 47–68.

Buntline, Ned. *The Volunteer; or the Maid of Monterey.* Boston: F. Gleason, 1847.

Clappe, Louise Amelia Knapp Smith. *The Shirley Letters from the California Mines, 1851–1852.* Ed. Marlene Smith-Baranzini. Berkeley: Heyday Books, 1998. Selections.

Delany, Martin. *Blake; or, the Huts of America.* Boston: Beacon Press, 1970.

Douglass, Frederick. "The War with Mexico," *North Star,* January 21, 1848.

Fuller, Margaret. *"These Sad But Glorious Days": Dispatches from Europe, 1846–1850.* Ed. Larry J. Reynolds and Susan Belasco Smith. New Haven: Yale University Press, 1991. Selections.

Joaquin Murieta, the Brigand Chief of California. Fresno, CA: Valley Publishers, 1969. Reprint of the 1932 Grabhorn Press edition.

Lippard, George. *Legends of Mexico.* Philadelphia: T. B. Peterson, 1847.

Marx, Karl and Frederick Engels. *The Communist Manifesto*. London: Verso, 1998.

O'Sullivan, John. "The Great Nation of Futurity." *United States Magazine and Democratic Review* 6, no. 23 (November 1839): 426–30.

Prescott, W. H. *History of the Conquest of Mexico*. New York: Modern Library, 1998. Selections.

Ridge, John Rollin. *The Life and Adventures of Joaquín Murieta*. Norman: University of Oklahoma Press, 1955.

Ruiz de Burton, María Amparo. *The Squatter and the Don*. Ed. Beatrice Pita and Rosaura Sánchez. Houston: Arte Público Press, 1992.

Seguín, Juan Nepomuceno. *A Revolution Remembered: The Memoirs and Selected Correspondence of John N. Seguín*. Ed. Jesús F. de la Teja. Austin: State House Press, 1991. Selections.

Thoreau, Henry David. *Walden; and Resistance to Civil Government*. Ed. William Rossi. 2nd ed. New York: W. W. Norton, 1992. Selections.

Walker, William. *The War in Nicaragua*. Mobile: S. H. Goetzel, 1860. Selections.

Zeh, Frederick. *An Immigrant Soldier in the Mexican War.* Trans. William J. Orr. Ed. William J. Orr and Robert Ryall Miller. College Station, TX: Texas A&M University Press, 1995. Selections.

SECONDARY SOURCES

Almaguer, Tomás. "Ideological Distortions and Recent Chicano Historiography: The Internal Model and Chicano Historical Interpretation," *Aztlán* 18, no. 1 (Spring 1987): 7–28.

———. *Racial Fault Lines: The Historical Origins of White Supremacy in California*. Berkeley: University of California Press, 1994. Selections.

Foner, Philip, and Richard Winchester, eds. *The Anti-Imperialist Reader: A Documentary History of Anti-Imperialism in the United States*. Vol. 1. New York: Holmes and Meier, 1984.

Gutiérrez, David. *Walls and Mirrors: Mexican Americans, Mexican Immigrants, and the Politics of Ethnicity*. Berkeley: University of California Press, 1995. Selections.

———. "Significant to Whom?: Mexican Americans and the History of the American West." In *A New Significance: Re-Envisioning the History of the American West*, ed. Clyde A. Milner II. New York: Oxford University Press, 1996, 67–89.

Horsman, Reginald. *Race and Manifest Destiny: The Origins of American Racial Anglo-Saxonism*. Cambridge: Harvard University Press, 1981.

Johannsen, Robert. *To the Halls of the Montezumas: The Mexican War in the American Imagination*. New York: Oxford University Press, 1985. Selections.

Kaplan, Amy. " 'Left Alone with America': The Absence of Empire in the Study of American Culture." In *Cultures of United States Imperialism,* ed. Amy Kaplan and Donald Pease. Durham, NC: Duke University Press, 1993, 3–21.

Maddox, Lucy. "Civilization or Extinction." In *Removals: Nineteenth-Century American Literature and the Politics of Indian Affairs*. New York: Oxford University Press, 1991, 15–49.

Miller, Angela. *The Empire of the Eye: Landscape Representation and American Cultural Politics, 1825–1875*. Ithaca, NY: Cornell University Press, 1993. Selections.

Padilla, Genaro. *"My History, Not Yours": The Formation of Mexican American Autobiography*. Madison: University of Wisconsin Press, 1993. Selections.

Porter, Carolyn. "What We Know That We Don't Know: Remapping American Literary Studies." *American Literary History* 6 (1994): 467–526.

Rodriguez, Richard. "The Head of Joaquín Murrieta." In *Days of Obligation: An Argument with My Mexican Father*. New York: Viking, 1992.

Rogin, Michael. *Fathers and Children: Andrew Jackson and the Subjugation of the American Indian*. New Brunswick: Transaction Publishers, 1991. Selections.

Saldívar, José David. "Remapping American Cultural Studies." In *Border Matters: Remapping American Cultural Studies*. Berkeley: University of California Press, 1997. Selections.

Sánchez, Rosaura. *Telling Identities: The Californio Testimonios*. Minneapolis: University of Minnesota Press, 1995. Selections.

Saxton, Alexander. "Mines and Railroads." In *The Indispensable Enemy: Labor and the Anti-Chinese Movement in California*. Berkeley: University of California Press, 1971. Selections.

Slotkin, Richard. *The Fatal Environment: The Myth of the Frontier in the Age of Industrialization, 1800–1890*. Middletown, CT: Wesleyan University Press, 1985. Selections.

Wald, Priscilla. *Constituting Americans: Cultural Anxiety and Narrative Form*. Durham, NC: Duke University Press, 1995. Selections.

———. "Terms of Assimilation: Legislating Subjectivity in the Emerging Nation." In *Cultures of United States Imperialism*, ed. Kaplan and Pease, 59–84.

My Border Stories

Life Narratives, Interdisciplinarity, and Post-Nationalism in Ethnic Studies

Barbara Brinson Curiel

La necesidad desconoce fronteras.
Mexican proverb

A few years ago in Southern California, in response to a series of incidents in which border-crossers were hit by cars while fleeing across the highway from Immigration and Naturalization Service officers, a new traffic sign was installed to alert drivers to watch for people crossing the highway. It's a well-known sign to Southern Californians. In a bright yellow diamond, a silhouetted family is captured in mid-stride. At the head of the line of figures is a running man; at his heels is the outline of a woman with a bobbed hairdo who is wearing a skirt. She runs while pulling a child along by the hand, who looks to be about four years old, and has thin pigtails, which fly from the force with which her mother pulls her along. Her mother is moving so fast that the child's feet, with the exception of one toe, are pulled off the ground. I see myself in this child. As a young child, I had braids like that, and her clothes are like those I wore in the early sixties: Bermuda shorts and a cropped blouse with three-quarter sleeves.

That child demonstrates the force with which my forebears crossed borders, pulling me along in the process. She also signals the dominant cultural view, as well as the physical reality of border crossing: it is a dangerous enterprise in which one must be swift in order to avoid bodily harm. The signs posted immediately south of the San Onofre border checkpoint, one hundred miles north of the actual border, have two one-word amendments: on the top they signal "caution" to the presumably English-speaking drivers. Underneath, white signs subtitle the silhouette, "Prohibido," Prohibited, for the presumably Spanish-speaking pedestrians whose aim it is to cross the border against the will of the citizenry. South of the checkpoint, the silhouetted family runs from east to west, and north of the checkpoint, they run from west to east. It isn't only the north-south corridor which is *prohibido,* but all movement along these thoroughfares of American life: both the paved and the unpaved, the movement across borders, and certainly movement within them, is not allowed.

But, as Henry Yu writes in his essay in this volume, there are other signs in American culture about ethnicity, racial identity, and border-crossing, which tell a contradictory, welcoming story. Posted along California highways are adopt-a-highway signs in which businesses can sponsor litter clean-up along the roadway in exchange for having their names posted and advertised. It is the quintessential merging of core American experiences: freeway driving and advertising. The adopt-a-highway sign which immediately precedes the San Onofre border checkpoint is sponsored by the language instruction company Inglés sin Barreras (English without Borders). They sell videotapes and workbooks intended to teach English to Spanish-speaking immigrants, and are heavily advertised in the Spanish media. In their commercials they enact an American drama: a man wants to get ahead in his job, but because of his poor English, advancement is closed to him. He buys the Inglés sin Barreras series and studies it in the comfort of his own living room, with his wife and his children by his side. Later, at a family dinner, he announces that he has indeed been promoted. His wife is proud of him, and one of his children says something like "Dad, give me a high-five" in order to illustrate that, with his newly acquired English skills, the man can not only advance economically, but also communicate with his Americanized children. This other message about border-crossing, in this case about scaling the wall between languages, is integral to the American dream and is used to capture and influence the spending habits of Latino immigrants.

We are surrounded by border-crossings of the real and the metaphorical variety, which explains the presence of these highway signs and their simultaneous warning away from and siren call toward the American Dream. In the present day, Ethnic Studies is one place in academia where students learn to examine these contradictions of American life and culture.[1] One fundamental benefit to students of Ethnic Studies courses should be that they become more mindful of their borders and aware and accepting of the boundary transgressions in their own lives, and in the lives of those around them. They should also come to view their life experiences as particular, as well as part of the social patterns of various groups. Students make their first mental leap in Ethnic Studies when they stop viewing their own lives as normative, and instead start seeing them as part of a variety of complex social relationships and cultural patterns.

My own life narrative shapes and is shaped by the view of Ethnic Studies I've outlined here, and by my vision of how it should grow in order to become a more viable presence in higher education. Like many experienced teachers, I have cultivated a series of personal anecdotes which illustrate the abstract points I am trying to make. Like all stories, mine are character-ized by tropes, one of these being the border, a fitting metaphor for a dis-cussion of disciplinary, racial, and social boundaries. I come from a long line of border-jumpers, in the geographic as well as in other senses. My ma-ternal grandparents were refugees from the Mexican Revolution. Before there was a stringently enforced border, they came separately to the United States and met in San Francisco. My grandmother, who lived in this country for decades without documents, never returned to Mexico. She feared that should she go back, she would not be allowed to return. In a critical way, the border loomed frighteningly over her life.

My paternal grandparents were also border-jumpers, but of a slightly different kind. My grandmother was born in Tucson of a Sonoran family before Arizona became a state. To paraphrase Luis Valdez (who was, most likely, paraphrasing Malcolm X), she didn't come to the United States, but the United States came to her.[2] She was a smart, hard-working woman who, according to the custom of her times, married her first husband at sixteen. He gave her what we call *una mala vida,* "a bad life," but she was a strong woman who knew that work cures both spiritually and physically, so she worked. She and her husband went back and forth between Tucson and Los Angeles in the 1920s, in a fruitless search for work which her husband thought fit his status as the son of a Protestant minister and as the former driver for the sheriff of Tucson. But also being a Mexican American, he was continually dissatisfied with the opportunities available to him in each place, and he and my grandmother traveled back and forth repeatedly.

In Los Angeles, my grandmother worked as a laundress, on her feet, ironing linens with flat irons in the heat with other Mexican and Italian im-migrant women. One day on her way home from work, she met a Tucson friend on the streetcar who told her where they were selling houses for five hundred dollars. You got two rooms and a large lot. My grandmother bought the house, telling her husband that if he didn't agree, he could stay behind. Of course, he came along. In addition to her work in the laundry, she grew all the produce for her family on the lot—she proudly told me that she bought only sugar and flour. She also raised rabbits, which she sold. I have never met anyone else with my grandmother's capacity for work. When she was in her eighties, she still chopped wood for the stove.

But the internal migrations my grandmother made between Tucson and Los Angeles were only one kind of border crossing. After twenty years of marriage to her husband, again, a marriage characterized as *una mala vida,* my grandmother met my grandfather, her second husband. It seems she and husband number one were drinking in a bar.[3] Standing alongside them was my grandfather. My grandmother explained that at that time a lot of bartenders were women, and the woman behind the bar that day had set her eye on my grandfather. My grandfather, young, handsome, could be described as a young Henry Fonda type: chiseled features, tall, slim, he was in his early twenties. He was also an Anglo, a Texan, a Southerner whose family originated in Louisiana. My grandmother, as I mentioned, had already been married for twenty years, and was in her mid-thirties. The bartender didn't have a chance. My grandmother explained that my grandfather told her at that first meeting that he was in love with her, that one day he would marry her. Well, it happened. They ran away together to San Francisco, where my father was born and grew to adulthood.

I am decades and generations, if not a far geographical distance, from these events. I am writing this essay because I was a postdoctoral fellow at the University of California Humanities Research Institute, a prestigious research institute affiliated with a prestigious public university. To get to my office each day, I left my home in San Diego county and drove up Interstate 5, a main thoroughfare in Southern California. To get to my office I had to pass a very real border which is indicative of the borders in both my past and present life: the San Onofre border checkpoint. Every day, that yellow, diamond-shaped warning reminded me that, like my ancestors, I was crossing borders which for many, are still *prohibidos*. We live in an age in which regulating movement across the international border has become insufficient. The border checkpoint is used as a backup system, which presumably satisfies the concerns of those who find themselves feeling overrun by outsiders. Driving on the freeway, traffic comes to a dead stop in all lanes as the cars must first slow down, and then momentarily stop, as vehicles and people are given the once-over by Border Patrol officers, who stand between the traffic lanes, each officer scrutinizing two lanes of traffic. That Californians, proverbially in a hurry, especially on Southern California freeways, put up with being stopped in the middle of the freeway, is a testament to public fear of immigrants as well as a distrust of the efficacy of borders and boundaries in general. Because some people won't keep their place, these inconvenient enforcement measures are tolerated.

When I teach ethnic American autobiographies, I try to mimic what I have done here very simply with my reading of the highway sign. I emphasize that ethnic life narratives, autobiographies, biographies, and ethnographies, are hybrid signs which blend both lived experience and textual representation. I incorporate the subjectivity of the reader by acknowledging how this story resonates against the reader's preexisting life text. I teach that ethnic American autobiographies are fundamentally stories, signs which have an indirect, often condensed and always selected relationship to lived experience. In teaching life narratives it is important to remember that, as Cathy N. Davidson observes, "A memoir is not a transcript."[4] In using this foundation to teach ethnic life narratives, I also resort to using my own life as a text, and I encourage students to write texts from their own family histories and life experiences.

Given the cultural transformations of the last forty years, it has been especially difficult to remember that when dealing with ethnic life narratives, a memoir is indeed not a transcript. According to her own account, when Maxine Hong Kingston first sent the manuscript of *The Woman Warrior: Memoirs of a Girlhood Among Ghosts* out to publishers, she conceived of it as a collection of short stories. However, once it was accepted for publication, it was marketed as autobiography. Even today, the edition of the book I teach is labeled on the back "nonfiction/literature."[5] This categorization denotes the transgression of some generic border, although certainly there are many examples of "nonfiction literature" (without the slash), such as the essay. But that slash seems to indicate that the text is both true and invented, since "literature" is generally allotted the realm of the fictional, and since nonfiction is assumed by most readers to imply historical accuracy. Ultimately, the generic transformation of Kingston's text from fiction to memoir reflects a hunger in the marketplace for "true" narratives on the lives of ethnic minority people, a hunger which is so substantial that even abstract and magical texts, like Kingston's, are marketed and read for their supposed ability to reveal the broad social truths about representative members of a given racial or ethnic group. This search for the truth persists, even though Kingston's protagonist in *The Woman Warrior* laments her inability to know "what is Chinese tradition and what is the movies" (6). Like many of us, she is confounded by the distinctions between "reality" and its cultural representations.[6]

A parallel and more blatant example is Sandra Cisneros's *The House on Mango Street*, which, when it first appeared in 1984, was noted in *Booklist*, the publication of the American Library Association, as a work of autobiographical fiction.[7] The fact that this book received both the blurred genre and autobiographical designations so soon after its initial publication suggests that the collection—an intensely lyrical array of narratively interconnected prose poems—was marketed by its publisher, Arte Público Press, as autobiography. However, Cisneros herself has taken a stance similar to Kingston's in qualifying the autobiographical character of this book. When asked directly if *The House on Mango Street* is autobiographical, she states,

> That's a question that students always ask me because I do a lot of lectures in universities. They always ask: Is this a true story? or "How many of these stories are true?" and I have to say, "Well they're all true." All fiction is nonfiction. Every piece of fiction is based on something that really happened. On the other hand, it's not autobiography because my family would be the first one to confess: "Well it didn't happen that way." They always contradict my stories. They don't understand I'm not writing autobiography. What I'm doing is writing true stories. They're all stories I lived or witnessed or heard; stories that were told to me. I collected those stories and I arranged them in order so they would be clear and cohesive. Because in real life, there's no order.[8]

Although literary texts are generated under the conditions Cisneros describes, literary texts by writers of color are not always taught with these qualified truth claims in mind. The circumstances of Ethnic Studies' early development, wittingly or not, reinforced a search for social transparency in cultural texts. In part, the field's early emphasis on the social sciences overdetermined a tendency to quantify ethnic and racial minorities and their social position in the United States. The study of literature and the arts gained a later momentum. Given this social science tradition, as well as Ethnic Studies' political emphasis, in which applied knowledge leads to social transformation, cultural texts have been extensively used to illustrate social dynamics and broad group characteristics and experiences. In the 1980s, the push for interdisciplinarity in Ethnic Studies became particularly strong. Although interdisciplinarity is an important and vital tradition in Ethnic Studies, its half-hearted practice easily results in the use of cultural materials as illustrations, or case studies, of social science discussions of race and ethnicity. But interdisciplinarity, when practiced faithfully, broadens the scope of Ethnic Studies by incorporating a variety of disciplinary evidence. A faithful interdisciplinarity requires that texts from various disciplines not only be taught side by side, but also that they be studied using the critical strategies of more than one discipline. To use a novel, for example, in a social science course only to interrogate the material in social science terms, a common enough occurrence in Ethnic Studies, gives only the most cursory nod to Ethnic Studies' interdisciplinary tradition. However, when practiced conscientiously, interdisciplinarity remains one of Ethnic Studies' hallmarks.

The student bodies of Ethnic Studies departments have also influenced how cultural texts were used at different times. When I first took Chicano Studies classes as an undergraduate and graduate student, the enrollment in these courses was almost exclusively Chicano. Literary and artistic texts were used to empower students by providing what were offered as cultural mirrors which would inspire students to forge individual and collective ethnic pride and identity. However, reading these texts to forge cultural nationalist sentiments, along with a sense of the typical and collective, made it almost impossible to read these texts critically for their perspectives on the more contentious topics of gender and sexuality. This reading practice went largely unquestioned at this time. When I taught Chicano Studies in California in the early 1980s, the course enrollments were still mostly Chicano, but an increasing number of non-Chicanos enrolled, thus marking the beginnings of a new generation of Ethnic Studies students, and complicating the discipline's approach and objectives.

The 1980s also saw the rise of Women's Studies as a discipline, and the increased consciousness of the feminist and the gay and lesbian rights movements. The prominence of these lines of inquiry automatically raised in Ethnic Studies classrooms those previously evaded topics of gender and sexuality. In addition, new texts emerged which considered race and ethnicity in their complex interconnections to gender, sexuality, and class. The best example of this new direction may be *This Bridge Called My Back: Writings by Radical Women of Color,* edited by Cherrie Moraga and Gloria Anzaldúa, which heralded in an era in which Ethnic Studies became the multifocused, comparative discipline it is today.[9]

From 1991 to 1996, I taught Ethnic Studies at California State University, San Marcos, a new state university in a suburban Southern California community. This institution has a strong ideological commitment to diversity and multiculturalism. Like a lot of colleges and universities, it has adopted requirements for general education which send large numbers of students to Ethnic Studies who would not have enrolled in these courses otherwise. In my first years, most of the students in my Introduction to Ethnic and Multicultural Studies course where white, as were most of the students enrolled at this institution. Most students took Ethnic Studies to fulfill the general education requirements satisfied by the course. However, more diverse populations of students also now pursued Ethnic Studies as a valuable course of study because of perceived benefits academically and in the job market. This trend is especially noticeable among teacher education students, given the significant demand for teachers in urban school districts with large minority populations. Toward the end of my tenure at San Marcos, the student body became more racially diverse, and the course enrollments also diversified, but satisfaction of the general education requirements was still the primary incentive bringing students to the discipline. The motive of forging ethnic identity for students of color had waned, although students of color who take Ethnic Studies still respond to the focus on their communities with a broadened understanding and respect, which have personal significance.

There was a time when taking Ethnic Studies was a badge of political commitment by ethnic minority students. There was also a time when Ethnic Studies was viewed by students, faculty, and staff as a significant retention tool for minority students, because it created a context in which students could forge social bonds among themselves and with faculty of the same racial-ethnic group. Ethnic Studies departments have frequently been seen as vehicles for minority student recruitment and retention. It would be more honest to say, however, that getting students of color into colleges and universities and retaining them is a complex dynamic of economic and educational policy, and increasingly—in light of the University of California Regents' decision to abolish affirmative action—political factors. Even though Ethnic Studies and its curricula have significant roles to play in achieving equal access to education for all students, this particular responsibility of Ethnic Studies departments has been overemphasized at the expense of neglecting other areas of higher education with similar responsibility for equal educational access and opportunity.

In addition, student attitudes toward university life, the meanings they attach to their ethnic identities, as well as their notions of political action, have changed. For example, in 1997 I visited California State University, Chico, where students explained to me that although there is a Chicano enrollment of several hundred students, MEChA, the Chicano student organization, competes for members with several sororities and fraternities, a dispersal of student extracurricular effort unimagined twenty years ago. Similarly, many students of color no longer see enrollment in Ethnic Studies courses as a duty or as part of their cultural and political development.

Student disinterest in politics and social activism is also illustrated by a survey conducted annually over the past thirty years by the University of California, Los Angeles. This survey of 250,000 college freshmen at four-year institutions noted a growing indifference toward social issues. Only 17 percent of 1997–98 college freshmen expressed interest in "influencing the political structure."[10] These shifts in student attitudes underscore the importance of Ethnic Studies' tradition of and roots in political activism. Reminding students of the discipline's history may nurture a renewed sense of student political empowerment. But these anecdotes and statistics show us that as a discipline, Ethnic Studies no longer has an already self-identified audience and that many students are even antagonistic to the very idea of Ethnic Studies.

Because of shifting student attitudes, the articulation of Ethnic Studies as an important area of study for all students, as well as the incorporation of Ethnic Studies into general education requirements, has been critical to its institutional survival. Those programs that have taken both of these steps—gotten across the message that Ethnic Studies is for all students in all disciplines and successfully built Ethnic Studies into general education requirements, or even into the requirements for other majors—are currently the most institutionally secure. Institutions that have not taken these steps, like my current institution, Humboldt State University, are among the many where Ethnic Studies is at a critical crossroads. At Humboldt, the relatively low (for California) minority student enrollment and the lack of an ethnically diverse local community are often cited as reasons for the currently anemic state of Ethnic Studies on campus. The absence of minority bodies is often the explanation for a seriously understaffed program which, due to a lack of course offerings, has lost its curricular coherence. However, student demographics are not the only predictor of the health of efforts aimed at promoting diversity.[11]

Population and attitude shifts both at universities and in Ethnic Studies classrooms, as well as the broadening of general education to include Ethnic Studies requirements, have made many scrutinize the older pedagogical and curricular models. The project of teaching intercultural knowledge and political activism must now be accomplished in a much more diverse environment, and more and more frequently with a student body which comes to the classroom convinced that the course materials will have nothing to do with them or with their experience. In Ethnic Studies classrooms across the country, students who are in varying degrees resistant to the discipline and everything it represents in the recent culture wars sit next to students who seek, in the interest of global awareness, a cosmopolitan multiculturalism.

Given the way that Ethnic Studies has been institutionalized in the general education requirements at some universities and colleges, and the ways that minority student enrollments have plateaued and in some cases begun an anticipated decline because of the erosion of affirmative action, the consumers of Ethnic Studies have changed dramatically from the early days. Coupled with these institutional realities, the advent of cultural studies and the shift of English from a text-based to a broader cultural field in which film and popular culture are also objects of study have changed the humanities and literary studies in unprecedented ways. This disciplinary shift in English can be helpful when considering some of the challenges currently facing us in teaching both literature and life narratives in the Ethnic Studies classroom to an increasingly diverse student body. These shifts have complicated our teaching of texts in ways that are ultimately helpful. From the earlier model of the literary text by an ethnic minority writer as principally a social document, the emerging body of work in cultural studies looks at texts in all disciplines to see how they construct knowledge and public identity in deliberate and strategic ways, often in contested social environments.

An example from literature may explain the related problems of teaching biography and autobiography in these new circumstances. I like to teach the play *The Wash* by Philip Kan Gotanda.[12] It's about an elderly Japanese American couple who are separated and eventually divorced. In an interdisciplinary Ethnic Studies course, I like to discuss the references to the internment of Japanese Americans during World War II, and I examine the dramatic structure of the play, its characters, and the symbols which give us clues to their interrelated evolutions. I also use this text to talk about the institution of the American family and its traditional organization around patriarchal authority. Some students recognize that Gotanda is using a culturally specific scenario which is also widespread beyond Japanese America. Other students, however, focus on the ethnicity of the characters. The husband, Nobu, exemplifies all of the attributes of the hegemonic male ideal. He is domineering, aggressive, noncommunicative, and always gets his way by exerting his socially accepted authority over his family. There is nothing exclusively Japanese American about this, and in fact Gotanda goes to great lengths to establish Nobu as American, as well as Japanese, in his attitudes and views. He tells us that Nobu is Nisei, American-born, and that he was interned as a young man during the war. In the opening scene of the film version of the play, Nobu eats a hot dog with chop sticks, indicating his hybrid American and Japanese identity. Yet this text trips up many students in a classic way. They read one text in which the characters are of a given ethnic group and, given their hunger for the "facts" about a group of people with which many of them have had limited contact, everything read is related to an essential cultural, even racial, quality distinct from the reader's.

Students are frequently inclined to view Nobu as flawed, because he is insufficiently "Americanized," due to his age and generational status. This is the case even though the model for the sensitive "modern" man in this play is a man of Nobu's generation. In addition, a much younger Sansei character, Brad, exhibits many of the same views toward women that Nobu does, in spite of his apparent "Americanness" and youth. Despite all these elements in Gotanda's play, many students are inclined to read this text within what Lisa Lowe calls the "master narratives of generational conflict and filial relation [which essentialize] Asian American culture."[13] As Lowe argues, the reduction of the problems of Asian American and other marginalized groups into familial and generational disputes reduces the complexities of history and structural inequality to family squabbles which are purely cultural in origin and which can be remedied by adequate assimilation into America's culture and value systems.

When we read life narratives, these problems of essentializing and reduction are magnified, because biography and autobiography are read by almost all undergraduate students as historical and truthful. These assumptions, when they are made by students in an only nominally integrated Ethnic Studies classroom in an only nominally integrated university, in a highly segregated community, ultimately can reinforce as many racial stereotypes as they attempt to undo. To use life narratives as social evidence of the quantifiable borders between ethnic and racial groups runs counter to the objectives of Ethnic Studies. It reduces individuals to representatives of groups, which are presumed to be easily characterized and classified.

James Clifford's and George Marcus's critique of anthropology, *Writing Culture: The Poetics and Politics of Ethnography,* gets students to see the traditions of racialized representation in scholarship, which, regardless of its efforts to achieve cultural representation, cannot avoid writerly tropes and storied fictional elements.[14] In his introduction, Clifford states that the main project of ethnographic writing, the tradition of anthropological writing about cultures and peoples, invents rather than represents culture. He points out that many of the strategies of this cultural invention have been strongly literary. Because of the constraints of writing, ethnographers, like other writers, "cannot avoid expressive tropes, figures, and allegories that select and impose meaning as they translate it" (7). The end result is an ethnographic text with the character of fiction, which has been fashioned or crafted, as is the work of any writer. Because of the way writing imposes meaning, Clifford labels traditional ethnographic texts "economies of truth," which operate through exclusion and rhetoric (7). In other words, ethnographic truths are by their nature partial, and cultural studies can no longer claim to reflect a transparent and complete cultural picture.

One mode of partial truth construction, the allegorical projection of the self through the object of study, is the subject of Clifford's own essay in the volume, "On Ethnographic Allegory." In this essay Clifford proposes that all ethnographic texts are allegorical because they assume a basic human or cultural similarity that permits differences to be understood. Clifford identifies both historical allegories and humanist allegories in ethnographic literature. In the historical allegory, other cultures are cast as earlier versions of the culture of the observer. On the other hand, humanist allegories establish "elemental or transcendent levels of truth" (102). Clifford shows that ethnographic texts are as a whole allegorical, because their writing "enacts a redemptive western allegory": the simultaneous rescue and loss of transferring events and speech into text (99). Clifford points out that the complexity of culture and experience is much greater than writing's capacity to represent it: "Authentic culture is not . . . something . . . to be gathered up in its fragile, final truth by an ethnographer or by anyone else" (119).

Several essays in *Writing Culture* address how the language of cultural representation contains both truth claims and assertions of power, which undergird structures of social domination even as they claim authorial detachment and scientific neutrality. In her essay "Fieldwork in Common Places," Mary Louise Pratt explores how some tropes of ethnographic writing derive from earlier discursive traditions, especially travel writing. She asserts that ethnography has largely defined itself in opposition to this important cultural and literary antecedent. Pratt also demonstrates how the notion of ethnographic accuracy relies on a specific relationship between the four variables of "ethnographic authority, personal experience, scientism, and originality of expression" (29). If any of these variables is atypically configured, the veracity of the whole study is questioned. Anticipating her more recent postcolonial work, Pratt also points out the relationship between ethnographic writing and colonial discourse. In many ethnographic texts, colonialism is at once justified as the salvation of a people on the brink of extinction and effaced when constructing the history of groups ostensibly untouched by outsiders.

Pratt's later work addresses not only those texts constructed by "expert" observers of cultural others, but also those texts produced by authors in culturally and politically compromised situations due to colonization. Her essay "Transculturation and Autoethnography: Peru 1615/1980" offers, among several important concepts, the term *autoethnography,* which is the genre in which colonized (and racialized) individuals construct textual identities which engage and selectively appropriate the representations that members of more powerful groups have made about them.[15] Understanding the complexity of representation as well as how life-narrative writers respond to existing social dialogues and power arrangements helps students to see ethnic life narratives in a new, more intellectually complex light. As Pratt points out, autoethnographies are constructed in dialogue with other representations of subordinated groups and selectively incorporate the concepts of the more powerful culture. Autoethnographies belong to the space of colonial encounters that Pratt terms the "contact zone."

Ruth Behar's *Translated Woman: Crossing the Border with Esperanza's Story* is both a valuable ethnographic text and an insightful document about both the production of ethnography and the evolution of cultural identity in dialogue with members of other cultural groups.[16] In teaching the problems of the life narrative, one can have no better example of both the potential and the limits of these stories. In *Translated Woman,* Behar documents her unfolding relationship with her ethnographic subject, the Mexican peddler woman Esperanza, who tells Behar the story of her life. Behar frames Esperanza's story very deliberately by writing openly about her years of taping conversations and about how the tapes had to be edited and shaped into a coherent form that responds both to Esperanza's original life story and Behar's own evolving sense of self as a Latina feminist scholar and writer. Behar identifies her text as an *historia.* Much like Esperanza's original oral narrative, *Translated Woman* combines both the elements of history and story. Esperanza's story is shaped, as Behar points out, by narratives to which she was exposed in her life: Christian narratives of suffering, popular narratives like *fotonovelas,* and the testimonies of healing she hears in her popular spiritual practice. Throughout her text, Behar is faithful to the idea of narrative as a cultural product which is not transparent. She echoes my own concern when she observes, "It worries me that one does violence to the life history as a story by turning it into the disposable commodity of information" (13).

In teaching life narratives, I try to introduce students to the ways that cultural studies scholars have opened up for questioning the possibility of adequately representing lived experience through texts. Teaching students that the creation of texts necessarily involves strategic narrative choices as well as the construction of the writer's authority helps them to see these texts and others in more complex ways. One of the main benefits of this approach is that students become much more sophisticated readers, who question and weigh both the content and context of the texts they study. Problematizing autobiographical narratives in this way also brings into the open questions of audience: Whom do these texts address? Who then might be best equipped to interpret them? When we look at ethnic life narratives in this way, we get outside the circular discussion of these texts as culturally "authentic" materials, which can best be understood by or have the most significant meaning for "authentic" cultural insiders. Earlier ideas of cultural authenticity have been complicated in the classroom by many factors, including the vocal presence of "mixed race" students and others who feel that their own racial-ethnic identity is not easily reflected in what Du Bois eloquently refers to as the trilogy of color, hair, and bone. Stuart Hall, Frantz Fanon, and Cherrie Moraga, among others, have pointed out that beneath the text of the body lies another text, which Hall describes as "stories, anecdotes, metaphors, images" that constitute a significant but more elusive part of the relationship among bodies and social and cultural space—a dynamic overlooked when we accept racial and cultural boundaries as absolutes.[17]

This relationship between the corporeal text and that other, submerged narrative is illustrated very potently by Michael Eric Dyson in the preface to his book, *Making Malcolm*.[18] He describes how a group of African American male students disrupted his seminar on Malcolm X with their insistent claims to exclusive rights to attach meaning to Malcolm, based on their commonality of race and gender. As Dyson describes it, "Several black males . . . appealed to Malcolm's masculinity, his blackness, and his ghetto grounding as the basis for their strict identification with him. In their eyes, such a strategy lent their interpretations of the leader a natural advantage" (xi). The problem with this, Dyson observes, is that it leads to a "rancid Aristotelian regression back to a mythic 'real blackness' that spins on endlessly, but borrows from a peculiarly European quest for racial purity" (xii). What Dyson calls for instead is attention to that narrative submerged within the body, which he articulates in his own moving autobiographical narrative, pointing deliberately to his similarity of experience with Malcolm as a Michigan native, as a clergyman, and as someone who has close knowledge of the prison experience, similarities which he indicates are more substantial than the corporeal text.

Considerations such as these prime students to think about the construction of their own narratives of experience and the gaps in the family narratives they have heard all their lives. I once heard a presentation in which a Women's Studies professor expressed her distaste for the personal essay written by students. She said that she found it a useless task to ask students to write personal experience essays, because students she had taught had so little experience about which to write. I feel that, on the contrary, students have a lot of experience to write about, but they must be taught to be critical about their experiences, and they must be taught that in constructing a narrative version of their lives, they are necessarily making critical selections from a range of things they could say. In addition, they must know that their narratives exist in dialogue with other, similar narratives written by other students and by published writers over time.

In Ethnic Studies, the personal experience essay has been a staple from the beginning. It serves many purposes, principally the generation of new narratives by members of groups whose experience has been insufficiently documented. These essays have affirmed the life experiences of ethnic minority students and illustrated social and demographic trends in the face of a scarcity of research. They have also instilled personal pride in students who, perhaps for the first time in their educations, have been asked to value their own life experiences and those of their peers, rather than attempt to replicate a foreign model of accomplishment and education.

In 1996 Thomas Dublin published a collection of student essays written at the University of California, San Diego, and at the State University of New York, Binghamton.[19] Written in response to an assignment to "think about their family within the broader context of immigration and ethnicity in the nation's history," these essays were part of Dublin's undergraduate course on American immigration and ethnicity, which he taught first at UCSD and then at SUNY between 1977 and 1994 (5). Dublin's intentions echo my own in asking students to write this kind of autoethnography, an option I've used in several courses. He also notes that "despite their differences, . . . students are all involved in the same fundamental activity: constructing an identity that is both personal and social, private and public" (2). Although Dublin emphasizes how these essays allow students to connect their personal and family experiences to "broader social processes," he does take into account the storied character of the family history as a source for these narratives and allows that "we will probably never know if the stories they tell . . . are true . . . " (2–3). Yet, as Dublin notes, these stories do have meaning, because some version of a family history is significant to the student's life narrative at the time that the essay is written.

Aside from his discussion of the life narrative as a teaching tool, I appreciate how Dublin addresses the issue of disseminating student writing. Although in publishing his volume, Dublin has elected a route with limited potential for other educators, he describes how he initiated the "publication" of these essays by having some students read their essays in class. I have taken this option one step further by warning students in advance that these texts are intended for public consumption and that they will be shared with their classmates. I then allow time in class for students to read as many of their peers' essays as possible, by handing them to each other around the room. What students learn from this, as one student told me, is how different they all are. Sharing these essays reinforces the notion that presumed similarities and differences based on race, class, ethnicity, or gender are unreliable. They also learn that their own lives fit imperfectly into predictably widespread patterns. Students also learn through this exercise that presenting a public textual identity involves a selection from among the various truths of a life.

Another good idea that Dublin offers is his own experience in archiving student essays in the university libraries, so that they may be available to others and form a historical record of that institution's student body. Dublin's book is made up of selections of archived student papers at both of the institutions where he taught his immigration and ethnicity course. In thinking about how to archive these essays and how to make them available to the campus community at my institution, I have increasingly come to favor the idea of posting them on a web page dedicated to the course. In this way, they could be accessible to both present and future students of the course, as well as to the student body at large.

Life narratives which consider our relationships to social, cultural, and political boundaries illustrate the borders that many of us navigate in the course of our lives. They show that lives, like texts, are not transparent, that what you see says a lot about you—and your borders. These stories illustrate how the impulse to quantify and totalize, which was an early strategy in Ethnic Studies, excludes people and constituencies which will inform and shape Ethnic Studies into the next generation: mixed bloods, women, gays, and lesbians, among others. When Ethnic Studies is used as a vehicle for a totalizing reinscription of what it is to be a cultural other, it mirrors the ways that people of color were totalized by stereotypical representations in the first place. It is not that we can't point to patterns of social experience, but that we can no longer use these patterns as rigid litmus tests of identity. Nor can we accept them as justifications for programmatic and disciplinary division. And we, ethnic minority scholars, can no longer use our own cultures' materials to establish these barriers. Ethnic narratives, like Ethnic Studies as a discipline, must be taught not only as responses to hegemonic American culture, but also in light of other cultural and economic communities and institutions, which must be considered in light of their own complex histories. Border stories also show that a faithful practice of interdisciplinarity should be much more common that it has been: we have been crossing much bigger borders for generations.

My border stories are told here to illustrate ideas about teaching, literature, ethnographic texts, and the disciplinary and institutional structures within which I work as an academic. I want to claim the new scholarly interest in post-nationalist American Studies as one intimately related to the practices and traditions of trans-border work in Chicano Studies and in Ethnic Studies as a whole.[20] Border-crossing is part of our heritage, in more ways than we have yet fully reckoned with. In invoking my own history, I want to claim the crossing of racial and national borders as a traditional path in Ethnic Studies which can be mimicked with institutional structure and program design.

The vitality of current Ethnic Studies scholarship—its rigorous interdisciplinarity and cross-cultural impulses—has unevenly penetrated institutions whose principal mission is teaching. In many programs, relatively few permanent faculty hires have been made since these departments were instituted, and once vacated, many positions go unfilled for long periods of time. It is the task of those of us currently at these institutions to demonstrate how Ethnic Studies is a conduit through which students learn important critical skills, as well as gain intercultural knowledge across both disciplinary and racial lines. We also must seriously debate models of Ethnic Studies programs and move in innovative directions, once given the opportunity.

At Humboldt State University one part of the current debate over the future of Ethnic Studies is over program design. In recent years the department was staffed by one full-time faculty member, whose teaching responsibilities were dedicated exclusively to Ethnic Studies, by adjuncts, and by faculty from other departments who cross-listed courses on a volunteer basis. The original program model calls for one full-time faculty member to teach subjects related to each of four ethnic/racial groups: African Americans, Latinos/Chicanos, Asian Americans, and Native Americans. After a two-year search, in the fall of 1999 we hired a new department chair, who is now the second full-time faculty member in the Ethnic Studies department. In the committee entrusted to steer the program over this current crisis, we often discuss what Ethnic Studies should look like, given our current limitations, and the reality that it may be several years until the department is fully staffed. One contentious issue has been whether or not we should replicate the old program design of courses focused principally on one of the four ethnic groups traditionally addressed in the program.

My position is that we should not repeat this model. In a small Ethnic Studies department there is no reason to devote the bulk of course offerings to single groups, especially on the lower-division level. The effectiveness of the old model, even in the old days, is questionable. It reinforces the view that barriers of race are essential and insurmountable. Divisions and boundaries, both self-imposed by nationalist necessity and imposed from above, have terrorized our thinking long enough. Just as we need to do more cross-disciplinary teaching, we need to do more cross-group teaching and look seriously at programs like the one at the University of California, San Diego, where Ethnic Studies is taught both across racial and ethnic group lines, across disciplines, and in a comparative way. That this approach might be more easily achieved without a full range of faculty in different disciplines devoted to each ethnic group makes it attractive as well. Of course skeletal staffs cannot offer a substantial academic program, and the fact that the successful UCSD program has a faculty of ten scholars is evidence of this, but those of us involved in the many floundering programs across the country are pressed to do what we can to offer a coherent and attractive program to students without waiting for the day when we have fully staffed faculties representative of and versed in a given group, and practitioners of an adequate range of necessary disciplines. Instead we must remember that border-crossing, ingenuity, and the ability to "hacer milagros," as my mother says, to make miracles from very little, is in our collective heritage.

A number of neglected Ethnic Studies programs are currently at a crossroads. Administrators, reluctant to make an unpopular decision to eliminate these programs, given vocal support by students and other interested constituencies, are willing to direct resources to the reconfiguration, and hopefully, the stabilization, of Ethnic Studies programs. It is up to those of us involved in Ethnic Studies at these campuses to try new configurations which may seem risky. To remain invested in the status quo, or in old configurations under which Ethnic Studies did not thrive, is also to give up the struggle for Ethnic Studies as an established entity in our institutions which can teach students to think and act critically in response to complex and interrelated cultural and social questions.

NOTES

1. The term "Ethnic Studies," I realize, is problematic. It reinforces the counterproductive idea that whites and the middle class have no culture, and that only some ("other") groups of people have noteworthy social and cultural experiences. The rest share some normative experience from which culture, particularly, is absent. Therefore, the reasoning goes, these groups are not subjects in the discipline. Nonetheless, I use the term Ethnic Studies to talk about a field which has evolved through the study of specific, and shifting, American cultural, racialized, and socioeconomic groups, which has been institutionalized in American universities and colleges most typically under the Ethnic Studies rubric.

2. Luis Valdez, "Introduction: 'La Plebe,' " in *Aztlan: An Anthology of Mexican American Literature*, ed. Luis Valdez and Stan Steiner (New York: Vintage Books, 1972), p. xxxiii.

3. This signals another trope in my story: the trope of drinking and alcoholism, which has remained for me, as it has for many people who grew up with or live with alcoholics, a story told only in highly selective contexts, even though it remains an ever-present narrative undercurrent. As novelist Carolyn See observes in *Dreaming* (Berkeley: University of California Press, 1995), the drama of addiction "may be the unwritten history of America" (p. xvi).

4. Cathy N. Davidson, "Critical Fictions," *PMLA* 111 (1996): 1071.

5. Maxine Hong Kingston, *The Woman Warrior: Memoirs of a Girlhood Among*

Ghosts (New York: Vintage, 1989); originally published in hardcover by Alfred A. Knopf, 1976. Page numbers subsequently cited in text.

6. This blurring of fiction and nonfiction is apparently at the root of the famed dispute between Kingston and fellow Chinese-American writer Frank Chin. According to an essay by journalist Edward Iwata, "In 1976, Kingston and her editor asked Chin [at that time the more celebrated writer] to endorse her soon-to-be-published book. The book was conceived as a fiction collection, but Kingston's publisher, Knopf, felt it would sell better as an autobiography. They titled it, *The Woman Warrior: Memoirs of a Girlhood Among Ghosts.* . . . Chin wrote Kingston that her prose was moving and lyrical. But he couldn't back this book that purported to be a nonfiction account of a Chinese American. He argued that autobiographies by Asian Americans were cloying bids for white acceptance. 'I want your book to be an example of yellow art by a yellow artist,' he wrote, 'not the publisher's manipulation of another Pocahontas.' A dismayed Kingston wrote Chin that she was 'experimenting' with genres, blending the novel and memoir. 'Who knows whether the stories are real or not?' she explained" ("Word Warriors," *Los Angeles Times,* June 24, 1990, pp. E1, 9). For a history of the Chin-Kingston debate, see Sau-ling Cynthia Wong, ed., *Maxine Hong Kingston's* The Woman Warrior: A Casebook (New York: Oxford University Press, 1999). See also Wong's excellent discussion of the autobiographical misreading of this text in her own contribution to the casebook, "Autobiography as a Guided Chinatown Tour? Maxine Hong Kingston's *The Woman Warrior* and the Chinese American Autobiographical Controversy," 29–53.

7. *Booklist,* Oct. 15, 1984, p. 281.

8. Pilar E. Rodríguez Aranda, "On the Solitary Fate of Being Mexican, Female, Wicked, and Thirty-three: An Interview with Sandra Cisneros," *The Americas Review,* 18, no. 1 (1990): 64–80.

9. Cherríe Moraga and Gloria Anzaldúa, eds., *This Bridge Called My Back: Writings by Radical Women of Color* (Watertown, MA: Persephone Press, 1981).

10. Rene Sanchez, "College Freshmen Called the Laziest in a Generation," *San Francisco Chronicle,* January 12, 1998, p. A4.

11. With twenty-three campuses and an enrollment in 1996 of 336,803 students, the California State University is the largest system of senior higher education in the country. In Fall 1996, the systemwide enrollment was as follows: 7.5 percent African American, 1.2 percent American Indian, 15.5 percent Asian, 4.7 percent Filipino, 15.5 percent Mexican American, 5.7 percent other Latino, 0.5 percent Pacific Islander, and 49.2 percent White (*1997 Facts about the California State University,* published by the CSU Office of the Chancellor). In comparison, the Humboldt campus, situated in a remote, rural part of the state, is considered by some to be a campus representing "white flight" from the high-minority enrollments in the urban campuses such as those at Los Angeles and San Francisco. In Fall 1997, Humboldt had an enrollment of 7,492, which included 3.3 percent Asian, 1.7 percent Black, 8.3 percent Hispanic, 2.8 percent Native American, 0.3 percent Pacific Islander, 67.4 percent White, 2.8 percent other and 13.4 percent unknown (Analytic Studies Fast Facts, compiled by Humboldt State University).

12. Philip Kan Gotanda, *The Wash* (Portsmouth, NH: Heinemann Educational Books, 1992). Film version: *The Wash,* dir. Michael Toshiyuki Uno, perf. Mako, Nobu McCarthy, Patti Yasutake, Marion Yue. An American Playhouse Theatrical Film Presentation; screenplay by Philip Kan Gotanda, 1988.

13. Lisa Lowe, *Immigrant Acts: On Asian American Cultural Politics* (Durham, NC: Duke University Press, 1996), p. 63.

14. James Clifford and George Marcus, eds., *Writing Culture: The Poetics and Politics of Ethnography* (Berkeley: University of California Press, 1986). Page numbers subsequently cited in text.

15. Mary Louise Pratt, "Transculturation and Autoethnography: Peru 1615/1980," in *Colonial Discourse/Postcolonial Theory,* ed. Francis Barker, Peter Hulme, and Margaret Iversen (New York: Manchester University Press, 1994), p. 28. See also Mary Louise Pratt, *Imperial Eyes: Travel Writing and Transculturation* (New York: Routledge, 1992).

16. Ruth Behar, *Translated Woman: Crossing the Border with Esperanza's Story* (Boston: Beacon, 1993). Page numbers subsequently cited in the text.

17. Stuart Hall, *Race: The Floating Signifier* (Media Education Foundation, 1996).

18. Michael Eric Dyson, *Making Malcolm: The Myth and Meaning of Malcolm X* (New York: Oxford University Press, 1995). Page numbers subsequently cited in the text.

19. Thomas Dublin, ed. *Becoming American, Becoming Ethnic: College Students Explore Their Roots* (Philadelphia: Temple University Press, 1996). Page numbers subsequently cited in text.

20. See, for example: José David Saldívar, *Border Matters: Remapping American Cultural Studies* (Berkeley: University of California Press, 1997), and *The Dialectics of Our America: Genealogy, Cultural Critique, and Literary History* (Durham, NC: Duke University Press, 1991); Lowe, *Immigrant Acts;* and Paul Gilroy, *The Black Atlantic: Modernity and Double Consciousness* (Cambridge, MA: Harvard University Press, 1993).

Syllabus RACE AND GENDER IN AMERICAN AUTOBIOGRAPHY

Instructor: Barbara Brinson Curiel

In this class we will explore life writings that address the issues of culture, race, gender, class, and nation. We will read a selection of texts and examine the possibilities and the limits of biographical and autobiographical forms. We will look at how authors establish credibility in the eyes of their readers, as well as how authors challenge their readers' preexisting views. We will also contrast the varying representations of what culture, race, class, and gender mean in the author's narrative rendition of his or her life. Finally, we will examine the shifting and expanding definitions of "America" and "American" reflected in these texts.

TEXTS

Behar, Ruth. *Translated Woman: Crossing the Border with Esperanza's Story.* Boston: Beacon, 1993.

Wolff, Tobias. *This Boy's Life.* New York: Harper and Row, 1990.

Campbell, Maria. *Halfbreed.* Lincoln: University of Nebraska Press, 1973.

Haley, Alex. *The Autobiography of Malcolm X.* New York: Random House, 1965.

Note: Many other titles could be rotated into this course. Some I have taught include: Ernesto Galarza, *Barrio Boy* (Notre Dame, Indiana: University of Notre Dame Press, 1971); Maya Angelou, *I Know Why the Caged Bird Sings* (New York: Random House, 1979); Fatima Mernissi, *Dreams of Trespass: Tales of a Harem Girlhood* (New York: Addison-Wesley, 1994); Anna Lee Walters, *Talking Indian: Reflections on Survival and Writing* (Ithaca, New York: Firebrand Books, 1992); Sara Lawrence Lightfoot, *Balm in Gilead: Journey of a Healer* (New York: Addison-Wesley, 1988); and Michiko Tanaka, *Through Harsh Winters: The Life of a Japanese Immigrant Woman* (Novato, California: Chandler and Sharp, 1981). Texts I would like to teach in this course in the future include Dianne Walta Hart, *Undocumented in L.A.* (Wilmington, Delaware: Scholarly Resources, 1997); and David Mura, *Turning Japanese: Memoirs of a Sansei* (New York: Anchor Books, 1992). I usually find beginning with Behar indispensable to laying a critical framework for the other books.]

TOPICS AND MATERIALS FOR EACH TEXT

Translated Woman

Other Materials

Timothy Dow Adams, *Telling Lies in Modern American Autobiography* (Chapel Hill: University of North Carolina Press, 1990).

Ruth Behar, "Writing in My Father's Name: A Diary of *Translated*

Woman's First Year," in *Women Writing Culture,* ed. Ruth Behar and Deborah A. Gordon (Berkeley: University of California Press, 1995).

James Clifford, "Introduction: Partial Truths," and "On Ethnographic Allegory," in *Writing Culture: The Poetics and Politics of Ethnography,* ed. James Clifford and George Marcus (Berkeley: University of California Press, 1986).

Topics and Questions

What is the relationship between "fact" and "fiction" in narrative? What is the relationship between autobiography and therapy? What are the structural and thematic elements of Esperanza's story? Of Ruth Behar's? How does the bilingualism of the text influence its reading? What many kinds of "border-crossing" are referred to by the title? What are the interrelationships between Esperanza's narrative and the author's? How does Ruth Behar evolve in the narrative from a "good gringa anthropologist" into a "bruja gusana?"

This Boy's Life

Other Materials

Bonnie Lyons and Bill Oliver, "An Interview with Tobias Wolff," *Contemporary Literature* 31, no. 1 (Spring 1990): 1–16.

Peter J. Bailey, " 'Why Not Tell the Truth?': The Autobiographies of Three Fiction Writers," *Critique* 32, no. 4 (Summer 1991): 211–21.

Geoffrey Wolff, *The Duke of Deception: Memories of my Father* (New York: Random House, 1979).

Copies of *Boy's Life* magazine.

Suzanne Pharr, "Homophobia as a Weapon of Sexism," in *Race, Class, and Gender in the United States: An Integrated Study,* ed. Paula S. Rothenberg (New York: St. Martin's, 1995), pp. 481–90.

Topics and Questions

How does Wolff's representation of geographical movement speak to other treatments of this same theme (e.g., *Pilgrim's Progress* and Manifest Destiny)? How does Wolff's treatment of guns, homosexuality, and male violence constitute a critique of hegemonic masculinity? Since the narrator is an admitted liar, how does the reader interpret the truthfulness of his story? According to this text, what is the true character of identity? How does this text challenge core American myths of class mobility, self-invention, and heroic citizenship? How does this book constitute a critique of the Vietnam War? How does Wolff's narrative complicate concepts of ethnicity?

Halfbreed

Other Materials

Michael Omi and Howard Winant, *Racial Formations in the United States: From the 1960s to the 1980s* (New York: Routledge, 1986).

Michael M. J. Fischer, "Ethnicity and the Post-Modern Arts of Memory," in *Writing Culture*, ed. Clifford and Marcus.

Mary Louise Pratt, "Transculturation and Autoethnography," and *Imperial Eyes: Travel Writing and Transculturation* (New York: Routledge, 1992).

Topics and Questions

In what ways are national boundaries insufficient to contain this book? How is this a Canadian text, and how is it not? How does this text, like Wolff's, also subvert the typical pilgrimage motif? In what ways does Campbell use her story to confront the stereotype of the drunken Indian? How does the term *halfbreed* come to have new meaning in the text? How is this story shaped by, and how does it offer a commentary on, the genre of the recovery narrative? Although Campbell is critical of Christianity, how is her narrative shaped by Christian tropes? How does Campbell conceive of race? Gender?

Malcolm X

Other Materials

Stuart Hall, *Race: The Floating Signifier* (Northampton, MA: Media Education Foundation, 1996).

Michael Eric Dyson, *Making Malcolm: The Myth and Meaning of Malcolm X* (New York: Oxford University Press, 1995).

Joe Wood, ed., *Malcolm X: In Our Own Image* (New York: St. Martin's, 1992).

Henry Louis Gates, ed., *"Race," Writing, and Difference* (Chicago: University of Chicago Press, 1985).

Topics and Questions

What does Alex Haley do in the narrative to authorize his version of Malcolm X? What is Malcolm's concept of the nature of identity? Can we argue that, ultimately, Malcolm's story reflects a quest for a father to replace the one he lost in childhood? What strategies are employed to make the more inflammatory race and gender views palatable to readers? How do these strategies influence the shape of the overall narrative?

Assignments

One five-page essay on each book, written in response to questions provided by the instructor. As an option, substitute your own life narrative for one essay. In writing your personal narrative, try to capture the "narrative truth" of your life. Pick a central metaphor or organizing feature. For example, in *Translated Woman,* Esperanza uses the progression from suffering to *coraje,* or rage, to organize her story. Malcolm X relies on his repeated transformations of identity as a structuring device. Use your life narrative to prove a political or ideological point, as Behar and Malcolm do. Be creative. Be selective.

How Tiger Woods Lost His Stripes

*Post-Nationalist American Studies as a
History of Race, Migration, and the
Commodification of Culture*

Henry Yu

As the summer waned in 1996, the world was treated to the coronation of a new public hero. Eldrick "Tiger" Woods, the twenty-year-old golf prodigy, captured his third straight amateur championship and then promptly declared his intention to turn professional. The story became a media sensation, transferring the material of sports page headlines to the front page of newspapers in a way usually reserved for World Series championships or athletes involved in sex and drug scandals. Television coverage chronicled every step of Tiger's life, debating his impact upon the sport, and wondering if he was worth the reported $40 million which Nike was going to pay him for an endorsement contract. The strange career of Tiger Woods said much about the current situation of race, ethnicity, and capitalism in the United States. It also spoke to the still relatively unexamined ways in which definitions of racial and cultural difference in the United States connect to the global market of consumption and production.

Woods's eagerly anticipated professional debut was hailed in August 1996 as a multicultural godsend to the sport of golf. As a child of multiracial heritage, Woods added color to a sport that traditionally appealed to those who were white and rich. A multicolored Tiger in hues of black and yellow would forever change the complexion of golf, attracting inner-city children to the game in the same way that Michael Jordan had for basketball. Nike's initial T.V. ad campaign emphasized the racial exclusivity that has marked golf in the United States, stating that there were golf courses at which Tiger Woods still could not play. A Tiger burning bright would change all of that, of course, with a blend of power, grace, skill, and sheer confidence that could not be denied. "Hello World," Tiger Woods announced in another T.V. spot, asking America and the world whether they were ready for the new partnership of Tiger and Nike. The answer to the challenge seemed to be a resounding yes. A year later, in October of 1997, a poll published in *USA Today* reported that Nike's campaign featuring Tiger Woods was by far the most popular advertising campaign of the year.[1]

In this essay, I would like to discuss Tiger Woods' commercial debut as a way of examining how race, ethnicity, and the mass market in the United States can no longer be understood (and perhaps was never properly understood) without the context of global capitalism that frames definitions of cultural and national difference. Notions of ethnic and cultural difference in the United States have always depended upon transnational connections and comparisons. The increasing awareness recently among scholars and the mass media of global perspectives has been marked by a hope that globalization will lead to a decrease in tribalism and ethnicity. Consequently, the practice of a "post-nationalist American Studies" might be construed as an act of self-immolation, erasing national identity formation by pointing towards a future without nations. For me, such a vision would be misguided and dangerously deluded. National formation, and the concurrent practices of cultural and racial differentiation, have always been transnational in character, and they have always called for a perspective that can link ethnic formation with processes that transcend national borders. A post-nationalist American Studies, therefore, should strive to place nation formation within transnational contexts of racial and cultural differentiation.

Tiger Woods's story exemplifies the crossroads between the commercialization of sport in the United States and the production of racial and cultural difference. Golf is perhaps the epitome of a commodification of leisure that characterizes the current global success of American capitalism, and like many of the multibillion dollar sports and entertainment industries (cultural productions such as movies, television, music, etc.), golf is marked by representations of racial and cultural hierarchies. Perhaps more than any other sport, golf stands for white male privilege and racial exclusion. Some of the fascination with Tiger Woods can be explained by how acts of conspicuous leisure and consumption have become essential to both racial and class distinction in the United States. For its very significance as a bastion of hierarchy, golf has also become a marker of the opposition to racial and class exclusion. Similar to how Jackie Robinson's entry into baseball symbolized for Americans more than just the eventual desegregation of baseball but also that of American society, Tiger Wood's entry into golf was heralded as the entry of multiculturalism into the highest reaches of country-club America.

The manner in which observers initially explained Tiger's potential appeal was very revealing. A *Los Angeles Times* article on Tuesday, August 27, 1996, the day after Woods turned pro, declared that Tiger had a "rich ethnic background," calculating that his father was "a quarter Native American, a quarter Chinese, and half African American," and that his mother was "half

Thai, a quarter Chinese, and a quarter white." How did we arrive at these fractions of cultural identity? Did they mean that he practiced his multicultural heritage in such a fractured manner, eating chow mein one day out of four, soul food on one of the other days, and Thai barbecue chicken once a week? Obviously not. The exactness of the ethnic breakdown referred to the purported biological ancestry of Woods' parents and grandparents.

The awkward attempts to explain Tiger's racial classification showed the continuing bankruptcy of languages of race in the United States. The racial calculus employed by both print and television reporters to explain Tiger's heritage reminds us uncomfortably of the biological classifications used in the Old South. The law courts of Louisiana tried for much of the nineteenth and twentieth centuries to calculate a person's racial makeup in the same precise manner, classifying people as mulatto if they were half white and half black, a quadroon if they were a quarter black, an octoroon if an eighth, and so on. The assumption was that blood and race could be broken down into precise fractions, tying a person's present existence in a racially segregated society with a person's purported biological ancestry. The upshot was that a single drop of black blood made a person colored, and no amount of white blood could overwhelm that single drop to make a person pure again.[2]

What was disturbing about the reception of Tiger Woods is how little we have changed from that conception of biological identity. Within American conceptions of race, Tiger Woods is an African American. The intricate racial calculus that broke Tiger into all manner of stripes and hues was a farce not only in terms of its facile exactitude, but also in its false complexity. According to the calculations, Tiger Woods is more Asian American than African American (a quarter Chinese on the father's side, plus a quarter Chinese and a half Thai on the mother's side, for a total of one-half Asian in Tiger, versus only half African American on the father's side, for a total of one-quarter black in Tiger . . .).[3] But this is an empty equation because social usage, and the major market appeal of Tiger, classifies him as black. "How Tiger Woods lost his stripes" describes the process by which the complexities of human migration and intermingling in this country become understood in the simplifying classifications of race.[4]

In his trek from the sports page to the front page, Tiger Woods quickly became another example of a black man making it in America because of his athletic skill. Woods earned his success through his prodigious accomplishments, but his popular apotheosis as black male hero fits him into generic modes of understanding African American masculinity. The strange way in which multinational sports corporations value minority sports stars is indicative of the more general American craving for individual black heroes to redeem its ugly history. Whether it is Jackie Robinson, Michael Jordan, Colin Powell, or Tiger Woods, we constantly fantasize that a single person will save us from racial problems which are endemic and built into the structure of U.S. society.

Tiger Woods combined a number of standard ways in which African American men are perceived as safe and nonthreatening. His Green Beret father, like Colin Powell, was a war hero, embodying the safe black man who sacrifices himself for the nation. Tiger's father correctly channeled the violent masculinity that popular imagery ascribes to African American males, forsaking the alleged criminality (drug dealing, drive-by shooting, gang-banging) that is the negative twin of the figure of the black war hero. Better yet, Tiger's father directed the dangerous, sexual desirability of his black masculinity not toward white women, but toward the safe option of a foreign, Asian war bride. Tiger himself, as the son of a black veteran who applied military discipline to create a black male sports hero, served to connect the appeal of the safe black male body as sports star to a lineage of the black male as military hero. In the light of how popular culture has overdetermined the meaning of his body, how could Tiger not have lost his stripes? After all, classified as a black male, he combined the social virtues of Michael Jordan with those of Colin Powell.[5]

More than blackness, however, Tiger Woods was seen to transcend racial division within his own body. As the sports star progeny of the black male military hero and the Asian wife picked up in the United States's foray into Vietnam, he added racial diversity into his black body. Media imagery, though, could not quite manage to represent this added complication. When Tiger Woods won his first professional golf tournament, and again when he won the prestigious Masters, newspaper photographs overwhelmingly showed him hugging his father. His mother Kultida was either cropped from the frame or blocked by the powerful imagery of the black American military father triumphantly joined with his black American sports star son. Along with the disappearing stripes of Tiger's racial complexity, Thai American Kultida Woods faded into black.

The attempt to see within Tiger Woods the embodiment of multiculturalism was a valiant attempt to contain within a single body all of the ethnic diversity in the social body that multiculturalism claims to represent. The awkwardness of description, and its inevitable failure, resulted both from a flawed conception of ethnic origins and from our inability to leave behind an obsession with the idea that race is a biological category represented by individuals. It is possible to describe a person's racial history in terms of fractions, because each of those fractions was supposedly a whole person one or two generations before. Tiger Woods as a single body, however, cannot express the fractions within—like almost all children of supposed mixed heritage in this country, his whole quickly becomes his darkest part.

Woods himself, as a child, attempting to rebut his reduction by others to a state of blackness, came up with the term "Cablinasian" (CAucasian +

BLack + INdian + ASIAN) to encapsulate his mixed makeup. Mentioned briefly by the press, the term achieved no currency or usage. Since the power of racial categories comes from their work of tying a number of people together under a single description, a label such as Cablinasian that serves only to describe Woods' own individual admixture has little use. Indeed, though Woods had found a name for his own unique brand of pain, he might as well have used his own name "Tiger" to label what was in the end a virtually singular racial description.

The confusion of tongues regarding how to name Tiger's complex heritage is a direct result of the confusion over race that continues to bedevil this country. Multiculturalism in the form embraced by corporate America is no more than this tired language with an added commodification of ethnicity. We want racial and cultural categories to be neatly represented by individuals, so that a multicultural Benetton or Calvin Klein advertisement will have a number of visible people of color—an African American, an Asian American, a Latino or Latina—and an assortment of generic white people. Multiculturalism is about different individuals getting along, and this is the version which is being sold by multinational corporations like Nike, in the hopes that all of these differing people will buy the same objects in a shared market of goods.[6] Nike's ad campaign showing young children of various visible minorities chanting the mantra of "I am Tiger Woods" ostensibly offered Tiger as the role model for multicultural America, but it also managed to call forth a world market ready to consume Nike's products. Like Nike's earlier slogan for basketball icon Michael Jordan, "I want to be like Mike," the phrase "I am Tiger Woods" could be translated by consumers as "My body is black and I am up and coming just like him," but more likely it meant "I want to wear what Tiger wears."

Tiger Woods serves as an example to introduce some issues concerning race and culture in an international perspective, particularly in terms of the interaction among ethnicity, national definition, and global capitalism. There has been a great deal of exciting scholarship in recent years exploring transnational perspectives, and my account is not meant to survey these works, but to sketch some suggestive issues which I see arising out of them. I want first to think about multicultural narratives as shorthand histories for international migration, and then to tie this to the perceived international appeal of Tiger's mixed ethnicity.

The awkward attempts to describe Woods's heritage bear the legacy of Old South notions of race, but they also arise from the late-nineteenth-century context of massive international labor migration.[7] Culture as a theory describing human difference can be linked to two particular historical developments of the nineteenth century: national formation and the rise of migrant labor to satisfy the expanding production that resulted from expanding capitalist development. The rise and triumph of the concept of culture at the beginning of the twentieth century supposedly eclipsed earlier biological definitions of race, but in some ways the idea of culture, and of multiculturalism, is little more than the grafting of nonbiological claims onto preexisting categories of race. Moreover, like the category of biological race, the culture concept erases history, suppressing into static categories the historical origins of how some people become defined as different.

Theories of biological race that arose in the nineteenth century emphasized belonging to some fictive category (for instance, Negroid, Mongoloid, Caucasoid) that collapsed racial type and geographical location. This mythic tie between race and spatial location called forth an epic history stretching back to prehistoric ancestors, tying racial difference to origins deep in time. We still operate with a version of this classificatory scheme when we identify some physical features as "Asian" (straight black hair) and others as "African" (brown skin) or "European" (light skin).[8] American Studies has acquired a central awareness of how racial theories that attributed variations in behavior and in physical and mental abilities to differences in racial type have for centuries served as justification for social oppression and hierarchy.

An anthropological conception of culture that came to the fore in the early twentieth century redefined variety in human behavior and practice as a consequence of social processes. Meant to eliminate any association of mental capacity with biological race, the theory of culture proved relatively successful as a way of attacking biological justifications for social hierarchy. The culture concept as it has been used in theories of multiculturalism, however, has mirrored the suppositions of racial theories about the centrality of biological ties to the past. Particularly in the way differences in behavior between people whose ancestors have come from Africa, Asia, or Europe have been explained as cultural in origin, cultural difference has paralleled the boundaries of earlier definitions of racial difference.

Created by anthropologists visiting exotic locales, culture as an intellectual concept has always been riven by the contradiction that it has come to be an *object* of description (the actual practices of various "cultures") at the same time that it has really only been the description of practices. Culture, as it was defined by early theorists such as Franz Boas, is transferred among physical human bodies through social means of communication. Embodied in social rituals and practices, culture was a way of life, reproduced by social groups that were bound together by such acts. As a set of descriptions, ethnographies were claimed by anthropologists to describe actual "cultures," but the differentiation between what was unique to one culture versus another always depended upon the perspective of Europeans or Americans implicitly comparing their objects of study to other ways of life (often, unwittingly, their own). Arising out of a systematic awareness of differences, the concept of culture is undermined when users forget its origin as a description. *Culture* as a word is continually used as if it were an object with causal powers ("Franz did that because his culture is German"), rather than a product of the very act of describing that is the way of life of anthropologists and those who see the world anthropologically ("Franz, in comparison with other people I have known, does things differently, and I make sense of that difference by describing those acts and linking them to my awareness that he and other people I have known who do things that way all come from Germany"). Unfortunately, in popular language such as that of multiculturalism, the word *culture* has come to have universal significance at the same time that it signifies less and less.

Despite the ability to perform cultural practices described as being the embodiment of some particular culture (for instance, "German culture"), we are constantly faced with examples of how cultural membership has very little to do with performance ability. Take, for instance, the examples of white American missionaries in Japan and Japanese immigrants in the United States during the nineteenth and twentieth centuries. There were a number of children of American missionaries to Japan who were born and raised in Japan, and came to be adept at speaking the local language and understanding and practicing local customs and ways of life. They knew how to use chopsticks; they wore "native" dress; they were allowed to play the same Japanese games as their childhood friends. Were they, by any definition, Japanese? Perhaps with a definition that is restricted to functional ability at performing cultural practices, but in any other sense they are anomalies, freaks of culture that serve to uphold the notion of culture as nonbiological ("they know what Japanese culture is") at the same time that they point to the not-so-hidden reliance of cultural differentiation on legal nationality and biological definitions of race.

Such a reliance is highlighted by the example of Japanese immigrants who came to the United States during the same period, parallel emigrés traveling in opposite directions. Children of theirs born in the United States were invariably raised in American schools, adept at American customs and the local language of English. They ate hamburgers and french fries; they wore Boy Scout uniforms and shouted the Pledge of Allegiance; they were allowed to play in American games with their childhood friends. Legal standards of national citizenship categorized them as American. But if internment of a whole people on the basis of ancestry during World War II means anything, questions of national loyalty, cultural performance, and racial biology have been so confused in U.S. history that the maintenance of culture as a separate category of analysis gains little more payback than a perverse sense of irony. Japanese Americans, despite the possibility of being described as culturally similar to other Americans, were still treated as if they were racially different and nationally suspect.

Lest we think that such examples are anomalous or irrelevant today, we should consider Korean-born orphans adopted by "white" Americans in Minneapolis. How are the new parents to treat the "cultural" heritage of their children? Should they deny that the biological link has a cultural expression, and thus pretend that the children are like any white children? Such a utopian fantasy would be principled, idealistic, and most likely psychologically cruel, for there can be little doubt that the children will receive repeated and stark messages from other people that they are not white. To immerse the children in their "Korean heritage" might prove a practical defense against a debilitated sense of self-worth, but it would be a child-rearing also based on a specious link between culture and biology.

Cultural differentiations, like the biological notions of race that they purportedly replace, rely upon an historical narrative of population migration. No matter how much even the most astute observers believe that culture is a purely social phenomenon, divorced from biology, there are presumed links to histories of the physical migration of human bodies that lead to generalizations based upon physical type. On the whole, these links have practical functions, connecting individual human bodies to histories of population migration. Seeing a body, and being trained to perceive that it shares particular physical characteristics with those descended from individuals who live in Asia, allows fairly accurate suppositions about biological ancestors from somewhere in Asia.

But almost inevitably false assumptions are made concerning the cultural knowledge and practices of such a person, and the relation of culture to the body's biological origin. So children of American missionaries in China, never having set foot in the United States until the age of eighteen or nineteen, can get off a boat in San Francisco and instantly be American in the legal and cultural senses. The norm of American identity has been so equated historically with whiteness that the very term *white American* in most situations is repetitive and redundant. Americans of color require a modifying term such as African or Asian or Hispanic. The term *European American* has been invented to extend the logic of geographic origins for different races, but in the absence of any color modifier, the term *American* means white.

The children, grandchildren, and great-grandchildren of Chinese immigrants to the United States will always be seen as possessing Chinese culture, no matter how inept they are at what it means to be Chinese in China (and in America)—they will be asked whether they know how to translate Chinese characters, how to cook chow mein, and to discuss the takeover of Hong Kong. Orphans from Korea who grew up in Minneapolis with Scandinavian American parents, no matter how young they were when they were transported from South Korea, will always be linked to Korean culture—they will allowed to discover their real culture or rediscover their culture. At worst, and in a manner reminiscent of the internment of Japanese

Americans, airport security officers or the FBI will suspect Arab Americans of being terrorists because of the way they spell their names, the clothes they wear, or the color of their skin. At the heart of all of these distinctions is not race as a biological category or culture as a nonbiological category, but a presumed history of population migrations.

Multiculturalism in the United States has had a long history of making transnational connections. If it really is because someone's grandfather came from Croatia and someone else's came from Canada that one is different from the other, then present cultural differences echo past national differences. Since there is an assumption that what makes someone different here in the United States is their link to some other place in the world, origins and biological heritage are all-important. Even when the differences are supposedly racial, they still presume a difference today arising from a difference in origin yesterday. Tiger Woods's formula of admixture, for instance, reveals a foundation in national, racial, and cultural difference. His Thai portion is national and/or cultural in origin. The Chinese would presumably be the same, with a hint of racial determinism (his Chinese grandparents were probably legally Thai in a national sense, with an indeterminately long history of living in Thailand). His African and Native American parts most certainly fixate on (some notion of) biological race with an assumption that there would be some accompanying cultural differences. His Caucasian (or white) heritage is racial and cultural in the same sense as his blackness, presuming an illusory tie to some mountains in Eastern Europe.

As an historical narrative defining the origins of difference, multiculturalism has linked the politics of the present to a biological genealogy of the individual body's past. This narrative has been a program for political empowerment, because it opposes the racial descriptions it mirrors, but in overturning the exclusion of those previously left out by promising their inclusion, multiculturalism as a political ideology has curiously reiterated the very "foreign" nature of those left out. Multiculturalism has valued those who were previously excluded by turning the terms of their exclusion into the terms of their inclusion. Embracing the foreign nature of ethnicity rather than sending foreigners packing, cultural pluralists have replaced nativism with exoticism.

Multiculturalism, like the narrative of biological race that it opposes, reveals the defining power of imperialism, when Europeans surveyed populations of the world and marked the boundaries between them. Long histories of continual population migration and movement were erased as bodies were given the attribute of "native"—mapping them into a "local" origin that was assigned to them by European knowledge.[9] Categorized by abstract identities such as race, nation, and culture, individuals and social groups all over the globe were defined and came to define themselves through such identifications.[10] The power of these identities for the last two centuries in creating imagined social and institutional ties is undeniable, but there is always the danger of missing the underlying demographic changes that lay at the base of such arbitrary ties.

There are myriad ways in which people are similar and different—male or female, position in a family, age, sexuality, height, shoe size, on and on. One of these ways is where one's grandparents came from, but if the reason someone has been treated differently in the United States is that their grandfather came from China, this tie is important less because of what was unique and native to China (both in the nineteenth century and now) and more because of how racial difference and animosity have been defined in North America; how, in other words, people in the United States have come to define "whiteness" by European origin and linked otherness in racial and cultural terms with non-European origin. Racial, cultural, and national categorization therefore have been inextricably linked in history, and in the most foundational sense these linkages have depended upon an awareness of population migration. Ultimately, however, these definitions of race and culture have not actually been about the migration histories of biological bodies; the definition of whiteness in opposition to other racial types, at its core, has been about the social privileges of not being considered colored. The strange conundrum of culture as a theory is that it assumes and then hides the same links between physical bodies and migration that biological theories of race did. In attempting to define more fairly in this way, we may end up reproducing the logic of justifying white privilege in the United States.

I SING THE BODY ECLECTIC?
TRANSNATIONAL FRACTIONS AND NATIONAL WHOLES

The fractional nature of the racial and cultural categories in Tiger Woods was as arbitrary as the classification of him as African American. The key factor that undermines Tiger Woods's racial formula is the fiction that somehow his ancestors were racially or culturally whole. When he was broken up into one-fourth Chinese, one-fourth Thai, one-fourth African American, one-eighth American Indian, and one-eighth Caucasian, the lowest common denominator of one-eighth leads to a three-generation history. Tracing a three-step genealogy of descent back to an original stage of pure individuals places us at the end of the nineteenth century. If we were to consider other striped, Tiger Woods–like bodies in a similar manner, they might be described as containing fractions like a sixteenth or even a thirty-second. But in any case the individuals who are imagined to live at the beginning point of the calculations are whole only because they have been assumed to originally exist in a shared moment of purity.

The timing of this moment of imagined purity is partly founded upon the coincidence of migration with national identity. The illusion of ethnic and racial wholeness of a grandparent's generation marks the importance of nineteenth-century nationalism in defining bodies. Emigrating from established or emergent nations, migrants during the nineteenth and early twentieth centuries had their bodies marked by nationality—Irish, Chinese, Japanese, Italian, German. That their bodies were whole in a national sense allowed for a consequent holistic definition of their racial and cultural origin.

Both race and culture as categories of belonging have often presupposed a biological genealogy of national origin. This view was legally enshrined in the 1924 National Origins legislation, when each nation was given a maximum quota for migrants to the United States. Every immigrant entering and every body already in the United States was defined by a national past. A migrant body was marked as a member of a single nation, and thus a national purity was conveyed regardless of a person's heterogeneous or complicated origins. Immigrants may have come from a place that did not exist as a political and legal nation, or they may have gone through numerous national entities before entering the United States, any of which could come to be defined as their "national origin." For instance, migrants from the area now known as South Korea were in the early part of the twentieth century counted as Japanese nationals. Virtually all Koreans understood that as a colonized and subject people they were not Japanese in a cultural or biological sense, but their legal status according to the National Origins Act meant that they had to have a national origin, and like other members of the nation of Japan, they were to be excluded from the United States on the basis of national categories.

Even with the supposed eclipse of biological notions of race in the twentieth century, we cling to definitions of national and cultural origin as a shorthand for describing biological origin. If you are a descendent of Asian immigrants to this country, for instance, you are forever being asked where you are originally from, regardless of whether you were born in Los Angeles, Denver, or New York. The confusion is not over whether an individual is American-born or not, since those asking are inevitably not satisfied with the answer of Los Angeles, Denver, or New York. What they are looking for is national origin, and therefore biological origin, even if the moment of origination is an act of migration undertaken by a grandparent. What they want to know is whether you are Japanese, Korean, Chinese, or Vietnamese (I suppose that they believe they can tell if you are from the Philippines, Polynesia, or India and therefore do not have to ask).[11]

The three-generation history of intermarriage that the one-eighth fractions ostensibly revealed actually described a family tree arbitrarily truncated. The hypothetically whole grandparents, given their own family genealogies of ancestry, would have themselves pointed to a past of intermingling population migrations. Further and further back in time, these genealogies would reveal that there has never been a set of racially whole individuals from which we have all descended. Whether in purportedly mixed or pure fashion, biological descent that invokes racially whole individuals in the past is an illusion.

With the possibility that future U.S. Census surveys will no longer restrict individuals to single racial categories (allowing people to check more than one box for categories of racial belonging), perhaps American views of racial and cultural descent will finally leave the notion of pure, whole individuals behind. But this is doubtful. The new problem of complex logarithms and formulae to try to convert the new fractions of identity into whole numbers still results from the same need to produce data that makes sense to demographers. How will all those who rely on population calculations from the U.S. Census use totals that are not the sum of whole numbers of individuals, but crazy totals like 234,574.375 that themselves reflect the sum of a string of fractions such as three-fourths, an eighth, and a sixty-fourth? Or if we are to count partial blood as equivalent to being a full member of a race, we will create tallies that count Tiger Woods four times, as an African American, and again as an Asian American, and again as a white American, and again as a Native American, so that the sum of our parts will no longer add to the same whole number as our total population. The census could remain with the principle of the darkest blood winning out, forcing Tiger Woods to be black, or it could allow him to choose his own category of belonging. He could even choose to be white, even if it is highly unlikely anyone would let him get away with it.

If American understandings of culture still depend largely upon presumed biological origins, and in particular have been tied to nineteenth-century nation-states, what should a post-nationalist American Studies be doing? Since definitions of race and culture have always depended upon the idea that ethnic populations in the United States are somehow linked biologically and/or culturally to foreign populations somewhere else on the globe, is thinking about transnational connections really that new? The answer to both questions is that a post-nationalist perspective on American Studies should not aim to transcend national differentiation, but to reaffirm the need to make apparent the very reliance of narratives of American race, culture, and nation upon transnational phenomena.

More studies need to be done on the salience of transnational migration for American nationalism and on the presumptions of national identity which undergird notions of racial and cultural origin in the United States. Histories of diaspora that underemphasize the importance of nationalism in the attempt to highlight a continuity of shared cultural origin risk missing one of the foundational elements of transnational population migration— the state and all its legal powers of definition and coercion. Nationalist institutions and national identity in transnational perspective, therefore, must be primary concerns of post-nationalist study. At the same time, we need to put racial and cultural differentiation at the center of processes of production and commodification in the international economy.

A number of fine studies have been conducted under the rubric of Asian American Studies, for instance, that might serve as models for a post-nationalist American Studies. Like other work in Ethnic Studies, such as Chicano Studies, Border Studies, and works on the African Diaspora, Asian American Studies has often emphasized transnational perspectives that examine the multiple locations of diasporic migration. At its most fundamental level, an examination of one place as home and another as workplace can invoke the transnational connections of labor migration. For instance, Madeline Hsu examined how Cantonese, male migrant workers formed families even though fathers were on opposite sides of the Pacific from wives and children. These overseas families, despite long absences and a lack of shared residence to tie them together, became standard family practice in particular parts of southern China. Embodied in the practice of financial remittances from the father in the United States to the wife and children in China, Hsu's study of these functioning families serves as an example of how normative conceptions of family can evolve outside the geography of the nation form. Studies such as Hsu's show the porous nature of borders and the arbitrary nature of definitions of national difference; they do not, however, dissolve notions of national identity. Indeed, charting the history of these transnational families further reinforces how historically powerful national borders have been, even when they belied almost every facet of a person's lived experience. The migrants' sense of home (whether in China, where the wives and children resided, or in America, where the migrants resided), was still shaped by the policies of national inclusion and exclusion practiced within both nations.

A post-nationalist American Studies must see past unexamined national discourses such as those on the family that can discount or label as aberrations innumerable social practices. Susan Koshy's work on migrants from India in the United States and Britain shows how studying South Asian diasporic communities in a comparative fashion can reveal the marked differences in how nations treat immigrants and the consequences of these differences. In the realm of culture, Shu-mei Shih's analysis of Taiwanese-American director Ang Lee's reception in both Taiwan and the United States highlights the powerful effects of nationalism in a global economy of cultural production.[12]

There are examples as well from the Atlantic world, but being a scholar of Asian American Studies concerned with the long neglect of the Pacific world, I highlight scholarship on the Pacific. An example of a scholar who has used the insights of Asian American Studies to re-envision the history of the Atlantic world is Kariann Yokota, whose research on the early American republic as a postcolonial society uses many of the transnational perspectives of Asian American history to analyze white colonists at the end of the eighteenth century. Trying to prove their worth in a transatlantic world dominated by British culture, postcolonial Americans created definitions of whiteness that both celebrated and denigrated what was perceived to be native to the United States. Yokota's research suggests how concerns about the status of the new American nation in a transnational Atlantic world formed one of the foundations for a virulent racism among whites.[13]

Just as transnational perspectives on early Chinese immigrant families help us to understand the power of national definition in nineteenth-century life, so transnational perspectives on contemporary society will most likely reveal the continuing power of nationalism. As the public furor in 1996 over television celebrity Kathy Lee Gifford's line of children's clothing demonstrates, an awareness among many observers of the international connections in capitalism can lead not to a diminution of national identity, but to the reinforcement of it. When allegations were made that children's clothing sold under Kathy Lee Gifford's name was being made by child labor in Central America, a long-standing debate resurfaced about whether or not Americans should buy foreign-manufactured clothing. One answer to the incident was that clothing should be made by union labor in the United States—"Buy American" and avoid the problems of oppressive labor conditions in foreign countries.

Besides avoiding the issue of how manufacturing production has been farmed out to low-wage regions around the globe and within the United States, such reactions echo the historical way in which low-wage competition has been racialized as foreign in order to draw the border between those within and without the nation.[14] Irish American labor agitator Dennis Kearney organized California workers in the 1870s by appealing to their solidarity as "whites" and as "Americans," in direct contrast to the "Chinese" and "foreign" workers who worked alongside them. That Kearney and the group of "whites" his appeal created were labor migrants to North America just as much as the Chinese was subsumed under the entwined categorizations of racial difference and of native versus foreigner. What connects the rhetorical construction of the "foreign" Chinese American worker in the 1870s to the "foreign" Central American worker in 1996 are the same processes of racialization and national exclusion. Asian American immigrant workers in the United States just happen to have embodied this classification of the perpetual foreigner, joining racial and national exclusion in a single body.

The xenophobic nationalism of "Buying American" is a duplicitous rhetoric of saving the other by saving ourselves. It says little about what should happen to workers in Honduras, Guatemala, Indonesia, and

Malaysia—just that Americans should not buy products made by them. If it is terrible that foreigners should be made to work in oppressive situations, then the solution should be to buy products made in situations where fair labor practices can be guaranteed—these happen, of course, to be in the United States.

Transnational awareness is not the end of national identity, and in fact it has always been the root process for national awareness. The field of American Studies, which has as its subject American culture and society, has always necessitated transnational perspectives, whether it has practiced such analyses or not. What is needed in the future is a meaningful engagement with the issues of racial and cultural commodification in an international context.

The first step, however, in building something that might be labeled an institutional practice of post-nationalist American Studies is to be certain of why we might want to pursue such a practice and, in particular, who might be interested in the knowledge created. We must be careful to understand the ways in which academics in the United States have themselves come to understand and value exotic knowledge and cultural difference. If we are to achieve a post-nationalist American Studies, it cannot be founded on a lack of awareness of how intellectuals in the United States are themselves American and prize their bourgeois professional status.

The cosmopolitan perspective of many academics in the United States, so valuable as a critical viewpoint that distances them from the practices of American nationalism, should not be mistaken for some truly non-national point of view removed from the provincial national identities they critique. Embedded in a bourgeois world where they are allowed to produce cosmopolitan knowledge for each other's consumption, American intellectuals at times seem to live in a fantasy world of mystified intellectual and cultural production. Creating knowledge of the exotic and the unknown seemingly for the sake of Knowledge itself, or for the sake of a critique that is blind to their own class position and relationship to the world they describe, many academics lack a sense of the market in knowledge and status embodied by American institutions of higher education.[15] Or, if they are aware of their relations to the means of intellectual production, they are compelled by their own places in the institutional structure to continue to produce knowledge, albeit in an ironic mode, artfully distracting themselves from the utility of their actions and the privilege of their positions with the same sly smirk.

Perhaps more unsettling than labor organizers, who shout, "Buy American" in response to the oppression of foreign workers, is the outlook of elites in the United States who link the exploitation of indigenous workers to the loss of their traditional cultures.[16] Narrated as a desire to protect native culture from eventual loss and extinction, this love of the exotic native reduces in the end to some version of "save the other for our own consumption." British and American imperial anthropologists earlier in this century rushed into the South Pacific alongside missionaries and gunboats in order to write descriptions of societies being changed by the very forces they themselves represented. Claiming that they were helping to save native cultures from extinction, the anthropologists produced ethnographies for the edification (and commodification) of British and American academies of higher learning. The anthropologists valued the exotic traditions of "disappearing" cultures—the people themselves were often disappearing due to disease and dislocation, but anthropologists' interest in the extinct nature of their "ways of life" had to do with their fascination in a culturally pure, traditional world that existed before white men arrived. The ways in which indigenous people were adapting, or not adapting, to changes were less interesting than the "lost" world they were trying to save.

There are perilous parallels between academic consumption of the exotic and commercial commodification. The marketing of the dream of a lack of intrusion on traditional culture, a sampling of exoticism without spoiling its pristine nature, still defines the views of much scholarship on ethnicity. The culture concept, as the product of a description of difference, has expired as a useful theory and acquired its greatest utility as a commodity. Imperial anthropology may be gone, but the act of producing ethnographic descriptions of the exotic in order to save them for Knowledge from the despoliation of modernity still remains a scholarly agenda. Related to this process of exotic cultural consumption is a nationalist arrogance, which is often unself-conscious and held by people who otherwise think of themselves as lacking national identifications.

The dilettantism of American academic knowledge is founded upon a conjunction of class privilege and national power. What relation do university scholars have to the means of production? What privileged conditions in their own lives allow them the luxury of a cosmopolitan embrace of diverse local cultures? What fetishizing and collecting of "native" cultural products do they practice, and what allows them to indulge in such practices? Are they independently wealthy in the United States? Are U.S. academics allowed to travel the world as alienated intellectuals because of the enormous diplomatic power of their national citizenship? How does their national identity, even as they act as critics of nationalism, grant them the capability of incorporating multicultural products and perspectives into their lives for their own display and benefit? How does a nationalist enterprise of incorporating knowledge in the interests of national power allow American intellectuals the fantasy of the creation of Knowledge as an unquestioned good? Rooms full of "oriental" vases and hand-crafted products from Southeast Asia may fill scholars' rooms in upper-middle-class homes in the United States, but they have always had the luxury of being able to acquire them "outside" of the tourist market of mass consumption and production. The elitist fantasy is that such native crafts are outside of capitalism, as if their very value were not wholly dependent upon the opposition constructed between mass-produced artifacts and authentic, traditional products prized as different and thus valued.[17]

If the 1960s radical injunction to "think globally, act locally" succeeded in turning American insularity into an awareness of international context, perhaps it also signaled an embrace of the global to such an extent that the national lost significance or became important only as an enemy to be defeated. In some ways, the radical anti-Americanism of much radical dissent allowed for a critical view of American nationalism from a point outside of nationalist ideology, but it may also have deracinated the critic. Just as American children don't really believe in the link between the local and the global when they hear the mothers' cliché, "Eat your beans, because kids are starving in India," so American national power is often erased or forgotten when perspectives outside of the nation become central. A critical perspective situated outside and against nationalist ideology does not equate with being a starving Indian rather than a child of American abundance. Being an intellectual in the United States locates one's critical perspectives in specific class, institutional, and national positions. Neither disagreeing with national policy nor renouncing one's class status results in abandoning the comfortable and privileged position that American academics enjoy.

NATIONAL DIVERSITY AND INTERNATIONAL MARKETING

The processes of national and racial differentiation have contemporary resonance in a time when claims of a new globalism resound. The tying of what is ethnic here in the United States to what is native there in some other nation in the world is what makes Tiger Woods so appealing as a marketing force for corporations looking for global sales. Multinational corporations have already disaggregated every step of production and farmed each out to whatever specific locations in the world offer the cheapest production and labor costs. If the production side is no longer linked to singular nation-states, the consumption side perhaps never has been. The desire for international markets for goods is not a recent dream for capitalists—mercantilists three hundred years ago looked to national exports as a way of creating favorable balances of trade, and European and American manufacturers in the late nineteenth century fantasized about the vast China market long before companies like Nike dreamed about a billion pairs of Air Jordans being purchased by Chinese.

Understanding the perception of so many people that Tiger Woods had the potential for foreign marketing involves connecting international sales with an American-born, mixed racial or cultural body, and the narrative that allows that connection is a multicultural ideology that identifies the origins of his ethnic fractions with foreign nations. The potential of developing Asian markets for golf wear and athletic products is tied to the international appeal of Tiger's partial Asian heritage. Lost in the blackness of America's perception of Tiger, his Asian stripes can be earned on the global market, parlayed into increased sales for Nike in Southeast Asia and other growth markets for Nike's leisure products. If Michael Jordan has been the best ambassador for the international growth of basketball as a marketing vehicle, then Tiger Woods can be golf's equivalent, instantiating such global possibilities in his body. The image of Woods also serves to hide the idealization in golf of white male hierarchy by providing a nonwhite, multiracial body as a fantasy pinnacle.

There is a perverse irony in selling products back to the places where capital has gone to find cheap labor. Marketing golf in Thailand, Indonesia, and other Southeast Asian nations, such as Vietnam, evokes the ultimate capitalist dream of pouring relatively little capital into a location in order to produce products for export to places that will pay a healthy mark-up on production costs, and also recouping as much as possible from those very sites of production. Of course, it's not the women and children being paid thirteen cents an hour in Indonesia who will be able to play golf and buy Nike shoes. But even if it is local elites who make their portion of the profit from managing the cheap labor and creating the professional services and infrastructure for production, the dream remains of new markets springing up alongside labor sites.

Initial indications are that Nike's fantasy of Tiger Woods creating global markets is achieving mixed results. Jan Weisman's work on Thai perceptions of Tiger Woods suggests that the attempt to market Woods as a Thai hero was eagerly embraced by a number of sectors of Thai society. Upon his initial visit as a professional golfer in 1997, newspapers hailed him as native son, and the Thai prime minister met his entourage. Unfortunately, racial hierarchies in Thailand cut against Tiger's inclusion into an imagined Thai social body, and in particular his blackness made constructions of him as Thai difficult.

As in the United States, Tiger's African American military father became the defining characteristic of Tiger's mixed heritage, but within the historical context of U.S. military presence in Thailand during the Vietnam war, Tiger's blackness also painted his mother with questionable moral stripes. Despite widespread efforts to portray Tiger's father as an elite Green Beret and thus different from the morally suspect GIs who had created a flourishing sex-trade industry in Thailand, Kultida Woods was trapped by the prejudices against Thai women who had sex with American soldiers, in particular black GIs. Though Woods's father was an elite officer, his mother was still marked with a low social status by such an association. Tiger Woods also did not act like a Thai national, neither speaking the language nor expressing the proper humility and devoutness of Thai Buddhism. In the end, Woods's triumphant visit to Thailand succeeded in publicizing him as a sports superstar and marketing icon, but it failed to establish him as a native Thai.

More important than his inability (or unwillingness, since Tiger went out of his way to mark himself as American) to perform culture in a manner that would allow his inclusion, categories of color hierarchy threatened the extinction of Tiger's value as Thai. In a society which mirrored an American fetishization of white purity, Wood's Thai heritage was lost in his father's blackness. The globalization of American leisure products has also exported the commodity of whiteness. Weisman's fascinating research contains an analysis of how partial "white" heritage has been commodified in Thai beauty pageants. A recent Miss Universe from Thailand, for instance, was originally recruited to be a Miss Thailand contestant because of her perceived "white" physical features.[18]

The spreading awareness of global perspectives as somehow explaining changes in contemporary society has led to interesting narrative variations. In the recent book *Jihad vs. McWorld,* Benjamin R. Barber argues that the twin forces of global homogenization and ethnic tribalism are tearing the world apart.[19] Enabled by technological advances in communications and transportation, the bland plasticity and homogenization of capital is embodied in the international spread of McDonald's. Combined with the mass production of superficial images that conflate culture with advertising, a world has been created in which leisure, consumption, and happiness all fall within the range between sports and MTV.[20] Opposed to such globalization, but often partaking in the spread of capital, has been the politics of identity, fragmenting nations and fomenting fratricide and genocide. Globalism and tribalism, both destructive in their own way, each threaten to end democracy and free citizenship as we know it.

Of course, if racial differentiation is seen as a foundational element in the formation of national citizenship, then it is clear that democracy and free citizenship are, contrary to Barber's view, future goals that history teaches us have always been ideals built on racial and gender oppression. It might seem a trite point that American democracy, the globe's shining example of egalitarian society, was built upon the self-evident freedom of white men to rule everyone else,[21] but it points out how such narratives of nostalgic longing for a golden age of democracy are empty gestures. Barber may fancy himself a Cassandra warning of the decline of democracy in the face of globalism and ethnic fragmentation, but he resembles Chicken Little decrying a falling firmament that was never that heavenly.

Decline, however, might be preferable to narratives of progress and modernity that assume global capitalism is bringing a better and brighter world. Each and every day we are all becoming better people, closer to and more like each other, or so the story goes. The resistance to global tendencies from ethnic tribalism thus easily produces the idea that identities

based on difference are somehow impeding the progress of global humanity. Whether racial, cultural, or national, an awareness of difference seems
to buck the trend towards world peace and togetherness. The dream of
Tiger Woods as the future thus resides in his embodiment of racial, cultural and national fusion, allowing for the equation of "We are Tiger
Woods" and "We are the world."

The classic tale of Western progress, with its concurrent descriptions of
development and underdevelopment, has been almost the sole narrative of
global history. There have also been a number of powerful explanations for
the global connections of capitalist production and consumption that critique the dominance of the West—world systems theory and dependency
theory being the foremost.[22] In the end, however, all of them are united in
a shared belief that capitalism has become a global phenomenon, disagreeing only on when exactly this happened, and whether it is a desirable development. Whether the global spread of capitalism signals the progress of
universal modernity or whether it encapsulates an oppressive Western system foisted upon the world, it is a global phenomenon nonetheless.[23]
Whether we chase the spirit of capitalism, or decry the specter of commodification, we live in a world that has structured its life around production
and consumption.

I have tried in this essay to suggest a number of different ways in which
recognizing transnational connections can lead to interesting questions for
a post-nationalist American Studies. Race and culture are not sociological
categories, but definitions predicated upon historical narratives of identity.
Definitions of what someone is now are tied biologically to a national origin in the past; these definitions were made in localized contexts, defining
who belonged to a particular geographical locale and who else was a foreigner from somewhere else. But even though the distinctions were made
in specific sites, they always invoked the international by imagining foreign
nations with theoretically homogenous populations from which migrants
originally came. Population migrations have always produced definitions
of the difference between the local and the foreign, imagining a set of
movements between here and somewhere else.

Racial and cultural differentiation has been at the center of such distinctions between the local and foreign. As languages that have served as
shorthands for national origin and for who belonged and who did not, definitions of race and culture have always been based upon transnational
comparisons and connections. Even in periods such as that between 1924
and 1965, when international immigration to the United States was virtually cut off, earlier transnational migrations were assumed in narratives of
racial and cultural difference. Migration and the imagined comparisons
between here and there that were linked to the movements of people and
objects lie at the heart of American history. A post-nationalist American

Studies that takes into account such a perspective, therefore, is a call for an examination of the importance of the transnational migrations that have defined racial and cultural differences in the United States. More than just recognizing the role of these migrations, however, we must also pay attention to the expansion of labor markets and capitalist production and consumption that have at times created these movements of people, and at other times have commodified the cultural differences they are seen to embody. In the end, I also contend that the position of the scholar must be considered, since the definitions and classifications that have resulted from the movements of history have marked us all, and to deny their relevance for the producers of knowledge only blinds us to the operations of power.

NOTES

Thanks to the members of the UCHRI research group and Hazel Carby, Michael Denning, Patricia Pessar, Andrés Resendez, Jace Weaver, and Bryan Wolf of the Race, Ethnicity, and Migration Program brown-bag colloquium at Yale for their helpful comments. Walter Johnson of NYU showed me an unpublished paper. Special acknowledgment to Kariann Yokota for her multiple, careful readings and large-scale additions to the subject matter and body of this essay, as well as numerous suggestions on the applicability of postcolonial theory to U.S. history.

1. "Money" section report on popularity of Tiger Woods advertising campaign, *USA Today* (October 20, 1997); James K. Glassman, "A Dishonest Ad Campaign," *Washington Post* (Sept. 17, 1996); Larry Dorman, "We'll Be Right Back, after This Hip and Distorted Commercial Break," *New York Times*, 145, sec. 8 (Sept. 1, 1996; hype surrounding entrance into professional golfing world of twenty-year-old Tiger Woods); Robert Lipsyte, "Woods Suits Golf's Needs Perfectly," *New York Times*, 145, sec. 1 (Sept. 8, 1996); David Segal, "Golf's $60 Million Question: Can Tiger Woods Bring Riches to Sponsors, Minorities to Game?" *Washington Post* (August 31, 1996); Ellen Goodman, "Black (and White, Asian, Indian) like Me," *Washington Post* (April 15, 1995; golfer Tiger Woods is multiracial); Ellen Goodman, "Being More Than the Sum of Parts: When Tiger Woods Speaks of His Background as Multiracial, He Speaks for a Generation That Shuns Labels," *Los Angeles Times*, 114 (April 14, 1995); "Tiger, Tiger, Burning Bright," *Los Angeles Times*, 113 (Sept. 1, 1994; Tiger Woods wins U.S. Amateur Golf Championship).

2. Virginia Domínguez, *White by Definition: Social Classification in Creole Louisiana* (New Brunswick, NJ: Rutgers University Press, 1986).

3. Somewhat in jest, but further revealing the absurdity of such calculations, this is not even counting as Asian American the one-eighth American Indian coursing through his veins, a legacy of the original immigrants from Asia crossing over the Bering land bridge.

4. The phrase "how Tiger lost his stripes" was suggested to me by George Sánchez.

5. Thanks to Hazel Carby and Michael Denning for suggesting the importance of Tiger Woods's father as military hero, and the connections between such representations of safe black male bodies and the dangerous criminalized black male in popular culture. See Hazel Carby, *RACEMEN* (Cambridge: Harvard University Press, 1998).

6. On different types of multiculturalism, see David Palumbo-Liu's "Introduction," in *The Ethnic Canon: Histories, Institutions, and Interventions* (Minneapolis: University of Minnesota Press, 1995). The marketing of diversity has been the subject of numerous newspaper articles, including the following: Patrick Lee, "As California's Ethnic Makeup Changes, Companies Are Facing New Challenges in Serving Diverse Customers," *Los Angeles Times*, 113 (Oct. 23, 1994); "So Long, Betty," *Christian Science Monitor,* 87 (Sept. 21, 1995); George White, "The Ethnic Side of Sears: Retailer Leads in Effort to Reach Diverse Markets," *Los Angeles Times*, 114 (Jan. 29, 1996); Walter C. Farrell, Jr., and James H. Johnson, Jr., "Toward Diversity, and Profits," *New York Times*, 146, sec. 3 (Jan. 12, 1997; workplace diversity makes both moral and economic sense).

7. There has been a good deal of interesting literature already on transnational movements of labor and how these diasporic movements have been at the heart of ethnic identity within the nation-states which arose at the same time. The United States was like many nations in the nineteenth century that derived part of their sense of national homogeneity from racializing and excluding diasporic labor from definitions of the national body.

8. Ashley Montagu, *Man's Most Dangerous Myth: The Fallacy of Race*, 5th ed. (New York: Oxford University Press, 1974).

9. Mary Louise Pratt, *Imperial Eyes: Travel Writing and Transculturation* (New York: Routledge, 1992); Margaret Hunt, "Racism, Imperialism, and the Traveler's Gaze in Eighteenth-Century England," *Journal of British Studies* 32 (October 1993): 333–57.

10. Postcolonial scholarship, such as that of South Asian scholars on India and partition, has described how nations arose in the wake of decolonization, and the problems of ethnicity within states which were abstract entities created by colonial mapmakers' fantasies of geographic and administrative order. A well-known example of this scholarship is Benedict Anderson's *Imagined Communities*, 2nd ed. (London: Verso, 1991), which includes an interpretation of the end of Dutch rule in the islands of the East Indies and the creation of the nation of Indonesia out of a myriad of diverse peoples, united by armed and political struggle, but also by an imagined unity that came out of a shared history of domination by Dutch colonizers. See also Jan Nederveen Pieterse and Bhikhu Parekh, eds., *The Decolonization of Imagination: Culture, Knowledge, and Power* (Atlantic Highlands, NJ: Zed Books, 1995); Arif Dirlik, ed., *The Postcolonial Aura: Third World Criticism in the Age of Global Capitalism* (Boulder: Westview Press, 1997), in particular the essay by Ann Stoler, " 'Mixed-bloods' and the Cultural Politics of European Identity in Colonial Southeast Asia," pp. 128–48; Arif Dirlik, *What's in a Rim? Critical Perspectives on the Pacific Region Idea* (Boulder: Westview Press, 1993), in particular the introduction, "Introducing the Pacific," and the essays by Alexander Woodside, "The Asia-Pacific Idea as a Mobilization Myth," pp. 13–28; Bruce Cumings, "Rimspeak: Or, the Discourse of the 'Pacific Rim,' " pp. 29–49; Neferti Xina M. Tadiar, "Sexual Economies in the Asia-Pacific Community," pp. 183–210; and Meredith Woo-Cumings, "Market Dependency in U.S.-East Asian Relations," pp. 135–57.

11. If a shared Asian American identity is formed for the most part from the experience of being treated as "Orientals" in a similar manner by other Americans, including being mistaken for each other, perhaps one of the largest reasons for the continued practice of excluding South Asians and most Filipinos and Pacific Is-

landers from a sense of identity with Asian Americans is that they are not mistaken for migrants from East Asia.

12. Madeline Hsu, "Between Diaspora and Native Place: Evolutions in the Relationship between Taishan County and Overseas Taishanese, 1849–1989"; Susan Koshy, "Category Crisis: South Asian Diasporic Negotiations of Racial Categories"; and Shu-mei Shih, "Globalization, Minoritization, and Ang Lee's Films"; all of these are unpublished papers given at the 1998 Association for Asian American Studies, Fifteenth Annual Conference, Honolulu, Hawaii. Hsu's and Koshy's research will be published in forthcoming books. See also Lisa Lowe, *Immigrant Acts: On Asian American Cultural Politics* (Durham, NC: Duke University Press, 1996).

13. Kariann Yokota's research appears in her doctoral dissertation in history, which is in progress at the University of California, Los Angeles.

14. Paul Ong, Edna Bonacich, and Lucie Cheng, eds., *The New Asian Immigration in Los Angeles and Global Restructuring* (Philadelphia: Temple University Press, 1994); Edna Bonacich et al., eds., *Global Production: The Apparel Industry in the Pacific Rim* (Philadelphia : Temple University Press, 1994); I. S. A. Baud, *Form of Production and Women's Labour: Gender Aspects of Industrialisation in India and Mexico* (Newbury Park: Sage, 1992); Michiel Scheffer, *Trading Places: Fashion, Retailers, and the Changing Geography of Clothing Production* (Utrecht: Department of Geography, 1992); Lisa Lowe and David Lloyd, eds., *The Politics of Culture in the Shadow of Capitalism* (Durham, NC: Duke University Press, 1998).

15. Anne McClintock, *Imperial Leather: Race, Gender, and Sexuality in the Colonial Contest* (New York: Routledge, 1995); Berth Lindfors, "Ethnological Show Business: Footlighting the Dark Continent," in Rosemarie G. Thomson, ed., *Freakery: Cultural Spectacles of the Extraordinary Body* (New York: New York University Press, 1996), pp. 207–18. On Saartjie Baartman, the San woman exhibited in 1810–11 as the "Hottentot Venus," and on the previous topic, see Sander Gilman, "Black Bodies, White Bodies," *Critical Inquiry* 12 (1985): 204–42; *Exhibiting Cultures: The Poetics and Politics of Museum Display* (Washington, DC: Smithsonian, 1991); Johannes Fabian, *Time and the Other: How Anthropology Makes Its Object* (New York: Columbia University Press, 1983); Marianna Torgovnik, *Gone Primitive: Savage Intellects, Modern Lives* (Chicago: University of Chicago Press, 1990); Edward Said, *Culture and Imperialism* (New York: Random House, 1993); Ann Stoler, *Race and the Education of Desire: Foucault's History of Sexuality and the Colonial Order of Things* (Durham, NC: Duke University Press, 1995); on the disinterested knower, see Etienne Balibar, *Masses, Classes, and Ideas* (London: Verso, 1994); Robert Young, *White Mythologies: Writing History and the West* (New York: Routledge, 1990); Nicholas Canny and Anthony Pagden, eds., *Colonial Identity in the Atlantic World, 1500–1800* (Princeton: Princeton University Press, 1987).

16. Rob Wilson and Arif Dirlik, eds., *Asia/Pacific as Space of Cultural Production* (Durham, NC: Duke University Press, 1995).

17. Pierre Bourdieu, *Distinction* (Cambridge: Harvard University Press, 1984); James Clifford, "On Collecting Art and Culture," in *The Predicament of Culture* (Cambridge: Harvard University Press, 1988).

18. Jan Weisman, "Multiracial Amerasia Abroad: Thai Perceptions and Constructions of Tiger Woods," a paper given at the 1998 Association for Asian American Studies, Fifteenth Annual Conference, Honolulu, Hawaii. Weisman's research

can be found in her 1998 doctoral dissertation in anthropology at the University of Washington.

19. Benjamin R. Barber, *Jihad vs. McWorld : How the Planet Is Both Falling Apart and Coming Together—and What This Means for Democracy* (New York: Times Books, 1995).

20. Frederic Jameson, *Postmodernism: Or, the Cultural Logic of Late Capitalism* (Durham, NC: Duke University Press, 1991).

21. For histories of the role of race in early American and Jacksonian democracy, see Edmund Morgan, *American Slavery, American Freedom: The Ordeal of Colonial Virginia* (New York: Norton, 1975); Alexander Saxton, *The Rise and Fall of the White Republic: Class Politics and Mass Culture in Nineteenth-Century America* (London: Verso, 1990); David Roediger, *The Wages of Whiteness: Race and the Making of the American Working Class* (London: Verso, 1991).

22. Patrick Wolfe, "Review Essay: History and Imperialism: A Century of Theory, from Marx to Postcolonialism," *American Historical Review* 102, no. 2 (April 1997): 388–420; Amy Kaplan and Donald Pease, eds., *Cultures of United States Imperialism* (Durham, NC: Duke University Press, 1993); John Tomlinson, *Cultural Imperialism: A Critical Introduction* (Baltimore: Johns Hopkins University Press, 1991); "Imperialism—A Useful Category of Historical Analysis?" *Forum in Radical History Review* 57 (1993). On modernization theory, see Walter W. Rostow, *The Stages of Economic Growth: A Non-Communist Manifesto* (Cambridge: Cambridge University Press, 1960); Partha Chatterjee, *Nationalist Thought and the Colonial World: A Derivative Discourse?* (Minneapolis: University of Minnesota Press, 1993), and *The Nation and Its Fragments: Colonial and Postcolonial Histories* (Princeton: Princeton University Press, 1993); Immanuel Wallerstein, *The Modern World-System,* vol. 1, *Capitalist Agriculture and the Origins of the European World-Economy in the Sixteenth Century* (New York: Academic Press, 1974), and vol. 2, *Mercantilism and the Consolidation of the European World-Economy, 1600–1750* (New York: Academic Press, 1980); see also his *The Capitalist World-Economy* (New York: Academic Press, 1989).

23. See Francis Fukuyama, *End of History and the Last Man* (New York: Free Press, 1992), for a prominent example of such a universal narrative of history and capitalism; on the foisting of capitalism on other societies, see Reinhold Wagnleitner, *Coca-Colonization and the Cold War,* trans. Diana Wolf (Chapel Hill: University of North Carolina Press, 1994). For a trenchant critique of the narratives of progress, see Dipesh Chakrabarty, "Postcoloniality and the Artifice of History: Who Speaks for 'Indian' Pasts?" *Representations* 37 (1992): 1–26.

Syllabus BUYING AND SELLING THE EXOTIC
Transnational Culture and Global History

Instructor: Henry Yu

An undergraduate- or graduate-level course might organize an examination of post-nationalist issues into three main themes: migration and movement, the consciousness of cultural difference, and commodification. An examination of migration, either actual physical bodies or imagined movements, is a good starting point to ground the previous two hundred years of history. Colonialism, empire, labor migration—all can be charted demographically and in imaginary productions. The consciousness of the exotic, of cultural, racial, and national difference, can be seen as attendant effects of migration and movement. Finally, cosmopolitan anti-nationalism can be examined for its connections to new forms of commodification—in particular, how imagined cultural difference has been sold. Whether the products are sold to tourists traveling abroad or brought to cosmopolitan buyers sitting at home, cultural forms, images, and representations are constructed as seemingly exotic objects which cross national borders.

READINGS

Books

Arjun Appadurai, *Modernity at Large: Cultural Dimensions of Globalization* (Minneapolis: University of Minnesota Press, 1996).

Benjamin R. Barber, *Jihad vs. McWorld : How the Planet Is Both Falling Apart and Coming Together—and What This Means for Democracy* (New York: Times Books, 1995).

Cynthia Enlou, *Bananas, Beaches, and Bases* (Berkeley: University of California Press, 1990).

Shelly Errington, *The Death of Authentic Primitive Art and Other Tales of Progress* (Berkeley: University of California Press, 1998).

Frederic Jameson, *Postmodernism: Or, the Cultural Logic of Late Capitalism* (Durham, NC: Duke University Press, 1991).

Lisa Lowe, *Immigrant Acts: On Asian American Cultural Politics* (Durham, NC: Duke University Press, 1996).

Mary Louise Pratt, *Imperial Eyes: Travel Writing and Transculturation* (New York: Routledge, 1992).

Essays

Dipesh Chakrabarty, "Post-coloniality and the Artifice of History: Who Speaks for 'Indian' Pasts?" *Representations* 37 (1992): 1–26.

Akhil Gupta and James Ferguson, "Beyond 'Culture': Space, Identity, and the Politics of Difference," *Cultural Anthropology* 7 (February 1992), 6–23.

Lisa Lowe and David Lloyd, eds., *The Politics of Culture in the Shadow of Capitalism* (Durham, NC: Duke University Press, 1998).

Karl Marx, *1844 Manuscripts* (sections on commodification).

CONTRIBUTORS

Barbara Brinson Curiel is an assistant professor of English at Humboldt State University, where she teaches American Literature, Ethnic Studies, Women's Studies, and Creative Writing. Her poetry has been widely anthologized, including in the recent volume, *The Floating Borderlands: Twenty-Five Years of U.S. Hispanic Literature,* ed. Lauro Flores (University of Washington Press, 1998). Her current research project is on the construction of transnational Latina identity in the literary works of U.S. Latina writers.

David Kazanjian is assistant professor of English at Queens College and visiting professor of English at the Graduate School and University Center, City University of New York. He is the author of "Racial Governmentality: Thomas Jefferson and the African Colonization Movement in the United States," *Alternation* 5:1 (Durban, South Africa: CSSALL, 1998), and "Notarizing Knowledge: Paranoia and Civility in Freud and Lacan," *Qui Parle* 7: 1 (Fall/Winter 1993). He has also recently coauthored, with Anahid Kassabian, "Melancholic Memories and Manic Politics: Feminism, Documentary, and the Armenian Diaspora," in *Feminism and Documentary,* ed. Diane Waldman and Janet Walker (Minneapolis: University of Minnesota Press, 1999), and is currently coediting, with David L. Eng, an anthology, *Loss: On the Social and Psychic Work of Mourning.*

Katherine Kinney teaches American Literature, African American Literature, and Film in the English department at the University of California, Riverside. She is the author of *Friendly Fire: American Identity and the Literature of the Vietnam War* (New York: Oxford University Press, forthcoming).

Steven Mailloux is professor of English and Comparative Literature at the University of California, Irvine. He is the author of *Interpretive Conventions* (Ithaca, NY: Cornell University Press, 1982) and *Rhetorical Power* (Ithaca, NY: Cornell University Press, 1989), editor of *Rhetoric, Sophistry, Pragmatism* (New York: Cambridge University Press, 1995), and coeditor (with Sanford Levinson) of *Interpreting Law and Literature* (Evanston, IL: Northwestern University Press, 1988). His most recent book is *Reception Histories: Rhetoric, Pragmatism, and American Cultural Politics* (Ithaca, NY: Cornell University Press, 1998).

Jay Mechling is professor of American Studies at the University of California, Davis. The author of over seventy-five articles and book chapters spanning his interdisciplinary interests, from history and literary criticism to folklore and rhetorical criticism, he received the Distinguished Teaching Award at the University of California, Davis, in 1993 and the American Studies Association's 1998 Mary Turpie Prize for distinguished achievement in teaching and curricular development. He was chair of the California Council for the Humanities from 1994–96.

John Carlos Rowe teaches the literatures and cultures of the United States and Critical Theory at the University of California, Irvine. He is the author of *Literary Culture and U.S. Imperialism: From the Revolution to World War II* (New York: Oxford University Press, 2000), *The Other Henry James* (Durham, NC: Duke University Press, 1998), *At Emerson's Tomb: The Politics of Classic American Literature* (New York: Columbia University Press, 1997), *The Theoretical Dimensions of Henry James* (Madison: University of Wisconsin Press, 1984), *Through the Custom-House: Nineteenth-Century American Fiction and Modern Theory* (Baltimore: Johns Hopkins University Press, 1982), *Henry Adams and Henry James: The Emergence of a Modern Consciousness* (Ithaca, NY: Cornell University Press, 1976), and the editor of *"Culture" and the Problem of the Disciplines* (New York: Columbia University Press, 1998), *New Essays on The Education of Henry Adams* (New York: Cambridge University Press, 1996), and (with Rick Berg) *The Vietnam War and American Culture* (New York: Columbia University Press, 1991). His new book, *A Future for American Studies,* will be published by the University of Minnesota Press in the fall of 2000.

George J. Sánchez is associate professor of History and the Program in American Studies and Ethnicity at the University of Southern California. He also serves as the director of the Chicano/Latino Studies Program at USC. His book, *Becoming Mexican American: Ethnicity, Culture, and Identity in Chicano Los Angeles, 1900–1945* (New York: Oxford University Press, 1993), received numerous awards, including the Robert Athearn Book Prize of the Western History Association, the Theodore Saloutus Memorial Book Award from the Immigration History Society, and the Local History Award from the Southern California Historical Society. His latest publications include "Reading Reginald Denny: The Politics of Whiteness in the Late Twentieth Century," *American Quarterly* 47 (September 1995), and "Face the Nation: Race, Immigration, and the Rise of Nativism in Late-Twentieth-Century America," *International Migration Review* 31: 4 (Winter 1997). His current project is a sociocultural study of the ethnic interaction of three groups—Mexican Americans, Japanese Americans, and Jews—in the Boyle Heights area of East Los Angeles, California, throughout the twentieth century.

Shelley Streeby is an assistant professor in the Literature Department at the University of California, San Diego. Her essays have appeared in *Criticism* and *boundary* 2. She is currently completing a book called *American Sensations: Class, Empire, and the Production of Popular Culture.*

Henry Yu is an assistant professor in the History Department, as well as a member of the Asian American Studies Center, at the University of California, Los Angeles. He received his B.A. from the University of British Columbia, and his M.A. and Ph.D. in history from Princeton. Yu teaches modern U.S. intellectual history and Asian American history; he is finishing a book entitled, *Thinking Orientals,* due to be published by Oxford University Press. Yu was born in Canada and raised in Vancouver and on Vancouver Island in British Columbia.

INDEX

Abu-Lughod, Janet, 8
Acholonu, Catherine Obianuju, 161n54
Affirmative action, 1, 12, 49, 52, 54, 206, 208
African-American masculinity, 225–226
Afrocentrism, 45, 46
Agnew, Jean-Christophe, 20n27
Alarcón, Norma, 36n17
Alien Labor Act (1931), 183
Allen, Ray, 79n22
Almaguer, Tomás, 166, 177, 194n30
American exceptionalism, 2, 3, 5, 6, 23, 29,
    41, 47, 55, 75, 77, 85, 110, 111, 112
American Federation of Labor, 183
American Legion, 183
American pragmatism, 25. See also James,
    William
American Quarterly, 6, 7, 14, 64
American Studies Association, 6, 30, 41
Ames, Fisher, 130–131, 144, 150
Anderson, Benedict, 91, 244n10
Andrews, William, 133
Antiwar movements (U.S.), 21n35, 50
Anzaldúa, Gloria, 206
Appadurai, Arjun, 17n1
Arrighi, Giovanni, 8, 137
Articles of Confederation, 131
Atomic bomb. See World War Two
Autoethnography. See Pratt, Mary Louise

Baker, Houston A., Jr., 8, 133–134
Balderrama, Francisco, 195n55
Balibar, Etienne, 136–137, 169, 190

Barber, Benjamin, 241
Bass, Randy, 33
Bataan (1943), 91, 105n27
Bauerlein, Mark, 34n5
Behar, Ruth, 79n17, 211
Bell, Daniel, 49
Bellah, Robert, 71, 72–73. See also Habits of
    the Heart
Berger, Peter, 63, 65, 66, 67, 68–69
Berkhofer, Robert, 26
Berlant, Lauren, 2, 194n45
Bhabha, Homi, 94
Birmingham School, 26
Black Atlantic, 30, 31, 37n21. See also Gilroy,
    Paul
Black nationalism, 46. See also Afrocentrism;
    Black Panthers; Black Power movement
Black Panthers, 50, 103
Black Power movement, 5, 9
Bloch, Marc, 8
Boas, Franz, 228
Bolster, W. Jeffrey, 163n60
Boorstin, Daniel, 5
Bourdieu, Pierre, 245n17
Braudel, Fernand, 8
Bretnor, H. H., 193n20
Brewer, John, 20n27
Brimelow, Peter, 48
Brouwer, Steve, 78n3
Brown, Wendy, 159n39
Buell, Lawrence, 36n18
Burns, Walter Noble, 182, 184–185

Cain, William, 124n18
California, propositions: Proposition 187, 1, 47; Proposition 209, 47, 54; Proposition 227, 47
California American Studies Association, 30
California State University, Chico: students, 207
California State University, San Marcos: Ethnic Studies, 206
Californios, 174–178
Caputo, Philip, 86, 97
Carter, Dan, 58n31
Casanova, José, 78n3, 79n35
Chakrabarty, Dipesh, 246n23
Cheney, Lynne, 46, 124n12
Chiang, Mark, 19n22
Chicano/a movement, 5, 9
Chin, Frank, 217n6
China (communist revolution), 85
Chinese Exclusion Laws, 15, 87
Chinosole, 133–134
Christian Science, 68, 70
Cisneros, Sandra, 204
Civil Rights movement, 5, 21n35, 48, 49, 50, 69
Civil War (U.S.), 4, 166
Clifford, James, 18n19, 79n17, 196n69, 209–210, 245n17
Clough, Michael, 33, 37n20
Cohen, Lizbeth, 57n9
Cold War, 2, 5, 49, 50, 85, 90, 92, 94, 97, 98
Columbia Online Project, 37n24
Columbia University, 43
Columbus, Christopher, 86
Contact zone. See Pratt, Mary Louise
Coolidge, Dane, 182
Cooppan, Vilashini, 20n26
Crèvecoeur, J. Hector St. John de (Michel-Guillaume Jean de), 6
Crowe, Michael, 123n10
Csikszentmihalyi, Mihaly, 65
Cultural authenticity, 212
Culture, theories of, 228–232

Danish West Indies, 145–146
Davidson, Cathy, 203
Davidson, Donald, 121
Davis, Angela, 162n57
Declaration of Independence, 135
Delano, Alonzo, 193n23

Denning, Michael, 57n9
Deportations of "illegal immigrants," 183, 186
Derrida, Jacques, 162n56
Desmond, Jane, 7–8
Dewey, John, 115
Dick, Steven, 123n10
Dickens, Charles: A Christmas Carol (film adaptations), 76
Didion, Joan, 84–85, 86, 90, 99–102, 104
Dirlik, Arif, 245n16
Dizon, Lily, 106n33
Dominguez, Manuel, 177
Domínguez, Virginia, 7–8, 243n2
Dornan, Robert, 2–3
Dower, John, 88, 94
Drinnon, Richard, 18n9, 26
Dublin, Thomas, 213–214
Du Bois, W. E. B., 4, 212
Dutch United Provinces, 136
Dyson, Michael Eric, 212

Elliot, Emory, 27, 35n12
Ellis, Richard, 123n8
Eng, David, 19n22, 20n26
Engelhardt, Tom, 105n19
Enloe, Cynthia, 188
Equiano, Olaudah, 131–134, 137, 142–152
Ewen, Stuart, 20n27

Fanon, Frantz, 212
Farber, David, 58n29
Farquhar, Francis, 193n20
Faulkner, Harold, 153n7
Federal Land Law of 1851, 175
Feld, Steven, 79n22
Feldman, Stephen, 80n43
Fichtelberg, Joseph, 143, 153n9, 155n20
Finlay, Jeff, 33
First Amendment, 70
Fish, Stanley, 124n11
Fitzsimons, Thomas, 130–131, 150
Foreign Miner's Tax (1850), 175, 176
Foucault, Michel, 8, 133, 170, 171
Fox, Richard Wightman, 20n27
Fox-Genovese, Elizabeth, 155n23
Frank, André Gunder, 19n21
Frankfurt School, 13, 25, 26
Fraser, Nancy, 70
Fukuyama, Francis, 246n23
Full Metal Jacket (1987), 91

Gales, Joseph, Sr., 152n2
Gay rights movement, 5
Geertz, Clifford, 67
Genovese, Eugene, 155n23
Gerstle, Gary, 49, 57n10, 58n44
Ghost (1990), 77
Gifford, Paul, 78n3
Gilbert, James, 80n44
Gilroy, Paul, 37n21, 134, 152
Gitlin, Todd, 47, 50–52, 53, 54
Glendon, 70, 74
Gold Rush, California, 166–167, 175–176, 178, 186. *See also* Foreign Miner's Tax
Goldwater, Barry, 51
Gomes, Leonard, 158n27
Gonzáles, Pedro, 185–186
Gonzales, Rodolfo "Corky," 180
Gordon, Avery, 55, 182
Gordon, Deborah, 79n17
Gotanda, Philip Kan, 208–209
Grable, Betty, 88, 89
Great Depression, 4, 183
Green, James, 153n9
Guerin-Gonzalez, Camille, 183
Gulf War, 27
Gunn, Giles, 35n13
Gutiérrez, David, 183, 194n39, 196n65
Gutiérrez-Jones, Carl, 192n13, 195n62
Gutman, Herbert, 45

Habermas, Jürgen, 70
Habits of the Heart, 67, 73, 74, 75
Hall, Stuart, 212
Hamilton, Alexander, 136
Handelman, Don, 65
Harvey, David, 1
Herr, Michael, 86
Herrera-Sobek, María, 186–187
Hersey, John, 89–90
Hill, William, 153n7
Hill, Winifred Storrs, 194n29
Hinds, Elizabeth Jane Wall, 153n9
Hirsch, Arnold, 58n30
Hirsch, E.D., Jr., 24, 29
Hittell, John, 194n28
Hobsbawm, Eric, 20n27
Hollinger, David, 47, 52–54
Hom, Alice, 19n22
Home Alone (1990), 76
Honey, Michael, 45
Horsman, Reginald, 26

Horwitz, Richard, 35n10
Hsu, Madeline, 235
Hu Shih, 115
Hugill, Peter J., 8
Humboldt State University: Ethnic Studies, 215; minority students, 207
Hunt, Margaret, 244n9
Hunter, James Davison, 79n25

Identity politics, 5–6, 44–45, 52, 55, 69
Ijsseling, Samuel, 124n11
Independence Day (1996), 40–41, 52, 54
Inglès sin Barreras (English without Borders), 201
Internal colonization model, 9, 166
Internet: American Crossroads electronic discussion, 14, 33; American Studies, resources for, 32–33; *Interroads* listserv, 24, 27; T-Amstudy listserv, 14
Intersectionality, intersectional studies, 16, 123n3
Ito, Akiyo, 153n9
It's a Wonderful Life (1946), 76

James, C.L.R., 17n6
James, William, 63, 65, 66, 67, 117
Jameson, Frederic, 246n20
Jeffords, Susan, 86, 105n27

Kammen, Michael, 49
Kant, Immanuel, 113–114
Kaplan, Amy, 4, 35n8
Kearney, Dennis, 236
Keil, Charles, 79n22
Kelley, Robin, 45, 51
Kensinger, Kenneth, 113, 119, 122, 123n9
Kerber, Linda, 7
Kerr, Clark, 55
Kessler-Harris, Alice, 27
Kingston, Maxine Hong: *China Men*, 86, 90, 96–99, 104; *The Woman Warrior*, 204
Klette, Ernest, 182
Kogawa, Joy, 86, 90, 92–94, 96, 104
Kolodny, Annette, 26
Korean War, 85–86, 98
Koshy, Susan, 235
Kouwenhoven, John, 5
Kovic, Ron, 86, 97

Labor movements, 5, 51
Laclau, Ernesto, 8

Lao-Tze, 115
Larrain, Jorge, 19n21
Lauter, Paul, 27, 34n4
Leal, Luis, 182, 185, 190
Lears, T. Jackson, 20n27
Lee, Ang, 19n22, 235
Lee, Benjamin, 7
Lewis and Clark, 86
Lewis, R. W. B., 5
Limerick, Patricia, 4
Limón, José, 181
Lind, Michael, 47, 48–50, 52, 53
Lindfors, Berth, 245n15
Linenthal, Edward, 105n19
Lipsitz, George, 2, 9, 45, 58n30, 79n22
Literature Online, 37n24
Lloyd, David, 37n19
Los Madrugadores, 185–186, 188
Lott, Eric, 167
Lowe, Lisa, 87, 123n2, 159n39, 196n66, 209
Luckmann, Thomas, 78n5
Lye, Colleen, 20n26
Lyotard, Jean-François, 116, 121–122

MacArthur, Arthur, 88
MacArthur, Douglas, 88
McClintock, Anne, 91, 245n15
Madison, James, 129–131, 144, 150
Manifest Destiny, 4, 75, 167
Marcus, George, 79n17, 209
Marren, Susan, 153n9
Marshall Plan, 27
Martí, José, 4, 17n5
Marx, Leo, 5, 16
Marxism: neo-Marxist theories of fetishism
    and alienation, 13; relation to religion,
    64; theory of value 133, 137–142, 144.
    See also Frankfurt School
May, Elaine Tyler, 89
Mechling, Jay, 78n13
Melville, Herman, 167
Merelman, Richard, 79n28
Mills, C. Wright, 5
Miller, James, 58n23
Miller, Perry, 4, 154n12
Minority Discourse Studies, 9
Mirabeau, Marquis de, 156n24
Miracle on 34th Street (1947), 76
Miyoshi, Masao, 17n3
Modernism, 91
Monroe Doctrine (1823), 3

Monroy, Douglas, 194n33
Montag, Susan, 123n9
Montagu, Ashley, 244n8
Moore, R. Laurence, 80n39
Moraga, Cherrie, 180, 206, 212
Mormons, 68
Mott, Frank Luther, 193n19
Murphey, Murray, 63
Murphy, Joseph, 79n21
Murrieta, Joaquín, 167–168, 172, 180, 181,
    182, 183, 187; *California Police Gazette* ver-
    sion, 168–175, 177–180, 181, 186,
    188–189; *corridos*, 168–170, 180,
    181–183, 185–190; John Rollin Ridge
    version, 167–169, 171–173, 179, 181,
    182, 186, 188–189
Muslims, 68
Myerhoff, Barbara, 67
Myth and symbol school, 5, 16, 23, 25

Nash, Gary, 46, 52
National Origins Legislation (1924), 233
Nazism, 89
Nelson, Cary, 35n7
Neo-pragmatism. *See* Rorty, Richard
Neuhaus, Richard John, 68–69
New Deal, 45, 49
New Historicism, 25
New York University: American Studies, 14
Newfield, Chris, 55
Nissenbaum, Stephen, 80n43
North Atlantic Free Trade Agreement
    (NAFTA), 2
Novak, Michael, 74–75, 76, 77

O'Brien, Tim, 86
Ogude, S. E., 162n54
Omi, Michael, 17n4, 176–177, 191n4

Padilla, Genaro, 166
Paredes, Américo, 17n6, 186, 187
Pease, Donald, 17n1
Personal experience essay, classroom use of,
    212–213
Philippine-American War, 27, 28, 85, 88
Phillips, Jayne Ann, 86, 90, 94–96, 99, 104
Pita, Beatrice, 166
Pitt, Leonard, 175, 194nn34, 36, 38
Plato, 114–115, 117
Poirier, Richard, 34n5
Polanyi, Karl, 8

Polynesian Cultural Centre on Oahu, 20n28
Porter, Carolyn, 167
Porter, Roy, 20n27
Potter, David, 5
Pratt, Mary Louise, 28, 210–211, 244n9;
    "autoethnography," 210–211; "contact
    zone," 28, 29, 30, 33, 211
Primitivism, 36n18
Princeton University: American Studies, 44
Protagoras. *See* Sophists
Puritan Origins school, 23
Puritans, 3; "City on the Hill," 3, 85, 87;
    Winthrop, 3

Race, biological theories of, 228
Ranger, Terence, 20n27
Reagan, Ronald, administration, 46, 50; Rea-
    gan-Bush era, 76
Reinhardt, Mark, 123n8
Religious Freedom Restoration Act of 1993,
    70
Republican Party, 49, 51
Ridge, John Rollin. *See* Murrieta, Joaquín
Robbins, Bruce, 123n8
Rockwell, Norman, 89
Rodriguez, Raymond, 195n55
Rodriguez, Richard, 180–181
Roeder, George H., Jr., 105n16
Roediger, David, 45, 160n45
Rogin, Michael, 4, 56n2, 89, 167
Rohrbough, Malcolm, 191n3
Roman Catholic Church, 68
Rorty, Richard, 65, 111–113, 115, 116,
    117–122; neo-pragmatism, 111, 112
Rose, Susan, 78n3
Rosenthal, Joe, 87
Rossinow, Doug, 58n29
Rousseau, Jean-Jacques, 72
Rowe, John Carlos, 11, 104n2, 110
Royce, Josiah, 176–177

Said, Edward, 91, 99
Saldaña-Portillo, María Josefina, 20n26
Saldívar, José David, 166, 167
Saldívar, Ramón, 181
Sánchez, George, 11, 69, 71, 186, 195n57
Sánchez, Jesús, 185–186
Sanchez, Loretta, 3
Sánchez, Rosaura, 166, 194n28
Sánchez, Víctor, 182, 185–186, 190
Sands, Kathleen, 78n13

Santa Clause, The (1994), 76
Santería, 68, 70–71
Santino, Jack, 80n43
Scarry, Elaine, 87
Schlesinger, Arthur, Jr., 24, 48
Schmidt, Leigh Eric, 80n43
Scientology, 68
Scrooged (1988), 76
See, Carolyn, 216n3
Sharp, Jenny, 9
Shell, Marc, 34n1
Sheridan, Richard, 135
Shih, Shu-mei, 235
Silverman, Kaja, 105n16
Skurski, Julie, 189
Slotkin, Richard, 18n9, 26, 105n11
Smith, Adam, 156n24
Smith, Anna Deavere, 102–104
Smith, Henry Nash, 5
Smith, Tony, 80n42
Sobel, Mechal, 79n19
Socrates, 114
Sollers, Werner, 24
Sophists, 114–115
Spanish-American War, 27, 75, 85
Spiller, Robert, 154n12
Spivak, Gayatri Chakravorty, 159n40
Stamp Act repeal (1766), 148–150
Standart, Sister Mary Colette, 194nn32, 38
Stanford University: Modern Thought and
    Literature Program, 14
Star Trek: The Next Generation, 113–114,
    116–117, 119–122
Strachwitz, Chris, 195n60
Straubel, Daniel, 193n18
Students for a Democratic Society (SDS), 50
Subaltern Studies Collective, 7
Sugrue, Thomas, 58n30
Sumner, Charles Graham, 75

Takaki, Ronald, 26
Tariff of 1789, 131, 132, 136, 150
Taussig, F. W., 152n1, 153n7, 158n27
Teng Shih, 115
Thébaud, Jean-Loup, 124n16
Tocqueville, Alexis de, 6
Tompkins, Jane, 26
Treaty of Guadalupe Hidalgo. *See* United
    States–Mexican War
Turner, Frederick Jackson: Turner thesis,
    3–4

United States Census, 234
United States Congress, 129, 130, 136
United States Department of Defense, 31
United States Information Agency, 12, 27
United States–Mexican War, 4, 166–167,
    170, 171, 176, 178, 179–180, 186, 188;
    California State Constitution, racial defi-
    nitions, 175; Treaty of Guadalupe Hi-
    dalgo (1848), 166, 175
University of California, Los Angeles: Ethnic
    Studies, 47
University of California, San Diego: Ethnic
    Studies, 215–216
University of California, Santa Cruz: Ameri-
    can Studies, 43
University of Colorado: American Studies, 43
University of Michigan: Program in Ameri-
    can Culture, 42
University of Pennsylvania: American Civi-
    lization program, 11

Valdez, Luis, 180, 202
Varley, James, 193n25
Vasquez, Jesse, 37n22
Veterans of Foreign Wars, 183
Vietnam Veterans Memorial, 86
Vietnam War, 5, 28, 84, 85–86, 91, 94–97,
    98–102

Wagnleitner, Reinhold, 20n29, 246n23;
    "coca-colonization," 28; Coca-Colonization
    and the Cold War, 10
Walker, Cheryl, 192n9
Wallace, George, 51

Wallerstein, Immanuel, 8, 143
War of 1812, 136
Warner, Stephen, 79n20
Washington, George: "Farewell Address"
    (1796), 3
Washington, Mary Helen, 41
Weisman, Jan, 240, 241
Westbrook, Richard, 88
White, Richard, 4
Wiegman, Robyn, 123n3
Wilentz, Sean, 29
Williams, Raymond, 192n11
Willis, Ellen, 49
Wilson, David, 63
Wilson, John, 124n12
Wilson, Rob, 245n16
Winant, Howard, 17n4, 176–177, 191n4
Winthrop, John, 3
Wise, Gene, 4
Wittner, Judith, 79n20
Women's movement, 5
Wong, Sau-ling Cynthia, 217n6
World War Two, 85–97, 99; atomic bomb,
    89, 90, 92, 94, 98; internment of Japa-
    nese Americans, 229
Wuthnow, Robert, 75, 76

X, Malcolm, 50, 202, 212

Yadav, Alok, 17n3
Yokota, Kariann, 236
Yu, Henry, 201

Zwick, Jim, 27

                    Text: 10/12 Baskerville
                 Display: Baskerville
             Composition: Binghamton Valley Composition
    Printing and binding: Maple-Vail